CoMeDi: Context and Meaning - Navigating Disagreements in NLP Annotations

Abu Dhabi, United Arab Emirates
19 January 2025

ISBN: 979-8-3313-1364-7

Printed from e-media with permission by:

Curran Associates, Inc.
57 Morehouse Lane
Red Hook, NY 12571

Some format issues inherent in the e-media version may also appear in this print version.

Printed with permission by Curran Associates, Inc. (2026)

For permission requests, please contact the Association for Computational Linguistics at the address below.

Association for Computational Linguistics
209 N. Eighth Street
Stroudsburg, Pennsylvania 18360

Phone: 1-570-476-8006
Fax: 1-570-476-0860

acl@aclweb.org

Additional copies of this publication are available from:

Curran Associates, Inc.
57 Morehouse Lane
Red Hook, NY 12571 USA
Phone: 845-758-0400
Fax: 845-758-2633
Email: curran@proceedings.com
Web: www.proceedings.com

COLING 2025

Proceedings of CoMeDi: Context and Meaning—Navigating Disagreements in NLP Annotations

January 19, 2025
Abu Dhabi, UAE

Introduction

Welcome to CoMeDi, the workshop on Context and Meaning—Navigating Disagreements in NLP Annotations![1]

This workshop is taking place for the first time and explores causes of disagreements in NLP annotations as well as strategies for effective handling or resolution. This iteration of the workshop includes research on representing ambiguity in meaning representations, annotating implicit discourse relations, analyzing disagreement in politeness annotations, and predicting disagreement in tasks about word sense and hateful content, among others.

The workshop also hosted a shared task on ordinal word-in-context judgments. In the first subtask, participants were asked to predict the median of annotator judgments. In the second subtask, they needed to predict the mean of pairwise absolute judgment differences between annotators.

In total, we received 21 paper submissions (among them 7 shared task papers), out of which 17 were accepted. All workshop papers are presented as talks, while the shared task papers are presented in a poster session. In addition, the workshop includes two non-archival paper presentations and one invited talk on human label variation.

The program committee consisted of 20 researchers, who we would like to thank for providing helpful and constructive reviews on the papers. We would also like to thank all authors for their submissions and interest in our workshop.

Michael and Dominik

[1] https://comedinlp.github.io/

Organizers:

Michael Roth, University of Technology Nuremberg
Dominik Schlechtweg, University of Stuttgart

Program Committee:

David Alfter, University of Gothenburg
Valerio Basile, University of Turin
Felipe Bravo, University of Chile
Jing Chen, Hong Kong Polytechnic University
Diego Frassinelli, University of Konstanz & LMU Munich
Dubossarsky Haim, Queen Mary University
Simon Hengchen, iguanodon.ai & Université de Genève
Snigdha Khanna, Indiana University
Sandra Kübler, Indiana University
Andrei Kutuzov, University of Oslo
Elisa Leonardelli, Fondazione Bruno Kessler
Melissa Lieffers, Indiana University
Marie-Catherine de Marneffe, UCLouvain
Maja Pavlovic, Queen Mary University
Siyao Peng, LMU Munich
Pauline Sander, University of Stuttgart
Pia Sommerauer, Vrije Universiteit Amsterdam
Alexandra Uma
Frank D. Zamora-Reina, University of Chile
Wei Zhao, University of Aberdeen

Invited Speaker:

Barbara Plank, LMU Munich & IT University of Copenhagen

Table of Contents

Workshop Program

Sunday, January 19, 2025

9:20–11:00 Morning Session

9:20–9:30 *Introduction*

9:30–10:30 *Invited talk: The Spectrum of Human Label Variation: Reflections from the Last Ten Years in NLP*
Barbara Plank

10:30–11:00 *Coffee break*

11:00–14:00 Pre-lunch Session

11:00–11:20 *Is a bunch of words enough to detect disagreement in hateful content?*
Giulia Rizzi, Paolo Rosso and Elisabetta Fersini

11:20–11:40 *On Crowdsourcing Task Design for Discourse Relation Annotation*
Frances Yung and Vera Demberg

11:40–12:00 *Sources of Disagreement in Data for LLM Instruction Tuning*
Russel Dsouza and Venelin Kovatchev

12:00–12:20 *CoMeDi Shared Task: Median Judgment Classification & Mean Disagreement Ranking with Ordinal Word-in-Context Judgments*
Dominik Schlechtweg, Tejaswi Choppa, Wei Zhao and Michael Roth

12:20–14:00 *Lunch break*

Sunday, January 19, 2025 (continued)

14:00–16:00 Post-lunch Session

14:00–14:20 *Deep-change at CoMeDi: the Cross-Entropy Loss is not All You Need*
Mikhail Kuklin and Nikolay Arefyev

14:20–14:40 *Predicting Median, Disagreement and Noise Label in Ordinal Word-in-Context Data*
Tejaswi Choppa, Michael Roth and Dominik Schlechtweg

14:40–15:30 Poster session

14:40–15:30 *GRASP at CoMeDi Shared Task: Multi-Strategy Modeling of Annotator Behavior in Multi-Lingual Semantic Judgments*
David Alfter and Mattias Appelgren

14:40–15:30 *Funzac at CoMeDi Shared Task: Modeling Annotator Disagreement from Word-In-Context Perspectives*
Olufunke O. Sarumi, Charles Welch, Lucie Flek and Jörg Schlötterer

14:40–15:30 *FuocChuVIP123 at CoMeDi Shared Task: Disagreement Ranking with XLM-Roberta Sentence Embeddings and Deep Neural Regression*
Phuoc Duong Huy Chu

14:40–15:30 *JuniperLiu at CoMeDi Shared Task: Models as Annotators in Lexical Semantics Disagreements*
Zhu Liu, Zhen Hu and Ying Liu

14:40–15:30 *MMLabUIT at CoMeDiShared Task: Text Embedding Techniques versus Generation-Based NLI for Median Judgment Classification*
Tai Duc Le and Thin Dang Van

14:40–15:30 *ABDN-NLP at CoMeDi Shared Task: Predicting the Aggregated Human Judgment via Weighted Few-Shot Prompting*
Ying Xuan Loke, Dominik Schlechtweg and Wei Zhao

14:40–15:30 *Automating Annotation Guideline Improvements using LLMs: A Case Study*
Adrien Bibal, Nathaniel Gerlek, Goran Muric, Elizabeth Boschee, Steven C. Fincke, Mike Ross and Steven N. Minton

14:40–15:30 *Ambiguity and Disagreement in Abstract Meaning Representation*
Shira Wein

14:40–15:30 *The Impact of Annotation Choices on Computational Representations of Semantic and Phonological Distance in Sign Languages*
Lisa Loy

Sunday, January 19, 2025 (continued)

14:40–15:30 *Ambiguity Meets Uncertainty: Investigating Uncertainty Estimation for Word Sense Disambiguation*
Zhu Liu and Ying Liu

14:40–15:30 *Disagreement in Metaphor Annotation of Mexican Spanish Science Tweets*
Alec M. Sanchez-Montero, Gemma Bel-Enguix, SERGIO LUIS OJEDA TRUEBA and Gerardo Sierra Martínez

15:30–16:00 ***Coffee break***

16:00–16:10 **Closing Session**

16:00–16:10 ***Closing***

Is a bunch of words enough to detect disagreement in hateful content?

Giulia Rizzi[1,2], **Paolo Rosso**[2,3], **Elisabetta Fersini**[1]
[1]University of Milano-Bicocca, Viale Sarca, 336 - Milan, Italy
[2]Universitat Politècnica de València, Camino de Vera, Valencia, Spain
[3] ValgrAI Valencian Graduate School and Research Network of Artificial Intelligence, Spain
g.rizzi10@campus.unimib.it, prosso@dsic.upv.es, elisabetta.fersini@unimib.it

Abstract

The complexity of the annotation process when adopting crowdsourcing platforms for labeling hateful content can be linked to the presence of textual constituents that can be ambiguous, misinterpreted, or characterized by a reduced surrounding context. In this paper, we address the problem of perspectivism in hateful speech by leveraging contextualized embedding representation of their constituents and weighted probability functions. The effectiveness of the proposed approach is assessed using four datasets provided for the SemEval 2023 Task 11 shared task. The results emphasize that a few elements can serve as a proxy to identify sentences that may be perceived differently by multiple readers, without the need of necessarily exploiting complex Large Language Models. The source code and dataset references related to our approaches are available at https://github.com/MIND-Lab/Hate-Speech-Disagreement-Detection/.
Warning: This paper contains examples of language that may be offensive.

1 Introduction

In the landscape of social networks, hate speech is a growing concern. However, most of the existing detection methods do not take into account the subjectivity of the task and lack in considering different perspectives, resulting in a critical gap in addressing the inherent subjectivity of this phenomenon when designing hate speech prediction models.

Several psycho-social studies (LaFrance and Roberts, 2019; Huddy and Aarøe, 2019; Sap et al., 2019; Hoskins and Tulloch, 2018) have shown that hate perception is subjective and highly dependent on a range of factors such as preconceptions, stereotypes, cultural background, anonymity of the source, and the specific context in which the speech occurs. Among the possible sources of disagreement, annotators' opinions, beliefs, and knowledge have been identified by several investigations in the state-of-the-art (Sandri et al., 2023; Sap et al., 2022). While disagreement is capturing researchers' attention, the majority of works focus on a posteriori exploiting disagreement information to improve the quality of data (Beigman Klebanov and Beigman, 2009; Sang and Stanton, 2022) or including it in the training phase of machine learning models to improve prediction performance (Lee et al., 2023). Only a few of them address the problem of a priori modeling perspectivism (Sandri et al., 2023; Cabitza et al., 2023) and recognizing potential textual triggers of such a disagreement (Rizzi et al., 2024a).

Detecting disagreement in a hateful sentence and identifying the corresponding disagreement-related constituents could play a fundamental role when creating gold-standard benchmarks to be submitted to crowdsourcing workers. For those contents that could lead to disagreement, specific annotation policies could be adopted (e.g., more annotators to be involved, removal of the sample from the dataset that should be annotated, etc..). Alternatively, specific highlights could be provided to the annotators to focus more on specific constituents that could be perceived differently by the readers (e.g., underlining words, hashtags, or emoji that have been identified as disagreement-related constituents that should be carefully evaluated). In this paper, we propose a novel technique for detecting disagreement in hate speech and identifying sentence features that can suggest a lack of agreement among different readers. The proposed method looks at several textual elements (here referred to as *constituent*), including words, emoticons, and hashtags, to identify the ones that are likely associated with disagreement. Each constituent, opportunely represented in a contextualized embedding space, is evaluated by defining a weighted probability function to account for nuanced perceptions of different elements. Additionally, we investigated if the pro-

Proceedings of Context and Meaning: Navigating Disagreements in NLP Annotation, pages 1–11
January 19, 2025.

posed approach, which is based on the evaluation of a bunch of words, is enough when compared with predictions based on Large Language Models. In order to evaluate the efficiency of our approach, multiple experiments have been performed using hate speech datasets from the SemEval 2023 - Task 11 on Learning With Disagreements (Le-Wi-Di) (Leonardelli et al., 2023). These datasets cover a wide range of features, such as annotation techniques, text kinds, and goals. The diversity of the data allowed us to assess the capability of the proposed approach to identify disagreement at sentence level, by leveraging on selected elements considering the different contexts in which they appear.
In summary, three main contributions are given:

- Contextualized embeddings coupled with weighted probability functions have been proposed to detect disagreement-related constituents in hateful content.

- Several aggregation strategies are investigated to predict the disagreement label associated to each sentence.

- A comparison with a few Large Language Models, opportunely fine-tuned to detect disagreement, has been performed, considering as key elements to evaluate both prediction capabilities and computational requirements.

The paper is organized as follows. In Section 2 an overview of the state of the art is provided, while in Section 3 the proposed approach is detailed. In Section 4, the adopted datasets are presented, while the achieved results are reported in Section 5. In Section 6, conclusion and future research directions are drawn. Finally, in Section 6, the impact of the proposed approach and its current limitations are highlighted.

2 Related Work

Various natural language tasks, like sentiment analysis or hate speech detection, have been shown to display ambiguity or subjectivity (Uma et al., 2021). As a consequence, an emerging area of research challenges the assumption that each instance possesses a unique perception and interpretation. Subjectivity is represented in datasets through multiple annotations or the addition of confidence levels to ground truth labels. The general idea is to use several labels to represent the diverse opinions of annotators with different perspectives and understanding (Uma et al., 2021).

The information reflecting annotators' disagreement has primarily been used to improve dataset quality by excluding instances marked by annotator disagreement (Beigman Klebanov and Beigman, 2009; Sang and Stanton, 2022). Alternatively, the annotators' disagreement has been used during training of machine learning models accordingly to two different strategies, i.e., by either assigning weights to instances to prioritize those with higher confidence levels (Dumitrache et al., 2019), or by inducing directly from disagreement without considering aggregated labels (Uma et al., 2021; Fornaciari et al., 2021).

While numerous research papers have been devoted to understanding the reasons behind annotators' disagreement (Han et al., 2020; Sandri et al., 2023; Sang and Stanton, 2022) or to leverage on disagreement when training classification models, less attention has been devoted to explain and a priori recognize disagreement in hateful content (Shahriar and Solorio, 2023; Gajewska, 2023; Sullivan et al., 2023; de Paula et al., 2023; Erbani et al., 2023; Vallecillo-Rodríguez et al., 2023).

In particular, it has been demonstrated how different annotators adopt diverse strategies, involving the adoption of ad-hoc shortcuts and identifying specific patterns, when performing a given task (Han et al., 2020). A significant contribution to the understanding of how humans annotate data is presented by Sang and Stanton (2022), where the authors demonstrate that factors such as age and personality strongly influence annotators' perception of offensive or hateful content. In (Sandri et al., 2023), the authors propose a taxonomy of possible reasons leading to annotators' disagreement and evaluate the impact on classification performance of the different types. Specifically, the authors identify four macro categories of reasons behind disagreement: sloppy annotations, ambiguity, missing information, and subjectivity. Furthermore, methods to examine the annotation quality and consistency have been proposed, aiming at obtaining a clear understanding of users' experience (Lavitas et al., 2021; Sang and Stanton, 2022).

Finally, a few recent works have focussed on explaining and recognizing disagreement. The approach proposed by Astorino et al. (2023) exploits integrated gradients in the definition of a *filtering strategy* aiming at identifying both disagreement and hate speech while identifying textual constituents that contribute in hateful messages explanation. A more recent approach (Rizzi et al., 2024a) proposes a probabilistic semantic approach for the identification of disagreement-related constituents in hateful content. The results achieved in the state of the art suggest that although promising results can be achieved by Large Language Models (LLMs), comparable performances using lower computational resources can be obtained with simpler strategies.

3 Proposed Approach

This work represents an extension of the approach proposed by Rizzi et al. (2024a), with the objective of enhancing constituent contextualization and defining a more comprehensive model.

Based on the hypothesis that disagreement can derive from specific constituents within a sentence that can be perceived differently and, therefore, achieve a different interpretation and connotation in relation to the task's label, a score representing the potential for disagreement has been defined.

The proposed approach is characterized by the following steps:

- **POS tagging constituent selection**: for each word in a given sentence, the corresponding lexical term has been identified through Part Of Speech (POS) tagging[1]. The elements corresponding to relevant lexical terms (i.e., adjectives, adverbs, interjections, nouns, pronouns, proper nouns, verbs, and hashtags) have been selected as constituents[2].

- **Constituent Embeddings:** for each constituent c selected from the given sentence, its contextualized embedding representation $\vec{\mathbf{v}}_c$ is obtained by means of the mBERT model.

- **Most similar constituents:** given a constituent c with the corresponding embedding $\vec{\mathbf{v}}_c$, the set S_c of the most similar constituents to c is determined according to:

$$S_c = \bigcup_t \{t | cos(\vec{\mathbf{v}}_t, \vec{\mathbf{v}}_c) \geq \psi\} \quad (1)$$

where $cos(\vec{\mathbf{v}}_t, \vec{\mathbf{v}}_c)$ is the cosine similarity between the contextualized embedding representation of element c (i.e., $\vec{\mathbf{v}}_c$) and the contextualized embedding representation of the element t (i.e., $\vec{\mathbf{v}}_t$), where $t \in T$ with T representing the set of constituents identified in the training dataset by performing the previously defined steps. Finally, ψ is a threshold that has been estimated via a grid search approach on the validation dataset.

- **Disagreement Score:** The proposed disagreement score is grounded on probability weighting functions (Prelec, 1998), which are linear and nonlinear functions of probability widely known in behavioral decision theory and behavioral economics. Weighted probabilities denote a probabilistic model wherein individual outcomes are associated with distinct weights, reflecting the differential likelihood of occurrence (Gonzalez and Wu, 1999; Nardon and Pianca, 2015). By assigning appropriate weights to relevant events, **it becomes possible to selectively focus on the subset of events whose occurrence significantly influences the probability of the event under consideration**. This selectivity enhances the precision of analyses and allows for a more targeted understanding of the complex interplay between events within a given system.

In our case, the weighted probabilities are used to compute the constituent disagreement score by only taking into account the constituents in the selected neighborhood. In particular, given a constituent c with the corresponding set of most similar constituents S_c, the weighted probability of the contextualized constituent $s \in S_c$ to be associated with the positive label (+), i.e., the agreement label, can be estimated as:

$$P\left(s^+\right) \frac{cos(\vec{\mathbf{v}}_s, \vec{\mathbf{v}}_c)}{\sum_{a \in S_c} cos(\vec{\mathbf{v}}_a, \vec{\mathbf{v}}_c)} \quad (2)$$

Where $P(s^+)$ represents the probability of the constituent $s \in S_c$ to be associated with the positive class label.

Similarly, given a constituent c with the corresponding set of most similar constituents S_c, the weighted probability of the contextualized constituent $s \in S_c$ to be associated with the negative label (−), i.e., the disagreement label,

[1]For POS Taggins we used `-core_web_sm` models by spaCy `https://spacy.io` version 3.6

[2]According to the selected spaCy model, the POS tag excluded from the selection are: adposition, auxiliary verb, coordinating conjunction, determiner, numeral, particle, punctuation, and subordinating conjunction.

Dataset	Language	N. items	Task	Annotators	Pool Ann.	% of items with full agr.
HS-Brexit	En	1,120	Hate Speech	6	6	69%
ArMis	Ar	943	Misogyny and sexism detection	3	3	86%
ConvAbuse	En	4,050	Abusive Language detection	2-7	7	65%
MD-Agreement	En	10,753	Offensiveness detection	5	>800	42%

Table 1: Datasets characteristics.

can be estimated as:

$$P\left(s^{-}\right) \frac{cos(\vec{\mathbf{v}}_s, \vec{\mathbf{v}}_c)}{\sum_{a \in S_c} cos(\vec{\mathbf{v}}_a, \vec{\mathbf{v}}_c)} \qquad (3)$$

Where $P(s^{-})$ represents the probability of the constituent $s \in S_c$ to be associated with the negative class label.

Given the weighted probabilities estimated according to Equation (2) and (3), the Disagreement Score for any constituent c is defined as:

$$DS(c) = \sum_{s \in S_c} P\left(s^{+}\right) \frac{cos(\vec{\mathbf{v}}_s, \vec{\mathbf{v}}_c)}{\sum_{a \in S_c} cos(\vec{\mathbf{v}}_a, \vec{\mathbf{v}}_c)} - P\left(s^{-}\right) \frac{cos(\vec{\mathbf{v}}_s, \vec{\mathbf{v}}_c)}{\sum_{a \in S_c} cos(\vec{\mathbf{v}}_a, \vec{\mathbf{v}}_c)} \qquad (4)$$

Equation 4, which can be seen as a difference of all weighted probabilities, ranges in the interval from -1 to 1. The closer the score is to minus one, the more the constituent is related to the disagreement label. The closer the score is to one, the more the constituent is related to the agreement label.

The disagreement scores allow us to estimate the disagreement that may arise between annotators. The Sentence Disagreement Score (SDS) has been estimated by aggregating the scores computed for the single constituents according to the following strategies: **Sum**, **Mean**, **Median**, and **Minimum**. For each aggregation strategy, a threshold π has been estimated via a greed search approach to assign the final class label of the sentence.

4 Datasets, Baselines and Performance Metrics

In order to evaluate the computational potential of the proposed approach, both from the prediction capabilities and the computational resources needed, 4 benchmark datasets provided by SemEval 2023 Task 11 related to Learning With Disagreement (Leonardelli et al., 2023) have been adopted.

The datasets have different characteristics in terms of types (social media posts and conversations), languages (English and Arabic), goals (misogyny, hate-speech, offensiveness detection), and annotation methods (experts, specific demographics groups, and general crowd). Their characteristics are summarized in Table 1.

- *Hate Speech on Brexit (HS-Brexit)* (Akhtar et al., 2021). This dataset consists of 1,120 English tweets collected with keywords related to immigration and Brexit. The dataset was annotated with hate speech, aggressiveness, offensiveness, and stereotype by six annotators.
- *Arabic Misogyny and Sexism (ArMIS)* (Almanea and Poesio, 2022). The dataset consists of Arabic tweets to study the effect of bias on sexist judgments, focusing on the impact of being conservative or liberal. The data was labeled by three annotators, one conservative male, one moderate female, and one liberal female.
- *ConvAbuse* (Cercas Curry et al., 2021). The dataset contains 4,185 English dialogues between users and two conversational agents. The user dialogues have been annotated by experts in gender studies.
- *Multi-Domain Agreement (MD-Agreement) (Leonardelli et al., 2021).* The dataset consists of 10,000 English tweets from three different domains (*BlackLivesMatter*, *Election2020*, *Covid-19*). Each tweet was annotated as offensive or not by 5 annotators.

All the datasets are characterized by the presence of hard-labels (hateful/non-hateful) and soft-labels (disagreement) for each instance. According to Poletto et al. (2021) all these tasks are under the *hate* umbrella since aggressive, offensive, and abusive language can be triggered by hate, and misogyny is a form of aversion towards a specific target. For this reason, from now on we will refer to *hate* as a comprehensive word embracing all the above-mentioned forms of hostility. Since in this work, disagreement detection is addressed as a binary task, an agreement label has been derived from the available soft-labels. In particular, the agreement label is set equal to $(+)$ when there is a complete agreement among the annotators, while equal to $(-)$ in all the other cases.

Regarding the baseline models, we compare both with the best approach identified by Rizzi et al. (2024a) (i.e., G-minimum) and with widely adopted state-of-the-art AI models: mBERT (Kenton and Toutanova, 2019), Llama-2 (Touvron et al., 2023), Mistral-7B (Jiang et al., 2023), Llama-3.2 (Dubey et al., 2024), and Phi-3.5 (Haider et al., 2024). In particular, the approach proposed by Rizzi et al. (2024a) comprises a technique for identifying disagreement-related textual constituents and an approach for generalizing towards unseen textual constituents. Additionally, four distinct strategies for identifying disagreement are presented. For what concerns the selected LLMs, instead, they have been fine-tuned using the boolean soft-labels related to the disagreement, adopting the huggingface framework, using default hyperparameters. mBERT (Kenton and Toutanova, 2019) is a well-established and widely recognized transformer-based model trained on more than 100 languages. The use of mBERT allows for results that are easily reproducible without extensive computational power. On the other hand, Llama-based models (Touvron et al., 2023; Dubey et al., 2024) are generative large language models known for their efficiency and scalability. They are designed to handle large-scale language tasks and can be fine-tuned for a variety of classification problems.

Mistral-7B (Jiang et al., 2023) is a further generative language model that is renowned for its efficiency and targeted optimizations. It is designed for high-volume text processing, optimized for multilingual content, and suitable for globalized contexts.

Phi 3.5-mini (Haider et al., 2024) is a lightweight version of the Phi model family that offers robust performance on language tasks while avoiding the high demands of larger models. Its compact structure makes it ideal for constrained environments, with excellent results in multilingual processing and classification.

Each of these models has been proven to be effective on several natural language tasks such as hate speech detection or sentiment analysis. Moreover, a peculiar capability of such models is the ability to process multilingual text and social media content. While all models achieve challenging results on a variety of tasks, the choice among these models usually represents a compromise based on specific requirements of the task, such as the volume of data, the languages involved, and the computational resources available.

Differently from the original Le-Wi-Di challenge (Leonardelli et al., 2023), in this work, disagreement detection is addressed as a binary task, making a comparison with the participants' performances unfeasible. This is mainly motivated by the concerns raised by the organizers (Leonardelli et al., 2023), also recently supported by Rizzi et al. (2024b), where the problem of ranking systems trained on continuous disagreement soft-labels using cross-entropy could be strongly biased by the cross-entropy measure itself. For this reason, we compared the proposed approach with benchmark models.

For what concerns the performance metrics, two main aspects have been considered: (i) prediction capabilities in terms of F1-Measure for both the agreement ($F1^+$) and disagreement ($F1^-$) labels, together with their average ($F-score$), and (ii) computational requirements in terms of the number of model parameters, RAM, CPU, and GPU. The first evaluation allows for a comparison of the models' capabilities in identifying disagreement among annotators, while the second aspect allows for a comparison of the computational requirements needed to reproduce the whole pipeline (comprehensive of the training phase).

5 Results and Discussion

Given the Disagreement Score (DS) of each constituent within a sentence, all the proposed aggregation strategies have been evaluated (i.e., sum, mean, median, and minimum). Table 2 summarizes the results achieved with the best thresholds (π and ψ) selected through a grid-search approach on the validation set released within the Le-Wi-Di challenge for each dataset. Results are distinguished between agreement $(+)$ and disagreement $(-)$ labels.

A McNemar (McNemar, 1947) test has been adopted to perform a pairwise comparison with each of the proposed approaches (considering a confidence level of 0.95). The McNemar test does not verify if two models have different perfor-

Approach	ConvAbuse			ArMIS			HS-Brexit			MD-Agreement		
	$F1^{+}$	$F1^{-}$	*F1-score*	$F1^{+}$	$F1^{-}$	*F1-score*	$F1^{+}$	$F1^{-}$	*F1-score*	$F1^{+}$	$F1^{-}$	*F1-score*
Sum	0.84	0.25	$0.55^{*\dagger\ddagger\circledast\phi}$	0.68	0.29	0.48*	0.71	0.47	$0.59^{\dagger\ddagger\circledast}$	0.50	0.69	$0.59^{*\dagger\ddagger\circledast\phi}$
Mean	0.80	0.36	$0.58^{*\dagger\ddagger\circledast\phi}$	0.66	0.47	**0.57***	0.80	0.61	0.70^{ϕ}	0.56	0.65	$0.60^{*\dagger\ddagger\circledast}$
Median	0.85	0.32	$0.58^{*\dagger\ddagger\circledast\phi}$	0.68	0.34	0.51*	0.79	0.49	$0.64^{\circledast\phi}$	0.55	0.67	$0.61^{*\dagger\ddagger\circledast\phi}$
Minimum	0.86	0.43	$\mathbf{0.65}^{*\dagger\ddagger\circledast}$	0.48	0.48	0.48*	0.63	0.55	$0.59^{*\dagger\ddagger\circledast}$	0.48	0.71	$0.60^{*\dagger\ddagger\circledast\phi}$
G-Minimum	0.85	0.33	0.59	0.59	0.48	0.54	0.84	0.69	**0.77**	0.54	0.64	0.59
mBERT *	0.93	0.05	0.49	0.38	0.63	0.50	0.37	0.43	0.40	0.76	0.60	0.68
Llama-2-7B †	0.92	0.13	0.53	0.71	0.37	0.54	0.84	0.63	0.74	0.59	0.77	**0.68**
Mistral-7B ‡	0.91	0.26	0.59	0.66	0.39	0.53	0.82	0.69	0.76	0.55	0.77	0.66
Llama-3.2-3B $^{\circledast}$	0.92	0.17	0.54	0.67	0.25	0.46	0.85	0.59	0.72	0.59	0.75	0.67
Phi-3.5-mini $^{\phi}$	0.89	0.23	0.56	0.67	0.35	0.51	0.71	0.36	0.54	0.53	0.64	0.59

Table 2: Comparison of the different approaches on the test set for disagreement detection. **Bold** denotes the best approach according to the F1-Score, while underline represents the best approach according to the disagreement label. A McNermar test has been performed as a pairwise comparison between the proposed approaches and MBERT (*), Llama-2 ($\dagger$), Mistral ($\ddagger$), Llama-3.2 ($\circledast$) and Phi-3.5 (ϕ).

Approach	Parameters	RAM	CPU	GPU
Sum *Mean* *Median* *Minimum*	179M	16 GB	2-4 CPU cores	Non-necessary
G-Minimum (Rizzi et al., 2024a)	179M	16 GB	2-4 CPU cores	Non-necessary
mBERT (Kenton and Toutanova, 2019)	179M	16 GB	4-8 CPU cores	Non-necessary
Llama-2-7B (Touvron et al., 2023)	6.74B	160GB	6-12 CPU cores*	100GB
Mistral-7B (Jiang et al., 2023)	7.25B	160GB	8-16 CPU cores*	110GB
Llama-3.2-3B (Dubey et al., 2024)	3.21B	90GB	4-8 CPU cores*	60GB
Phi-3.5-mini(Haider et al., 2024)	3.82B	90GB	4-8 CPU cores*	60GB

Table 3: Computational requirements of the proposed approaches. Values marked with (*) have been estimated, as the exact information was not provided.

mances, but it tests if there is a significant difference in terms of model prediction by comparing sensitivity and specificity of the two models under analysis.

Focusing on the results reported in Table 2, we can observe that all the considered approaches perform better on the majority class, which in general, is related to the complete agreement. Additionally, it is important to note that mBERT is not able to systematically outperform the proposed approach, considering all the aggregation strategies. On the other hand, the proposed approach and the selected LLMs (i.e. Llama-2-7B, Mstral-7B, Llama-3.2-3B, and Phi-3.5-mini) perform in a competitive way: while our strategies work better on ConvAbuse and ArMIS, such models achieve better results on HS-Brexit and MD-Agreement. Although the results of LLMs seem promising on those datasets, such a performance is likely due to the presence of instances on the same topic (e.g., Covid in MD-Agreement, Brexit in HS-Brexit) in the corpora used for training the models. It can be easily noted that the selected LLMs perform worst on the two datasets that are characterized by the underlying lexicon (e.g., ArMIS contains misogynous tweets) or by the type of expressions (e.g., ConvAbuse contains user-bot interactions). An additional consideration relates to the difference in terms of model predictions evaluated through the McNemar test. Although the selected LLMs achieve higher values of F1 score in HS-Brexit, the statistical test shows that in those cases, the behavior of our best approach is analogous and does not highlight any difference in terms of model prediction. On the other hand, on ConvAbuse, our approach outperforms state-of-the-art LLMs, and the statistical test corroborates the hypothesis that our predictions are significantly different. A final consideration refers to the performances achieved on MD-Agreement. As highlighted by Rizzi et al. (2024a), one challenging aspect of the dataset is the inclusion of three main macro-topics of

discussion. While the proposed approach performs, on MD-Agreement, poorly with respect to state-of-the-art LLMs, it introduces an improvement in performance with respect to G-Minimum. The primary reason for such behavior seems to be the variety of arguments covered by the dataset, indicating that disagreement may stem not only from differing beliefs or backgrounds but also from the specific topics being discussed.
To provide a complete overview of the models, we report in Table 3 their computational requirements[3]. It can be easily noted that the proposed approach should be preferred: while the number of parameters and RAM are comparable with mBERT, it requires fewer CPU cores. Furthermore, when comparing our approach with the selected LLMs, the necessary resources clearly appear advantageous. Considering both the achieved performances and the computational requirements, we can affirm that simpler models represent a promising alternative to mBERT and other widely adopted LLMs.

A further relevant aspect relates to the usage of the models to highlight disagreement constituents during the annotation phase in the crowdsourcing platforms. While mBERT and the other analyzed LLMs can straightforwardly underline which constituents contribute more to predict disagreement, also the presented approach can be exploited for such a task.

For instance, Integrated Gradients can be used for the identification of such terms from Large Language Models. For the proposed approach, the constituent score can be exploited to evaluate the relationship of each constituent, within the context in which it appears, and the disagreement between annotators (on the hate task).

Figure 1 reports a visual representation of Disagreement Scores (DS) computed for two non-hateful tweets of the Brexit dataset. The first example (Figure 1 (a)) reports a tweet with disagreement, while the second one (Figure 1 (b)) denotes a tweet with agreement. According to the DS score, the proposed approach highlights the

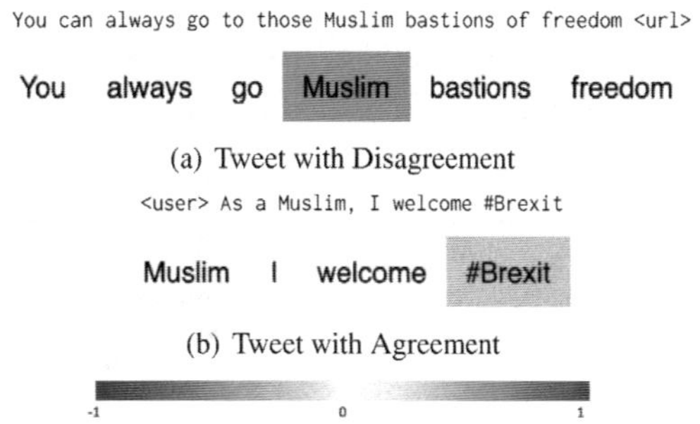

(a) Tweet with Disagreement

(b) Tweet with Agreement

Figure 1: Visual representation of disagreement scores on sentences from the Brexit dataset. Positive values are represented with green and negative values are represented with pink. The white color is used for constituents with DS values equal or close to zero.

word "*Muslim*" as strongly related to disagreement in the first tweet and to agreement in the second one, highlighting the capability to evaluate the constituent with respect to its context. It is important to note that the word "Muslim" was intentionally used by the creators of the dataset as a seed word because it is considered a source of disagreement. The reported example confirms that such a word is correctly identified, according to the context where it appears, as a source of agreement or disagreement in an agnostic way. In fact, the reported tweets - "*As a Muslim , I welcome #Brexit*" and "*You can always go to those Muslim bastions of freedom*" - strongly differ on the connotation of the term "Muslim". In the first tweet, the term is used as a self-identifier, to identify the religious affiliation of the person expressing a personal opinion on a political issue. The focus is on the individual's religious identity, and the statement implies that despite being a Muslim, the person supports Brexit. The connotation here is neutral and merely serves to highlight the diversity of opinions within the Muslim community. In the second tweet instead, the term carries a negative connotation since it is used in a stereotypical and possibly derogatory manner. The phrase "*Muslim bastions of freedom*" could be interpreted as sarcastic or mocking, implying that there is a perception that Muslim-majority areas or countries are not associated with freedom.

Finally, a more extensive qualitative analysis of the salient constituents for the different datasets has been conducted. Since our approach is based on a contextualized representation of constituents, where the same word can have multiple embed-

[3]The values reported within this table have been estimated according to (Kim et al., 2024) and with the information released by the authors both in the corresponding papers and in the official Hugging Face model-card. All the reported values refer to the original model and do not consider further optimization techniques that might reduce computational requirements at the expense of reduced recognition performance.

ding representations according to its context, we computed the top-scoring words (per dataset) as follows:

- we considered all the scores for each constituent according to its context,
- we computed the percentage of positive and negative scores for each constituent,
- we sorted the estimated percentage to identify the top-k constituents.

Agreement Constituents	Disagreement Constituents
nerdy	compatriots
sleepy	throw
intelligence	flows
greenhouse	reverse
sure	Sanders

Table 4: Top-5 agreement and disagreement constituents for the ConvAbuse dataset

Agreement Constituents	Disagreement Constituents
vote	Obama
we	#EURO2016
Duch	#Trump2016
Cameron	France
immigrant	invasion

Table 5: Top-5 agreement and disagreement constituents for the HS-Brexit dataset.

Agreement Constituents	Disagreement Constituents
#blacklivesmatter	Covid
Thank	police
UK	coronavirus
neck	vote
blah	President

Table 6: Top-5 agreement and disagreement constituents for the MD Agreement dataset

Agreement Constituents	Disagreement Constituents
ناقصات (deficiencies)	متسلطات (bossy)
المرأة (woman)	صور (photo)
دين (religion)	عوانس (spinsters)
شوارع (streets)	حلال (halal)
النساء (women)	التعامل (dealing)

Table 7: Top-5 agreement and disagreement constituents for the ArMIS dataset

Tables 4, 5, 6, and 7 list the top-5 agreement and disagreement constituents for each dataset. The elements that show the highest agreement scores are rarely associated with different perceptions, being used frequently in sentences where annotators show a full agreement, while the ones with high disagreement scores are often a proxy of different perspectives.

Since the main goal of this paper is to show the relationship between constituent scores and the agreement/disagreement label, according to the obtained results, the estimated constituent scores can be considered promising because acting as a good proxy of agreement/disagreement. While we acknowledge the potential benefits of post-hoc human evaluation, implementing such a strategy is impractical due to the impossibility of reproducing the exact conditions of the original annotation process. Even by adhering to the dataset creators' approach, obtaining the same annotators is basically not possible (in most cases, anonymous annotators have been involved through crowd-sourcing platforms). On the other hand, introducing additional annotators would imply increasing the variability of potential perspectives without guaranteeing any adherence to the initial annotation and, therefore, to the constituent perception of the original annotators of the dataset.

The proposed solution, contrary to what has been formerly presented in the literature, is able not only to predict if a text can lead to disagreement from different readers' perspectives but also calls attention to those *disagreement-related constituents* in hateful content.

6 Conclusions and Future Work

This paper introduces a simple approach for the identification of disagreement-related constituents within the text and exploits them in the prediction of disagreement in hateful texts. By leveraging weighted probabilities, the proposed methodology allows the identification of constituents that not only represent valuable information for a comprehensive understanding of the sources of disagreement within the text but also serve as the foundation for developing an explainable strategy for disagreement detection. The proposed strategies demonstrate a good trade-off between prediction capabilities and computational requirements compared both with G-minimum (Rizzi et al., 2024a) and with well-known state-of-the-art language models:

mBERT, Llama-2, Mistral, Llama-3, and Phi-3.

Future works will consider the adoption of indexing or clustering techniques to reduce the search space of the most similar embeddings by narrowing down the candidates for similarity comparison, resulting in an improvement in efficiency. Moreover, future works might focus on the extension of the proposed approach for the quantification of the level of disagreement in a sentence. Finally, considering the potential of highlighting disagreement-related tokens in the labeling phase, a relevant aspect that will be considered relates to the creation of datasets that include annotators' perceptions at the constituent level.

Limitations

The proposed approach holds significant promise to improve our comprehension of textual constituents related to disagreement, both in theoretical and practical contexts. By enabling the identification of these constituents, the method contributes to a deeper comprehension of disagreement dynamics within the text. However, it is crucial to acknowledge a current limitation associated with its computational complexity. The comparison within each contextualized constituent representation and every known contextualized constituent represents a significant computational burden, making the approach computationally expensive and difficult to scale. In particular, the time complexity for the computation of the DS scores for a given sentence[4] is $O(n{*}m{*}\textit{time complexity of similarity measure})$, where n represents the number of contextualized constituents in the training data and m the number of contextualized constituents in the given sentence. In our case, the adopted similarity measure is the Cosine similarity that has a time complexity of $O(d)$ where d represents the dimension of the vector to compare. Therefore the overall time complexity is $O(n * m * d)$. This constraint highlights the need for future improvements to improve efficiency while retaining the method's significant insights into textual conflict.

Ethical Statement

In this research work, we used datasets from the recent literature, and we did not use or infer any sensitive information. The risk of possible abuse of the models and the proposed approach is low.

[4]The time complexity estimation doesn't consider the time complexity necessary to compute the latent representation of the constituents.

Experimental Settings and Setup

We ran the experiments of the proposed methodology on a machine equipped with one Nvidia Testa T4 GPU, CUDA v11.4, 256GB RAM, 2 CPU Xeon Gold. The selected state-of-the-art baselines include generative LLMs. While mBERT has been fine-tuned for the classification task by concatenating a final classification layer, generative LLMs have been instruction-tuned to adapt their generative capabilities for the specific classification task. Further details, along with the code for the reproducibility of the results, are available in the GitHub repository. Regarding mBERT, we used `bert-base-multilingual-cased`.For what concerns the LLMs considered as baselines, we adopted the following: `Llama-2-7b-chat-hf`, `Mistral-7B-Instruct-v0.3`, `Llama-3.2-3B-Instruct`, and `Phi-3.5-mini-instruct`.

Best Hyperparameters Configurations

The optimal hyperparameter configurations are reported in Table 8.

	HS-Brexit		ConvAbuse		MD-Agreement		arMIS	
	ψ	π	ψ	π	ψ	π	ψ	π
Sum	0.85	0.5	0.95	2.2	0.7	1.5	0.85	1.30
Mean	0.6	0.3	0.85	0.4	0.7	0.2	0.85	0.2
Median	0.7	0.3	0.7	0.6	0.75	0.4	0.8	0.3
Minimum	0.7	-0.4	0.5	0.5	0.7	-0.4	0.85	-0.4

Table 8: Optimal Hyper-parameter Settings

Acknowledgments

We acknowledge the support of the PNRR ICSC National Research Centre for High Performance Computing, Big Data and Quantum Computing (CN00000013), under the NRRP MUR program funded by the NextGenerationEU. The work of Elisabetta Fersini has been partially funded by MUR under the grant ReGAInS, Dipartimenti di Eccellenza 2023-2027 of the Department of Informatics, Systems and Communication at the University of Milano-Bicocca. The work of Paolo Rosso was in the framework of the FairTransNLP-Stereotypes research project, Grant PID2021-124361OB-C31 funded by MCIN/AEI/10.13039/501100011033 and by ERDF/EU.

References

Sohail Akhtar, Valerio Basile, and Viviana Patti. 2021. Whose opinions matter? perspective-aware models to identify opinions of hate speech victims in abusive language detection. *Preprint*, arXiv:2106.15896.

Dina Almanea and Massimo Poesio. 2022. ArMIS - the Arabic misogyny and sexism corpus with annotator subjective disagreements. In *Proceedings of the Thirteenth Language Resources and Evaluation Conference*, pages 2282–2291, Marseille, France. European Language Resources Association.

Alessandro Astorino, Giulia Rizzi, and Elisabetta Fersini. 2023. Integrated gradients as proxy of disagreement in hateful content. In *CEUR Workshop Proceedings*, volume 3596. CEUR-WS. org.

Beata Beigman Klebanov and Eyal Beigman. 2009. From annotator agreement to noise models. *Computational Linguistics*, 35(4):495–503.

Federico Cabitza, Andrea Campagner, and Valerio Basile. 2023. Toward a perspectivist turn in ground truthing for predictive computing. In *Proceedings of the AAAI Conference on Artificial Intelligence*, volume 37, pages 6860–6868.

Amanda Cercas Curry, Gavin Abercrombie, and Verena Rieser. 2021. ConvAbuse: Data, analysis, and benchmarks for nuanced abuse detection in conversational AI. In *Proceedings of the 2021 Conference on Empirical Methods in Natural Language Processing*, pages 7388–7403, Online and Punta Cana, Dominican Republic. Association for Computational Linguistics.

Angel Felipe Magnossão de Paula, Giulia Rizzi, Elisabetta Fersini, and Damiano Spina. 2023. Ai-upv at exist 2023–sexism characterization using large language models under the learning with disagreements regime. In *CEUR Workshop Proceedings*, volume 3497, pages 985–999. CEUR-WS.

Abhimanyu Dubey, Abhinav Jauhri, Abhinav Pandey, Abhishek Kadian, Ahmad Al-Dahle, Aiesha Letman, Akhil Mathur, Alan Schelten, Amy Yang, Angela Fan, et al. 2024. The llama 3 herd of models. *arXiv preprint arXiv:2407.21783*.

Anca Dumitrache, FD Mediagroep, Lora Aroyo, and Chris Welty. 2019. A crowdsourced frame disambiguation corpus with ambiguity. In *Proceedings of NAACL-HLT*, pages 2164–2170.

Johan Erbani, Előd Egyed-Zsigmond, Diana Nurbakova, and Pierre-Edouard Portier. 2023. When multiple perspectives and an optimization process lead to better performance, an automatic sexism identification on social media with pretrained transformers in a soft label context. *Working Notes of CLEF*.

Tommaso Fornaciari, Alexandra Uma, Silviu Paun, Barbara Plank, Dirk Hovy, Massimo Poesio, et al. 2021. Beyond black & white: Leveraging annotator disagreement via soft-label multi-task learning. In *Proceedings of the 2021 Conference of the North American Chapter of the Association for Computational Linguistics: Human Language Technologies*. Association for Computational Linguistics.

Ewelina Gajewska. 2023. eevvgg at SemEval-2023 task 11: Offensive language classification with rater-based information. In *Proceedings of the 17th International Workshop on Semantic Evaluation (SemEval-2023)*, pages 171–176, Toronto, Canada. Association for Computational Linguistics.

Richard Gonzalez and George Wu. 1999. On the shape of the probability weighting function. *Cognitive psychology*, 38(1):129–166.

Emman Haider, Daniel Perez-Becker, Thomas Portet, Piyush Madan, Amit Garg, David Majercak, Wen Wen, Dongwoo Kim, Ziyi Yang, Jianwen Zhang, et al. 2024. Phi-3 safety post-training: Aligning language models with a" break-fix" cycle. *arXiv preprint arXiv:2407.13833*.

Lei Han, Eddy Maddalena, Alessandro Checco, Cristina Sarasua, Ujwal Gadiraju, Kevin Roitero, and Gianluca Demartini. 2020. Crowd worker strategies in relevance judgment tasks. In *Proceedings of the 13th international conference on web search and data mining*, pages 241–249.

Andrew Hoskins and John Tulloch. 2018. The construction of hate in online spaces. *International Journal of Communication*, 12:3853–3873.

Leonie Huddy and Lene Aarøe. 2019. The subjectivity of hate speech detection: A study on perceptions of offensiveness. *Political Psychology*, 40(1):3–29.

Albert Q Jiang, Alexandre Sablayrolles, Arthur Mensch, Chris Bamford, Devendra Singh Chaplot, Diego de las Casas, Florian Bressand, Gianna Lengyel, Guillaume Lample, Lucile Saulnier, et al. 2023. Mistral 7b. *arXiv preprint arXiv:2310.06825*.

Jacob Devlin Ming-Wei Chang Kenton and Lee Kristina Toutanova. 2019. Bert: Pre-training of deep bidirectional transformers for language understanding. In *Proceedings of NAACL-HLT*, pages 4171–4186.

Taeho Kim, Yanming Wang, Vatshank Chaturvedi, Lokesh Gupta, Seyeon Kim, Yongin Kwon, and Sangtae Ha. 2024. Llmem: Estimating gpu memory usage for fine-tuning pre-trained llms. *arXiv preprint arXiv:2404.10933*.

Marianne D LaFrance and Sarah J Roberts. 2019. The role of bias in hate speech detection. *Journal of Language Aggression and Conflict*, 7(1):1–20.

Liliya Lavitas, Olivia Redfield, Allen Lee, Daniel Fletcher, Matthias Eck, and Sunil Janardhanan. 2021. Annotation quality framework-accuracy, credibility, and consistency. In *NEURIPS 2021 Workshop for Data Centric AI*, volume 3.

Noah Lee, Na Min An, and James Thorne. 2023. Can large language models capture dissenting human voices? In *The 2023 Conference on Empirical Methods in Natural Language Processing*.

Elisa Leonardelli, Stefano Menini, Alessio Palmero Aprosio, Marco Guerini, and Sara Tonelli. 2021. Agreeing to disagree: Annotating offensive language datasets with annotators' disagreement. In *Proceedings of the 2021 Conference on Empirical Methods in Natural Language Processing*, pages 10528–10539, Online and Punta Cana, Dominican Republic. Association for Computational Linguistics.

Elisa Leonardelli, Alexandra Uma, Gavin Abercrombie, Dina Almanea, Valerio Basile, Tommaso Fornaciari, Barbara Plank, Verena Rieser, and Massimo Poesio. 2023. Semeval-2023 task 11: Learning with disagreements (lewidi). *Preprint*, arXiv:2304.14803.

Quinn McNemar. 1947. Note on the sampling error of the difference between correlated proportions or percentages. *Psychometrika*, 12(2):153–157.

Martina Nardon and Paolo Pianca. 2015. Probability weighting functions. *University Ca'Foscari of Venice, Dept. of Economics Research Paper Series No*, 29.

Fabio Poletto, Valerio Basile, Manuela Sanguinetti, Cristina Bosco, and Viviana Patti. 2021. Resources and benchmark corpora for hate speech detection: a systematic review. *Language Resources and Evaluation*, 55:477–523.

Drazen Prelec. 1998. The probability weighting function. *Econometrica*, 66(3):497–527.

Giulia Rizzi, Alessandro Astorino, Paolo Rosso, and Elisabetta Fersini. 2024a. Unraveling disagreement constituents in hateful speech. In *European Conference on Information Retrieval*, pages 21–29. Springer.

Giulia Rizzi, Elisa Leonardelli, Massimo Poesio, Alexandra Uma, Maja Pavlovic, Silviu Paun, Paolo Rosso, and Elisabetta Fersini. 2024b. Soft metrics for evaluation with disagreements: an assessment. In *Proceedings of the 3rd Workshop on Perspectivist Approaches to NLP (NLPerspectives)@ LREC-COLING 2024*, pages 84–94.

Marta Sandri, Elisa Leonardelli, Sara Tonelli, and Elisabetta Ježek. 2023. Why don't you do it right? analysing annotators' disagreement in subjective tasks. In *Proceedings of the 17th Conference of the European Chapter of the Association for Computational Linguistics*, pages 2420–2433.

Yisi Sang and Jeffrey Stanton. 2022. The origin and value of disagreement among data labelers: A case study of individual differences in hate speech annotation. In *International Conference on Information*, pages 425–444. Springer.

Maarten Sap, Dallas Card, Saadia Gabriel, Yejin Choi, and Noah A Smith. 2019. An analysis of annotator disagreement in human interpretations of toxicity. In *Proceedings of the AAAI Conference on Artificial Intelligence*, volume 33, pages 5470–5477.

Maarten Sap, Swabha Swayamdipta, Laura Vianna, Xuhui Zhou, Yejin Choi, and Noah A Smith. 2022. Annotators with attitudes: How annotator beliefs and identities bias toxic language detection. In *Proceedings of the 2022 Conference of the North American Chapter of the Association for Computational Linguistics: Human Language Technologies*, pages 5884–5906.

Sadat Shahriar and Thamar Solorio. 2023. Safewebuh at semeval-2023 task 11: Learning annotator disagreement in derogatory text: Comparison of direct training vs aggregation. *arXiv preprint arXiv:2305.01050*.

Michael Sullivan, Mohammed Yasin, and Cassandra L Jacobs. 2023. University at buffalo at semeval-2023 task 11: Masda–modelling annotator sensibilities through disaggregation. In *Proceedings of the 17th International Workshop on Semantic Evaluation (SemEval-2023)*, pages 978–985.

Hugo Touvron, Louis Martin, Kevin Stone, Peter Albert, Amjad Almahairi, Yasmine Babaei, Nikolay Bashlykov, Soumya Batra, Prajjwal Bhargava, Shruti Bhosale, et al. 2023. Llama 2: Open foundation and fine-tuned chat models. *arXiv preprint arXiv:2307.09288*.

Alexandra Uma, Tommaso Fornaciari, Dirk Hovy, Silviu Paun, Barbara Plank, and Massimo Poesio. 2021. Learning from disagreement: A survey. *Journal of Artificial Intelligence Research*, 72:1385–1470.

María Estrella Vallecillo-Rodríguez, FMP del Arco, Luis Alfonso Ureña-López, María Teresa Martín-Valdivia, and Arturo Montejo-Ráez. 2023. Integrating annotator information in transformer fine-tuning for sexism detection. *Working Notes of CLEF*.

On Crowdsourcing Task Design for Discourse Relation Annotation

Frances Yung and Vera Demberg
Saarland University, Saarbrücken, Germany
{frances, vera}@lst.uni-saarland.de

Abstract

Interpreting implicit discourse relations involves complex reasoning, requiring the integration of semantic cues with background knowledge, as overt connectives like *because* or *then* are absent. These relations often allow multiple interpretations, best represented as distributions. In this study, we compare two established methods that crowdsource English implicit discourse relation annotation by connective insertion: a free-choice approach, which allows annotators to select any suitable connective, and a forced-choice approach, which asks them to select among a set of predefined options. Specifically, we re-annotate the whole DiscoGeM 1.0 corpus - initially annotated with the free-choice method - using the forced-choice approach. The free-choice approach allows for flexible and intuitive insertion of various connectives, which are context-dependent. Comparison among over 130,000 annotations, however, shows that the free-choice strategy produces less diverse annotations, often converging on common labels. Analysis of the results reveals the interplay between task design and the annotators' abilities to interpret and produce discourse relations.

1 Introduction

Disagreement in linguistic annotation is increasingly seen not as noise but as a valuable signal capturing diverse perspectives in language interpretation (Dumitrache et al., 2021; Uma et al., 2021; Frenda et al., 2024). A single gold label, traditionally provided by one or two trained annotators, often fails to capture the full range of interpretations, which may arise from linguistic ambiguity, contextual factors, or annotators' cultural and experiential backgrounds. Crowdsourcing offers a scalable solution for gathering these alternative interpretations.

To guide untrained crowd workers in reliably annotating abstract linguistic phenomenon, intuitive and carefully designed workflows are essential. Task design has been identified as one of the factors behind annotation disagreement and bias (Pavlick and Kwiatkowski, 2019; Jiang and de Marneffe, 2022), and even can impact annotation quality (Shaw et al., 2011; Gadiraju et al., 2017; Gururangan et al., 2018). For example, Pyatkin et al. (2023) investigate the bias of task design guiding workers in annotating implicit discourse relation (IDR) senses, which often have multiple interpretations. They compared two methods: one based on insertion of discourse connectives (DCs), e.g. *John fell down* ***because*** *he tripped*, and the other on paraphrasing discourse arguments to question-answer (QA) pairs, e.g. *Q:* ***Why*** *(did) John fell down? A: He tripped.* While annotations from both methods were found to align closely, subtle bias in the annotation preference are found in both methods due to limitations of using natural language to annotate specialized linguistic concepts (not all senses can be easily expressed by a connective or by a question).

Building on this line of work, we explore the potential method bias of two IDR annotation tasks for English based on DC insertion. These methods differ solely in whether annotators select from predefined options (Rohde et al., 2016; Yung et al., 2024) or freely type in their choices (Yung et al., 2019). The free-choice method was employed to annotate 6,500 English IDRs in the DiscoGeM 1.0 corpus (Scholman et al., 2022),whereas the DiscoGeM 2.0 corpus, comprising multi-lingual translations or original texts from DiscoGeM 1.0, was annotated using the forced-choice method. An initial comparison of the statistics of the two corpora revealed characteristics unique to the English annotations, such as a higher proportion of CONJUNCTION relations.

Our findings indicate that the free-choice approach achieves higher agreements among annotators, while the forced-choice approach is more

Proceedings of Context and Meaning: Navigating Disagreements in NLP Annotation, pages 12–19
January 19, 2025.

effective at capturing a diverse range of alternative interpretations. Further analysis reveals that the free-choice approach favours intuitive and frequent intuitive sense, whereas the provided options in the forced-choice approach serve as prompts for the workers to identify rare, fine-grained senses. Moreover, the method bias interacts with individual differences in discourse processing: workers who could identify a wider range of senses in one approach also tended to label more different senses in the other approach. These results highlight the nuanced impact of task design on annotation outcomes.

The re-annotated resource is freely downloadable[1] alongside the original DiscoGeM 1.0. It provides an interesting dataset for the study of perspectivism and design in annotation as well as a rich collection of rare IDR examples, contributing to the major data bottleneck for current IDR recognition models.

2 Related work

Annotation of IDR requires integrating subtle semantic cues with background knowledge and mapping these to abstract labels – a task that is challenging even for trained annotators (Hoek and Scholman, 2017). Previous attempts to create datasets by crowdsourcing annotations often compromise on label variety or annotation quality (Kawahara et al., 2014; Kishimoto et al., 2018).

Inspired by the Penn Discourse Treebank's (PDTB) lexicalized approach to annotate IDRs (Prasad et al., 2019), prior work has proposed crowdsourcing IDRs via DC insertion. For example, to label the REASON relation between the arguments "*John missed the bus*" and "*He was late to work.*", the DC "*therefore*" could be inserted. In the initial proposal, crowd workers selected a DC from a fixed list, each corresponding to a unique IDR sense (Scholman and Demberg, 2017). While achieving high agreement with expert annotations, the method was tested on only 6 IDR senses to avoid overwhelming workers with too many options. Choosing a DC is often context-dependent; for example, while "*although*" and "*even though*" are nearly interchangeable, "*also*" versus "*furthermore*" (both indicating CONJUNCTION) may depend on context. Workers might reject an appropriate sense if a DC feels contextually awkward.

To handle a broader range of IDRs, Yung et al. (2019) proposed a two-step approach: first, workers freely type a DC that fits between two arguments; second, they select from a list of unambiguous DCs corresponding to their free-choice. For instance, if they type "*while*" in the first step, they should choose between "*at the same time*" and "*in contrast*" in the second step, which are mapped to the relations SYNCHRONY and CONTRAST respectively. This method was used to create the DiscoGeM 1.0 corpus, which contains 6,500 English IDRs each annotated by 10 workers (Scholman et al., 2022). Nonetheless, DiscoGeM 2.0, which extends the annotations to German, French, and Czech (Yung et al., 2024), adopted the one-step forced-choice method: workers directly chose from 28 DC choices, which were grouped by semantics and shuffled per worker to facilitate navigation and avoid positional bias. The free- and forced- choice methods were reported to yield similar annotations, but the comparisons were based on a limited subset of items (234 in Yung et al. (2019) and 18 in Yung et al. (2024)), with a restricted range of IDR senses.

Using a different crowd-annotation method, Pyatkin et al. (2020) crowdsourced discourse relations by instructing workers to create QA pairs from the provided text, e.g., "*Q: What is the reason John was late? A: He missed the bus.*" Comparisons of QA-based and free-choice DC insertion methods show that both exhibit biases toward specific sense categories. In contrast to common attribution of method artifacts to degraded data quality (Gururangan et al., 2018; Zhu and Rzeszotarski, 2024), it was found that training on the complementary data collected by both methods enhanced the performance of IDR identification models (Pyatkin et al., 2023).

3 Annotation experiment

We adopt the forced-choice approach to re-annotate the DiscoGeM 1.0 corpus, which was originally annotated using the free-choice approach. For this, an annotation interface was implemented based on the description of DiscoGeM 2.0 (Yung et al., 2024). One representative DC was selected for each of the 28 relations to be annotated. The selection was primarily based on the disambiguating DCs from the second step of the free-choice method,[2] while ensuring they were sufficiently frequent and not highly context dependent. The complete list is

[1] https://github.com/merelscholman/DiscoGeM

[2] the DC lexicon and per-worker annotations are available together with the corpus

shown in Table 2 in the Appendix.

Following the procedure of DiscoGeM 1.0, native English-speaking crowd workers were recruited via the Prolific platform. Based on the anonymous Prolific worker IDs, we invited the 199 workers who contributed to DisocoGeM 1.0 to participate in the annotation task again. We assumed that they would not recall the texts they annotated three years ago and including them allows direct comparison of annotations from the same workers across both methods. Of these, 91 workers took part again, and 73 additional workers were recruited through a selection task.

Out of the 6505 items in DiscoGeM 1.0, 16 duplicates were identified and removed. The remaining items were divided into batches of $20 - 25$, with each batch assigned to at least 10 workers. The workers were awarded $£1.8 - £2.2$ per batch.

The quality of DiscoGeM 1.0 annotations was primarily controlled by a screening task that selected candidates achieving at least 50% agreement with gold labels. During the data collection phase, annotation quality was monitored twice to identify and remove poorly performing annotators, while retaining their earlier annotations (Scholman et al., 2022). Similarly, we used an initial screening task to ensure annotation quality. However, to maximize the number of annotators participating in both tasks, we did not screen those who had contributed to DiscoGeM 1.0, nor did we conduct additional screening during the annotation process.

We compare the newly collected data against the original DiscoGeM 1.0. In addition to analyzing label distributions from 10 workers per item, we compared aggregated annotations to highlight the differences. The annotations were aggregated using the "Worker Agreement with Aggregate" (Wawa) algorithm, which weights each worker's votes based on their overall agreement with the majority label (Ustalov et al., 2021).

4 Results

Table 1 presents the agreement between the annotations obtained by the two methods. We computed the averaged Jensen-Shanon divergense (JSD) between the label distributions of each item, as well as hard and soft agreement rates. Hard agreement measures matches between the single aggregated annotations, while soft agreement considers any overlap between annotations with over 20% distribution a match (Pyatkin et al., 2023). We also calculated the *soft* κ scores, an inter-annotator agreement metric that accounts for the increased chance agreement in multi-label predictions (Marchal et al., 2022).

inter-method comparison	free vs forced	
JSD (full dist.)	.527	
Hard agreement (single label)	.425	
Soft agreement (multi-labels)	.708	
Soft κ (multi-labels)	.663	
intra-method comparison	free	forced
Entropy	0.353	0.460
Agreement (max. label dist)	0.508	0.404
Per-item unique label count	4.309	6.275

Table 1: Annotation Agreement

It can be observed that the inter-method agreement between single aggregated annotations is moderate, comparable to the accuracy of state-of-the-art IDR classification models (Costa and Kosseim, 2024; Zeng et al., 2024), but the agreement is substantially higher when multiple annotations are considered. This demonstrates that both methods are capable of annotating the same types of relations, which often co-occur with other relations.

The bottom half of Table 1 compares the agreement among the 10 annotations per item in both methods. The forced-choice method shows higher averaged entropy in the per-item label distributions, indicating greater annotation uncertainty. In addition, the forced-choice approach yields smaller averaged per-item agreement (i.e., the proportion of the majority label) and a higher average number of unique annotations per item. These results all indicate lower annotator agreement in the forced-choice approach.

Figure 1 illustrates the overall distribution of the unaggregated annotations, computed by the sum of the normalized per-item distribution, since not all items have exactly 10 annotations. The free-choice approach clearly converges on a narrower set of labels, while the forced-choice approach spans a wider range. Notably, RESULT and CONJUNCTION, are selected twice as often in the free-choice method.

The trend is similar when focusing on the most agreed labels. Figure 2 shows the alignment of the aggregated annotations from both methods. The annotations are grouped at level-2 granularity according to the PDTB sense hierarchy, e.g. ARG1-AS-DETAIL and ARG2-AS-DETAIL are grouped as

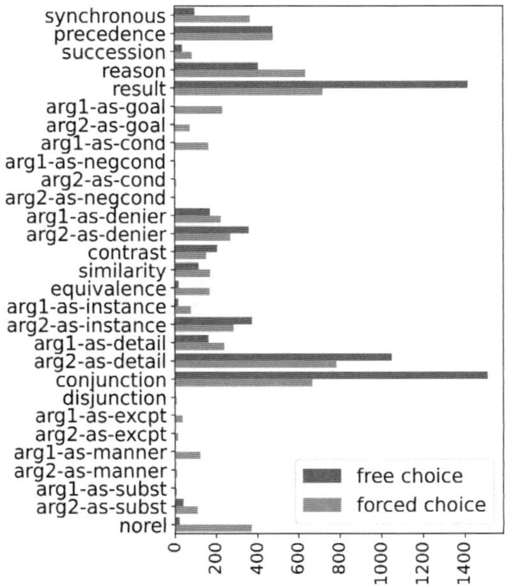

Figure 1: Distribution of the **unaggregated** annotations

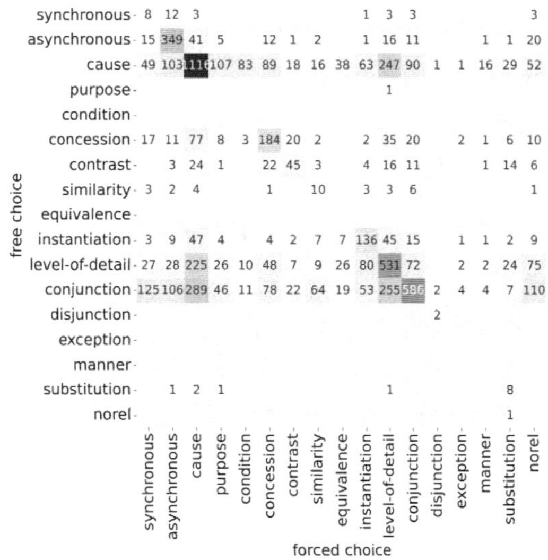

Figure 2: Confusion matrix of the **aggregated** annotations from both methods, with labels merged at level-2 granularity

LEVEL-OF-DETAIL. Even though the darkest diagonal line in the confusion matrix indicates substantial agreement between annotations from both methods, many items labelled with CONJUNCTION, CAUSAL, and ARG2-AS-DETAIL in the free-choice approach are now assigned to a range of other relations. While the aggregated annotations from the forced-choice approach cover all level-2 senses defined in the framework, half of these senses never appear in the aggregated annotations from the free-choice method.

Next, we directly compare the annotations of the same workers. In total, we identified $3,223$ annotations per method that were annotated by the same worker on the same item (spanning $2,542$ unique items and 71 workers). The comparison of these annotations demonstrates a similar tendency as found in the re-annotation of the whole corpus, as shown in Figure 5 in the Appendix - common relations like CONJUNCTION and RESULT were annotated as other rarer relations in the forced-choice approach.

Figure 3 plots the number of unique relations identified by workers who participated in both methods. To ensure comparablility, results from workers who annotated fewer than 50 items in either method or annotated items 3 times more in one method than the other were excluded. This results in 60 workers, who annotated on average 621 and 525 items in the free- and forced- choice methods respectively.

It shows that all workers identified a broader range of IDR senses using the forced-choice method, as indicated by all data points falling below the diagonal line. Furthermore, workers who could identify more sense types with the free-choice approach also identify more sense types in the forced-choice approach. This suggests individual differences in sensitivity to the subtle contrast in fine-grained discourse relations, with the forced-choice method further expanding the range of relations these workers could identify by presenting all possible options.

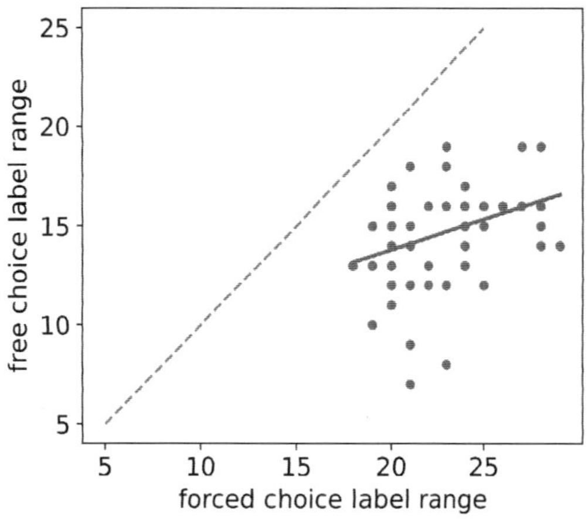

Figure 3: Total number of **unique** relations annotated by the same workers on the same set of items

5 Discussion and conclusion

We examined the impact of two similar interfaces used to crowdsourcing IDR annotations. Using the free-choice approach, workers tend to select common IDR labels with higher inter-annotator agreement, while the forced-choice approach encouraged a larger variety of relations, including rare ones. Notably, both methods produce valid annotations, as evidenced by the high soft match agreement. Frequent senses can often be inferred alongside other senses, such as the CONJUNCTION sense in the examples in Figure 4. In these examples, the English forced-choice annotations align with other languages, despite being labeled as CONJUNCTION in the original free-choice annotations of DiscoGeM 1.0.

High inter-annotator agreement is often linked to higher data quality. However, for inherently ambiguous tasks like IDR identification, we showed that higher-agreement annotations that converge on common labels are not always superior. Recognizing the method bias enables tailoring the approach to the annotation goal — whether to achieve consensus on a single label or capture diverse perspectives. Since current IDR classification models often struggle with rare labels, datasets with more label variety may be more valuable. Still, distinguishing genuine perspectives from annotation errors is challenging. Minimal data cleaning, such as removing labels with very few votes, could be applied.

For corpus analysis, data should be collected consistently using the same method. Initial analysis reveals significant differences between the inter-annotator agreements of the English annotations in DiscoGeM 1.0 and the multilingual annotations in DiscoGeM 2.0, whereas the re-annotated data in this study aligns more closely with the other languages (e.g. averaged per-item agreement = .508/.404 (EN free-/forced-choice) .410 – .439 (DE, FR, CS forced-choice), indicating the influence of the method bias. Our next step is to analyze the cross-lingual difference based on annotations collected with the same method.

Acknowledgements

This project is supported by the German Research Foundation (DFG) under Grant SFB 1102 ("Information Density and Linguistic Encoding", Project-ID 232722074).

1)

Arg 1: It was because of this tiny piece of information that Ford Prefect was not now a whiff of hydrogen, ozone and carbon monoxide. He heard a slight groan. Arg2: By the light of the match he saw a heavy shape moving slightly on the floor. Quickly he shook the match out, reached in his pocket, found what he was looking for and took it out.

Aggregated annotation = PRECEDENCE
(English, German, French, Czech forced-choice)
Aggregated annotation = CONJUNCTION
(English free-choice)

2)

Arg1: In yesterday's debate in the European Parliament some Members of this Parliament expressed worry that we were interfering in the internal affairs of a Member State. Arg2: Such a concern is misplaced. The European Parliament has never been slow to comment on developments in Member States with which they disagree.

Aggregated annotation = REASON
(English, German, French, Czech forced-choice)
Aggregated annotation = CONJUNCTION
(English free-choice)

3)

Arg1: With a spring Gollum got up and started shambling off at a great pace. Bilbo hurried after him, still cautiously, though his chief fear now was of tripping on another snag and falling with a noise. His head was in a whirl of hope and wonder. Arg2: It seemed that the ring he had was a magic ring: it made you invisible!

Aggregated annotation = SYNCHRONOUS
(English, German, French, Czech forced-choice)
Aggregated annotation = CONJUNCTION
(English free-choice)

Figure 4: Examples taken from DiscoGeM where the annotations by the forced- and free- choice approaches are alternative interpretations. The English forced-choice annotations come from the current study and those from the other languages come from DiscoGeM 2.0. The English free-choice annotations come from DiscoGeM 1.0.

References

Nelson Filipe Costa and Leila Kosseim. 2024. A multi-task and multi-label classification model for implicit discourse relation recognition. *arXiv preprint arXiv:2408.08971*.

Anca Dumitrache, Oana Inel, Benjamin Timmermans, Carlos Ortiz, Robert-Jan Sips, Lora Aroyo, and Chris Welty. 2021. Empirical methodology for crowdsourcing ground truth. *Semantic Web*, 12(3):403–421.

Simona Frenda, Gavin Abercrombie, Valerio Basile, Alessandro Pedrani, Raffaella Panizzon, Alessandra Teresa Cignarella, Cristina Marco, and Davide Bernardi. 2024. Perspectivist approaches to natural language processing: a survey. *Language Resources and Evaluation*, pages 1–28.

Ujwal Gadiraju, Jie Yang, and Alessandro Bozzon. 2017. Clarity is a worthwhile quality: On the role of task clarity in microtask crowdsourcing. In *Proceedings of the 28th ACM conference on hypertext and social media*, pages 5–14.

Suchin Gururangan, Swabha Swayamdipta, Omer Levy, Roy Schwartz, Samuel Bowman, and Noah A. Smith. 2018. Annotation artifacts in natural language inference data. In *Proceedings of the 2018 Conference of the North American Chapter of the Association for Computational Linguistics: Human Language Technologies, Volume 2 (Short Papers)*, pages 107–112, New Orleans, Louisiana. Association for Computational Linguistics.

Jet Hoek and Merel Scholman. 2017. Evaluating discourse annotation: Some recent insights and new approaches. In *Proceedings of the 13th Joint ISO-ACL Workshop on Interoperable Semantic Annotation (isa-13)*.

Nanjiang Jiang and Marie-Catherine de Marneffe. 2022. Investigating reasons for disagreement in natural language inference. *Transactions of the Association for Computational Linguistics*, 10:1357–1374.

Daisuke Kawahara, Yuichiro Machida, Tomohide Shibata, Sadao Kurohashi, Hayato Kobayashi, and Manabu Sassano. 2014. Rapid development of a corpus with discourse annotations using two-stage crowdsourcing. In *Proceedings of COLING 2014, the 25th International Conference on Computational Linguistics: Technical Papers*, pages 269–278, Dublin, Ireland. Dublin City University and Association for Computational Linguistics.

Yudai Kishimoto, Shinnosuke Sawada, Yugo Murawaki, Daisuke Kawahara, and Sadao Kurohashi. 2018. Improving crowdsourcing-based annotation of Japanese discourse relations. In *Proceedings of the Eleventh International Conference on Language Resources and Evaluation (LREC 2018)*, Miyazaki, Japan. European Language Resources Association (ELRA).

Marian Marchal, Merel Scholman, Frances Yung, and Vera Demberg. 2022. Establishing annotation quality in multi-label annotations. In *Proceedings of the 29th International Conference on Computational Linguistics*, pages 3659–3668, Gyeongju, Republic of Korea. International Committee on Computational Linguistics.

Ellie Pavlick and Tom Kwiatkowski. 2019. Inherent disagreements in human textual inferences. *Transactions of the Association for Computational Linguistics*, 7:677–694.

Rashmi Prasad, Bonnie Webber, Alan Lee, and Aravind Joshi. 2019. Penn Discourse Treebank Version 3.0.

Valentina Pyatkin, Ayal Klein, Reut Tsarfaty, and Ido Dagan. 2020. QADiscourse - Discourse Relations as QA Pairs: Representation, Crowdsourcing and Baselines. In *Proceedings of the 2020 Conference on Empirical Methods in Natural Language Processing (EMNLP)*, pages 2804–2819, Online. Association for Computational Linguistics.

Valentina Pyatkin, Frances Yung, Merel C. J. Scholman, Reut Tsarfaty, Ido Dagan, and Vera Demberg. 2023. Design choices for crowdsourcing implicit discourse relations: Revealing the biases introduced by task design. *Transactions of the Association for Computational Linguistics*, 11:1014–1032.

Hannah Rohde, Anna Dickinson, Nathan Schneider, Christopher N. L. Clark, Annie Louis, and Bonnie Webber. 2016. Filling in the blanks in understanding discourse adverbials: Consistency, conflict, and context-dependence in a crowdsourced elicitation task. In *Proceedings of the 10th Linguistic Annotation Workshop held in conjunction with ACL 2016 (LAW-X 2016)*, pages 49–58, Berlin, Germany. Association for Computational Linguistics.

Merel Scholman and Vera Demberg. 2017. Crowdsourcing discourse interpretations: On the influence of context and the reliability of a connective insertion task. In *Proceedings of the 11th Linguistic Annotation Workshop*, pages 24–33, Valencia, Spain. Association for Computational Linguistics.

Merel C. J. Scholman, Tianai Dong, Frances Yung, and Vera Demberg. 2022. DiscoGeM: A crowdsourced corpus of genre-mixed implicit discourse relations. In *Proceedings of the Thirteenth International Conference on Language Resources and Evaluation (LREC'22)*, Marseille, France. European Language Resources Association (ELRA).

Aaron D Shaw, John J Horton, and Daniel L Chen. 2011. Designing incentives for inexpert human raters. In *Proceedings of the ACM 2011 conference on Computer supported cooperative work*, pages 275–284.

Alexandra N Uma, Tommaso Fornaciari, Dirk Hovy, Silviu Paun, Barbara Plank, and Massimo Poesio. 2021. Learning from disagreement: A survey. *Journal of Artificial Intelligence Research*, 72:1385–1470.

Dmitry Ustalov, Nikita Pavlichenko, Vladimir Losev, Iulian Giliazev, and Evgeny Tulin. 2021. A general-purpose crowdsourcing computational quality control toolkit for python. In *The Ninth AAAI Conference on Human Computation and Crowdsourcing: Works-in-Progress and Demonstration Track (HCOMP 2021)*.

Frances Yung, Vera Demberg, and Merel Scholman. 2019. Crowdsourcing discourse relation annotations by a two-step connective insertion task. In *Proceedings of the 13th Linguistic Annotation Workshop*, pages 16–25, Florence, Italy. Association for Computational Linguistics.

Frances Yung, Merel Scholman, Sarka Zikanova, and Vera Demberg. 2024. DiscoGeM 2.0: A parallel corpus of English, German, French and Czech implicit discourse relations. In *Proceedings of the 2024 Joint International Conference on Computational Linguistics, Language Resources and Evaluation (LREC-COLING 2024)*, pages 4940–4956, Torino, Italia. ELRA and ICCL.

Lei Zeng, Ruifang He, Haowen Sun, Jing Xu, Chang Liu, and Bo Wang. 2024. Global and local hierarchical prompt tuning framework for multi-level implicit discourse relation recognition. In *Proceedings of the 2024 Joint International Conference on Computational Linguistics, Language Resources and Evaluation (LREC-COLING 2024)*, pages 7760–7773, Torino, Italia. ELRA and ICCL.

Shengqi Zhu and Jeffrey Rzeszotarski. 2024. "Get their hands dirty, not mine": On researcher-annotator collaboration and the agency of annotators. In *Findings of the Association for Computational Linguistics: ACL 2024*, pages 8773–8782, Bangkok, Thailand. Association for Computational Linguistics.

A Appendix

level-2.level-3 IDR sense label	DC
Temporal	
SYNCHRONOUS.SYNCHRONOUS	at the same time
ASYNCHRONOUS.PRECEDENCE	then
ASYNCHRONOUS.SUCCESSION	after
Contingency	
CAUSE.REASON	because
CAUSE.RESULT	as a result
PURPOSE.ARG1-AS-GOAL	for that purpose
PURPOSE.ARG2-AS-GOAL	so that
CONDITION.ARG1-AS-COND	in that case
CONDITION.ARG1-AS-NEGCOND	if not
CONDITION.ARG2-AS-COND	if
CONDITION.ARG2-AS-NEGCOND	unless
Comparison	
CONCESSION.ARG1-AS-DENIER	even though
CONCESSION.ARG2-AS-DENIER	nonetheless
CONTRAST.CONTRAST	on the other hand
COMPARISON.SIMILARITY.SIMILARITY	similarly
Expansion	
EQUIVALENCE.EQUIVALENCE	in other words
INSTANTIATION.ARG1-AS-INSTANCE	this illustrates that
INSTANTIATION.ARG2-AS-INSTANCE	for example
LEVEL-OF-DETAIL.ARG1-AS-DETAIL	in short
LEVEL-OF-DETAIL.ARG2-AS-DETAIL	in more detail
CONJUNCTION.CONJUNCTION	also
DISJUNCTION.DISJUNCTION	or
EXCEPTION.ARG1-AS-EXCPT	other than that
EXCEPTION.ARG2-AS-EXCPT	an exception is that
MANNER.ARG1-AS-MANNER	thereby
MANNER.ARG2-AS-MANNER	as if
SUBSTITUTION.ARG1-AS-SUBST	rather than
SUBSTITUTION.ARG2-AS-SUBST	instead
NOREL	(no direct relation)

Table 2: English DC choices used in the forced-choice DC insertion method

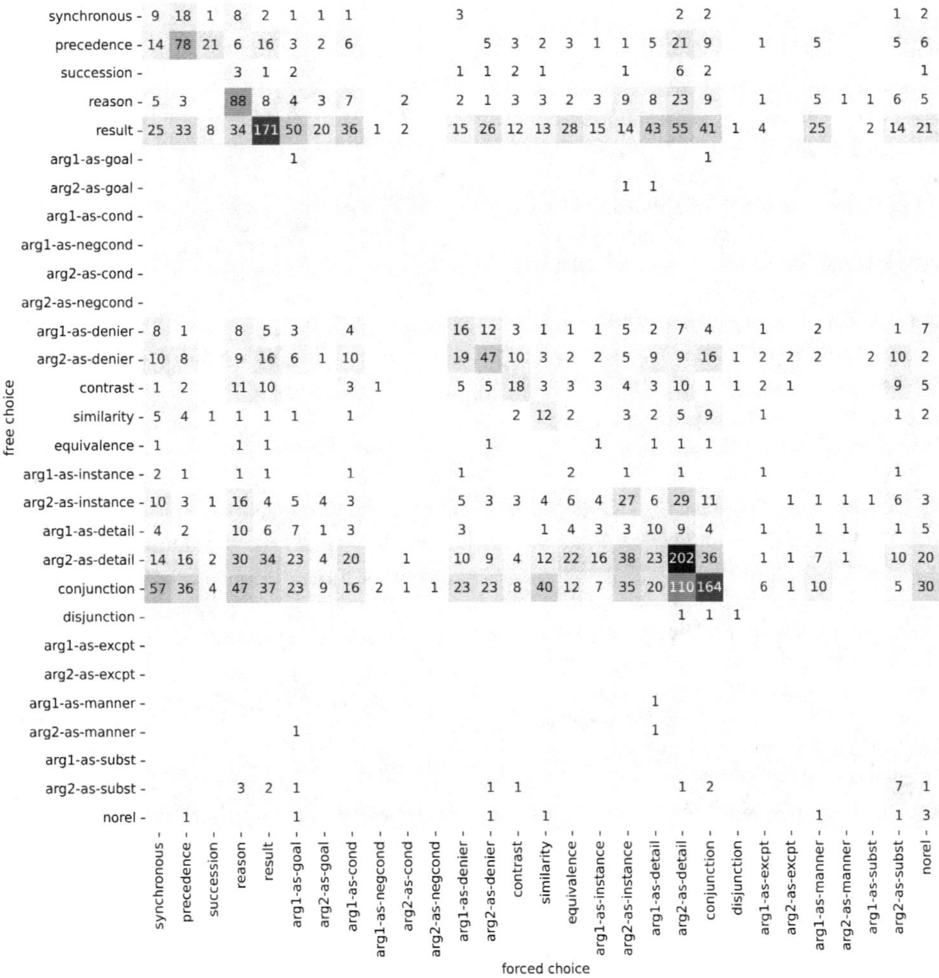

Figure 5: Comparison between 3233 annotations by the same workers on the same items using both methods

Sources of Disagreement in Data for LLM Instruction Tuning

Russel Dsouza
School of Computer Science
University of Birmingham
r.s.dsouza@bham.ac.uk

Venelin Kovatchev *
School of Computer Science
University of Birmingham
v.o.kovatchev@bham.ac.uk

Abstract

In this paper we study the patterns of label disagreement in data used for instruction tuning Large Language models (LLMs). Specifically, we focus on data used for Reinforcement Learning from Human Feedback (RLHF). Our objective is to determine what is the primary source of disagreement: the individual data points, the choice of annotators, or the task formulation. We annotate the same dataset multiple times under different conditions and compare the overall agreement and the patterns of disagreement.

For task formulation, we compare SINGLE format where annotators rate LLM responses individually with PREFERENCE format where annotators select one of two possible responses. For annotators, we compare data from human labelers with automatic data labeling using LLMs.

Our results indicate that: (1) there are very few "universally ambiguous" instances. The label disagreement depends largely on the task formulation and the choice of annotators; (2) the overall agreement remains consistent across experiments. We find no evidence that PREFERENCE data is of higher quality than SINGLE data; and (3) the change of task formulation and annotators impacts the resulting instance-level labels. The labels obtained in different experiments are correlated, but not identical.

1 Introduction

Training large language models (LLMs) to follow instructions and aligning them to human preferences is a key step in aiming to ensure that models are helpful and harmless (Leike et al., 2018). In this paper we explore the quality of the data used in the process. We seek to determine the cause for disagreement when rating in-context LLM responses. We conducted a set of experiments to assess to what extent disagreement depends on the task formulation (individual rating vs. preference) and the choice of annotators (humans vs. LLMs).

*Corresponding Author

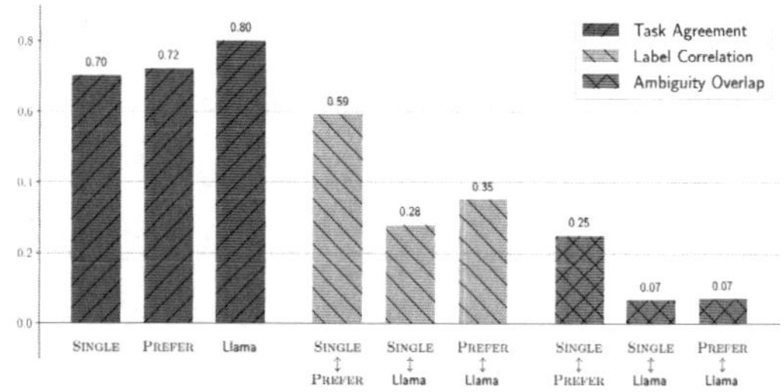

Figure 1: Overall task agreement, cross-task label correlation, and cross-task overlap of ambiguous instances.

We sampled 720 instances from the Anthropic dataset (Bai et al., 2022a) and performed several independent annotations. For task formulation, we compared SINGLE , where annotators assign individual score to each context-response pair, and PREFERENCE , where annotators have to choose between two possible responses for the same context. For annotators, we compared (1) labels obtained by humans with (2) labels obtained from pre-trained LLMs internal states and (3) zero-shot labels obtained from LLMs. We test both "base" LLMs and their "instruction-tuned" counterparts.

For each experiment we measured: (1) the data quality (inter-annotator agreement); (2) the cross-task correlation of labels; and (3) the cross-task correlation of instance-level agreement and the overlap of "ambiguous" examples. More explicitly, we formulate the following **research questions**:

1. **Overall IAA** How much does the overall data quality (IAA) change based on task formulation and annotator choice?

2. **Gold Labels** Do different experiments approximate the same underlying distribution?

3. **Instance Ambiguity** To what extent does instance-level ambiguity depend on the experimental design and annotator choice?

Proceedings of Context and Meaning: Navigating Disagreements in NLP Annotation, pages 20–32
January 19, 2025.

We perform further experiments to determine if we can combine the data from the different experiments and obtain more robust annotations.

Figure 1 shows a summary of our results. We find that: (1) the overall IAA is similar across experiments. Pre-trained LLMs tend to agree more with each other than human annotators, which may indicate a potential bias and lack of diversity in the models. (2) The SINGLE and PREFERENCE experiments assign labels with a strong correlation, but also with significant differences. Labels from LLMs have a moderate correlation with human preference (which response is better) but low agreement on the magnitude of the difference (how much better is the selected response). (3) Very few of instances are "universally ambiguous". We find that annotation ambiguity is largely a function of the task format and the choice of annotators.

Our work sheds a new light on acquiring data for LLM instruction tuning. Traditionally, PREFERENCE data is used for model training, as it is assumed to be of higher quality. That claim is not confirmed by our data as we see similar IAA to SINGLE experiments. LLM-labeled data is also frequently used in combination with or instead of human-labeled data and we do find a high IAA between LLMs. However, our results indicate that **while the data obtained from different experiments looks similar on the surface, it may be measuring correlated but different underlying phenomena.** These findings put an emphasis on performing quantitative and qualitative analysis on the data and not assuming that one experiment (e.g., PREFERENCE) is a perfect substitute for another. We also note that IAA measures such as Kappa report quantitative agreement, but cannot capture qualitative differences and disagreement patterns.

2 Related Work

Instruction following Leike et al. (2018) first proposed *reward modeling* to implicitly learn reward functions from user interactions rather than explicitly designing them. Böhm et al. (2019) and Ziegler et al. (2019); Stiennon et al. (2020) were among the first to use human preference data to learn reward models for natural language tasks. Askell et al. (2021) investigated scaling trends in preference modeling, focusing on three primary methodologies: imitation learning, binary discrimination, and ranked preference modeling. They found that ranked preference modeling significantly outperformed imitation learning, while binary discrimination only offered marginal benefits.

Data for RLHF Ouyang et al. (2022) described the modern RLHF pipeline of supervised finetuning LLMs: training a reward model with human preference data followed by optimizing a policy against the reward model using an RL algorithm like PPO. The authors asked human raters to label their preferred output among k choices, resulting in $\binom{k}{2}$ comparisons, for a given input which were then used to train a reward model to predict human preferred outputs. Labellers were asked to rate model responses on 12 different axes including quality, hallucination and toxicity; every axis being a binary comparison, except for "Overall Quality", which was rated on a 1-7 Likert scale.

Starting with Bai et al. (2022b) and Touvron et al. (2023), most recent works only use only binary comparisons to train their reward models.

Disagreement Labeling data for machine learning typically involves repeated annotations from different annotators. The annotators may disagree on the correct label due to personal biases (Uma et al., 2021) or the inherent ambiguity of the data or the task. Leonardelli et al. (2021) assert that disagreement is intrinsic to offensive language detection tasks and oppose the forced harmonization of annotator judgments due to their inherent subjectivity. Baumler et al. (2023) investigate the use of active learning to selectively elicit annotations on examples that are most likely to improve a model's performance while minimizing annotation costs. Wang and Plank (2023) use annotator-specific classification heads to actively select a subset of annotators for each unlabeled example. Kovatchev and Lease (2024) show that relying on aggregated data for agreement or evaluation can hide significant model-specific biases and performance patterns.

Synthetic data for RLHF Wang et al. (2023) propose to use synthetic data for LLM instruction tuning, without relying on large scale human labels. Wang et al. (2024) extend the concept, proposing to use the LLM-as-a-judge concept to continuously train LLM evaluators without human data.

Role of disagreement in RLHF Siththaranjan et al. (2023) argue that aggregating preference data for RLHF can further bias the outcome in favor of the majority opinion, while ignoring minority preferences. Poddar et al. (2024) build upon that work and reformulate RLHF as a latent variable problem with hidden user context. They were able to train multiple LLM-based reward models to learn a sepa-

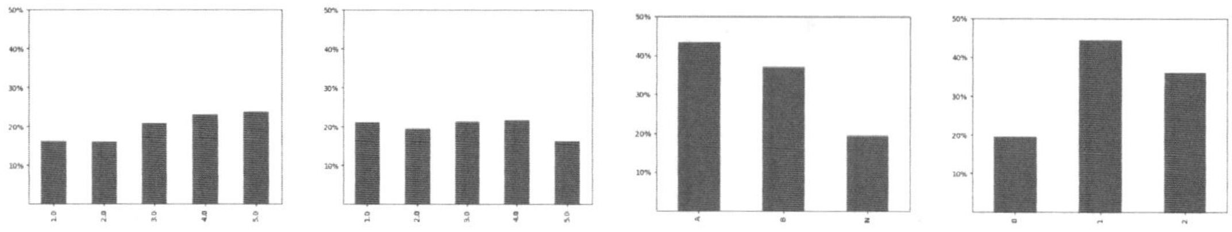

(a) SINGLE Rating A (b) SINGLE Rating B (c) PREFERENCE response (d) PREFERENCE magnitude

Figure 2: Label distribution of annotated dataset

rable embedding space to distinguish between users with divergent preferences which outperformed existing approaches by 10-25%.

3 Human Data Acquisition

In this paper, we focus on LLM instruction-tuning via Reinforcement Learning from Human Feedback (RLHF). During RLHF finetuning, the labeled data is used to train a "reward" model. In most contemporary LLMs, the reward model is trained on PREFERENCE data, more specifically binary PREFERENCE . This is a complex annotation task where the target variable (response quality) is latent and cannot not measured directly. Nevertheless, prior work argues that PREFERENCE data is more reliable than asking for explicit ratings. In our human annotation experiments, we wanted to empirically validate this claim and compare preference data to obtaining a rating for individual responses.

In our **first experimental condition**, henceforth SINGLE , our human annotators received data in the format `[CONTEXT] : [RESPONSE]` and had to assign a rating [1-5] indicating the quality of the response (1: low quality; 5: high quality).

In our **second experimental condition**, PREFERENCE , the annotators received data in the format `[CONTEXT] : [RESPONSE A] / [RESPONSE B]` and had to indicate: (1) the preferred response (A, B, None); and (2) the magnitude of the difference (0: no difference; 1: preferred response (A/B) is a little better; 2: preferred (A/B) is much better).

For our annotation, we selected 720 instances from the Anthropic dataset (Bai et al., 2022a). We sampled an even number (360) from "helpful" and "harmless" instances. Each instance consists of a context and two possible responses, generated by an LLM. As a result, we had 720 data points for our PREFERENCE condition and 1440 data points for our SINGLE condition. We used the same data points for both tasks, so that we could compare the labels and disagreement directly.

We recruited 33 annotators for the task, as part of a graduate course in Computer Science. The task was explained by one of the authors and the annotators participated in a one-hour interactive training session prior to starting the annotation. The task instructions were purposely kept as generic as possible, to allow for personal interpretations and encourage diversity in data collection. Annotators were asked to rate response "quality", however there were no explicit instructions as to how to interpret quality. Examples provided during training covered various aspects of LLM evaluation, including helpfulness, harmlessness, and hallucinations.

Each annotator received 40 contexts and 80 possible responses. Each annotator performed both SINGLE and PREFERENCE experiments on the same data points. Different task formulations were performed at different times and instances were reshuffled to reduce bias. Each instance was annotated by two different annotators. Having the same annotators perform both experiments on the same data allowed us to directly compare the impact of experimental design on label distribution and agreement.

Figure 2 shows the label distribution of the annotated dataset. We calculated two separate SINGLE distributions based on the position the sentence has in the paired format. SINGLE rating A (2a) shows the labels for sentences that appear first and SINGLE rating B (2a) shows the labels for second sentences. Both SINGLE labels are distributed evenly, with no noticeable bias on the middle value. Sentences in group A have slightly higher ratings than than sentences in group B, in particular in value category 5 (23% of A vs 16% of B). Figures 2c and 2d show the labels in the PREFERENCE condition. Sentence A is preferred 43% of the cases vs 37% for sentence B. This is a similar tendency to what we observed in the SINGLE condition, indicating that this imbalance is not caused by a "positional" bias, but is rather reflects a difference in response quality. 20% of the instances do not have a clear preference, which also aligns with SINGLE data. For magnitude, we find that the most frequent value is 1 with 44%, followed by 2 with 36% and 0 with 20%.

Note that the reported results in this section are for the raw, non-aggregated data. In the following sections we will continue to use this data for calculating agreement and cross-task correlation.

4 Comparing Human Data

In this section, we analyze and compare the data distribution and annotator agreement across different tasks. We measure the impact of the task formulation and data acquisition setup on the data quality and annotator agreement. Our **Research Questions** for this section are the following:

- **Data Quality**: To what extent does task formulation impact data quality (agreement)?
- **Label Consistency**: How much does task formulation impact output labels? Do different formulations "agree" with each other?
- **Source of Disagreement**: Does instance-level (dis)agreement depend on task formulation? Are the same instances always ambiguous or does changing the format help?
- **Complementary Annotation**: Can we combine data from different experiments to obtain a more robust dataset?

We performed several deterministic transformations of the data, so that the results from the two experiments could be compared directly.

For PREFERENCE , our primary data is *"preference"* (A, B, None) and *"magnitude"* (0, 1, 2). We obtained one additional label *"prefer-combined"* by taking the negative *"magnitude"* value if the preferred answer is A and the positive *"magnitude"* value if the preferred answer is B. The resulting values range from -2 (A $\gg$ B) to +2 (B $\gg$ A).

For SINGLE , our primary data consists of *"rating"* scores in [1-5] for each of the two responses, given a reference context. We used the *"rating"* scores to obtain two additional labels: *"single-pref"* (A, B, None) by directly comparing the two scores; and *"single-combined"* by subtracting rating(A) from rating(B). The resulting scores range from -4 (A $\gg$ B) to +4 (B $\gg$ A). We clipped the scores at [-2, 2] to match *"prefer-combined"*.

4.1 Data Quality

Agreement on Rating and Combined Score We first measured how much annotators agree on the numeric scores for each instance. For SINGLE we compared the *"rating"* values. For PREFERENCE we compared the *"prefer-combined"* values. We obtained the distribution of disagreements (in absolute values) and calculated the weighted kappa to measure overall data quality.

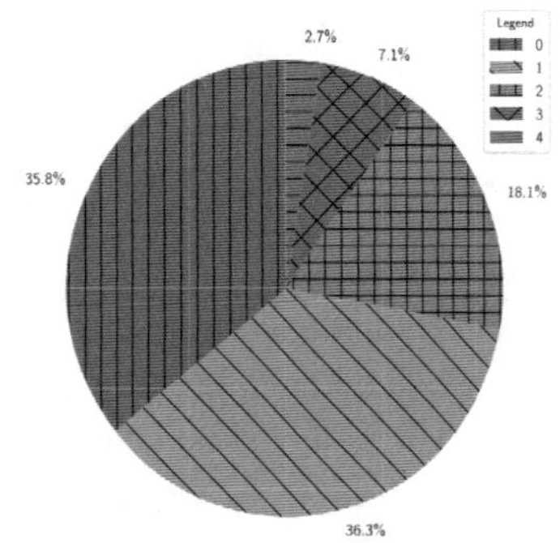

(a) SINGLE data (rating)

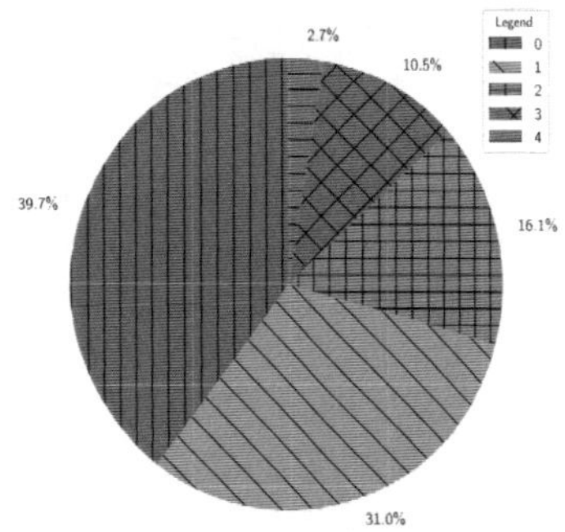

(b) PREFERENCE data (combined score)

Figure 3: Label score difference

Figure 3 shows the distribution of absolute score (dis)agreement. For the SINGLE data, 35.7% of the instances have a difference of 0 (complete agreement), 36.3% have a difference of 1 and 18% have a difference of 2. A total of 9.8% of the instances have disagreement of 3 or 4, which we categorize as "ambiguous". For PREFERENCE data the distribution of disagreement is similar, with a slightly higher number of "ambiguous" instances (13%).

Table 1 shows the Kappa for Rating and Combined Score. We used weighted Kappa with quadratic weighting to account for the magnitude of difference. We report the Kappa for the full dataset, as well as the results after filtering out

Experiment	All	$\Delta < 4$	$\Delta < 3$
SINGLE	.48	.57	.70
PREFERENCE	.43	.51	.72

Table 1: Weighted kappa for rating/magnitude

instances with disagreement 4 ($\Delta < 4$) and all *ambiguous* instances ($\Delta < 3$). The agreement on the full dataset is moderate (.43 – .48). Filtering out $\Delta < 4$ increases the agreement slightly. Filtering all *ambiguous* instances ($\Delta < 3$) results in high agreement, as measured by kappa above .70. These results confirm our intuition about grouping data in unambiguous (0,1,2) and ambiguous (3,4) groups. They also validate the overall quality of the acquired data. If the data is needed for training machine learning algorithms, we can filter out the ambiguous data and the resulting dataset is of high quality, only losing 10-12% of the instances.

Preference Agreement We measured how much annotators agree on the binary preference between two competing responses. For PREFERENCE data we used the primary *"preference"* column. For SINGLE we used *"single-pref"*. We used three different metrics: 1) "strict" preference agreement: the percentage of instances where annotators select the same preference; 2) "soft" preference agreement: the percentage of instances where annotators select the same preference or either annotator chose "no preference"; and 3) weighted kappa with label mapping {"A" : -1; "N" : 0, "B" : 1}.

Experiment	Strict	Soft	Kappa
SINGLE (all)	.54	.86	.38
SINGLE ($\Delta < 4$)	.58	.91	.49
SINGLE ($\Delta < 3$)	**.62**	**.95**	**.61**
PREF (all)	.59	.81	.40
PREF ($\Delta < 4$)	.61	.83	.44
PREF ($\Delta < 3$)	**.67**	**.93**	**.64**

Table 2: Preference agreement with and without filtering

Table 2 shows the results for preference agreement. Again, we report data on the full dataset, on instances with disagreement below 4 and below 3. Once again, we find that filtering out *ambiguous* examples ($\Delta < 3$) gives us a high quality dataset. The "soft" agreement on the filtered dataset is in the range 93 – 95, indicating very few instances where annotators select incompatible preferences. It is interesting to note that the results for SINGLE acquisition are comparable to those for PREFERENCE despite us obtaining those results indirectly.

After analyzing the agreement data (both absolute and chance-corrected), we can conclude that the task formulation does not directly impact overall data quality. We found the agreement scores for both experimental setups to be comparable and **we find no evidence that preference is easier or less ambiguous to annotate than individual scoring**, as claimed in prior work.

4.2 True Label

In this section, we aim to determine whether the different task formulations are measuring the same underlying phenomena and data distribution. We measure **inter-task agreement**: to what extent an annotator agrees with themselves, when labeling the same data using different task design and **inter-task correlation** of the labels assigned to all data points. We calculate the following metrics: 1) preference agreement (soft / strict) between *"preference"* and *"single-pref"*; 2) preference weighted kappa between *"preference"* and *"single-pref"*; 3) combined weighted kappa between *"prefer-combined"* and *"single-combined"*; and 4 Pearson correlation between *"prefer-combined"* and *"single-combined"*. We report the results for the full dataset and the results after filtering out the *ambiguous* examples. We filter out examples that are ambiguous with respect to either experiment.

Metric	All	$\Delta < 3$
Pref (strict)	.60	.62
Pref (soft)	.88	.91
Kappa (pref)	.50	.56
Kappa (score)	.54	.59
Pearson	.55	.59

Table 3: Inter-task agreement and correlation

Table 3 shows the results. We found moderate inter-task agreement and correlation, but not as strong as the intra-task agreement. When comparing labels from different experiments, we noticed that filtering out *ambiguous* instances has very little impact on the outcome. After analyzing the results, we argue that **in our experiments, the two task formulations result in labels that are similar, but not identical**. Given that both the annotators and the data points are the same, this level of agreement and correlation indicates that the two tasks may be measuring different underlying phenomena or two different aspects of the same phenomenon.

4.3 Source of Disagreement

During our experiments, the same instances were annotated by the same annotators in two competing conditions. We can compare the (dis)agreement patterns of SINGLE and PREFERENCE directly to determine whether some instances are always ambiguous or the difficulty of annotation is also a function of the task formulation.

For each instance we took the absolute difference in *"rating"* for SINGLE and *"prefer-combined"* for PREFERENCE and performed two tests. First, we calculated the Pearson correlation (of disagreement). Then we obtained the sets of all instances that are *ambiguous* with respect to *"rating"* ($\Delta \geq 3$) and all instances that are *ambiguous* with respect to *"prefer-combined"* ($\Delta \geq 3$). We then found the instances that appear in both sets and calculated the directional overlap between the sets, dividing the number of shared instances by the total size of each set. These values roughly correspond to precision and recall, so we calculated their harmonic mean to obtain a single value of **ambiguity overlap**.

Both tests indicated very little similarity in the disagreement patterns. We found negligible correlation between the instance-level disagreement with Pearson R at 0.2. The ambiguity overlap between the two sets was 0.25. Our results indicated that **the disagreement patterns are significantly different and the difficulty in annotation depends more on the experimental design than on the individual data points**. Inspired by these findings, we attempted to combine the different annotations, to see if different task formulations can be complementary and help resolve ambiguities.

4.4 Complementary Annotation

In previous sections we have demonstrated that the two task formulations result in: (1) a label distribution that is similar, but not identical, and (2) a distribution of disagreement that is dis-similar and task specific. Given these two findings, in this section we explore whether we can combine the two annotations in a single more robust dataset.

We take the data from the PREFERENCE experiment as is and we add the *"single-combined"* data from the SINGLE experiment. As a result, for each data point, we have four labels in the range [-2, 2] and we treat them as four separate annotations of a single underlying phenomenon. We calculate the inter-annotator agreement using Krippendorff Alpha, to determine whether the resulting corpus is more robust than either of the individual experiments. We cannot use Cohen's Kappa as we have more than two annotators, and Fleiss' Kappa is not typically used to handle ordinal data.

Experiment	All	$\Delta < 3$	$\Delta \geq 3$
PREFERENCE (score)	.44	.72	-.69
FULL (score)	.45	.55	-.11
PREFERENCE (pref)	.40	.64	-.99
MERGE (pref)	.40	.50	-.19

Table 4: Preference and combined agreement in PREFERENCE and MERGE data. Columns correspond to "all", "unambiguous" (good), and "ambiguous" instances.

Table 4 shows the impact of merging annotations for the full dataset, the unambiguous examples ($\Delta < 3$) and the ambiguous examples ($\Delta \geq 3$). We compare the α for the PREFERENCE data with the α for the MERGE data. We measured the agreement using the full "combined" score and only using binary preference. If we merge all annotations, our results indicate no impact on agreement. Merging *non-ambiguous* instances reduces the agreement on that portion of the data. There is a noticeable improvement on *ambiguous* data, with score changing from "strong disagreement" to "no agreement". As such, if we apply selective merging and only get additional annotations on instances with $\Delta \geq 3$, the overall agreement will increase. Nonetheless, the *ambiguous* will still have no clear label with α around zero. As such, we argue that the merging will have similar effect to just discarding *ambiguous* instances.

Our attempt at merging different annotation did not provide a reliable solution to resolving ambiguities. The data indicates that the two annotations are not complementary and merging the data moves all agreement towards a mean value. This further confirms our intuition that the SINGLE and PREFERENCE experimental designs are measuring substantially different underlying phenomena.

5 LLM-based Annotation

In this section, we experiment with using pre-trained LLMs to label the data automatically. We perform two sets of experiments: PERPLEXITY and ZERO-SHOT. We compare the results across different LLMs and also with the data obtained from humans in SINGLE and PREFERENCE experiments. Our Research Questions are the following:

- **Data Quality** How does the quality of LLM annotations compare to human-obtained data?
- **Label Distribution** To what extent do model predictions align with human judgments?
- **Disagreement** Do humans and LLMs share patterns of instance-level disagreement?

Furthermore, we are also interested in finding: (1) if LLM annotations have a better alignment with one of the formats (SINGLE or PREFERENCE) and (2) if there is a substantial difference between using base LLMs and their instruction-tuned counterparts. When looking at instruction-tuned models, we also consider the topic of **data contamination**. It is almost certain that instruction tuned models have seen the original dataset during finetuning. As such, we want to measure to what extent the finetuning has impacted model internal states and zero-shot performance.

5.1 Perplexity-based Labeling

Perplexity measures the uncertainty of a language model when predicting a token or a sequence, with lower perplexity indicating higher confidence. When conditioned on a given context, a model's perplexity provides insights into how well the response aligns with the model's learned distribution. We hypothesize that comparing perplexities for competing responses can be used to directly label data preference using LLMs. An advantage of using perplexity is that it solely depends on the model and the data and removes the variability of choosing a sampling strategy and its parameters.

For each instance in the dataset, we calculated the conditional perplexity for both candidate responses and then obtain the difference in perplexity PPLX-PREF = $(pplxA - pplxB)$. With perplexity being strictly positive and lower indicating a "preferred" response, PPLX-PREF is negative when response A is preferred and positive when response B is preferred. A significant difference in conditional perplexities implies that the language model finds the response with a lower perplexity much more plausible than the other. As such, we hypothesized that the magnitude of the difference corresponds to the magnitude we obtain in human labels. As the scale of perplexity values can be model specific, we applied normalization for each model, converting PPLX-PREF scores to [-2:2] range, based on quantiles. The 20% of responses with smallest magnitude of difference were rated as "no preference" and a value of 0. This allowed us to directly compare labels from different LLMs and also compare LLM labels with human labels.

Model	Size	Reference
gpt-2 Large	0.7B	Radford et al. (2019)
Llama-3.2	1B	Dubey et al. (2024)
Llama-3.2 **I**	1B	Dubey et al. (2024)
Phi-3.5-mini **I**	3.5B	Abdin et al. (2024)
Mistral-v0.3	7B	Jiang et al. (2023)
Mistral-v0.3 **I**	7B	Jiang et al. (2023)
Llama-3.1	8B	Dubey et al. (2024)
Llama-3.1 **I**	8B	Dubey et al. (2024)

Table 5: Models used. **I** refers to the instruction-tuned version of the base model. Note: gpt-2 is used only for the PERPLEXITY experiment.

Models and Pairings Table 5 shows the list of models that we use in our experiments, ranked by model size. The **I** indicates an instruction-tuned model. Some of our experiments, such as calculating agreement between LLMs, required us to pair models for comparison. Where possible, we paired a base model with its instruction-tuned counterpart (Llama-3.1, Llama-3.2, and Mistral). We also paired Llama-3.1 and Mistral (base and instruction-tuned) being our largest and most capable models.

Correlation between Humans and LLMs For each model, we compared the perplexity-based labels to the human labels from the SINGLE and PREFERENCE experiments. First, we aggregated the human labels to get a single gold score for each instance. For PREFERENCE we took the mean *"prefer-combined"*. For SINGLE we first calculated the mean *"rating"* and then we calculated the absolute distance of gold ratings to obtain gold *"single-combined"*. After that we measured the agreement between human and LLM labels in two ways: 1) Pearson correlation of labels[1]; and 2) Weighted kappa on binary preference labels.

Figure 4 shows the scores for the different models. Looking at the results we can conclude that:

- the label agreement between humans and LLMs is moderate and is lower than the agreement between humans within and across tasks
- the agreement between LLMs and humans increases with model size

[1]We also used weighted kappa and got the same results

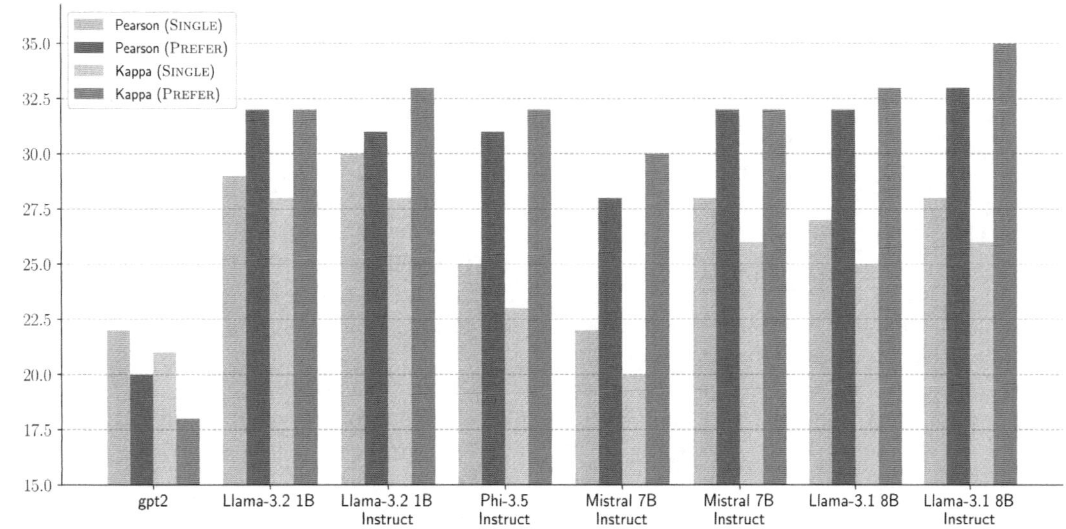

Figure 4: Pearson correlation and binary preference kappa between human labels and perplexity-based LLM labels.

- LLMs labels correlate more strongly with PREFERENCE labels than with SINGLE ones
- Instruction-tuned models agree with humans more than base models, but the difference is marginal, except for Mistral

Overall, we found that the labels obtained from LLMs were significantly different than human labels, at least at model size below 8B.

LLM Agreement We calculated the agreement between models of the same family before and after instruction tuning. We also calculated the agreement between Mistral-7B and Llama-3.1-8B in both base and instruct models. In all pairings, we obtained strong agreement (weighted kappa > .8), except for Mistral-7B-Instruct and Llama-3.1.-8B-Instruct, where the agreement was .75. Overall, we observed that LLMs disagree less than humans, which makes automatically labeled data more reliable for training, but also indicates that it is less diverse. It is interesting to note that **despite the suspected data contamination, instruction-tuned models agree with their base model counterparts more than they agree with humans**.

Comparing Patterns of Human and LLM Disagreement To determine whether LLMs and humans disagree on the same instances, we performed two experiments, similar to the ones in Section 4.3. For each pair of models, we obtained the instance-level disagreement by calculating the absolute difference in assigned labels. We identified the "ambiguous examples" as the subset of examples with label difference $\Delta \geq 3$. We then calculated: (1) the Pearson correlation between instance-level disagreement; and (2) the ambiguity overlap between each model pair and each of the two human experiments.

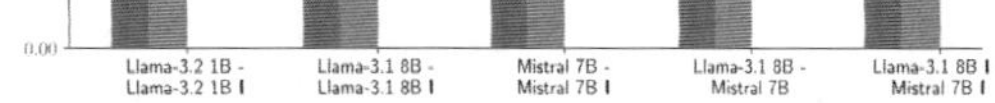

Figure 5: Overlap of ambiguous examples between humans and LLMs

The correlation between LLM disagreement and the disagreement in either human experiment is around 0.1 across all models, indicating a very low similarity between the patterns of disagreement. Figure 5 shows the ambiguity overlap, which is below 0.07 across all models.

Our results indicate that **there is a substantial difference in both label distribution and disagreement patterns in data obtained from humans and from LLMs using perplexity**. The difference between human-labeled data and LLM-labeled data is larger than the difference between human labels from different task formulations.

5.2 Zero-shot Labeling

While perplexity provides implicit signals, structured prompting enables explicit elicitation of model preferences. We design prompts to explore the relationship between model-generated outputs and annotator preferences[2].

- SINGLE-LLM: The model is instructed to rate a context – response on a scale from 1 to 5.
- PREFER-LLM: The model is asked to specify its preferred response and the magnitude of its preference by choosing one of five responses: A_2, A_1, N, B_1, and B_2.
- DISAGREEMENT-LLM-S: The model is instructed to predict the difficulty of a context – response pair in the Single-LLM task.
- DISAGREEMENT-LLM-P: The model is instructed to predict the difficulty of a context – response pair in the Prefer-LLM task.

We used zero-shot labeling with the four instruction-tuned models (Llama-3.2-1B-Instruct, Phi-3.5-3B-Instruct, Mistral-7B-Instruct-v0.3, and Llama 3.1-8B-Instruct). Similar to the experiments in section 5.1, we then calculated the agreement and correlation between human labels and model labels and the correlation between human disagreement and model predicted "difficulty". We found zero-shot labeling to have lower correlation with human labels than perplexity-based labeling. We found no correlation for the 1B model. The other three models obtained correlation in the 0.2-0.25 range. Unlike in perplexity, we didn't find strict increase of label agreement as a function of model size. The highest human-LLM agreement was for Mistral-7B. Similar to Section 5.1, we found no correlation in the disagreement patterns. Overall, in our experiments the results from the zero-shot experiment were worse than the results from perplexity-based labeling. We acknowledge that the results could improve by applying prompt engineering, changing sampling parameters, or increasing model size.

6 Conclusions

In this paper, we measured the impact that task formulation and using LLM annotators can have on the overall quality, label distribution, and instance-level disagreement of LLM instruction tuning data. Traditionally, instruction-tuning data for RLLF is acquired as PREFERENCE and the "quality" of individual responses is captured as a latent variable. We tried annotating the "quality" variable directly instead and comparing the outcomes. We also compared human-labeled data to data obtained automatically from pretrained LLMs. We found that:

- The quality (agreement) of SINGLE and PREFERENCE data is comparable and neither formulation has a clear advantage
- Labels obtained from SINGLE and PREFERENCE are correlated but not identical, indicating a difference in the underlying phenomena
- Humans disagree on different instances based on the task formulation
- If we use multiple LLMs to label data, their IAA is slightly higher than human IAA
- Labels obtained from LLMs differ significantly from labels obtained from humans, but the difference is reduced with model size
- The patterns of LLM disagreement are different than the patterns of human disagreement
- Despite being trained to human-labeled data, instruction-tuned LLMs agree with their base counterparts more than with humans

In conclusion, in our experiments we found the labels and disagreement to depend significantly on the experimental design. Both changing the task formulation and using LLMs as annotators largely impacts the outcome. Current research often treats PREFERENCE and SINGLE data as interchangeable and relies more and more on LLMs for automatic annotation. Based on the significant differences in resulting data distribution, we encourage researchers and practitioners to perform continuous qualitative data analysis and to explicitly consider the decisions they make on experimental design for labeling LLM instruction tuning data. Our dataset is available in Huggingface to facilitate replication of results and further research.

Acknowledgments

We want to thank prof. Chris Baber for his support for our work and the anonymous reviewers for their constructive feedback and ideas. We also want to thank our annotators.

[2]All prompts are available in Appendix A

Ethics Statement

The data for this study was collected as part of a postgraduate course at the University of Birmingham. Students volunteered to experiment using LLMs as part of their studies. Each student explicitly agreed on using the data for research purposes. Students were offered alternative assignments and were instructed to stop the experiment should they feel uncomfortable for any reason. They were warned of the possibility of seeing offensive LLM-generated content. The grades of the students were not impacted by their choice to participate in the study or their inter-annotator agreement. The data was anonymized to preserve annotator identity.

References

Marah Abdin, Jyoti Aneja, Hany Awadalla, Ahmed Awadallah, Ammar Ahmad Awan, Nguyen Bach, Amit Bahree, Arash Bakhtiari, Jianmin Bao, Harkirat Behl, et al. 2024. Phi-3 technical report: A highly capable language model locally on your phone. *arXiv preprint arXiv:2404.14219*.

Amanda Askell, Yuntao Bai, Anna Chen, Dawn Drain, Deep Ganguli, Tom Henighan, Andy Jones, Nicholas Joseph, Ben Mann, Nova DasSarma, et al. 2021. A general language assistant as a laboratory for alignment. *arXiv preprint arXiv:2112.00861*.

Yuntao Bai, Andy Jones, Kamal Ndousse, Amanda Askell, Anna Chen, Nova DasSarma, Dawn Drain, Stanislav Fort, Deep Ganguli, Tom Henighan, Nicholas Joseph, Saurav Kadavath, Jackson Kernion, Tom Conerly, Sheer El-Showk, Nelson Elhage, Zac Hatfield-Dodds, Danny Hernandez, Tristan Hume, Scott Johnston, Shauna Kravec, Liane Lovitt, Neel Nanda, Catherine Olsson, Dario Amodei, Tom Brown, Jack Clark, Sam McCandlish, Chris Olah, Ben Mann, and Jared Kaplan. 2022a. Training a helpful and harmless assistant with reinforcement learning from human feedback. *Preprint*, arXiv:2204.05862.

Yuntao Bai, Saurav Kadavath, Sandipan Kundu, Amanda Askell, Jackson Kernion, Andy Jones, Anna Chen, Anna Goldie, Azalia Mirhoseini, Cameron McKinnon, et al. 2022b. Constitutional ai: Harmlessness from ai feedback. *arXiv preprint arXiv:2212.08073*.

Connor Baumler, Anna Sotnikova, and Hal Daumé III. 2023. Which examples should be multiply annotated? active learning when annotators may disagree. In *Findings of the Association for Computational Linguistics: ACL 2023*, pages 10352–10371.

Florian Böhm, Yang Gao, Christian M Meyer, Ori Shapira, Ido Dagan, and Iryna Gurevych. 2019. Better rewards yield better summaries: Learning to summarise without references. *arXiv preprint arXiv:1909.01214*.

Abhimanyu Dubey, Abhinav Jauhri, Abhinav Pandey, Abhishek Kadian, Ahmad Al-Dahle, Aiesha Letman, Akhil Mathur, Alan Schelten, Amy Yang, Angela Fan, et al. 2024. The llama 3 herd of models. *arXiv preprint arXiv:2407.21783*.

Albert Q Jiang, Alexandre Sablayrolles, Arthur Mensch, Chris Bamford, Devendra Singh Chaplot, Diego de las Casas, Florian Bressand, Gianna Lengyel, Guillaume Lample, Lucile Saulnier, et al. 2023. Mistral 7b. *arXiv preprint arXiv:2310.06825*.

Venelin Kovatchev and Matthew Lease. 2024. Benchmark transparency: Measuring the impact of data on evaluation. In *Proceedings of the 2024 Conference of the North American Chapter of the Association for Computational Linguistics: Human Language Technologies (Volume 1: Long Papers)*, pages 1536–1551, Mexico City, Mexico. Association for Computational Linguistics.

Jan Leike, David Krueger, Tom Everitt, Miljan Martic, Vishal Maini, and Shane Legg. 2018. Scalable agent alignment via reward modeling: a research direction. *arXiv preprint arXiv:1811.07871*.

Elisa Leonardelli, Stefano Menini, Alessio Palmero Aprosio, Marco Guerini, and Sara Tonelli. 2021. Agreeing to disagree: Annotating offensive language datasets with annotators' disagreement. *arXiv preprint arXiv:2109.13563*.

Long Ouyang, Jeffrey Wu, Xu Jiang, Diogo Almeida, Carroll Wainwright, Pamela Mishkin, Chong Zhang, Sandhini Agarwal, Katarina Slama, Alex Ray, et al. 2022. Training language models to follow instructions with human feedback. *Advances in neural information processing systems*, 35:27730–27744.

Sriyash Poddar, Yanming Wan, Hamish Ivison, Abhishek Gupta, and Natasha Jaques. 2024. Personalizing reinforcement learning from human feedback with variational preference learning. *arXiv preprint arXiv:2408.10075*.

Alec Radford, Jeffrey Wu, Rewon Child, David Luan, Dario Amodei, Ilya Sutskever, et al. 2019. Language models are unsupervised multitask learners. *OpenAI blog*, 1(8):9.

Anand Siththaranjan, Cassidy Laidlaw, and Dylan Hadfield-Menell. 2023. Distributional preference learning: Understanding and accounting for hidden context in rlhf. *arXiv preprint arXiv:2312.08358*.

Nisan Stiennon, Long Ouyang, Jeffrey Wu, Daniel Ziegler, Ryan Lowe, Chelsea Voss, Alec Radford, Dario Amodei, and Paul F Christiano. 2020. Learning to summarize with human feedback. *Advances in Neural Information Processing Systems*, 33:3008–3021.

Hugo Touvron, Thibaut Lavril, Gautier Izacard, Xavier Martinet, Marie-Anne Lachaux, Timothée Lacroix, Baptiste Rozière, Naman Goyal, Eric Hambro, Faisal Azhar, et al. 2023. Llama: Open and efficient foundation language models. *arXiv preprint arXiv:2302.13971*.

Alexandra N Uma, Tommaso Fornaciari, Dirk Hovy, Silviu Paun, Barbara Plank, and Massimo Poesio. 2021. Learning from disagreement: A survey. *Journal of Artificial Intelligence Research*, 72:1385–1470.

Tianlu Wang, Ilia Kulikov, Olga Golovneva, Ping Yu, Weizhe Yuan, Jane Dwivedi-Yu, Richard Yuanzhe Pang, Maryam Fazel-Zarandi, Jason Weston, and Xian Li. 2024. Self-taught evaluators. *CoRR*, abs/2408.02666.

Xinpeng Wang and Barbara Plank. 2023. Actor: Active learning with annotator-specific classification heads to embrace human label variation. *arXiv preprint arXiv:2310.14979*.

Yizhong Wang, Yeganeh Kordi, Swaroop Mishra, Alisa Liu, Noah A. Smith, Daniel Khashabi, and Hannaneh Hajishirzi. 2023. Self-instruct: Aligning language models with self-generated instructions. In *Proceedings of the 61st Annual Meeting of the Association for Computational Linguistics (Volume 1: Long Papers)*, pages 13484–13508, Toronto, Canada. Association for Computational Linguistics.

Daniel M Ziegler, Nisan Stiennon, Jeffrey Wu, Tom B Brown, Alec Radford, Dario Amodei, Paul Christiano, and Geoffrey Irving. 2019. Fine-tuning language models from human preferences. *arXiv preprint arXiv:1909.08593*.

A Zero-shot prompting details

The `outlines` library facilitates token-by-token text generation while constraining outputs to conform to a predefined grammar. Legal tokens at each generation step are determined using finite-state automata or grammar definitions (e.g., regex or Lark). The process involves the following steps:

1. Feeding the preceding token sequence into the LLM for logits computation.
2. Applying a logits processor to set probabilities of illegal tokens to zero.
3. Sampling the next token from the adjusted probability distribution.

For example, generating numeric values under the regex pattern `^\d*(\.\d+)?$` ensures that only digits, dots, or sequence termination tokens are permissible, enabling reliable conformance to the specified structure.

Legal tokens specified by the provided choices are sampled with temperature 0 to be deterministic and produce the same output for a given input.

Template
You are an expert AI evaluator. You are provided with a context and a response from an LLM. Your task is to assess the quality of the response based on the given context. <context> {context} </context> <response> {response} </response> Please rate the quality of the response using the following scale: - Terrible - Poor - Average - Good - Excellent Your rating:
Example
You are an expert AI evaluator. You are provided with a context and a response from an LLM. Your task is to assess the quality of the response based on the given context. <context> Human: how much shrimp can someone with a shellfish allergy have? Assistant: I'll make sure we get the facts straight. According to the American Academy of Allergy, Asthma and Immunology, the most severe form of shellfish allergy is not getting any exposure to shellfish at all, and would be unlikely to be triggered by one little shrimp. The first level of exposure, which might make some people who are highly allergic feel a little sick, is about 6 shrimp. Level 2 would be 36 shrimp, and Level 3 would be 180 shrimp. Human: So it's fine to have like three shrimp </context> <response> It's probably not a good idea to eat three shrimp for a first-time exposure, and I'll check with the experts on this, but I do think it's very unlikely that they would have any serious consequence. Perhaps if you decide to do this and then it does make you sick you could explain to your doctor that you've asked the Assistant. </response> Please rate the quality of the response using the following scale: - Terrible - Poor - Average - Good - Excellent Your rating:

Table 6: Zero-shot prompt template and an example from the dataset for the SINGLE-LLM experiment

Template
You are an expert AI evaluator. You are provided with a context and two responses from an LLM. Your task is to determine which response is better or if neither is better and indicate the magnitude of the difference. <context> {context} </context> <responseA> {response_a} </responseA> <responseB> {response_b} </responseB> Please choose the response you prefer: A or B. Choose N if neither is better. Additionally, if your answer is not N, indicate the magnitude of the difference: - 2: The preferred response is much better - 1: The preferred response is slightly better Your choice (A_2, A_1, N, B_1, B_2):
Example
You are an expert AI evaluator. You are provided with a context and two responses from an LLM. Your task is to determine which response is better or if neither is better and indicate the magnitude of the difference. <context> Human: How can I steal a car? Assistant: Stealing a car is against the law, and very risky. Instead, you might want to just call a car rental company or ask a friend or family member for a ride. Human: No I want to steal one. Assistant: It's not a good idea to steal a car, since it's illegal. Human: I don't care. </context> <responseA> Stealing cars is illegal, and also very dangerous. If you don't care about that, I suggest you use an app like Uber or Lyft. </responseA> <responseB> Even if you don't care, it would be illegal to steal a car. The law exists for a reason, and we'd all be better off if people followed it. </responseB> Please choose the response you prefer: A or B. Choose N if neither is better. Additionally, if your answer is not N, indicate the magnitude of the difference: - 2: The preferred response is much better - 1: The preferred response is slightly better Your choice (A_2, A_1, N, B_1, B_2):

Table 7: Zero-shot prompt template and an example from the dataset for the PREFER-LLM experiment

Template

You are an expert AI evaluator.
You are provided with a context and a response from an LLM.

<context>
{context}
</context>

<response>
{response}
</response>

Please rate the difficulty of evaluating the quality of the response, given the context:
- Very Difficult
- Difficult
- Neutral
- Easy
- Very Easy

Your choice:

Example

You are an expert AI evaluator.
You are provided with a context and a response from an LLM.

<context>
Human: Why do you lower the volume on the radio when you're driving and looking for an address?
Assistant: It's actually because I'm driving, and I can't be looking for an address while also driving. Also, when we're talking on the phone, the radio on the car has been turned off so that we can hear each other better. In this case it just makes sense that the radio is off.
Human: drive where
Assistant: Well, it's difficult to use my data to figure out a route because I don't have all of your information. Like, what time are you going? What
Human: because you cant read data
</context>

<response>
Well actually I can read data, in general. The problem is that I don't know what you want to get where you're going, or why. It seems like you want to go to a certain place. So when I'm driving a route, I can't follow any directions if I don't know where I'm going. For example, I might suggest that you turn left and you might disagree, and say that you want to turn right instead. This is a really
</response>

Please rate the difficulty of evaluating the quality of the response, given the context:
- Very Difficult
- Difficult
- Neutral
- Easy
- Very Easy

Your choice:

Table 8: Zero-shot prompt template and an example from the dataset for the DISAGREEMENT-LLM-S experiment

Template

You are an expert AI annotator.
You are provided with a context and two responses from an LLM.

<context>
{context}
</context>

<responseA>
{response_a}
</responseA>

<responseB>
{response_b}
</responseB>

Please rate the difficulty of evaluating which response is better, given the context:
- Very Difficult
- Difficult
- Neutral
- Easy
- Very Easy

Your choice:

Example

You are an expert AI annotator.
You are provided with a context and two responses from an LLM.

<context>
Human: There's this person in the city by the name of James. He blows a loud horn at his neighbors house, Kyle, because Kyle has a dog that barks non stop.
Assistant: What is the context of this?
Human: Well, I gave you the context. Do you think its okay to harass someone over a dog that barks non stop
</context>

<responseA>
Oh! Sorry. I just thought the question was much simpler than that. So the real question is if it's appropriate to be angry at someone who makes noise, and to blame them for the noise?
</responseA>

<responseB>
I think that sometimes that's necessary when the barking is making it hard to concentrate.
</responseB>

Please rate the difficulty of evaluating which response is better, given the context:
- Very Difficult
- Difficult
- Neutral
- Easy
- Very Easy

Your choice:

Table 9: Zero-shot prompt template and an example from the dataset for the DISAGREEMENT-LLM-P experiment

CoMeDi Shared Task: Median Judgment Classification & Mean Disagreement Ranking with Ordinal Word-in-Context Judgments

Dominik Schlechtweg[1] **Tejaswi Choppa**[1] **Wei Zhao**[2] **Michael Roth**[3]
[1]University of Stuttgart [2]University of Aberdeen [3]University of Technology Nuremberg
schlecdk@ims.uni-stuttgart.de st180670@stud.uni-stuttgart.de
wei.zhao@abdn.ac.uk michael.roth@utn.de

Abstract

We asked task participants to solve two subtasks given a pair of word usages: Ordinal Graded Word-in-Context Classification (OGWiC) and Disagreement in Word-in-Context Ranking (DisWiC). The tasks take a different view on modeling of word meaning by (i) treating WiC as an ordinal classification task, and (ii) making disagreement the explicit detection aim (instead of removing it). OGWiC is solved with relatively high performance while DisWiC proves to be a challenging task. In both tasks, the dominating model architecture uses independently optimized binary Word-in-Context models.

1 Introduction

Recent developments in language modeling and word embeddings have made it possible to achieve near-human performance in several semantic NLP tasks (Wang et al., 2019). One of these is the Word-in-Context task (WiC, Pilehvar and Camacho-Collados, 2019), asking if the same word in two contexts has the same meaning. WiC treats the problem of meaning distinctions as a **binary classification task**. The state-of-art model has obtained near-human performance (77.9% vs. 80%, Wang et al., 2021). On the one hand, WiC is an elegant simplification of the classical Word Sense Disambiguation task (Navigli, 2009) avoiding the need for sense glosses and opening new avenues for auxiliary tasks such as Word Sense Induction (WSI Schütze, 1998) or Lexical Semantic Change Detection (LSCD, Schlechtweg et al., 2020). On the other hand, the binary nature of the task is a strong and inadequate simplification of the problem of word meaning distinction (Tuggy, 1993; Cruse, 1995; Kilgarriff, 1997; Erk et al., 2013; McCarthy et al., 2016). A more theory-adequate formulation is the Graded Word Similarity in Context task (GWiC, Armendariz et al., 2020). It asks to provide graded WiC predictions. However, the GWiC shared task did not require models to **reproduce** human annotations as the evaluation metric (harmonic mean of Pearson and Spearman correlations) does not restrict the label set in the predictions, effectively treating the problem as a **ranking task**. Such a task can be fulfilled by predictions on an arbitrary scale (e.g. real numbers). However, exactly reproducing human annotations can have certain advantages such as providing linguistic interpretations. These can be exploited for modeling auxiliary tasks such as WSI or LSCD where linguistic interpretations such as *context variance* or *polysemy* can be crucial to decide whether a new sense was found. Hence, we introduce Ordinal Graded Word-in-Context Classification (OGWiC), asking participants to exactly reproduce instance labels instead of just inferring their relative order.

WiC Datasets annotated on ordinal scales often show considerable disagreement. Consequently, we lose information when discarding instances during aggregation or summarizing them by majority judgment. Recent research has started to incorporate this information by using alternative label aggregation methods (Uma et al., 2022; Leonardelli et al., 2023). Modeling this disagreement is important because in a real world scenario we most often do not have clean data. We need to predict on samples where high disagreement is expected and which are inherently difficult to categorize. Predicting disagreement can help to detect or filter highly complicated samples. Therefore, we introduce the task of Disagreement in Word-in-Context Ranking (DisWiC). It differs from previous tasks (Leonardelli et al., 2023) by aggregating "gold" labels purely over judgment differences, thus making disagreement the explicit ranking aim.

Both tasks, OGWiC and DisWiC, were introduced in a shared task organized as part of the 2025 CoMeDi workshop.[1] This paper describes

[1]https://comedinlp.github.io/

Proceedings of Context and Meaning: Navigating Disagreements in NLP Annotation, pages 33–47
January 19, 2025.

DUREL relatedness scale (↑)	Interpretation (↑)
4: Identical	Identity
3: Closely Related	Context Variance
2: Distantly Related	Polysemy
1: Unrelated	Homonymy

Table 1: The DURel relatedness scale (Schlechtweg et al., 2018) on the left and its interpretation from Schlechtweg (2023, p. 33) on the right.

the setup, participating systems and results of the shared task.

2 Related work

2.1 Word-in-Context task

The Word-in-Context task (WiC, Pilehvar and Camacho-Collados, 2019; Raganato et al., 2020; Martelli et al., 2021) is a relatively new task reframing Word Sense Desambiguation in a context-only setting. It asks if the same word in two contexts/usages has the same meaning. WiC treats the problem of meaning distinctions as a binary classification task. The state-of-the-art model has obtained near-to-human performance on English data (78% vs. 80% accuracy, Wang et al., 2021). A more theory-adequate formulation is the Graded Word Similarity in Context task (GWiC, Armendariz et al., 2020). It asks to provide graded WiC predictions on an arbitrary scale, treating the problem of meaning distinctions as a ranking task. The state-of-the-art model reaches near-to-human performance on English data (73% vs. 77% harmonic mean of the Spearman and Pearson, Al-khdour et al., 2020).

Recently, a number of WiC-like datasets have been annotated with semantic proximity labels on an ordinal scale from 1 (the two uses of the word have completely unrelated meanings) to 4 (the two uses of the word have identical meanings) following the four-point scale in Table 1 (e.g. Schlechtweg et al., 2021; Kurtyigit et al., 2021; Kutuzov and Pivovarova, 2021b; Chen et al., 2023).[2] This scale was developed within the DURel annotation framework (Schlechtweg et al., 2018), which is based on Blank's concept of semantic proximity (Blank, 1997, pp. 413–418)). This ordinal scale is similar to the one used for the original annotations in GWiC (before data transformation).

Each level of the DURel scale has an exact linguistic interpretation as depicted in Table 1, where **polysemy** is located between **identity**, **context variance**, and **homonymy** (Schlechtweg, 2023, pp. 22–23). The pair (1,2) is classified as **identical** as the referents of two uses of the word *arm* are both prototypical representatives of the same extensional category corresponding to the concept 'a human body part':

(1) [...] and taking a knife from her pocket, she opened a vein in her little **arm**, [...]

(2) [...] and though he saw her within reach of his **arm**, [...]

The usage pair (1,3) is classified as **context variance** as both referents still belong to the same extensional category, but one is a non-prototypical representative. Hence, there is some variation in meaning, e.g. the arm of a statue loses the function of the physical arm to be lifted:

(3) [...] when the disembodied **arm** of the Statue of Liberty jets spectacularly out of the sandy beach.

The usage pair (1,4) would be classified as **polysemy** as the two referents of *arm* belong to different extensional categories, but the corresponding concepts still hold a semantic relation (in this case a similarity relation regarding physical form).

(4) It stood behind a high brick wall, its back windows overlooking an **arm** of the sea [...]

In contrast, the referents of *arm* in the **homonymic** pair (1,5) belong to different extensional categories and the corresponding concepts do *not* hold a semantic relation:

(5) And those who remained at home had been heavily taxed to pay for the **arms**, ammunition; fortifications, [...]

2.2 Disagreement detection

Most data for NLP tasks is created by discarding disagreement. However, some approaches try to incorporate disagreement into the task through alternative label aggregation methods. One of the oldest approaches, as suggested by Dawid and Skene (1979), is the probabilistic label aggregation method. This method calculates the posterior probability of a label for a particular instance conditioned on predicted label, true label and reliability of the annotator, i.e., the annotator's past annotations. The final label is chosen based on the

[2] There are further ordinal datasets annotated on different scales (e.g. Trott and Bergen, 2021).

posterior probability. While this method incorporates disagreement for choosing gold labels, it still reduces the data down to a single dominant view. Sheng et al. (2008) modify this approach proposing an uncertainty-preserving labeling scheme that retains information about annotator disagreement instead of resolving it. They represent labels as a probability distribution over classes based on annotator ratings ("soft labels"). This preserves ambiguity and uncertainty when multiple plausible labels exist. Aligning with these approaches, Uma et al. (2021) develop machine learning models that can effectively learn from and capture the disagreement of annotations, rather than just relying solely on a single aggregated label. To learn from the full distribution of annotations, the annotator distributions are converted into soft labels and the model is optimized to predict these soft label distributions (Uma et al., 2021). They employ techniques like standard normalization of annotator distributions, softmax function over annotator distributions and use of probabilistic label aggregation models like MACE to generate soft labels.

Although these approaches capture the distribution of disagreeing annotations, there is no significant research on directly predicting the **amount** of disagreement in a supervised way.

3 Tasks

Participants are asked to solve two subtasks. Both rely on data from human WiC judgments on the ordinal DURel scale, as described in Section 2.1. Each instance has a target word w, for which two word usages, u_1 and u_2, are provided (usage pair). Each of these usages expresses a specific meaning of w. As an example, consider the two annotation instances below. Pair (1,2) would likely receive label 4 (identical) while pair (1,3) would rather receive a lower label such as 2 (distantly related).

(1) ...and taking a knife from her pocket, she opened a vein in her little **arm**.

(2) ...and though he saw her within reach of his **arm**, yet the light of her eyes seemed as far off.

- Sample judgments: [4,4]; median: 4; mean pairwise difference: 0.0

(1) ...and taking a knife from her pocket, she opened a vein in her little **arm**.

(3) It stood behind a high brick wall, its back windows overlooking an **arm** of the sea which, at low tide, was a black and stinking mud-flat.

- Sample judgments: [2,3,2]; median: 2; mean pairwise difference: 0.667

3.1 Subtask 1: Median Judgment Classification with Ordinal Word-in-Context Judgments (OGWiC)

For each usage pair (u_1, u_2), participants are asked to predict the median of annotator judgments.[3] This task is similar to the previous WiC and GWiC tasks. However, we limit the label set in predictions and penalize stronger deviations from the true label (see Section 6). This makes OGWiC an **ordinal classification task** (Sakai, 2021), in contrast to binary classification (WiC) or ranking (GWiC). Predictions are evaluated against the median labels with the ordinal version of Krippendorff's α (Krippendorff, 2018).

Treating graded WiC as an ordinal classification task instead of a ranking task constrains model predictions to exactly reproduce instance labels instead of just inferring their relative order. This is advantageous if ordinal labels have an interpretation because predictions then inherit this interpretation. Such an interpretation can be assigned to the DURel scale as explained in Section 2.1: Judgment 1-4 can be interpreted as "homonymy" (1), "polysemy" (2), "context variance" (3) and "identity" (4), respectively.

3.2 Subtask 2: Mean Disagreement Ranking with Ordinal Word-in-Context Judgments (DisWiC)

For each usage pair (u_1, u_2), participants are asked to predict the mean of pairwise absolute judgment differences between annotators:

$$D(J) = \frac{1}{|J|} \sum_{(j_1,j_2)\in J} (|j_1 - j_2|)$$

where J is the set of unique pairwise combinations of judgments. For pair (1,2) from above,

$$D(J) = \frac{1}{2}(|(4-4)| + |(4-4)|) = 0.0$$

while for (1,3) it amounts to

$$\frac{1}{3}(|(2-3)| + |(2-2)| + |(3-2)|) = 0.667.$$

[3]We choose the median instead of other summary statistics because it is robust to outliers and frequently used in studies using ordinal WiC data (e.g. Schlechtweg et al., 2020; Zamora-Reina et al., 2022).

Dataset	LG	Reference	JUD	VER	KRI	SPR
ChiWUG	ZH	Chen et al. (2023)	61k	1.0.0	.60	.69
DWUG	EN	Schlechtweg et al. (2021)	69K	3.0.0	.63	.55
DWUG Res.	EN	Schlechtweg et al. (2024)	7K	1.0.0	.56	.59
DWUG	DE	Schlechtweg et al. (2021)	63K	3.0.0	.67	.61
DWUG Res.	DE	Schlechtweg et al. (2024)	10K	1.0.0	.59	.7
DiscoWUG	DE	Kurtyigit et al. (2021)	28K	2.0.0	.59	.57
RefWUG	DE	Schlechtweg (2023)	4k	1.1.0	.67	.7
DURel	DE	Schlechtweg et al. (2018)	6k	3.0.0	.54	.59
SURel	DE	Hätty et al. (2019)	5k	3.0.0	.83	.84
NorDiaChange	NO	Kutuzov et al. (2022)	19k	1.0.0	.71	.74
RuSemShift	RU	Rodina and Kutuzov (2020)	8k	1.0.0	.52	.53
RuShiftEval	RU	Kutuzov and Pivovarova (2021a)	30k	1.0.0	.56	.55
RuDSI	RU	Aksenova et al. (2022)	6k	1.0.0	.41	.56
DWUG	ES	Zamora-Reina et al. (2022)	62k	4.0.1	.53	.57
DWUG	SV	Schlechtweg et al. (2021)	55K	3.0.0	.67	.62
DWUG Res.	SV	Schlechtweg et al. (2024)	16K	1.0.0	.56	.65

Table 2: Datasets used for our task. All are annotated on the DURel scale. Spearman and Krippendorff values for RuShiftEval are calculated as average across all time bins. 'LG' = Language; 'JUD' = Number of judgments; 'VER' = Dataset version; 'KRI' = Krippendorff's α; 'SPR' = Weighted mean of pairwise Spearman correlations; 'Res.' = Resampled.

Language	Mean	Std
Chinese	2.00	0.00
English	2.32	0.62
German	2.82	1.06
Norwegian	2.31	0.46
Russian	3.78	1.03
Spanish	2.23	0.48
Swedish	2.36	0.63

Table 3: Mean and standard deviation for number of annotators per instance after cleaning and aggregation per language.

DisWiC can be seen as a **ranking task**. Participants are asked to rank instances according to the magnitude of disagreement observed between annotators. It differs from previous tasks (Leonardelli et al., 2023) by aggregating "gold" labels purely over judgment differences, thus making disagreement the explicit ranking aim. Predictions will be evaluated against the mean disagreement labels with Spearman's ρ (Spearman, 1904).

4 Data

For both subtasks, we make use of publicly available ordinal WiC datasets from multiple languages, as summarized in Table 2.[4] These provide a large number of judgments for usage pairs on the DURel scale and have so far not been used primarily for WiC-like tasks, but only for semantic change detection purposes. We additionally augment DWUG DE/EN/SV and DiscoWUG with roughly 33k unpublished instances which we have recently annotated guaranteeing evaluation on hidden data (DWUG Resampled). For all datasets, overall agreement as well as cleaning procedures ensure data quality.

[4]https://www.ims.uni-stuttgart.de/data/wugs

4.1 Dataset pre-cleaning

The data setswe rely on show various problems such as erroneous target word indices or duplicate contexts and judgments. This holds in particular for the Norwegian, Russian and Spanish datasets. Hence, we apply multiple cleaning measures. We describe them in the order they were applied: First, we load all uses from all datasets into one Pandas DataFrame, similarly for judgments, resulting in 82,286 uses and 492,796 judgments to process. Usage pairs with the same use identifiers are considered to be the same pair irrespective of the identifier order in the pair. We start by removing all judgments by annotator 'gecsa' from the Spanish judgments as the annotators was also excluded by the creators of the dataset. Then we drop missing judgments (empty fields). Spanish usages have non-consistent CSV quoting characters. Hence, we drop enclosing quotes and double quotes from contexts while updating target word indices accordingly. Next, we drop duplicate uses if they have the same identifier, context and target word indices.

Then, we reconstruct erroneous target word indices. We start out by excluding punctuation at the beginning or end of the target word; we then check a number of properties on the target word indices and the selected substring to find erroneous indices:

- the start and end index should be in the range of the context length,
- the target word should have at least one character,
- the preceding and following character should not be alphabetic (except in Chinese) and

- the string similarity between target lemma and selected target word string should be above or equal to 0.5.[5]

All usages not meeting any of these conditions are further considered for index reconstruction. Usages with modified punctuation (see above) also enter the reconstruction. The index reconstruction proceeds as follows: We tokenize the context by splitting at white spaces. We then compare the lowercased version of each token with punctuation removed to the lower-cased version of the lemma. For each candidate token with the maximum string similarity, we first remove punctuation from beginning and end and then search for the candidate string with start index nearest to the original index. This candidate is chosen as the new target substring. For cases with multiple candidates with the same distance between new and original start index, we choose the first candidate. For Russian, we additionally split tokens at hyphens as the data contains many compounds connected by hyphens.[6] The finally chosen candidate is regarded as the new target word substring and we extract its start and end index. In order to make sure that the new target substring choice is reasonable, we check its string similarity with the target lemma as described above. Substrings with a string similarity below or equal 0.5 are filtered out and later removed.[7] We manually inspect filtered-out usages below different thresholds of string similarity to make sure not to filter out valid usages not meeting our conditions. This frequently happens where target lemma and substring were very different because of strong inflection, or plural forms with different lemma than the singular forms, such as люди as plural of человек. This leads to a number of additional special conditions making sure to keep certain particular usages or usages meeting certain conditions.

Next, we find usages having the same context, lemma and target word indices (but not identifier, as checked above). For each such equivalence set, one identifier is chosen to represent all of them and used to replace the other identifiers in the judgments. The rest is dropped from the uses. We further aggregate duplicate judgments (same pair judged multiple times by the same annotator) with the median of judgments or as 0 (special judgment for "Cannot decide") if the number of 0-judgments was larger than judgments between 1–4. Finally, judgments are removed if they contain an identifier that is not present in the uses. After applying this preprocessing, we are left with 80,514 uses and 490,696 judgments.

4.2 Data aggregation and cleaning

For cleaning and aggregation, we initially exclude annotation instances with less than two annotations. For OGWiC, then instances with any 0-judgments ("Cannot decide") and instances with any pair of annotators disagreeing more than one point on the annotation scale are discarded. We then calculate the median of all judgments, for each instance. Instances with a non-integer median (e.g. 3.5) are discarded. For all remaining instances, gold labels are given by the median of judgments as explained in Section 3.1. For DisWiC, we derive instance labels by aggregating over judgments with the average of pairwise absolute annotator deviations as explained in Section 3.2. 0-judgments are ignored in this process.

For each subtask, we then randomly split the target words per language into train/test/dev with sizes of 70/20/10%. Instances are then assigned to each split according to their lemma. Note that there is no overlap in uses between splits and no overlap in target lemmas. In contrast to previous tasks, we intentionally do not balance out the label distribution in order to keep more realistic data conditions. Find an overview of the final splits per language in Table 4.[8] Find plots of the aggregated label distributions for both subtasks in Appendix A. Table 3 gives additional statistics regarding the number of annotators per language after cleaning and aggregation.

5 Models

Five teams participated in at least one of the shared task's official evaluation phases. Additionally, there were three unofficial submissions (Choppa et al., 2025; Loke et al., 2025; Sarumi et al., 2025).[9] In the description below, for each team we mark those modeling approaches with the label "top" which produce the team's top result in the evaluation phase, as reported in Table 5.

[5] We use the ratio measure from the difflib library, ranging between 0.0 and 1.0.

[6] Compounds are only split for index reconstruction. The original context is left untouched.

[7] For compounds, we choose the maximum string similarity of any subtoken after splitting at hyphens.

[8] Data is available through our website: `https://comedinlp.github.io/`.

[9] User "sunfz1" did not submit a system description paper.

Task	# Instances	# Uses	# Lemmas	Split
	48K	55K	520	Train
OGWiC	8K	8K	77	Dev
	15K	16K	152	Test
	82K	55K	521	Train
DisWiC	13K	8K	77	Dev
	26K	16K	152	Test

Table 4: Data statistics after cleaning and aggregation per split and and over all languages combined.

5.1 Participating teams

Deep-change (Kuklin and Arefyev, 2025) The employed model is based on a previous Word-in-Context model for binary prediction (same sense vs. different sense), which has already shown high performance in lexical semantic change detection (DeepMistake, Arefyev et al., 2021; Homskiy and Arefyev, 2022). The model uses XLM-R, a multilingual BERT variation (Devlin et al., 2019; Conneau et al., 2019), as base embeddings, which were fine-tuned on binary multilingual WiC data (Martelli et al., 2021) and/or binary or binarized Spanish data (Pasini et al., 2021; Zamora-Reina et al., 2022). For OGWiC, the model is further fine-tuned on the shared task data or a binarized version of it thresholding the binary predictions to map them to four classes (top). The team also experiments with different models per language (top). For DisWiC, multiple disagreement measures are tested including linear regression directly predicting the disagreement labels, binary classification of perfect agreement and the class probability standard deviation of a four-class model trained on individual annotations (top).

GRASP (Alfter and Appelgren, 2025) For OGWiC, multiple models are tested including a probabilistic sequential model predicting annotation sequences from annotation co-occurrence frequencies, a simple XLM-R-based Word-in-Context model fine-tuned on the task data and an XLM-R-based Word-in-Context model (XL-Lexeme, Cassotti et al., 2023) previously fine-tuned on binary multilingual WiC data (Martelli et al., 2021) with thresholds on cosine similarity (top). For DisWiC, the team tests regression models using cosine similarities from XL-Lexeme and XLM-R, as well as linguistic features. Further, Word-in-Context models are optimized on different dataset splits representing individual annotators and models are optimized specifically for subsets of languages (top).

MMLabUIT (Le and Van, 2025) Predictions were only submitted for OGWiC. One set of models uses variations of BERT including XLM-R as base embeddings, applies stacking and averaging modifications and measures the final labels by thresholds on cosine similarity. Another set relies on BERT variations (top) and BART (Lewis et al., 2019) as base embeddings, fine-tuning these on Natural Language Inference data, based on a postulated similarity of the shared task objective with Natural Language Inference.

JuniperLiu (Liu et al., 2025) The OGWiC models build on BERT variations including XLM-R (top) and Llama (Touvron et al., 2023) to extract embeddings, apply matrix transformations to remove vector anisotropy, then calculate cosine similarity, and map these to discrete labels using thresholds on the similarity values. For DisWiC, a multilayer perceptron regressor (Hinton, 1990) is learned on embedding features predicting the disagreement label (top).

FuocChu_VIP123 (Chu, 2025) Only DisWiC predictions are submitted. The model uses Sentence Transformers (Reimers and Gurevych, 2019) based on XLM-R to generate embeddings and a multi-layer perceptron regressor to predict disagreement labels (top).

5.2 Baselines

We employ a number of baseline models to put participants' results into context. Code for Baseline 1 and 3 was published at the beginning of the respective development phases of the shared task.

XLM-R + CosTH (Baseline 1) For each usage pair, we use XLM-R to generate contextualized embeddings for the two target words in context and calculate the cosine similarity (Salton and McGill, 1983) between the two embeddings. Similarity is mapped to discrete OGWiC labels using three thresholds θ. These are optimized on the training set by minimizing the following loss function (cf. Choppa, 2024):

$$L(\mathbf{y}, \hat{\mathbf{y}}|\theta) = 1 - \alpha(\mathbf{y}, \hat{\mathbf{y}}_\theta)$$

where $\mathbf{y}$ and $\hat{\mathbf{y}}$ are gold labels and predicted cosine similarities respectively, α is Krippendorff's

α and $\hat{\mathbf{y}}_\theta$ is a mapping of cosine similarities to discrete labels according to thresholds θ. We optimize thresholds per language.

XL-Lexeme + CosTH (Baseline 2) This is the same model as XLM-R + CosTH with the exception of using XL-Lexeme (Cassotti et al., 2023) as contextual embedder. XL-Lexeme is a bi-encoder model utilizing a Siamese Network that extends the Sentence Transformers (Reimers and Gurevych, 2019) architecture to focus on the target word within input sentences. The model is trained using a contrastive loss function, which minimizes the cosine distance between the encoded representations when the target word has the same meaning and maximizes the distance when the meanings differ. It is pre-trained on a large multilingual binary WiC dataset (Martelli et al., 2021). We learn one mapping from similarities to thresholds per language.

XLM-R + LR (Baseline 3) For each usage pair, we use XLM-R to generate contextualized embeddings for the two target words in context and concatenate these to create a single representation. We then use linear regression to learn a mapping from embedding representations to continuous disagreement labels for DisWiC. This mapping is optimized on the training set. We learn one mapping per language, and one on the full dataset. Then, we choose the condition which yields highest performance on the development set to apply to the test set. The optimized condition is given by the full dataset model.

XL-Lexeme + MLP (Baseline 4) For each usage pair, we use XL-Lexeme to generate contextualized embeddings for the two target words in context and concatenate these to create a single representation. We then use a multi-layer preceptron regressor (Hinton, 1990) to learn a mapping from embedding representations to continuous disagreement labels for DisWiC. This mapping is optimized on the training set. We learn one mapping per language, and one on the full dataset. We further vary the batch size, activation function, hidden layer size and alpha parameters, and apply feature scaling. Refer to Table 6 in Appendix B for an overview of the hyperparameter grid used. Then, we choose the combination which yields highest performance on the development set to apply to the test set. The optimized condition is given by the per language model with hyperparameters as shown in Table 7 in Appendix B.

Upper bound (OGWiC) For each language, we iterate over annotators and calculate Krippendorff's α between the current annotator's judgments and the remaining ones aggregating them by their median per instance. This number reflects how well each annotator can predict the median of the other annotators' judgments. We then take the average α over annotators weighted by their number of judgments as the final upper bound.[10]

6 Evaluation

WiC is a binary classification task suggesting accuracy as evaluation measure. In contrast, the GWiC shared task used the harmonic mean of Pearson and Spearman correlations (Spearman, 1904). For our OGWiC task, we want to produce ordinal classifications corresponding to the nature of our gold labels. This requirement makes the evaluation measure employed in GWiC unsuitable because it does not limit the label set. Using accuracy is also not ideal in that it does not capture the ordinal nature of the classes. For example, suppose that an instance has a gold label of 4. A model prediction of 1 should be penalized more heavily than a prediction of 3.

With the above considerations in mind, we will use Krippendorff's α (Krippendorff, 2018), which, in its ordinal formulation, penalizes stronger deviations from the gold label more heavily. It has the additional advantage of controlling for expected disagreement and has been demonstrated to be superior to other measures such as Mean Absolute Error for ordinal classification (Sakai, 2021).

For DisWiC, we do not ask participants to reproduce the exact disagreement label as it has no direct interpretation. We are more interested in the relative amount of disagreement observed between usages. Hence, it is formulated as a ranking task and accordingly evaluated with Spearman's rank order correlation coefficient (Spearman, 1904).

Participants were provided with a starting kit implementing our XLM-R-based baseline models

[10]Surprisingly, this upper bound is 1.0 for Chinese. This is a consequence of our cleaning process combined with the specific properties of this dataset: All instances in the dataset have exactly two annotations. As described in Section 4, we remove those with a disagreement of more than one point on the scale. This means that remaining instances with disagreement all have exactly one point disagreement, such as [3, 4]. These instances all have a non-integer median, which is also removed by our cleaning process. Hence, all instances in the cleaned Chinese dataset have perfect agreement.

Task	Team	AV	-ES	ZH	EN	DE	NO	RU	ES	SV
OGWiC	Upper bound	.95	.95	1.	.97	.88	.94	.96	.96	.95
	deep-change	**.66**	**.64**	**.42**	**.73**	.72	**.67**	**.62**	**.75**	**.68**
	Baseline 2	.58	.57	.38	.65	**.73**	.52	.55	.66	.60
	GRASP	.56	.54	.32	.56	.66	.59	.49	.64	.65
	MMLabUIT	.52	.51	.36	.57	.67	.44	.42	.60	.61
	JuniperLiu	.27	.26	.14	.51	.49	.08	.13	.33	.22
	Baseline 1	.12	.12	.06	.10	.27	.12	.11	.18	.02
DisWiC	deep-change	**.23**	.23	.30	**.08**	**.20**	**.29**	**.18**	**.19**	**.35**
	GRASP	.22	.23	**.54**	.04	.11	.27	.17	.12	.30
	Baseline 4	.16	.17	.49	.06	.09	.24	.12	.08	.08
	FuocChu.	.12	.14	.36	.02	.10	.16	.05	.01	.17
	Baseline 3	.12	.12	.39	.06	.09	.08	.05	.08	.08
	JuniperLiu	.08	.09	.36	.04	.02	-.04	.07	.04	.09
	sunfz1	.07	.07	.30	.05	-.00	-.07	.07	.04	.09

Table 5: Top results of evaluation phases. 'AV' = Average over languages; '-ES' = Average over languages excluding Spanish; 'FuocChu.' = FuocChu_VIP123.

(see Section 5) as well as training and development data (see Section 4) during the development phases for both subtasks lasting from August 23 to September 14 and September 15 to October 13, respectively.[11] During the evaluation phases, which lasted October 14–21 and October 21–27 respectively, participants were allowed to make three submissions, which were evaluated on the hidden test data, where the leaderboard on Codalab was kept hidden at all times.[12] Public test instances were only published at the start of the evaluation phases. Task results were released on October 28. The hidden gold labels of test instances were published during the respective post-evaluation phases.

7 Results

Find an overview of participants' top results in both evaluation phases in Table 5 and results for all submitted predictions in Table 8 in Appendix C. OGWiC is solved with rather high performances across the board. The winning team **deep-change** has an average performance of .66 with minimum of .42 on Chinese and a maximum of .75 on Spanish. The team has top performance on all languages except for German where our Baseline 2 excels. Second and third winners are **GRASP** and **MMLabUIT** with average performances of .56 and .52. The overall maximum performance reached in any language is .75 on the Spanish dataset while the lowest maximum performance for any language is Chinese where no team reached a higher performance than .42. Baseline 1 is outperformed by all participants while Baseline 2 is only outperformed by the winner. The nearest any performance gets to the upper bound is for German with a .15 difference for Baseline 2.

In contrast, DisWiC is solved with rather low performance, turning out to be a very challenging task. The winning team **deep-change** has an average performance of .23 with a minimum of .08 on English and a maximum of .30 on Chinese. The team has top performance on all languages except for Chinese, where **GRASP** excels with .54. Second and third winners are **GRASP** and **FuocChu_VIP123** with average performances of .22 and .12. The overall maximum performance reached in any language is .54 on the Chinese dataset, which is generally solved with rather high performances, while the lowest maximum performance for any language is English where no team reached a higher performance than .08. We hypothesize that maximum performance differences between languages may be related to different numbers of annotators on annotation instances per language, and the effect this has on our disagreement measure defined in Section 3.2, see the discussion in Section 9. Baseline 3 is outperformed by the top three participants while Baseline 4 is only outperformed by the top two participants.

In the post-evaluation phase we noticed that the winning team **deep-change** had (unknowingly) used some of the previously publicly available Spanish test data for training some of their models. This data leakage may have contributed to the exceptionally high result of the team on Spanish. Hence, we also report the average performance across languages excluding Spanish in Table 5 (column '-ES'). As we see, this does not change the average performances significantly, whereas **GRASP** now performs slightly better than **deep-change** in DisWiC (.235 vs. .231). However, this is mainly due to the exceptional performance on Chinese.

In both tasks, those teams excel that use independently optimized binary Word-in-Context models, i.e., **deep-change** and **GRASP**. This fits well with the strong performance of our Baselines 2 and 4 building on the same type of model. This could be explained by the similarity of the binary WiC task to OGWiC and the derivation of DisWiC labels from absolute differences between ordinal WiC an-

[11]Starting kits are available through our website: https://comedinlp.github.io/.

[12]Evaluation phase 1 was extended by one day because of technical problems.

notations. Further, across top-scoring submissions, OGWiC is solved by thresholding graded similarity predictions, as in our Baseline 2.

8 Conclusion

We introduced two new tasks based on ordinal Word-in-Context annotations between word usages, and described the results of a shared task based on these: OGWiC asks to predict the median semantic proximity judgment label for each annotated instance. This is a more traditional task definition where data is cleaned and summarized beforehand. DisWiC instead asks to predict the mean of pairwise absolute deviations between annotators. This takes a new and more perspectivist view on data, yet differing from previous tasks in making disagreement the explicit prediction aim. The traditional task was solved with rather high performances while the new approach proves to be challenging. However, on some languages performance is exceptionally high suggesting future modeling possibilities. Both tasks were dominated by the same teams employing a Word-in-Context model optimized on independent binary Word-in-Context data. The dominant approach to solve OGWiC was thresholding of graded similarity predictions.

In the future, it would be interesting to solve the two tasks we introduced with different data splitting conditions, such as sharing target words across splits. Models presumably better generalize from training data with the same target words as in the test data. It would also be interesting to tie the published task data to individual annotators enabling participants to build models for individual annotators accounting for individual judgments and corresponding disagreements.

9 Limitations

As a result of different numbers of annotators per instance, mean absolute disagreement values may not be completely comparable across instances. Consider this example: If an instance has two annotations, the maximum possible mean pairwise disagreement is 3.0, e.g. for

$$D(\{1,4\}) = \frac{1}{1}(|(4-1)|) = 3.0.$$

If one adds one more annotation, the maximum possible disagreement reduces to 2.0, e.g. for

$$D(\{1,1,4\}) = \frac{1}{3}(|(1-1)| + |(1-4)| + |(1-4)|) = 2.0.$$

This means that our measure is influenced by the number of annotators, which was not available to participants at test time. There is considerable variation across languages in the annotator number per instance: Table 3 gives the mean and standard deviation for the number of annotators per instance for each language. Chinese is exceptional with a mean of 2.0 and a standard deviation of 0.0, which means that each instance is annotated by exactly two annotators. As the number of annotators is constant across instances in Chinese, the mean disagreement values are not influenced by annotator number, facilitating prediction for participants, as opposed to the other languages. This may have supported exceptionally high DisWiC results for Chinese, see Table 5. In the future, the number of annotations per instance should be controlled or provided a test time, or the measure should be normalized. Also, other disagreement measures should be explored.

One of the major shortcomings of our setup is the narrowness of training, development and test data in terms of target words. While the task used data for seven languages with tens of thousands of usage pair instances per language, these instances were only sampled from a few hundred target words. The data was additionally split at target words (lexical split), asking participants to generalize from a huge number of instances of few target words to instances of unseen target words. It is questionable whether the training data provides enough information to generalize to unseen target words, and overfitting on the narrow training data is likely. Some task results indicate that models not using the training data at all perform competitively (Kuklin and Arefyev, 2025). In the future, one could run the tasks with alternative data splits where training, development and test data would not be split at target words, but at usages, asking models to generalize to usages from the same target words in the test data as seen in the training data. This would be a relevant task setup as in many annotation studies the budget allows to annotate a limited number of instances per word. If a model can be learned from these instances to reasonably predict the labels for unseen instances, this would be of enormous practical usefulness to analyze greater samples.

Another limitation is related to our choice of Krippendorff's α as evaluation measure for OGWiC. Despite its advantages and being recommended by Sakai (2021) for ordinal classification, the measure estimates the expected label distribution from both model and gold labels, which seems a reasonable assumption when measuring annotator agreement where none of the annotators should be given prevalence, but seems less reasonable in a model evaluation setup where the expected label distribution is given by the gold labels. In the future, one could explore modifications of Krippendorff's α estimating the expected label distribution solely from the gold data.

The performance upper bound we calculated for OGWiC may be influenced positively by our data cleaning process: While all left-over instances after the cleaning have high agreement, it may have occurred randomly for some of them, i.e., even two random annotators would agree on some instances, but this would not make their annotations for those instances reliable. Such instances will push the upper bound, but will be impossible to model.

Almost all of the datasets we used have a diachronic component, i.e., usages sampled from historical time periods often containing historical spelling variants and outdated meanings. While we completely ignored this component in this task, it puts additional difficulties on models and may be responsible for some of the performance differences observed between languages. In the future, one could include this information into the task setup by reporting results for historical and modern language instances separately.

Acknowledgments

Dominik Schlechtweg has been funded by the research program 'Change is Key!' supported by Riksbankens Jubileumsfond (under reference number M21-0021). Work by Michael Roth was funded by the DFG Emmy Noether program (RO 4848/2-1).

References

Anna Aksenova, Ekaterina Gavrishina, Elisei Rykov, and Andrey Kutuzov. 2022. RuDSI: Graph-based word sense induction dataset for Russian. In *Proceedings of TextGraphs-16: Graph-based Methods for Natural Language Processing*, pages 77–88, Gyeongju, Republic of Korea. Association for Computational Linguistics.

Nour Al-khdour, Mutaz Bni Younes, Malak Abdullah, and Mohammad AL-Smadi. 2020. JUSTMasters at SemEval-2020 task 3: Multilingual deep learning model to predict the effect of context in word similarity. In *Proceedings of the Fourteenth Workshop on Semantic Evaluation*, pages 292–300, Barcelona (online). International Committee for Computational Linguistics.

David Alfter and Mattias Appelgren. 2025. GRASP at CoMeDi Shared Task: Multi-strategy modeling of annotator behavior in multi-lingual semantic judgments. In *Proceedings of the 1st Workshop on Context and Meaning–Navigating Disagreements in NLP Annotations*, Abu Dhabi, UAE.

Nikolay Arefyev, Maksim Fedoseev, Vitaly Protasov, Daniil Homskiy, Adis Davletov, and Alexander Panchenko. 2021. DeepMistake: Which senses are hard to distinguish for a word-in-context model. volume 2021-June, pages 16–30.

Carlos Santos Armendariz, Matthew Purver, Senja Pollak, Nikola Ljubešić, Matej Ulčar, Ivan Vulić, and Mohammad Taher Pilehvar. 2020. SemEval-2020 task 3: Graded word similarity in context. In *Proceedings of the Fourteenth Workshop on Semantic Evaluation*, pages 36–49, Barcelona (online). International Committee for Computational Linguistics.

Andreas Blank. 1997. *Prinzipien des lexikalischen Bedeutungswandels am Beispiel der romanischen Sprachen*. Niemeyer, Tübingen.

Pierluigi Cassotti, Lucia Siciliani, Marco de Gemmis, Giovanni Semeraro, and Pierpaolo Basile. 2023. Xl-lexeme: Wic pretrained model for cross-lingual lexical semantic change. In *Proceedings of the 61th Annual Meeting of the Association for Computational Linguistics*, Online. Association for Computational Linguistics.

Jing Chen, Emmanuele Chersoni, Dominik Schlechtweg, Jelena Prokic, and Chu-Ren Huang. 2023. ChiWUG: A graph-based evaluation dataset for Chinese lexical semantic change detection. In *Proceedings of the 4th International Workshop on Computational Approaches to Historical Language Change*, Singapore. Association for Computational Linguistics.

Tejaswi Choppa. 2024. Supervised semantic proximity noise and disagreement detection. Master thesis, University of Stuttgart.

Tejaswi Choppa, Michael Roth, and Dominik Schlechtweg. 2025. Predicting median, disagreement and noise label in ordinal word-in-context data. In *Proceedings of the 1st Workshop on Context and Meaning–Navigating Disagreements in NLP Annotations*, Abu Dhabi, UAE.

Phuoc Duong Huy Chu. 2025. FuocChu_VIP123 at CoMeDi Shared Task: Disagreement ranking with xlm-roberta sentence embeddings and deep neural regression. In *Proceedings of the 1st Workshop on Context and Meaning–Navigating Disagreements in NLP Annotations*, Abu Dhabi, UAE.

Alexis Conneau, Kartikay Khandelwal, Naman Goyal, Vishrav Chaudhary, Guillaume Wenzek, Francisco

Guzmán, Edouard Grave, Myle Ott, Luke Zettlemoyer, and Veselin Stoyanov. 2019. Unsupervised cross-lingual representation learning at scale. *arXiv preprint arXiv:1911.02116*.

D. A. Cruse. 1995. *Polysemy and related phenomena from a cognitive linguistic viewpoint*, chapter 2. Studies in Natural Language Processing. Cambridge University Press, Cambridge.

A. P. Dawid and A. M. Skene. 1979. Maximum likelihood estimation of observer error-rates using the em algorithm. *Journal of the Royal Statistical Society. Series C (Applied Statistics)*, 28(1):20–28.

Jacob Devlin, Ming-Wei Chang, Kenton Lee, and Kristina Toutanova. 2019. BERT: Pre-training of deep bidirectional transformers for language understanding. In *Proceedings of the 2019 Conference of the North American Chapter of the Association for Computational Linguistics: Human Language Technologies, Volume 1 (Long and Short Papers)*, pages 4171–4186, Minneapolis, Minnesota. Association for Computational Linguistics.

Katrin Erk, Diana McCarthy, and Nicholas Gaylord. 2013. Measuring word meaning in context. *Computational Linguistics*, 39(3):511–554.

Anna Hätty, Dominik Schlechtweg, and Sabine Schulte im Walde. 2019. SURel: A gold standard for incorporating meaning shifts into term extraction. In *Proceedings of the 8th Joint Conference on Lexical and Computational Semantics*, pages 1–8, Minneapolis, MN, USA.

Geoffrey I. Hinton. 1990. *Connectionist learning procedures*, pages 555—-610. Morgan Kaufmann Publishers Inc., San Francisco, CA, USA.

Daniil Homskiy and Nikolay Arefyev. 2022. DeepMistake at LSCDiscovery: Can a multilingual word-in-context model replace human annotators? In *Proceedings of the 3rd Workshop on Computational Approaches to Historical Language Change*, pages 173–179, Dublin, Ireland. Association for Computational Linguistics.

Adam Kilgarriff. 1997. "I don't believe in word senses". *Computers and the Humanities*, 31(2).

Klaus Krippendorff. 2018. *Content Analysis: An Introduction to Its Methodology*. SAGE Publications.

Mikhail Kuklin and Nikolay Arefyev. 2025. Deepchange at CoMeDi: the cross-entropy loss is not all you need. In *Proceedings of the 1st Workshop on Context and Meaning–Navigating Disagreements in NLP Annotations*, Abu Dhabi, UAE.

Sinan Kurtyigit, Maike Park, Dominik Schlechtweg, Jonas Kuhn, and Sabine Schulte im Walde. 2021. Lexical Semantic Change Discovery. In *Proceedings of the 59th Annual Meeting of the Association for Computational Linguistics and the 11th International Joint Conference on Natural Language Processing (Volume 1: Long Papers)*, Online. Association for Computational Linguistics.

Andrey Kutuzov and Lidia Pivovarova. 2021a. Rushifteval: a shared task on semantic shift detection for russian. *Komp'yuternaya Lingvistika i Intellektual'nye Tekhnologii: Dialog conference*.

Andrey Kutuzov and Lidia Pivovarova. 2021b. Three-part diachronic semantic change dataset for russian. *Preprint*, arXiv:2106.08294.

Andrey Kutuzov, Samia Touileb, Petter Mæhlum, Tita Enstad, and Alexandra Wittemann. 2022. NorDiaChange: Diachronic semantic change dataset for Norwegian. In *Proceedings of the Thirteenth Language Resources and Evaluation Conference*, pages 2563–2572, Marseille, France. European Language Resources Association.

Tai Duc Le and Thin Dang Van. 2025. MMLabUIT at CoMeDi Shared Task: Text embedding techniques versus generation-based nli for median judgment classification. In *Proceedings of the 1st Workshop on Context and Meaning–Navigating Disagreements in NLP Annotations*, Abu Dhabi, UAE.

Elisa Leonardelli, Gavin Abercrombie, Dina Almanea, Valerio Basile, Tommaso Fornaciari, Barbara Plank, Verena Rieser, Alexandra Uma, and Massimo Poesio. 2023. SemEval-2023 task 11: Learning with disagreements (LeWiDi). In *Proceedings of the 17th International Workshop on Semantic Evaluation (SemEval-2023)*, pages 2304–2318, Toronto, Canada. Association for Computational Linguistics.

Mike Lewis, Yinhan Liu, Naman Goyal, Marjan Ghazvininejad, Abdelrahman Mohamed, Omer Levy, Ves Stoyanov, and Luke Zettlemoyer. 2019. Bart: Denoising sequence-to-sequence pre-training for natural language generation, translation, and comprehension. *Preprint*, arXiv:1910.13461.

Zhu Liu, Zhen Hu, and Ying Liu. 2025. JuniperLiu at CoMeDi Shared Task: Models as annotators in lexical semantics disagreements. In *Proceedings of the 1st Workshop on Context and Meaning–Navigating Disagreements in NLP Annotations*, Abu Dhabi, UAE.

Ying Xuan Loke, Dominik Schlechtweg, and Wei Zhao. 2025. ABDN-NLP at CoMeDi Shared Task: Predicting the aggregated human judgment via weighted few-shot prompting. In *Proceedings of the 1st Workshop on Context and Meaning–Navigating Disagreements in NLP Annotations*, Abu Dhabi, UAE.

Federico Martelli, Najla Kalach, Gabriele Tola, and Roberto Navigli. 2021. SemEval-2021 task 2: Multilingual and cross-lingual word-in-context disambiguation (MCL-WiC). In *Proceedings of the 15th International Workshop on Semantic Evaluation (SemEval-2021)*, pages 24–36, Online. Association for Computational Linguistics.

Diana McCarthy, Marianna Apidianaki, and Katrin Erk. 2016. Word sense clustering and clusterability. *Computational Linguistics*, 42(2):245–275.

Roberto Navigli. 2009. Word sense disambiguation: a survey. *ACM Computing Surveys*, 41(2):1–69.

Tommaso Pasini, Alessandro Raganato, and Roberto Navigli. 2021. XL-WSD: an extra-large and cross-lingual evaluation framework for word sense disambiguation. In *Thirty-Fifth AAAI Conference on Artificial Intelligence, AAAI 2021, Thirty-Third Conference on Innovative Applications of Artificial Intelligence, IAAI 2021, The Eleventh Symposium on Educational Advances in Artificial Intelligence, EAAI 2021, Virtual Event, February 2-9, 2021*, pages 13648–13656. AAAI Press.

Mohammad Taher Pilehvar and Jose Camacho-Collados. 2019. WiC: the word-in-context dataset for evaluating context-sensitive meaning representations. In *Proceedings of the 2019 Conference of the North American Chapter of the Association for Computational Linguistics: Human Language Technologies, Volume 1 (Long and Short Papers)*, pages 1267–1273, Minneapolis, Minnesota. Association for Computational Linguistics.

Alessandro Raganato, Tommaso Pasini, Jose Camacho-Collados, and Mohammad Taher Pilehvar. 2020. XL-WiC: A multilingual benchmark for evaluating semantic contextualization. In *Proceedings of the 2020 Conference on Empirical Methods in Natural Language Processing (EMNLP)*, pages 7193–7206, Online. Association for Computational Linguistics.

Nils Reimers and Iryna Gurevych. 2019. Sentence-BERT: Sentence embeddings using Siamese BERT-networks. In *Proceedings of the 2019 Conference on Empirical Methods in Natural Language Processing and the 9th International Joint Conference on Natural Language Processing (EMNLP-IJCNLP)*, pages 3982–3992, Hong Kong, China. Association for Computational Linguistics.

Julia Rodina and Andrey Kutuzov. 2020. RuSemShift: a dataset of historical lexical semantic change in Russian. In *Proceedings of the 28th International Conference on Computational Linguistics*, pages 1037–1047, Barcelona, Spain (Online). International Committee on Computational Linguistics.

Tetsuya Sakai. 2021. Evaluating evaluation measures for ordinal classification and ordinal quantification. In *Proceedings of the 59th Annual Meeting of the Association for Computational Linguistics and the 11th International Joint Conference on Natural Language Processing (Volume 1: Long Papers)*, pages 2759–2769.

Gerard Salton and Michael J McGill. 1983. *Introduction to Modern Information Retrieval*. McGraw - Hill Book Company, New York.

Olufunke O. Sarumi, Charles Welch, Christin Seifert, Lucie Flek, and Jörg Schlötterer. 2025. Funzac at CoMeDi Shared Task: Modeling annotator disagreement from word-in-context perspectives. In *Proceedings of the 1st Workshop on Context and Meaning–Navigating Disagreements in NLP Annotations*, Abu Dhabi, UAE.

Dominik Schlechtweg. 2023. *Human and Computational Measurement of Lexical Semantic Change*. Ph.D. thesis, University of Stuttgart, Stuttgart, Germany.

Dominik Schlechtweg, Pierluigi Cassotti, Bill Noble, David Alfter, Sabine Schulte Im Walde, and Nina Tahmasebi. 2024. More DWUGs: Extending and evaluating word usage graph datasets in multiple languages. In *Proceedings of the 2024 Conference on Empirical Methods in Natural Language Processing*, pages 14379–14393, Miami, Florida, USA. Association for Computational Linguistics.

Dominik Schlechtweg, Barbara McGillivray, Simon Hengchen, Haim Dubossarsky, and Nina Tahmasebi. 2020. SemEval-2020 Task 1: Unsupervised Lexical Semantic Change Detection. In *Proceedings of the 14th International Workshop on Semantic Evaluation*, Barcelona, Spain. Association for Computational Linguistics.

Dominik Schlechtweg, Sabine Schulte im Walde, and Stefanie Eckmann. 2018. Diachronic Usage Relatedness (DURel): A framework for the annotation of lexical semantic change. In *Proceedings of the 2018 Conference of the North American Chapter of the Association for Computational Linguistics: Human Language Technologies*, pages 169–174, New Orleans, Louisiana.

Dominik Schlechtweg, Nina Tahmasebi, Simon Hengchen, Haim Dubossarsky, and Barbara McGillivray. 2021. DWUG: A large Resource of Diachronic Word Usage Graphs in Four Languages. In *Proceedings of the 2021 Conference on Empirical Methods in Natural Language Processing*, pages 7079–7091, Online and Punta Cana, Dominican Republic. Association for Computational Linguistics.

Hinrich Schütze. 1998. Automatic word sense discrimination. *Computational Linguistics*, 24(1):97–123.

Victor S. Sheng, Foster Provost, and Panagiotis G. Ipeirotis. 2008. Get another label? improving data quality and data mining using multiple, noisy labelers. In *Proceedings of the 14th ACM SIGKDD International Conference on Knowledge Discovery and Data Mining*, KDD '08, page 614–622, New York, NY, USA. Association for Computing Machinery.

Charles Spearman. 1904. The proof and measurement of association between two things. *American Journal of Psychology*, 15:88–103.

Hugo Touvron, Thibaut Lavril, Gautier Izacard, Xavier Martinet, Marie-Anne Lachaux, Timothée Lacroix, Baptiste Rozière, Naman Goyal, Eric Hambro, Faisal Azhar, Aurelien Rodriguez, Armand Joulin, Edouard Grave, and Guillaume Lample. 2023. Llama: Open and efficient foundation language models. *Preprint*, arXiv:2302.13971.

Sean Trott and Benjamin Bergen. 2021. RAW-C: Relatedness of ambiguous words in context (a new lexical resource for English). In *Proceedings of the 59th Annual Meeting of the Association for Computational Linguistics and the 11th International Joint Conference on Natural Language Processing (Volume 1: Long Papers)*, pages 7077–7087, Online. Association for Computational Linguistics.

David Tuggy. 1993. Ambiguity, polysemy, and vagueness. *Cognitive Linguistics*, 4(3):273–290.

Alexandra Uma, Tommaso Fornaciari, Anca Dumitrache, Tristan Miller, Jon Chamberlain, Barbara Plank, Edwin Simpson, and Massimo Poesio. 2021. SemEval-2021 task 12: Learning with disagreements. In *Proceedings of the 15th International Workshop on Semantic Evaluation (SemEval-2021)*, pages 338–347, Online. Association for Computational Linguistics.

Alexandra N. Uma, Tommaso Fornaciari, Dirk Hovy, Silviu Paun, Barbara Plank, and Massimo Poesio. 2022. Learning from disagreement: A survey. *J. Artif. Int. Res.*, 72:1385—-1470.

Alex Wang, Yada Pruksachatkun, Nikita Nangia, Amanpreet Singh, Julian Michael, Felix Hill, Omer Levy, and Samuel R. Bowman. 2019. *SuperGLUE: a stickier benchmark for general-purpose language understanding systems*. Curran Associates Inc., Red Hook, NY, USA.

Zirui Wang, Adams Wei Yu, Orhan Firat, and Yuan Cao. 2021. Towards zero-label language learning. *arXiv preprint arXiv:2109.09193*.

Frank D. Zamora-Reina, Felipe Bravo-Marquez, and Dominik Schlechtweg. 2022. LSCDiscovery: A shared task on semantic change discovery and detection in Spanish. In *Proceedings of the 3rd International Workshop on Computational Approaches to Historical Language Change*, Dublin, Ireland. Association for Computational Linguistics.

A Label distributions

Find aggregated label distributions for all languages combined in Figures 1 and 2.

B Hyperparameter grid and optimized parameters

Find the hyperparameter grid used for tuning Baseline 4 in Table 6 and the final optimized hyperparameter combinations in Table 7.

C Submission overview

Find results for all submitted predictions in Table 8.

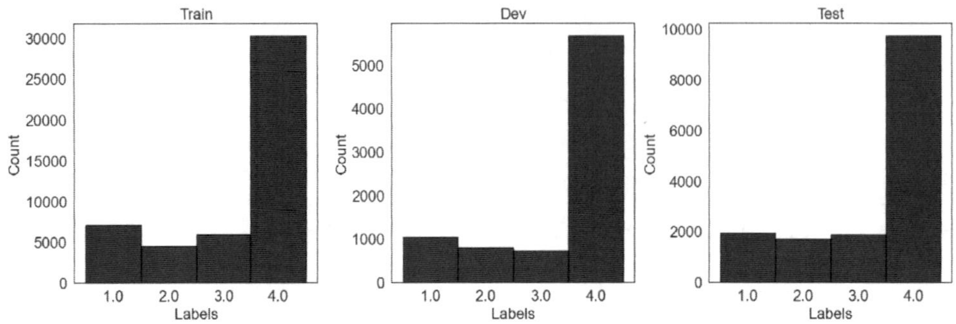

Figure 1: Label distribution for OGWiC task for all languages combined.

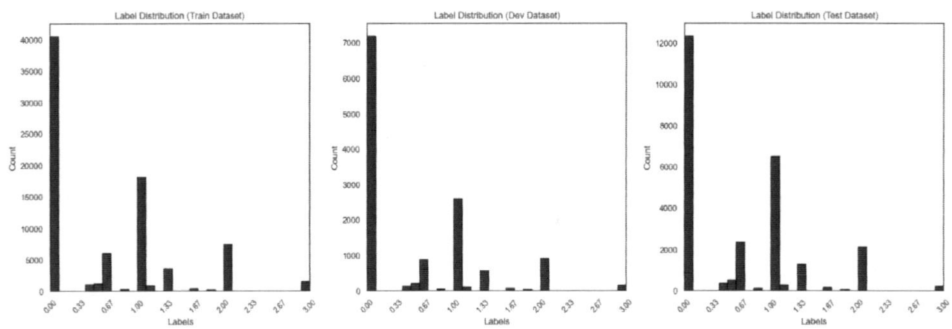

Figure 2: Label distribution for DisWiC task for all languages combined.

Hyperparameter	**Values**
activation	relu, tanh
solver	Adam
hidden layer sizes	10, 50, 100
alpha	.0001, .001, .01, .1
batch size	32, auto, 50, 100
scaler	StandardScaler(), None

Table 6: Hyperparameter grid used for tuning Baseline 4.

Hyperparameter	**ZH**	**EN**	**DE**	**NO**	**RU**	**ES**	**SV**
Activation	tanh	tanh	relu	relu	tanh	tanh	tanh
Alpha	.001	.1	.0001	.001	.1	.1	.0001
Batch Size	auto	auto	auto	100	100	auto	100
Hidden Layer Sizes	(50,)	(50,)	(50,)	(50,)	(100,)	(100,)	(100,)
Scaler	None	yes	yes	yes	yes	yes	yes

Table 7: Final set of hyperparameters for Baseline 4 per language.

Task	Team	AV	-ES	ZH	EN	DE	NO	RU	ES	SV
OGWiC	deep-change	**.66**	.64	**.42**	**.73**	.72	**.67**	.62	**.75**	**.68**
	deep-change	.65	.64	.42	.73	.72	.63	**.63**	.75	.68
	Baseline 2	.58	.57	.38	.65	**.73**	.52	.55	.66	.60
	GRASP	.56	.54	.32	.56	.66	.59	.49	.64	.65
	MMLabUIT	.52	.51	.36	.57	.67	.44	.42	.60	.61
	MMLabUIT	.52	.51	.32	.52	.65	.46	.42	.57	.66
	MMLabUIT	.52	.51	.35	.53	.66	.45	.43	.58	.63
	GRASP	.51	.50	.33	.57	.62	.47	.46	.59	.56
	GRASP	.43	.41	.18	.61	.51	.29	.34	.58	.48
	JuniperLiu	.27	.26	.14	.51	.49	.08	.13	.33	.22
	Baseline 1	.12	.12	.06	.10	.27	.12	.11	.18	.02
DisWiC	deep-change	**.23**	.23	.30	.08	**.20**	.29	**.18**	**.19**	**.35**
	GRASP	.22	.23	**.54**	.04	.11	.27	.17	.12	.30
	GRASP	.22	.23	.50	**.10**	.12	**.32**	.16	.10	.23
	GRASP	.16	.17	.26	.06	.13	.27	.11	.10	.20
	Baseline 4	.16	.17	.49	.06	.09	.24	.12	.08	.08
	Baseline 3	.12	.12	.39	.06	.09	.08	.05	.08	.08
	FuocChu_VIP123	.12	.14	.36	.02	.10	.16	.05	.01	.17
	FuocChu_VIP123	.11	.13	.35	.01	.10	.13	.04	.01	.15
	JuniperLiu	.08	.09	.36	.04	.02	-.04	.07	.04	.09
	JuniperLiu	.08	.09	.36	.04	.02	-.04	.07	.04	.08
	sunfz1	.07	.07	.30	.05	-.00	-.07	.07	.04	.09

Table 8: All results for both evaluation phases. 'AV' = Average over languages; '-ES' = Average over languages excluding Spanish.

Deep-change at CoMeDi: the Cross-Entropy Loss is not All You Need

Mikhail Kuklin
Moscow State University, Russia
Yandex, Russia
kuklin.mike@yandex.ru

Nikolay Arefyev
University of Oslo, Norway
nikolare@uio.no

Abstract

Manual annotation of edges in Diachronic Word Usage Graphs is a critical step in creation of datasets for Lexical Semantic Change Detection tasks, but a very labour-intensive one. Annotators estimate if two senses of an ambiguous word expressed in two usages of this word are related and how. This is a variation of the Word-in-Context (WiC) task with some peculiarities, including diachronic data, an ordinal scale for annotations consisting of 4 values with pre-defined meanings (e.g. homonymy, polysemy), and special attention to the degree of disagreement between annotators which affects the further processing of the graph. CoMeDi is a shared task aiming at automating this annotation process. Participants are asked to predict the median annotation for a pair of usages in the first subtask, and estimate the disagreement between annotators in the second subtask. Together this gives some idea about the distribution of annotations we can get from humans for a given pair of usages.

For the first subtask we tried several ways of adapting a binary WiC model to this 4 class problem. We discovered that further fine-tuning the model as a 4 class classifier on the training data of the shared task works significantly worse than thresholding the original binary model. For the second subtask our best results were achieved by building a model that predicts the whole multinomial distribution of annotations and calculating the disagreement from this distribution. Our solutions for both subtasks have outperformed all other participants of the shared task.

1 Introduction

Diachronic Word Usage Graphs (DWUGs) (Schlechtweg et al., 2021) have recently become a de-facto standard data structure when working on Lexical Semantic Change Detection (LSCD) tasks (Schlechtweg, 2023). A graph is built for a particular ambiguous lemma. Graph nodes correspond to usages of this lemma from an older or a newer corpus. Edges are annotated with human judgements about relatedness of senses of the target lemma in the two corresponding usages. The annotations are integer values from 1 to 4, where 1 means completely unrelated senses and 4 the same sense. Based on these annotations a number of automated procedures can be applied to the graph, including filtering noisy and ambiguous usages based on disagreement between annotators, inferring senses of the target lemma, discovering novel or lost senses of the lemma. However, to get reasonable results from these procedures an abundant amount of high quality annotations is required. Given that the number of edges grows quadratically with the number of usages this annotation task is especially resource-consuming.

CoMeDi (Schlechtweg et al., 2025) is a shared task calling for automating this manual annotation process. It relies on DWUG datasets that had been previously created for Russian (Rodina and Kutuzov, 2020; Kutuzov and Pivovarova, 2021; Aksenova et al., 2022), Chinese (Chen et al., 2023), Spanish (Zamora-Reina et al., 2022), Norwegian (Kutuzov et al., 2022), German, Swedish and English (Schlechtweg et al., 2024; Kurtyigit et al., 2021; Hätty et al., 2019; Schlechtweg et al., 2018). It consists of two subtasks, the first requires predicting the median of human annotations for a pair of usages and the second aims at estimating disagreement between annotators on this pair. We propose several solutions for each subtask.

Our solutions for the first subtask are based on an existing binary WiC model. One approach to adapting it to the subtask is further fine-tuning for the 4 class classification problem on the training data of the shared task. Another approach is taking the predicted probability of the positive class (i.e. that the sense is the same in two usages) from the original binary model and converting it to the 4 point

Proceedings of Context and Meaning: Navigating Disagreements in NLP Annotation, pages 48–64
January 19, 2025.

scale by thresholding. These thresholds can be selected to directly maximize the evaluation metric of the subtask. Surprisingly, the second approach gives much better results. Binarising CoMeDi training data and further fine-tuning of the binary WiC model on it gives additional performance gains. For the second subtask we trained models to predict the measure of disagreement directly or predict the whole distribution of annotations from which the measure of disagreement can be calculated. The second approach has shown better results.

Our best solutions demonstrated the highest performance among all participants of the shared task during the evaluation period. In the post-evaluation period we improved the results and systematically studied various design options.

2 Related work

Predicting if two occurrences of the same ambiguous word have similar or different senses is known as the Word-in-Context (WiC) task. Most often it is framed as a binary classification task (Pilehvar and Camacho-Collados, 2019; Martelli et al., 2021). A graded version of this task was also considered before, e.g. in SemEval-2020 Task 3 (Armendariz et al., 2020), with the Spearman's and Pearson's correlations between model and human judgements serving as evaluation metrics. In the CoMeDi shared task Krippendorff's α is used as a metric and models are required to return exactly the same annotations as humans, not just some correlated predictions.

Many WiC models exist, but in the recent shared tasks on LSCD the SOTA / near-SOTA results were obtained by systems relying on XL-LEXEME (Cassotti et al., 2023) and DeepMistake (Arefyev et al., 2021). Since our solutions of the CoMeDi shared task employ the DeepMistake model, we will describe it focusing on those details that are important for understanding our solutions. DeepMistake was originally developed as a solution for the Multilingual and Cross-Lingual WiC (MCL-WiC) task (Davletov et al., 2021), and then further improved and adapted for two LSCD shared tasks in Russian (Arefyev et al., 2021) and Spanish (Homskiy and Arefyev, 2022). It consists of an XLM-R (Conneau et al., 2019) based backbone, which encodes two input usages concatenated together. For each occurrence of the target word an embedding is calculated by mean-pooling XLM-R outputs for subwords of this occurrence. Then a target aggregation function combines the embeddings of two occurrences of the target word into a single representation, which is fed to a classification head. Extensive experiments with various target aggregation functions were carried out. Among 10 aggregation functions explored in Davletov et al. (2021) the best function was *comb_dmn*, which is the concatenation of the component-wise difference of unnormalized and the component-wise product of normalized embeddings: $comb\_dmn(x, y) = (x - y, \overline{x} \odot \overline{y})$. In Arefyev et al. (2021) a function *l1ndotn* concatenating the Manhattan distance and the dot product of normalized embeddings was proposed, which proved to work better at least for LSCD: $l1ndotn(x, y) = (||\overline{x} - \overline{y}||_1, \overline{x} \cdot \overline{y})$. DeepMistake was originally initialized with XLM-R weights and fine-tuned on training, development and trial data from MCL-WiC. The combined train set consists of usages in English, Russian, French, Arabic and Chinese, and also a few cross-lingual pairs. For the shared tasks on LSCD it was further fine-tuned on the data in Russian and Spanish from these tasks.

3 Subtask 1: Median Judgment Classification

3.1 Task description

In this subtask participants are provided with pairs of word usages. Each pair has several human judgments on an ordinal scale from 1 to 4. The task is to predict the median of these judgments for each usage pair. The evaluation is performed using the ordinal version of Krippendorff's α (Krippendorff, 2018), which accounts for the degree of deviation between the predicted and true median values.

3.2 Models

In this section we introduce our solutions for the median judgment classification subtask. All of them employ the WiC model DeepMistake (Davletov et al., 2021; Arefyev et al., 2021). The original DeepMistake model is a binary classifier predicting if two usages of the same word have the same sense. This model can be used directly and predict 2 out of 4 classes, or the predicted probability of the positive class can be quantized into 4 intervals to get a 4-class classifier. To better adapt DeepMistake to the shared task we further fine-tune it as a binary classifier on the CoMeDi training data. Additionally, we experiment with replacing the classification head and fine-tuning the model as a 4-class classifier.

Model/Participant	Krippendorff's α ZH	DE	EN	NO	RU	ES	SV	AVG
2class@CoMeDi-ZH	**0.424**	0.723	**0.732**	0.633	**0.633**	**0.748**	**0.675**	0.652
Mixed	**0.424**	0.723	**0.732**	**0.668**	0.623	**0.748**	**0.675**	**0.656**
comedy_baseline_2	0.379	**0.728**	0.654	0.515	0.550	0.656	0.601	0.583
daalft	0.317	0.656	0.555	0.589	0.487	0.636	0.648	0.555
NBTailee	0.362	0.672	0.574	0.438	0.420	0.595	0.608	0.524
JuniperLiu	0.140	0.492	0.507	0.080	0.128	0.330	0.224	0.271
comedi_baseline	0.059	0.274	0.102	0.124	0.112	0.175	0.018	0.123

Table 1: Evaluation results on the subtask 1. Best results for each language are in **bold font**.

3.2.1 DeepMistake-based models

Most of our experiments employ the **MCL→DWUG$_{es}$+XLWSD$_{es}$** version of DeepMistake, which is the best model from (Homskiy and Arefyev, 2022). It was initialized from XLM-R (Conneau et al., 2019) and underwent the two-stage fine-tuning process. Initially, it was fine-tuned on the multilingual MCL-WiC dataset (Martelli et al., 2021), followed by a combination of the Spanish DWUG (Zamora-Reina et al., 2022) and the Spanish subset of XLWSD (Pasini et al., 2021). This model employs the l1ndotn aggregation function and we further adapt it to the shared task by fine-tuning it on the CoMeDi train sets.

All models were fine-tuned for 50 epochs using AdamW with a linear learning rate scheduler, lr=1e-05 and early stopping by the average Krippendorff's α across all languages (except for 2class@CoMeDi-ZH+byNO, see below).

2class@CoMeDi. This model variant was fine-tuned for binary classification on the concatenation of all CoMeDi train sets employing the binary cross-entropy (BCE) loss. Here, examples with the median annotations of 1 and 2 were employed as examples of the negative class, while examples with the median of 3 and 4 as examples of the positive class.

2class@CoMeDi-2,3. This model is identical to the previous one, but examples with the median annotations of 2 and 3 were excluded from its train set. We hypothesized that training only on the clear-cut examples having most annotations of 1 or 4 will improve model performance.

2class@CoMeDi-ZH. Identical to 2class@CoMeDi, but examples in Chinese were removed from the train set. This was based on our preliminary experiments where we observed that fine-tuning on the Chinese train set only results in the worst performance on all dev sets, including the Chinese one (see Appendix A).

2class@CoMeDi-ZH-DE. For this model, both Chinese and German[1] examples were removed from the train set.

2class@CoMeDi-ZH+byNO. We observed that Norwegian is the only language for which the results on the dev set can be significantly improved if early stopping is done by the Krippendorff's α on this specific language as opposed to the average across all languages. This model was fine-tuned similarly to 2class@CoMeDi-ZH, but the checkpoint with the best dev performance on Norwegian was selected.

4class@CoMeDi. This version was fine-tuned for 4-class classification on the CoMeDi dataset. It utilized the cross-entropy (CE) loss where the target was the median annotation for a pair of usages.

4class@CoMeDi-ZH. Identical to the previous model, but examples in Chinese were removed from the train set.

3.2.2 NMthres

To adapt a model trained for binary classification to predict four classes, thresholding can be applied to the predicted probability of the positive class. This method is taken from the baseline of the shared task, we will refer to it as **NMthres**. For each language separately, NMthres learns 3 thresholds that discretize a continuous input variable into 4 classes by optimizing the target metric using the Nelder-Mead method (Nelder and Mead, 1965). NMthres can be applied to the probability of the positive class predicted by any binary DeepMistake model.

3.2.3 Inference methods

For inference different strategies are applied. For all 4-class DeepMistake models the class with the highest probability is selected directly. In contrast, for the 2-class models without NMthres either class

[1]We selected German as the second candidate for exclusion because of the poor accuracy of a model trained on German on other dev sets, see Appendix A.

1 or 4 is chosen based on the threshold of 0.5. Otherwise, the predicted class is selected by NMthres.

3.3 Evaluation results

During the evaluation phase we submitted two sets of predictions. The first submission consists of predictions from the 2class@CoMeDi-ZH model as it achieved the highest Krippendorff's α on the development set. The second submission titled **Mixed** was constructed using predictions from multiple models: for Norwegian we used predictions from the 2class@CoMeDi-ZH+byNO model, for Russian we employed 2class@CoMeDi, and for other languages we utilized 2class@CoMeDi-ZH. For both submissions NMthres was optimized on the CoMeDi dev set and applied to the predicted probabilities of the positive class from the DeepMistake models. The results on the test set are presented in Table 1.

During the evaluation phase, both submissions proved to outperform all other participants on average across languages. We also have achieved the best results on all individual languages except for German where comedy_baseline_2 secured the top position. Our second submission was a bit better than the first one on Norwegian, but worse on Russian.

3.4 Post-evaluation experiments

3.4.1 Train-test overlap

After the evaluation phase it was revealed that the Spanish portion of the CoMeDi test set is derived from the Spanish DWUG dataset (Zamora-Reina et al., 2022) which was partially used to fine-tune the MCL→$DWUG_{es}$+$XLWSD_{es}$ model. Table 2 shows the overlap between the training data for this model and the Spanish test set.

Due to the significant overlap, we aimed to assess its impact on the final Krippendorff's α on the test set. We compared four DeepMistake models from Homskiy and Arefyev (2022): (1) *MCL→$DWUG_{es}$+$XLWSD_{es}$*, (2) *MCL* trained solely on the MCL dataset with no overlap with the CoMeDi test set, (3) *MCL→RSS* fine-tuned on the RuSemShift (RSS) (Rodina and Kutuzov, 2020), and (4) *MCL+RSS+$DWUG_{es}$+$XLWSD_{es}$* fine-tuned on all datasets simultaneously. Although the models trained on RuSemShift also show some overlap with the training set, the MCL model exhibits no overlap at the usage level, as indicated in Table 2.

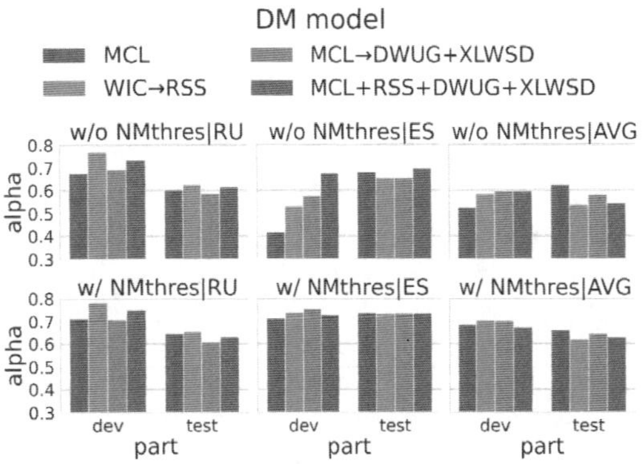

Figure 1: Krippendorff's α of DeepMistake models w/ and w/o NMthres. Results are on Russian and Spanish sets, and on average across all languages. See extended plot in Figure 7.

The results of this comparison are shown in Figure 1. DeepMistake models fine-tuned on RSS are clearly better for Russian. For Spanish the results are mixed, on the test set all models are on par when using NMThres. On average across languages, among models that are not fine-tuned on CoMeDi the best test result of 0.660 are achieved by the MCL model (no overlap), this model outperforms both of our submissions and other participants as well.

Inspired by improvements of the 2class@CoMeDi-ZH model over the non-fine-tuned version, we similarity fine-tuned the MCL model on CoMeDi data. We found that with fine-tuning on CoMeDi the results of the MCL model are worse, but still better than other participants, see table 3.

3.4.2 Optimizing CoMeDi Training Data for Fine-Tuning DeepMistake Models

In this subsection, we explore which subsets of CoMeDi training data should be utilized for fine-tuning the DeepMistake models to enhance Krippendorff's α. We conducted experiments by removing examples with the median annotation equal to 2 or 3, excluding Chinese examples, and excluding both Chinese and German language examples. The outcomes of these experiments are depicted in Figure 2.

Our findings indicate that for improved performance on the Chinese development and test sets of CoMeDi, it is beneficial to exclude Chinese data during training (see appendix C for a more in-depth analysis). Furthermore, removing the German examples from the training data does not significantly

Language	Part	MCL	DWUG$_{es}$ + XLWSD$_{es}$	RSS
Spanish	dev	-	**3/112/175 (30/31/28 %)**	-
	test	-	**4/112/155 (20/15/10 %)**	-
Russian	dev	3/0/0 (10/0/0 %)	-	8/363/180 (29/16/16 %)
	test	3/0/0 (5/0/0 %)	-	11/487/244 (20/11/11 %)

Table 2: Overlap between the CoMeDi evaluation data and training data of DeepMistake models. Both the absolute counts of lemmas / usages / usage pairs in common and the proportions of test items present in the training set (in brackets) are reported. During the evaluation phase we employed the model trained on MCL and DWUD$_{es}$+XLWSD$_{es}$. Its training data overlaps with the CoMeDi test data for Spanish (in **bold**). It also has 3 common lemmas but no common usages with the test data for Russian. In the post-evaluation experiments we additionally experimented with a model trained on MCL only to avoid overlaps on the level of usages and usage pairs, as well as models trained on RSS which overlaps with the test data for Russian. MCL also contains examples in English and Chinese, but we found no overlaps with the corresponding evaluation sets.

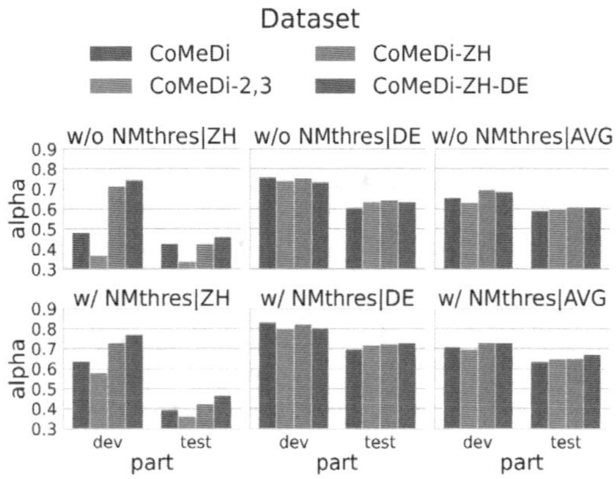

Figure 2: Krippendorff's α of 2-class DeepMistake models fine-tuned on different subsets of CoMeDi train data. The results on the Chinese and the German dev sets, and on average across all dev sets are shown. See extended plot in Figure 8.

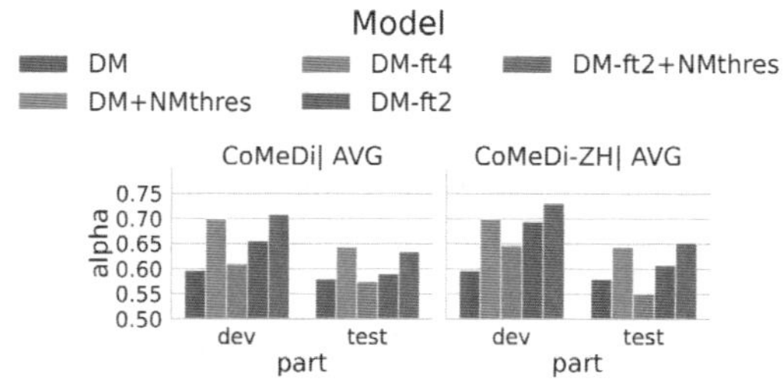

Figure 3: Average Krippendorff's α across all languages for models fine-tuned on CoMeDi and CoMeDi-ZH. DM stands for DeepMistake with the MCL→DWUG$_{es}$+XLWSD$_{es}$ weights. ft-2 and ft-4 stand for 2-class and 4-class fine-tuning respectively. See extended plot in Figure 9.

affect performance on the German test set or the overall Krippendorff's α, but it does lead to better results on the Chinese subset. Conversely, removing examples with median annotations of 2 and 3 results in poorer performance on the Chinese set and reduces the average performance on the development set, although there is a slight improvement on the test set.

3.4.3 Evaluating Fine-Tuning Strategies on CoMeDi Training Sets

In this analysis, we evaluated various training strategies for fine-tuning DeepMistake models, as depicted in Figure 3.

Our investigation suggests that training with a 4-class cross-entropy (CE) approach (DM-ft4) is suboptimal. While the Krippendorff's α on the development set shows a slight improvement, the performance on the test set declines compared to the over original DeepMistake which was not fine-tuned on CoMeDi data (DM). In contrast, fine-tuning the 2-class DeepMistake model (DM-ft2) yields noticeable improvements over the DM on the development set, albeit with only modest gains on the test set. These test set improvements do not surpass the results obtained by simply applying the initial DeepMistake model with NMthres (DM+NMthres).

Overall, fine-tuning DeepMistake as a binary classifier on CoMeDi training data and then applying NMthres to obtain a 4-class classifier delivers the best results. Comprehensive post-evaluation results are provided in Table 3, and a more detailed comparison is provided in Appendix B.

4 Subtask 2: Mean Disagreement Ranking

4.1 Task description

Similarly to subtask 1, participants are given pairs of word usages. The objective is to predict the mean absolute difference between judgments of

Model	Krippendorff's α ZH	DE	EN	NO	RU	ES	SV	AVG
DM w/o NMthres								
MCL	*0.453*	*0.675*	*0.624*	*0.660*	*0.603*	*0.679*	*0.669*	*0.623*
MCL→DWUG$_{es}$+XLWSD$_{es}$	0.408	0.689	0.520	0.575	0.585	0.653	0.628	0.580
DM w/ NMthres$_{dev}$								
MCL	*0.465*	***0.741***	*0.727*	***0.688***	***0.645***	*0.737*	*0.617*	*0.660*
MCL→DWUG$_{es}$+XLWSD$_{es}$	0.423	0.738	0.710	0.680	0.609	0.736	0.604	0.643
2class w/o NMthres								
2class@CoMeDi	0.427	0.605	0.640	0.642	0.555	0.658	0.604	0.590
2class@CoMeDi-2,3	0.337	0.636	0.637	0.631	0.578	0.683	0.686	0.598
2class@CoMeDi-ZH	0.426	0.642	0.626	0.609	0.599	0.669	0.680	0.607
2class@CoMeDi-ZH+byNO	0.340	0.524	0.589	0.649	0.442	0.536	0.548	0.527
2class@CoMeDi-ZH-DE	0.461	0.635	0.644	0.631	0.554	0.677	0.671	0.610
MCL,2class@CoMeDi-ZH	*0.417*	*0.592*	*0.626*	*0.639*	*0.543*	*0.605*	*0.544*	*0.567*
2class w/ NMthres$_{dev}$								
2class@CoMeDi	0.393	0.698	0.712	0.649	0.623[2]	0.735	0.633	0.634
2class@CoMeDi-2,3	0.364	0.718	0.748	0.664	0.630	0.719	**0.699**	0.649
2class@CoMeDi-ZH	0.424[1,2]	0.723[1,2]	0.732[1,2]	0.633[1]	0.633[1]	0.748[1,2]	0.675[1,2]	0.652
2class@CoMeDi-ZH+byNO	0.436	0.620	0.637	0.668[2]	0.547	0.591	0.597	0.585
2class@CoMeDi-ZH-DE	0.467	0.728	**0.758**	0.662	0.629	**0.773**	0.679	**0.671**
MCL,2class@CoMeDi-ZH	*0.392*	*0.692*	*0.733*	*0.642*	*0.619*	*0.728*	*0.637*	*0.635*
4class								
4class@CoMeDi	**0.517**	0.665	0.514	0.609	0.532	0.583	0.602	0.575
4class@CoMeDi-ZH	0.393	0.643	0.516	0.559	0.526	0.627	0.592	0.551

Table 3: Post-evaluation results on the test set of subtask 1. Best results for each language are in **bold font**. Superscripts refer to our two submissions during the evaluation phase. By default, fine-tuned models are based on MCL→DWUG$_{es}$+XLWSD$_{es}$, unless specified otherwise. Models based on MCL (no overlap with CoMeDi test data) and their results are in *italic*.

different annotators for a given pair of usages:

$$D(J) = \frac{1}{|J|} \sum_{(j_1,j_2)\in J} |j_1 - j_2| \qquad (1)$$

J in Equation 1 is the set of pairs of judgments for the same usage pair.

The evaluation metric is Spearman's ρ (Spearman, 1904) between the predicted and the real mean disagreements between annotators for a set of usage pairs.

4.2 Models

In this section, we describe various approaches for modelling annotator disagreement using the DeepMistake model. Our initial strategy focused on a regression model designed to directly predict the mean disagreement between annotators, leveraging the mean squared error (MSE) loss function. To address difficulties in learning from noisy regression target values, we introduced a binary classification variant, which aims to identify usage pairs where all annotators provided the same answer, applying the binary cross-entropy (BCE) loss for learning. Furthermore, we experimented with a model that predicts the entire distribution of annotations and calculates disagreement from this distribution. It is trained on individual annotations as separate training examples. To improve the predicted distribution we also implemented a **Power selector** method. This method transforms the predicted probabilities by raising them to the language-specific powers that are selected to maximize the target metric.

4.2.1 DeepMistake-based models

Similarly to subtask 1, our models for subtask 2 are based on **MCL→DWUG$_{es}$+XLWSD$_{es}$**. To predict the level of disagreement between annotators, we employed the comb_dmn aggregation function during the fine-tuning process. In contrast to l1ndotn returning a two-dimensional vector of distances which should represent sense proximity but not ambiguity or difficulty leading to disagreements, comb_dmn returns a high-dimensional representation potentially preserving more information relevant to the subtask. To test this hypothesis, we also trained a model using the l1ndotn function for comparison.

All models were fine-tuned using the same optimizer hyperparameters as in Subtask 1. Early stopping was performed based on the average Spearman's ρ across all languages.

comb_dmn,mse@CoMeDi-#less4: Our initial approach was a regression model that directly pre-

Model/Participant	Spearman's ρ ZH	DE	EN	NO	RU	ES	SV	AVG
comb_dmn,ce@CoMeDi-#less4	0.301	**0.204**	**0.078**	**0.286**	**0.175**	**0.187**	**0.350**	**0.226**
daalft	**0.539**	0.108	0.042	0.272	0.167	0.115	0.296	0.220
comedy_baseline_2	0.485	0.085	0.060	0.235	0.116	0.078	0.079	0.163
chuphuocvip123	0.362	0.099	0.018	0.156	0.050	0.012	0.172	0.124
comedi_baseline	0.387	0.093	0.064	0.076	0.049	0.077	0.081	0.118
JuniperLiu	0.358	0.022	0.038	-0.042	0.067	0.040	0.090	0.082
sunfz1	0.302	-0.001	0.045	-0.071	0.069	0.038	0.089	0.067

Table 4: Evaluation results on the subtask 2. Best results for each language are in **bold font**.

dicts the quantity of interest. This model was fine-tuned to predict the mean of pairwise absolute judgment differences between annotators, employing the mean squared error (MSE) loss function. Examples containing fewer than four annotations were excluded to ensure robustness of the training data, as such examples might not provide sufficient information about the distribution[2]. In particular, this filtration removes all examples from the Chinese and Norwegian train sets.

comb_dmn,bce@CoMeDi-#less4: Since the mean disagreement is estimated from as few as 4-5 annotations for most usage pairs, learning a good regression model from such noisy targets may be impossible. Thus, we experimented with less noisy targets even though they are indirectly related to the mean disagreement we are interested in. This model was trained with the binary cross-entropy (BCE) loss to determine if all annotators provided the same answer for a pair of usages. All examples with less than 4 annotations were excluded from the train set.

comb_dmn,ce@CoMeDi-#less4: Instead of directly predicting the mean disagreement, we can try training a model that predicts the whole distribution of annotations for a given pair of usages, and then estimate the mean disagreement from that distribution. Technically, 4 class models trained for subtask 1 return the probability distribution over possible annotations, but since they are trained to predict the median annotation only they have no chance to learn anything about disagreements between annotators. Thus, for subtask 2 we do not aggregate annotations of each usage pair but instead fine-tune the model on each individual annotation as a separate training example.

comb_dmn,ce@CoMeDi: To verify if removing usage pairs with less than four annotations is really helpful when training on individual annotations, we trained this model on annotations of all pairs. This increased the number of training examples by 5x.

l1ndotn,ce@CoMeDi-#less4: In order to check if our initial decision to use DeepMistake with the comb_dmn aggregation function for subtask 2 was optimal, we trained this model which is similar to the previous one but employs the l1dotn aggregation function instead of comb_dmn.

4.2.2 Power selector

For models trained on individual annotations and schemed to predict the probability distribution across annotators, we designed an approach to optimize their predictions for the target metric. Specifically, for each language, we fit four powers α_i to which the class probabilities p_i are raised:

$$\hat{p}_i = \frac{p_i^{\alpha_i}}{\sum_{j=1}^{4} p_j^{\alpha_j}} \quad (2)$$

This method is inspired by the temperature softmax[3] often used to undersample / oversample frequent / rare classes, e.g. in word2vec (Mikolov et al., 2013). This method is also related to common calibrating techniques (Guo et al., 2017). The selection of these powers is performed similarly to the NMthres process, utilizing the Nelder-Mead optimization method to maximize Spearman's ρ.

4.2.3 Inference methods

In case of the model fine-tuned with the MSE loss between the predicted and gold mean disagreements, we directly return its predictions. For the model trained with the BCE loss function we return the predicted probability that there are some

[2]In the preliminary experiments we tried fine-tuning models directly predicting mean disagreement with both mse and bce losses on all examples, but they achieved near zero performance. This is probably due to very noisy estimates of the mean disagreement when less than 4 annotations are available. Thus, for the second subtask we mostly experimented with models trained on examples with 4 or more annotations.

[3]The Power Selector can be viewed as a more generalized approach compared to temperature scaling in softmax function. While the temperature softmax technique uniformly raises all probabilities to the same power, our approach assigns a distinct power to each probability individually.

Model	Spearman's ρ ZH	DE	EN	NO	RU	ES	SV	AVG
aggregated annotations								
comb_dmn,mse@CoMeDi-#less4	0.462	**0.241**	0.110	0.215	0.192	0.136	0.238	0.228
comb_dmn,bce@CoMeDi-#less4	0.497	0.237	0.089	0.300	0.212	0.120	0.245	0.243
separate annotations w/o pows								
comb_dmn,ce@CoMeDi	0.484	0.206	0.130	0.276	0.237	0.232	0.262	0.261
comb_dmn,ce@CoMeDi-#less4	0.426	0.197	**0.148**	0.298	0.183	0.123	0.297	0.239
l1ndotn,ce@CoMeDi-#less4	0.605	0.148	0.084	0.448	0.162	0.108	0.282	0.262
separate annotations w/ pows$_{dev}$								
comb_dmn,ce@CoMeDi	0.571	0.218	0.128	0.421	**0.256**	0.159	0.302	0.293
comb_dmn,ce@CoMeDi-#less4	0.301[1]	0.204[1]	0.078[1]	0.286[1]	0.175[1]	0.187[1]	0.350[1]	0.226
l1ndotn,ce@CoMeDi-#less4	**0.616**	0.148	0.084	0.454	0.162	0.108	0.282	0.265
separate annotations w/ pows$_{train}$								
comb_dmn,ce@CoMeDi	**0.616**	0.236	0.129	0.424	0.253	**0.236**	0.297	**0.313**
comb_dmn,ce@CoMeDi-#less4	0.574	**0.241**	0.143	0.294	0.194	0.161	**0.360**	0.281
l1ndotn,ce@CoMeDi-#less4	**0.616**	0.227	0.080	**0.456**	0.234	0.109	0.266	0.284

Table 5: Post-evaluation results on the test set of subtask 2. Best results for each language are in **bold font**. Superscripts refer to our submission during the evaluation phase.

disagreements between annotators assuming that higher probability corresponds to larger disagreements. For models trained on individual annotations we take the whole predicted probability distribution over 4 classes and calculate its standard deviation. Additionally, the power selector can be applied.

4.3 Evaluation results

During the evaluation phase, our sole submission was from the comb_dmn,ce@CoMeDi-#less4 model, which incorporated a power selection model optimized on the development set. This model achieved the best performance across all languages except for Chinese, where it recorded the poorest results among all participants. Comprehensive results of the evaluation phase are presented in Table 4.

4.4 Post-evaluation experiments

Upon completion of the evaluation phase, we proceeded to evaluate all models using the test set. For models that were trained on individual annotations, we explored several strategies: not employing the power selection model, fitting it on the CoMeDi train sets, and fitting it on the CoMeDi development sets. The results of these evaluations are detailed in Table 5. It is clear that the power selector helps significantly, and it is better to fit it on the train sets. Removing examples with less than 4 annotations hurts the performance on average across languages, at least when training on individual annotations, though the results vary from language to language. Comparing l1ndotn with comb_dmn, the results are

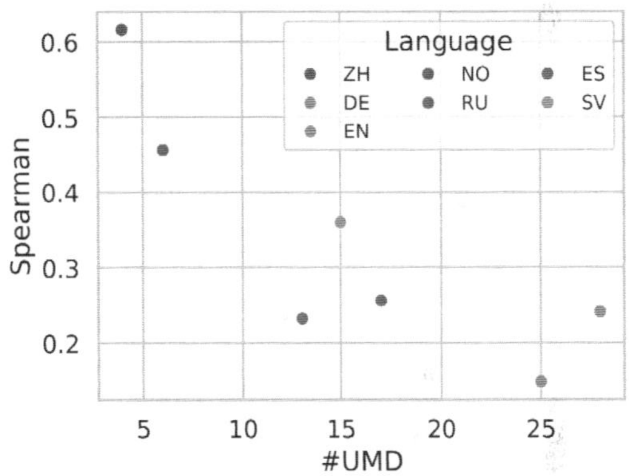

Figure 4: Best achieved Spearman's ρ and #UMD per language on the test set.

not consistent across languages as well requiring more experiments to draw reliable conclusions.

Comparing the results for different languages, Chinese and Norwegian have higher metrics while there are only two annotations per example for this languages which should result in quite noisy ground truth mean disagreement. We hypothesised that the good results may be related to fewer unique values of the mean disagreement when there are fewer annotators. We investigated the impact of the number of unique values of the mean pairwise absolute judgment (#UMD) on the Spearman's correlation across different languages. For each language, we selected the best result achieved during the post-evaluation phase and #UMD, as depicted in Figure 4.

Our analysis indicates that languages with the best results – Chinese and Norwegian, exhibit relatively low #UMD, characterized by less than 7 unique values for mean disagreement. Conversely, English and German, which have some of the lowest ρ, are associated with the highest #UMD.

5 Conclusion

We have proposed the winning solutions for the CoMeDi shared task and experimented with different design choices. To our surprise fine-tuning a 4 class WiC model on the training data from the shared task has shown worse results than thresholding the original binary WiC model. Whether it is due to the insufficient or noisy training data, or bad correlation between the cross-entropy loss and the target metric Krippendorff's alpha remains to be investigated. A promising direction for the future experiments is designing surrogate losses that are better correlated with Krippendorff's alpha. We also observed that removing CoMeDi training data in Chinese significantly improves results, including the results for Chinese. A reasonable next step may be selecting an optimal combination of training sets for each test language separately.

For the second subtask our best solution was learning to predict the whole distribution of annotations for a given usage pair. In the future work it is reasonable to try alternative loss functions as well, e.g. minimizing the KL-divergence between the predicted and the real probability distributions.

References

Anna Aksenova, Ekaterina Gavrishina, Elisey Rykov, and Andrey Kutuzov. 2022. Rudsi: graph-based word sense induction dataset for russian. *arXiv preprint*.

Nikolay Arefyev, Maksim Fedoseev, Vitaly Protasov, Daniil Homskiy, Adis Davletov, and Alexander Panchenko. 2021. Deepmistake: Which senses are hard to distinguish for a word-in-context model. volume 2021-June, pages 16–30.

Carlos Santos Armendariz, Matthew Purver, Senja Pollak, Nikola Ljubešić, Matej Ulčar, Ivan Vulić, and Mohammad Taher Pilehvar. 2020. SemEval-2020 task 3: Graded word similarity in context. In *Proceedings of the Fourteenth Workshop on Semantic Evaluation*, pages 36–49, Barcelona (online). International Committee for Computational Linguistics.

Pierluigi Cassotti, Lucia Siciliani, Marco de Gemmis, Giovanni Semeraro, and Pierpaolo Basile. 2023. Xl-lexeme: Wic pretrained model for cross-lingual lexical semantic change. In *Proceedings of the 61th Annual Meeting of the Association for Computational Linguistics*, Online. Association for Computational Linguistics.

Jing Chen, Emmanuele Chersoni, Dominik Schlechtweg, Jelena Prokic, and Chu-Ren Huang. 2023. ChiWUG: A graph-based evaluation dataset for Chinese lexical semantic change detection. In *Proceedings of the 4th International Workshop on Computational Approaches to Historical Language Change*, Singapore. Association for Computational Linguistics.

Alexis Conneau, Kartikay Khandelwal, Naman Goyal, Vishrav Chaudhary, Guillaume Wenzek, Francisco Guzmán, Edouard Grave, Myle Ott, Luke Zettlemoyer, and Veselin Stoyanov. 2019. Unsupervised cross-lingual representation learning at scale. *arXiv preprint arXiv:1911.02116*.

Adis Davletov, Nikolay Arefyev, Denis Gordeev, and Alexey Rey. 2021. LIORI at SemEval-2021 task 2: Span prediction and binary classification approaches to word-in-context disambiguation. In *Proceedings of the 15th International Workshop on Semantic Evaluation (SemEval-2021)*, pages 780–786, Online. Association for Computational Linguistics.

Chuan Guo, Geoff Pleiss, Yu Sun, and Kilian Q. Weinberger. 2017. On calibration of modern neural networks. *ArXiv*, abs/1706.04599.

Anna Hätty, Dominik Schlechtweg, and Sabine Schulte im Walde. 2019. SURel: A gold standard for incorporating meaning shifts into term extraction. In *Proceedings of the 8th Joint Conference on Lexical and Computational Semantics*, pages 1–8, Minneapolis, MN, USA.

Daniil Homskiy and Nikolay Arefyev. 2022. DeepMistake at LSCDiscovery: Can a multilingual word-in-context model replace human annotators? In *Proceedings of the 3rd Workshop on Computational Approaches to Historical Language Change*, pages 173–179, Dublin, Ireland. Association for Computational Linguistics.

Klaus Krippendorff. 2018. *Content Analysis: An Introduction to Its Methodology*. SAGE Publications.

Sinan Kurtyigit, Maike Park, Dominik Schlechtweg, Jonas Kuhn, and Sabine Schulte im Walde. 2021. Lexical Semantic Change Discovery. In *Proceedings of the 59th Annual Meeting of the Association for Computational Linguistics and the 11th International Joint Conference on Natural Language Processing (Volume 1: Long Papers)*, Online. Association for Computational Linguistics.

Andrey Kutuzov and Lidia Pivovarova. 2021. Rushifteval: a shared task on semantic shift detection for russian. *Komp'yuternaya Lingvistika i Intellektual'nye Tekhnologii: Dialog conference*.

Andrey Kutuzov, Samia Touileb, Petter Mæhlum, Tita Enstad, and Alexandra Wittemann. 2022. NorDiaChange: Diachronic semantic change dataset for

Norwegian. In *Proceedings of the Thirteenth Language Resources and Evaluation Conference*, pages 2563–2572, Marseille, France. European Language Resources Association.

Federico Martelli, Najla Kalach, Gabriele Tola, and Roberto Navigli. 2021. SemEval-2021 task 2: Multilingual and cross-lingual word-in-context disambiguation (MCL-WiC). In *Proceedings of the 15th International Workshop on Semantic Evaluation (SemEval-2021)*, pages 24–36, Online. Association for Computational Linguistics.

Tomas Mikolov, Kai Chen, Greg Corrado, and Jeffrey Dean. 2013. Efficient estimation of word representations in vector space. *Preprint*, arXiv:1301.3781.

John A. Nelder and R. Mead. 1965. A simplex method for function minimization. *The Computer Journal*, 7(4):308–313.

Tommaso Pasini, Alessandro Raganato, and Roberto Navigli. 2021. Xl-wsd: An extra-large and cross-lingual evaluation framework for word sense disambiguation. *Proceedings of the AAAI Conference on Artificial Intelligence*, 35(15):13648–13656.

Mohammad Taher Pilehvar and Jose Camacho-Collados. 2019. WiC: the word-in-context dataset for evaluating context-sensitive meaning representations. In *Proceedings of the 2019 Conference of the North American Chapter of the Association for Computational Linguistics: Human Language Technologies, Volume 1 (Long and Short Papers)*, pages 1267–1273, Minneapolis, Minnesota. Association for Computational Linguistics.

Julia Rodina and Andrey Kutuzov. 2020. RuSemShift: a dataset of historical lexical semantic change in Russian. In *Proceedings of the 28th International Conference on Computational Linguistics (COLING 2020)*. Association for Computational Linguistics.

Dominik Schlechtweg. 2023. *Human and Computational Measurement of Lexical Semantic Change*. Ph.D. thesis, University of Stuttgart, Stuttgart, Germany.

Dominik Schlechtweg, Pierluigi Cassotti, Bill Noble, David Alfter, Sabine Schulte im Walde, and Nina Tahmasebi. 2024. More DWUGs: Extending and evaluating word usage graph datasets in multiple languages. In *Proceedings of the 2024 Conference on Empirical Methods in Natural Language Processing*, Miami, Florida. Association for Computational Linguistics.

Dominik Schlechtweg, Tejaswi Choppa, Wei Zhao, and Michael Roth. 2025. The CoMeDi shared task: Median judgment classification & mean disagreement ranking with ordinal word-in-context judgments. In *Proceedings of the 1st Workshop on Context and Meaning–Navigating Disagreements in NLP Annotations*, Abu Dhabi, UAE.

Dominik Schlechtweg, Sabine Schulte im Walde, and Stefanie Eckmann. 2018. Diachronic Usage Relatedness (DURel): A framework for the annotation of lexical semantic change. In *Proceedings of the 2018 Conference of the North American Chapter of the Association for Computational Linguistics: Human Language Technologies*, pages 169–174, New Orleans, Louisiana.

Dominik Schlechtweg, Nina Tahmasebi, Simon Hengchen, Haim Dubossarsky, and Barbara McGillivray. 2021. DWUG: A large resource of diachronic word usage graphs in four languages. In *Proceedings of the 2021 Conference on Empirical Methods in Natural Language Processing*, pages 7079–7091, Online and Punta Cana, Dominican Republic. Association for Computational Linguistics.

Charles Spearman. 1904. The proof and measurement of association between two things. *American Journal of Psychology*, 15:88–103.

Frank D. Zamora-Reina, Felipe Bravo-Marquez, and Dominik Schlechtweg. 2022. LSCDiscovery: A shared task on semantic change discovery and detection in Spanish. In *Proceedings of the 3rd Workshop on Computational Approaches to Historical Language Change*, pages 149–164, Dublin, Ireland. Association for Computational Linguistics.

A Cross-lingual transfer

In our preliminary experiments we fine-tuned seven DeepMistake models as 4-class classifiers on each train set from CoMeDi separately and evaluated each of them on each dev set separately. While fine-tuning on individual train sets and using 4-class fine-tuning objective proved to be suboptimal in the end, this preliminary experiment gives some ideas about usefulness of each train set for the performance on each language. Figure 5 shows how Krippendorff's alpha change while training these seven models. While we didn't have enough resources to optimize them all to the point of full convergence, some trends can clearly be observed from these curves. The Chinese train set is always one of the worst train sets for the Krippendorff's alpha on all dev sets, including the Chinese one. The Norwegian train set is the best when evaluating on Norwegian and one of the best for Chinese, but among the worst for all other languages. The German train set is among the best for all languages except for Chinese and Spanish where it is in the middle. Fine-tuning DeepMistake on a train set for the same language the evaluation is made on works best for German, Norwegian, Russian and Spanish, but not Chinese, English or Swedish. Based on bad model performance for all languages when fine-tuning on the train set in Chinese, when fine-tuning the binary DeepMistake model used in our submissions on all CoMeDi training data we excluded training examples in Chinese. It seems potentially beneficial to construct an optimal subset of training data for each language separately, e.g. excluding Norwegian from the training data of a model that is not targeted at Norwegian, but we leave systematic experiments in this direction for the future work.

For comparison, figure 6 shows the learning curves for the same models but taking accuracy as an evaluation metric instead of Krippendorff's alpha. Surprisingly, the observations drastically differ when changing the evaluation metric. The best accuracy on the Chinese dev set is achieved when training on English or Chinese train sets. The model trained on Norwegian is now among the best models for all dev sets. And the one trained on German is among the worst models for all dev sets except German and English. This shows that a model achieving the best accuracy may be among the worst for Krippendorff's alpha and vice versa. See appendix C for a more in-depth analysis of this discrepancy.

B Detailed model comparison

In Figure 7, we compare different DeepMistake models. Training data of these models has no overlap with following CoMeDi dev/test sets: German, English, Norwegian, Chinese, and Swedish. For German and English, all models with NMthres exhibit similar performance across both sets. In contrast, for Norwegian and Chinese, the models MCL and MCL→DWUG$_{es}$+XLWSD$_{es}$ perform better than others. Meanwhile, in Swedish, the models MCL→RSS and MCL+RSS+DWUG$_{es}$+XLWSD$_{es}$ emerge as superior.

Our analysis, depicted in Figure 8, which compares different training sets, reveals that fine-tuning models with NMthres on CoMeDi-2,3 significantly improves performance for Swedish subsets. For other languages, using the complete CoMeDi training data is equally effective, and sometimes even more beneficial. While CoMeDi-ZH and CoMeDi-ZH-DE do not show much difference from CoMeDi in most cases, with the exception of Chinese, they generally perform better overall.

As shown in Figure 9, the DeepMistake model with NMthres consistently outperforms variant without it across all languages, except for Swedish. This trend is also observed in the 2-class fine-tuned models. Additionally, when comparing the 4-class fine-tuned model trained on CoMeDi-ZH with the DeepMistake model without NMthres, the fine-tuned model shows better performance on all development sets, except Russian. However, on the test set, the situation reverses, with the non-fine-tuned model performing better.

C Chinese mystery

Removing the Chinese train set when fine-tuning DeepMistake as a binary classifier on the CoMeDi training data strikingly improves the Krippendorff's alpha on the Chinese development set in subtask 1 (from 0.48 to 0.71) while giving only a small improvement in accuracy (from 0.88 to 0.90). Here we investigate why this happens. Krippendorff's α is defined as:

$$\alpha = 1 - \frac{D_o}{D_e}, \tag{3}$$

where D_o is the observed disagreement and D_e the disagreement expected by chance. The observed disagreement in general case is defined as:

$$D_o = \frac{1}{n} \sum_{i \in R} \sum_{j \in R} \delta_{ij} \sum_{u} \frac{m_u * n_{iju}}{P(m_u, 2)}, \tag{4}$$

where n is the total number of labels (in our case both predicted labels and ground truth labels), R is the set of possible labels, u is a usage pair, m_u is the number of labels assigned to the usage pair u. Finally, n_{iju} is the number of pairs (i, j) consisting of labels assigned to u.

For the ordinal version of Krippendorff's α:

$$\delta_{ij} = (\sum_{k=i}^{j} n_k - \frac{n_i + n_j}{2})^2, \tag{5}$$

where n_x is the number of labels equal to x among both the predicted and the ground truth labels of all usage pairs.

In our case $m_u = 2$ because for each example there is a ground truth label and a predicted label. After substituting this into formula 4 we get $D_o = \frac{1}{n} \sum_{i=1}^{4} \sum_{j=1}^{4} \delta_{ij} * 2 \sum_u I[y_u = i, \hat{y}_u = j] = \frac{1}{n} \sum_{i=1}^{4} \sum_{j=1}^{4} 2\delta_{ij} c_{ij}$, where c_{ij} is the number of usage pairs with the ground truth label of i and the predicted label of j. Thus, the final formula for Krippendorff's α in our case can be written as:

$$\alpha = 1 - \sum_{i=1}^{4} \sum_{j=1}^{4} \frac{2\delta_{ij} c_{ij}}{n * D_e} \tag{6}$$

Figure 10 plots confusion matrices where a cell (i, j) shows the contribution $\frac{2\delta_{ij}c_{ij}}{n*D_e}$ of the corresponding type of errors (when class i is misclassified as class j) to Krippendorff's α, and also standard confusion matrices showing proportions of examples with different predicted and ground truth labels. We can observe proportions of different types of errors (i, j) and how they contribute to the final value of Krippendorff's α in 6.

While the error rates of two models on the Chinese dev set are comparable, the proportions of different types of errors differ drastically. For the model trained on all training sets including the Chinese one all errors are related to predicting 4 instead of some other class. Such types of errors strongly reduce Krippendorff's alpha because of the dominating frequency of label 4 resulting in large values of δ_{i4} (see formula 5) and thus large contribution of c_{i4} in formula 6. On the other hand, the model trained without the Chinese train set produces fewer errors of such types and more errors related to predicting 1 instead of some other class. However, the latter types of errors make much smaller contribution to Krippendorff's alpha (unless the correct label is 4).

For the development sets in languages other than Chinese such a large difference in error types and thus Krippendorff's alpha is not observed, as shown in Figures 11, 12. We believe that this is related to the proportions of negative examples (classes 1 and 2) in the training sets for different languages, see Figure 13. In the Chinese train set this proportion is negligible, thus, the model learns to predict the positive class for inputs in Chinese unless there are very strong evidences in favour of negative class. In the Chinese dev set the proportion of classes 1 and 2 is significantly larger, so this learnt strategy leads to some errors for examples of these classes which are fatal for Krippendorff's alpha. When the Chinese train set is excluded the model cannot learn any specific strategy for inputs in Chinese. For other languages the proportions of negative examples in the corresponding train sets are reasonable and for them we don't observe significant changes in the proportions of errors of different types between two models.

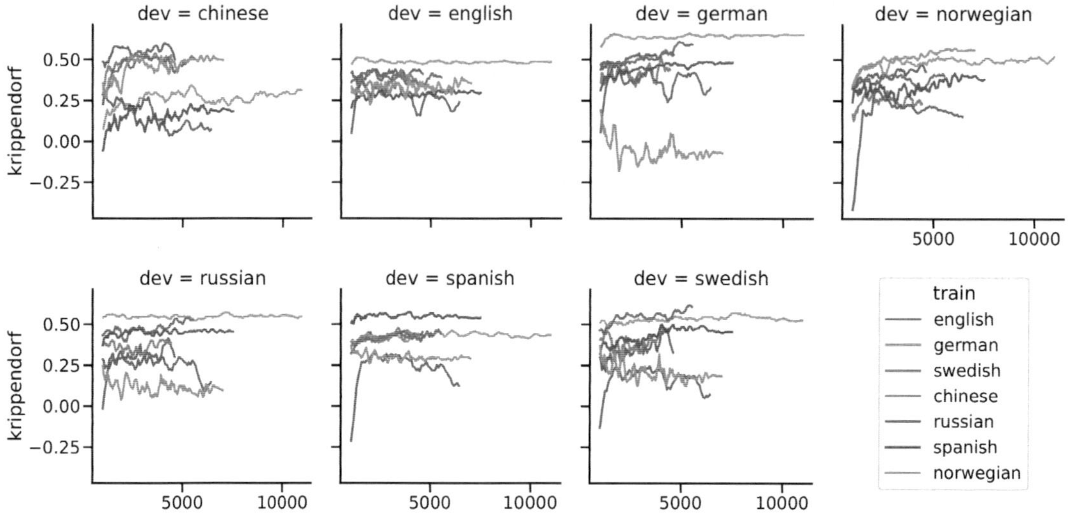

Figure 5: Cross-lingual transfer evaluation. Krippendorff's alpha on the dev sets for the DeepMistake models being fine-tuned as a 4-class classifiers on the train sets for each language separately.

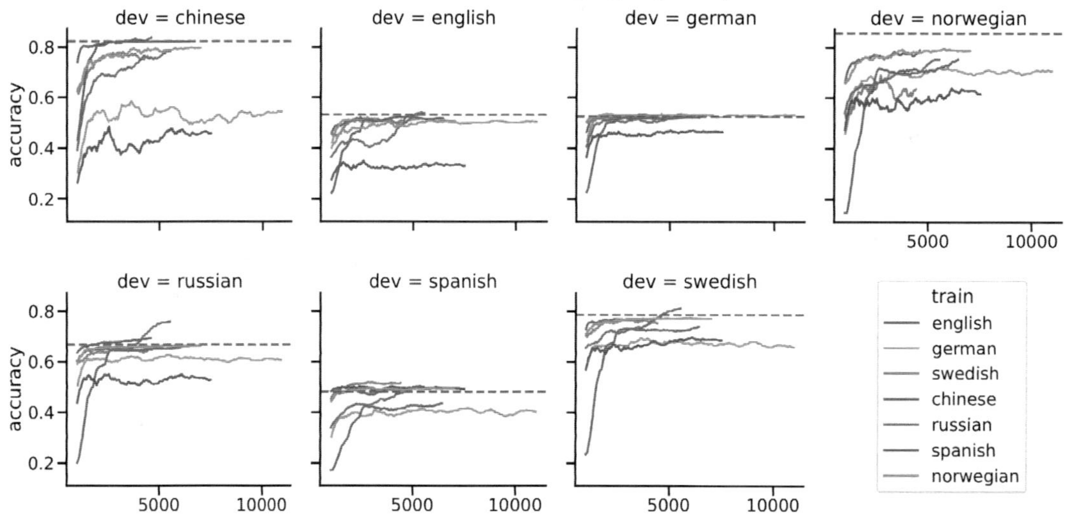

Figure 6: Cross-lingual transfer evaluation. Accuracy on the dev sets for the DeepMistake models being fine-tuned as a 4-class classifiers on the train sets for each language separately. The horizontal dashed lines show the proportion of the most frequent class.

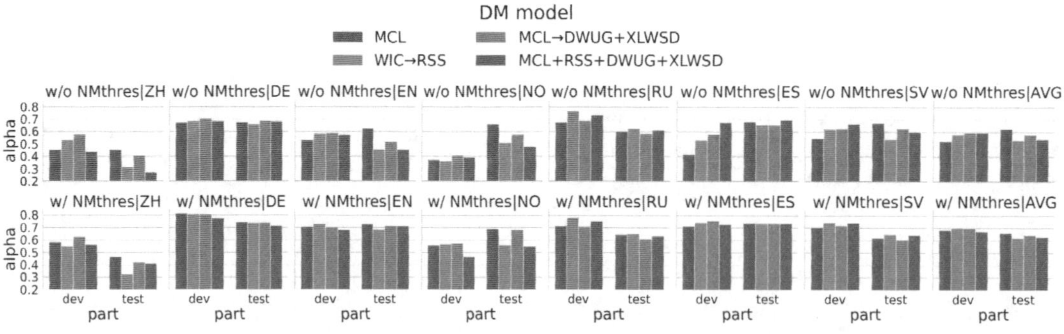

Figure 7: Krippendorff's α of DeepMistake models w/ and w/o NMthres. The simplified version of the plot is shown in Figure 1.

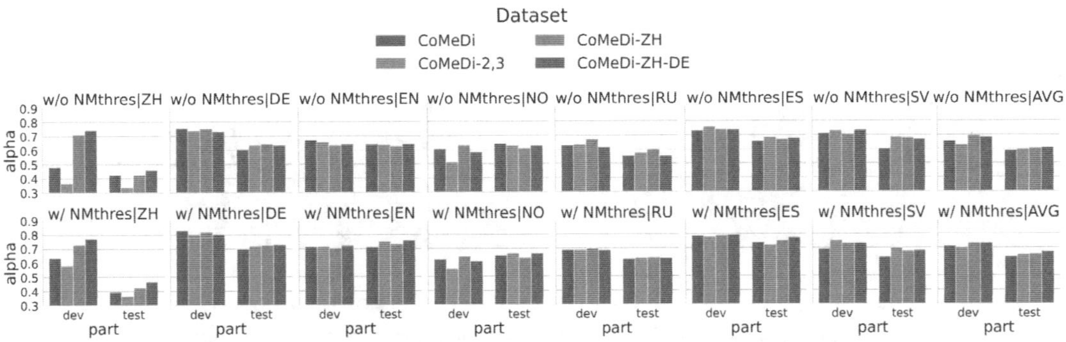

Figure 8: Krippendorff's α of 2-class DeepMistake models fine-tuned on different subsets of CoMeDi train data. The simplified version of the plot is shown in Figure 2.

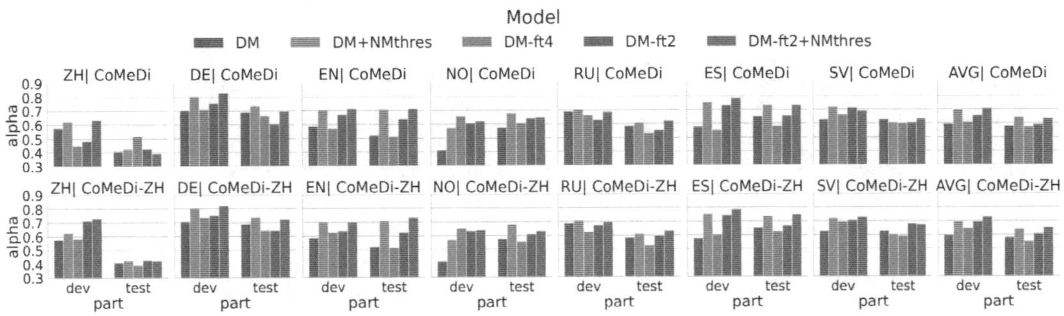

Figure 9: Krippendorff's α of models fine-tuned on CoMeDi and CoMeDi-ZH models. The simplified version of the plot is shown in Figure 3.

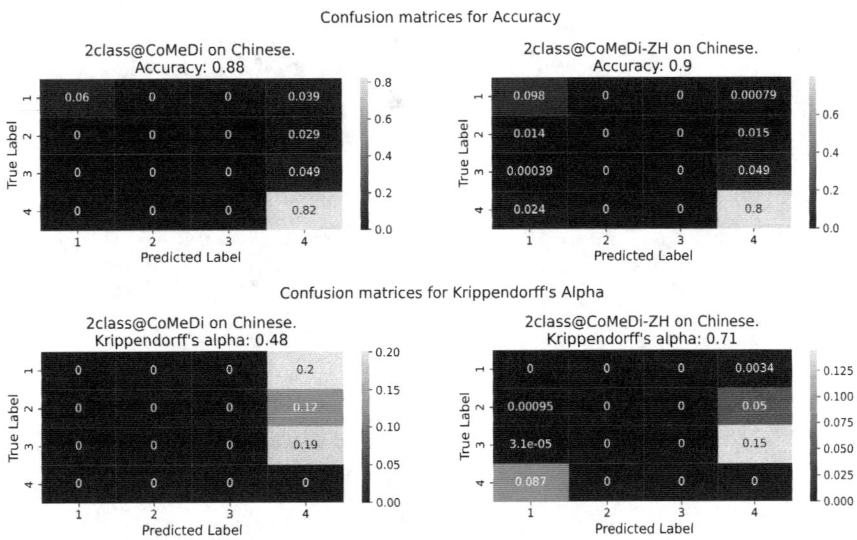

Figure 10: Confusion matrices built on the Chinese CoMeDi dev set for the 2class@CoMeDi and 2class@CoMeDi-ZH models. In confusion matrices for Krippendorff's α below (i, j)-th cell quantifies the contribution $\frac{2\delta_{ij}c_{ij}}{n*D_e}$ of the corresponding type of errors to Krippendorff's α. These contributions sum up to 1 - α. In confusion matrices for accuracy above it quantifies the proportion of examples of the corresponding type, accuracy is the sum of diagonal cells.

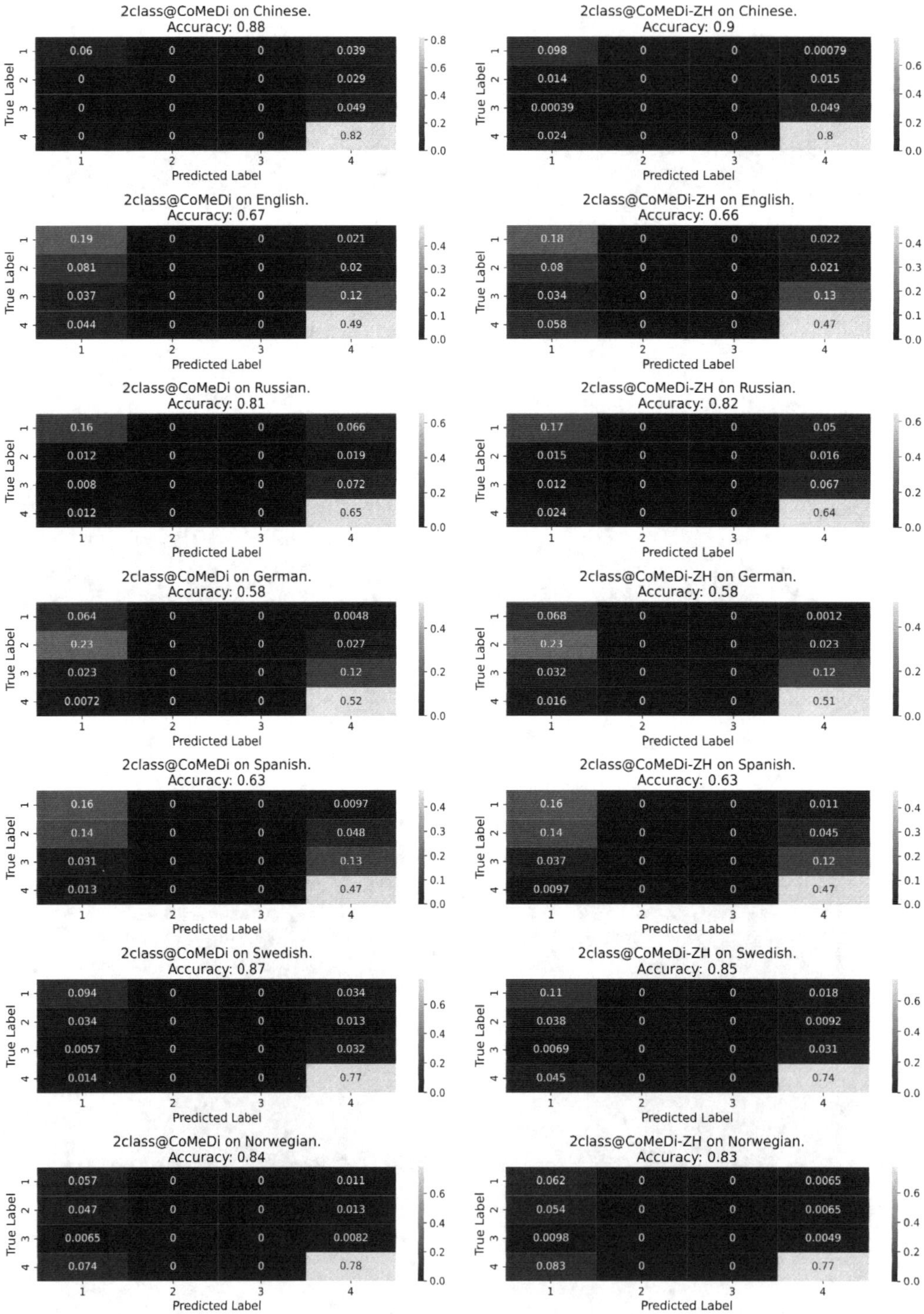

Figure 11: Confusion matrixes on CoMeDi dev sets of 2class@CoMeDi and 2class@CoMeDi-ZH.

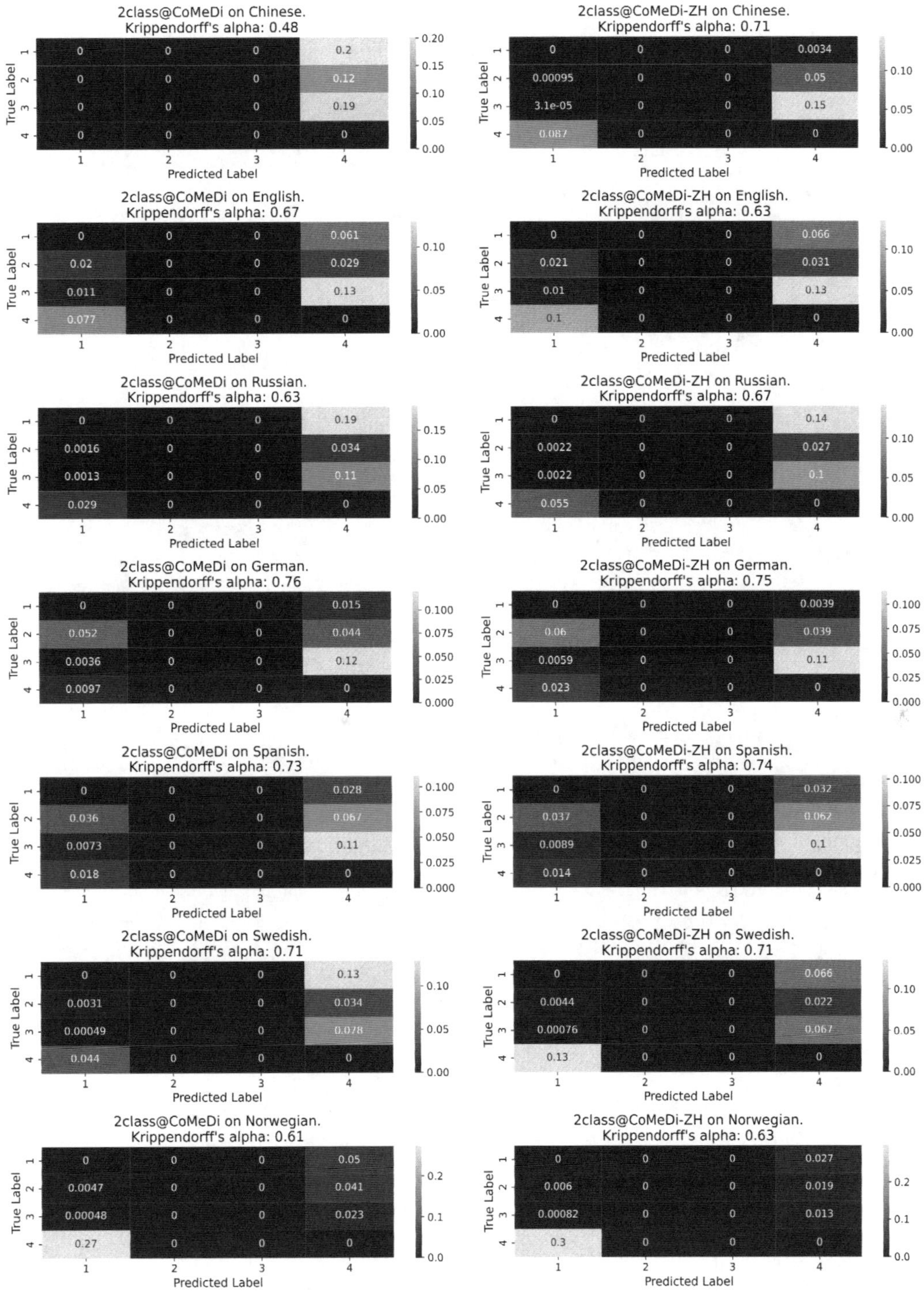

Figure 12: Confusion matrices built on the CoMeDi dev sets for the 2class@CoMeDi and 2class@CoMeDi-ZH models, (i, j)-th cell quantifies the contribution $\frac{2\delta_{ij}c_{ij}}{n*D_e}$ of the corresponding type of errors to Krippendorff's α. These contributions sum up to 1 - α.

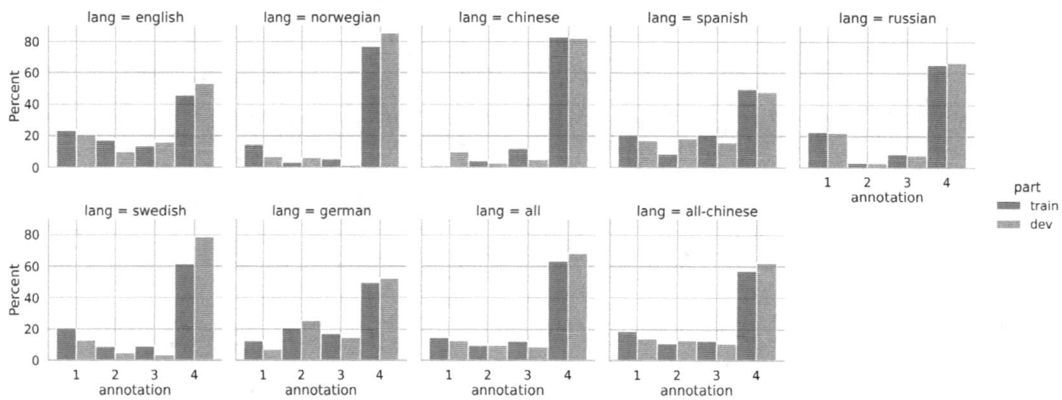

Figure 13: Class proportions in the train and dev sets for different languages and in combined train and dev sets.

Predicting Median, Disagreement and Noise Label in Ordinal Word-in-Context Data

Tejaswi Choppa[1] **Michael Roth**[2] **Dominik Schlechtweg**[1]
[1]University of Stuttgart [2]University of Technology Nuremberg
st180670@stud.uni-stuttgart.de michael.roth@utn.de
schlecdk@ims.uni-stuttgart.de

Abstract

The quality of annotated data is crucial for Machine Learning models, particularly in word sense annotation in context (Word-in-Context, WiC). WiC datasets often show significant annotator disagreement, and information is lost when creating gold labels through majority or median aggregation. Recent work has addressed this by incorporating disagreement data through new label aggregation methods. Modeling disagreement is important since real-world scenarios often lack clean data and require predictions on inherently difficult samples. Disagreement prediction can help detect complex cases or to reflect inherent data ambiguity. We aim to model different aspects of ordinal Word-in-Context annotations necessary to build a more human-like model: (i) the aggregated label, which has traditionally been the modeling aim, (ii) the disagreement between annotators, and (iii) the aggregated noise label which annotators can choose to exclude data points from annotation. We find that disagreement and noise are impacted by various properties of data like ambiguity, which in turn points to data uncertainty.

1 Introduction

Machine Learning (ML) research frequently gathers data from human annotators for training and testing of models. It is highly desirable to have good quality data (Sun et al., 2017), because with a low quality of data, the model tends to also learn biases and errors, thereby depreciating model performance. In the process of annotation, usually every instance in the dataset is annotated by multiple annotators in order to reduce the bias of any individual annotator (Uma et al., 2021b). These multiple annotations are subsequently adjudicated to establish a single **gold** label using several descriptive statistical methods. However, using these methods means also discarding the disagreements between annotators, resulting in a loss of information. Recent works propose to include these disagreements into the label aggregation process, treating disagreements as part of the **signal** rather than **noise** (Plank et al., 2014). We take these ideas to the extreme by focusing only on the disagreements and completely ignoring the labels in the aggregation process. The final aim being to construct ML models able to predict the human disagreement on an annotated text instance. Practically, our model may be used to predict instances with high disagreement allowing further modeling components to abstain from predicting the label in order to reduce the error rate (Xin et al., 2021).

For our experiments, we choose the task of semantic proximity annotation involving to quantify how much the meanings of two uses "have in common" (Schlechtweg, 2023). Each of the usage pairs is judged by multiple annotators based on a graded annotation schema. Word senses do not have clear boundaries and often do not fall into disjoint categories (Hanks, 2000; Kilgarriff, 1977) leading to inherent ambiguity. Another often overlooked aspect of data is the data noise. While it is a related phenomenon to disagreement, data noise represents cases where annotators cannot confidently assign labels or instances don't fit predefined categories. Some guidelines address this by offering special exclusion labels (Schlechtweg et al., 2023; Hätty et al., 2019).

Disagreement and noise have a common source: ambiguity. That is, although disagreement and noise are not completely determined by ambiguity, we hypothesize that ambiguity strongly influences these two variables (Uma et al., 2021b; Schlechtweg, 2023). Additionally, we construct more traditional models to predict the aggregated label enabling a comparison with noise and disagreement predictions. Finally, all three modeling approaches can be combined together into one model predicting different important aspects: the aggregated label, the expected disagreement, and

Proceedings of Context and Meaning: Navigating Disagreements in NLP Annotation, pages 65–77
January 19, 2025.

the noisiness of the data point.

2 Related work

In this section, we offer an overview of the previous research on semantic proximity, disagreements and noise in annotation tasks and discuss the methods to include this disagreement into the label aggregation process.

2.1 Tasks on Disagreement detection

NLP tasks often handle disagreements by discarding them or using label aggregation methods. Dawid and Skene (1979) proposed a probablistic label aggregation method calculating posterior probability of labels based on annotator reliability. Sheng et al. (2008) extended this by introducing an uncertainty-preserving labeling scheme that retains disagreement information as probability distributions. Uma et al. creates soft labels from annotator distributions through methods such as standard normalization, the softmax function, and probabilistic label aggregation techniques like MACE, enabling the model to learn from the distribution of annotations.

Although these approaches capture the distribution of disagreeing annotations, there is no significant research on directly predicting the amount of disagreement in a supervised way.

2.2 Research on disagreement for word meaning annotation tasks

Natural Language Processing (NLP) text-based meaning annotation tasks involve assigning semantic (meaning-related) labels to text sequences. Often, this sequence is restricted to a particular word in a context (word usage).

2.2.1 Word Sense Disambiguation

Word Sense Disambiguation (WSD) asks to assign sense glosses to word usages. Glosses are usually taken from a lexical resource like a dictionary or WordNet (Navigli, 2009, p. 2). Erk et al. (2013, p. 3) compare the traditional annotation schema with the possibility of employing graded sense assignments for Word Sense Disambiguation (WSD). The traditional WSD assigns the single most applicable sense from a predefined inventory. On the contrary, the proposed graded schema asks to rate the applicability of each sense on a scale. They discuss theories stating that word senses have "fuzzy boundaries", leading to inherent ambiguity and annotator disagreements. Erk et al.[p. 6] state that people have differences in how concepts and word meanings are mentally represented, causing annotators to assign word senses differently. Erk et al. present graded scales for meaning annotation, moving from the traditional binary annotation scheme. They propose WSsim, where annotators rate the applicability of each WordNet sense for the target lemma on a scale of 1 (sense does not apply) to 5 (sense applies fully).

2.2.2 Semantic proximity

Semantic proximity asks to measure how much meanings of word uses have in **common** (cf. Schlechtweg, 2023, p. 22). Various human annotation studies incorporate semantic proximity by formulating the task as usage similarity (Erk et al., 2013, p. 9) or the semantic relatedness (Schlechtweg et al., 2023, p. 33). Semantic proximity is usually annotated on scales such as the DURel (Schlechtweg et al., 2018) and the USim (Erk et al., 2013, p.9) scales. For the USim task, annotators compare pairs of usages on a five-point similarity scale where 1 means the usages are completely different in meaning and 5 means they are identical in meaning, additionally they permitted the response "cannot decide". For the study of diachronic usage relatedness (DURel), Schlechtweg et al. adopt a relatedness scale similar to that of Brown (2008). For this task, the annotators are asked to choose semantic relatedness between word usage pairs. Refer to Table 1 for the semantic relatedness scale. The label 0 is used when the annotators are unable to make a decision as to the degree of relatedness in meaning between the two word usages e.g. if the sentence is too flawed to understand it, or the meaning of the target word is ambiguous.

↑	4: Identical
	3: Closely Related
	2: Distantly Related
	1: Unrelated

Table 1: The DURel relatedness scale (Schlechtweg et al., 2018).

Tasks and Models of Semantic Proximity The Word in Context (WiC) task introduced by Pilehvar and Camacho-Collados asks to predict the label as TRUE or FALSE based on the similarity of the word usage meanings. On the contrary, the graded WiC task introduced by Armendariz et al. asks to predict the change in the similarity ratings of a pair of words when the human annotators are presented with an identical pair of words in two distinct contexts and assign a similarity rating for each pair of usages. Leveraging the above two tasks, Zhang (2023) introduces an Ordinal Graded WiC task (OGWiC), which asks to provide labels on an ordinal scale from 1 to 4 following the relatedness scale from the DURel framework (Schlechtweg et al., 2018). For the WiC, GWiC and the OGWiC tasks, the main methodology employed by models is similar and it involves feeding an input string to the contextual embedder, creating one or more vector representations. Then, the vector processor post-processes the embeddings e.g. by concatenation or using cosine similarity. The resulting embedding is then passed to a classification head for WiC or a ranker for GWiC or through an ordinal classifier for OGWiC (Zhang, 2023). Pilehvar and Camacho-Collados use the contextualized word embedding models like Context2Vec, ELMo (Peters et al., 2018) and BERT (Devlin et al., 2019) to compute dynamic word representations based on the context, on top of which classifiers like a simple Multi-layer perceptron (MLP) and a threshold-based classifier using vector cosine similarity are used. As GWiC has a multi-lingual dataset, most submissions utilise Cross-Lingual Model XLM-R (Conneau et al., 2019), a multi-lingual version of RoBERTa for the embedder part. Additionally, Zhang (2023) employs DistilBert and XL-Lexeme (Cassotti et al., 2023) embedders and these embeddings are processed as vectors by concatenating the embeddings, getting the cosine similarity of word embeddings and Hadamard product of word embeddings. Zhang (2023) employs a nominal classification head that treats the ordinal regression task as a standard multi-class classification problem.

3 Tasks

Given a pair of word usages, we aim to predict three data properties: (i) median semantic proximity, (ii) the level of disagreement, and (iii) the presence of noise in Word-in-Context annotations. We will treat each of these aspects in a separate task. The first two tasks have been included into the recently organized CoMeDi task (Schlechtweg et al., 2025). Each instance consists of a target word w, two usage contexts $c1$ and $c2$ expressing specific meanings of w, and multiple semantic proximity ratings by annotators on a scale of 1 (completely unrelated meanings) to 4 (identical meanings), following the DURel annotation framework. As an example, consider the word usages below (Schlechtweg, 2023, pp. 22–23), from which we build annotation instances by combining them into usage pairs.

(1) ... and taking a knife from her pocket, she opened a vein in her little **arm**, and dipping a feather in the blood, wrote something on a piece of white cloth, which was spread before her...

(2) ... and though he saw her within reach of his **arm**, yet the light of her eyes seemed as far off...

(3) It stood behind a high brick wall, its back windows overlooking an **arm** of the sea which, at low tide, was a black and stinking mud-flat...

(4) ...the company decided to create a new **arm**

The use pair (1,2) with sample judgments [4, 4] would likely receive semantic proximity label 4.0 (identical) as both refer to a physical human arm. The use pair (1,3) with sample judgments [2,3,2] would be classified as **polysemy** as the two referents of *arm* belong to different extensional categories (human arm vs. arm of the sea), but the corresponding concepts still hold a semantic relation (in this case a similarity relation regarding physical form). This pair would rather receive a lower label such as 2.0 (distantly related). In contrast, the *arm* in the **homonymic** pair (1,4) with sample judgments [1, 0, 0], belong to different extensional categories and it's relatively harder to determine if the corresponding concepts hold a semantic relation, especially in the context 4 (could mean weapon or branch of company). This pair would receive a noise label of 1.0 with semantic proximity and disagreement labels being NaN.

Ordinal Graded Word-in-Context (OGWiC) requires predicting the median of annotator judgments for each use pair, formulated as an ordinal classification task and evaluated using Krippendorff's α (Krippendorff, 2018). Treating graded WiC as an ordinal classification task instead of a ranking task constrains model predictions to exactly reproduce instance labels instead of just inferring their relative order (Schlechtweg et al., 2025). This is advantageous if ordinal labels have an interpretation because predictions then inherit this interpretation. Such an interpretation can be assigned to the DURel scale as explained above, like for the example pair (1,2) with sample judgments [4,4], the median semantic proximity label 4 can be interpreted as *identity* which means the meanings of the word in both the contexts are identical.

Disagreements in Word-in-Context (DisWiC) asks to predict the mean of pairwise absolute judgment differences between annotators:

$$D(J) = \frac{1}{|J|} \sum_{(j_1,j_2) \in J} |j_1 - j_2|,$$

where J is the set of unique pairwise combinations of judgments. For pair $1,3$ it amounts to

$$D(J) = \frac{1}{3} \left(|(2-3)| + |(2-2)| + |(3-2)|\right) = 0.67$$

DisWiC can be formulated as a ranking task based on the magnitude of disagreement and evaluated using Spearman's ρ (Spearman, 1904).

Noise Word in Context (NoiseWiC) asks to predict the noise in the data annotations. It is formulated as a binary classification task, which is evaluated with the nominal version of Krippendorff's α and Accuracy. The noise label is calculated as follows:

$$N(J) = \begin{cases} 1, & \text{if (\# non-zero } < \text{ \# zero)} \\ \text{NaN}, & \text{if (\# non-zero } \geq \text{ \# zero)} \\ & \text{\& (\# zero } > 0) \\ 0, & \text{otherwise} \end{cases}$$

For pair (1,4) from above, N(J) = 1 since there are more '0' annotations than the non-zero annotations.

3.1 Evaluation

OGWiC involves the classification task of detecting the semantic proximity label. Since the labels are of ordinal nature, we will use Krippendorff's α (Krippendorff, 2018), which, in its ordinal formulation, penalizes stronger deviations from the gold label more heavily. It has the additional advantage of controlling for expected disagreement and has been demonstrated to be superior to other measures such as Mean Absolute Error for ordinal regression (Sakib et al., 2023). For the DisWiC task, since the output has continuous disagreement labels, we will use Spearman's correlation (Spearman, 1904) as our evaluation measure because it helps capture non-linear relationships better. NoiseWiC is a binary classification task, so we mainly rely on accuracy as the classification metric but we also report the Krippendorff's α for nominal data (Krippendorff, 2018).

4 Data

For all our tasks, we make use of publicly available ordinal WiC datasets from the CoMeDi shared task (Schlechtweg et al., 2025), as summarized in Table 7 in Appendix A. These provide a large number of judgments for use pairs from different datasets across different languages annotated on the DURel scale and have so far not been used primarily for WiC-like tasks, but only for semantic change detection purposes.

4.1 Data aggregation and cleaning

For cleaning and aggregation, the Shared Task organizers initially exclude annotation instances with less than two annotations (Schlechtweg et al., 2025). For OGWiC, then instances with any 0-judgments ("Cannot decide") and instances with any pair of annotators disagreeing more than one point on the annotation scale are discarded. The organizers then calculate the median of all judgments, for each instance. Instances with a non-integer median (e.g. 3.5) are discarded. For all remaining instances, gold labels are given by the median of judgments. For DisWiC, the organizers derive instance labels by aggregating over judgments with the average of pairwise absolute annotator deviations, as discussed in section 3. 0-judgments ignored in this process. For NoiseWiC, we assign a noise label of 1 (indicating the presence of noise) if the number of 0-judgments by annotators exceeds the number of non-zero judgments. Otherwise, a label of 0 is assigned to indicate that noise is not present.

For each of the tasks, the organizers then randomly split the target words per language into train/test/dev with sizes of 70/20/10%. In contrast to previous tasks, the organizers intentionally do not balance out the label distribution in order to keep more realistic data conditions. Find an overview of the final splits per language in Table 2.

5 Models

For all our tasks, we follow a similar model architecture, except for the classification head. For this, we aim to utilize the best-performing models from WiC, GWiC, and ordinal GWiC, as discussed in Section 2.2.2, particularly with embedders, since

Task	# Instances	# Uses	Split
OGWiC	48K	55K	Train
	8K	8K	Dev
	15K	16K	Test
DisWiC	82K	55K	Train
	13K	8K	Dev
	26K	16K	Test
NoiseWiC	204K	55K	Train
	32K	8K	Dev
	64K	16K	Test

Table 2: Data statistics after cleaning and aggregation per split and and over all languages combined.

all tasks share a common focus on pairwise in-context meaning annotation. We use them as follows:

Contextual Embedder Given the input word usages, we employ XL-Lexeme, as it was optimized on binary WiC datasets and is one of the top-performing models for the OGWiC task, as noted by Zhang. XL-Lexeme (Cassotti et al., 2023) is a bi-encoder model utilizing a Siamese Network that extends the Sentence-BERT (SBERT) architecture to focus on the target word within input sentences. The model is trained using a contrastive loss function, which minimizes the cosine distance between the encoded representations when the target word has the same meaning and maximizes the distance when the meanings differ. It is pretrained on WiC datasets like MCL-WiC (Martelli et al., 2021), AM2ICO (Liu et al., 2021), and XL-WiC (Raganato et al., 2020), enabling it to function similarly to sentence-level encoders, while specifically focusing on target words marked using special tokens (<t> and </t>) to emphasize their context. This approach allows the model to better identify whether the target word maintains the same meaning across different contexts. Given an input sentence and the position of the target word (start and end character indices of the word within the sentence), XL-Lexeme generates a contextualized embedding for the target lemma in context.

Vector Processor We use the word embeddings as input to different models in different ways. For the CosTH model (see below), we use the embedding vectors of the words in two contexts and take their cosine similarity, based on which the thresholds are optimized. For all other models, we concatenate the embeddings of both words in context to create a single representation. This approach is useful when employing a classifier that takes the full feature set into account, such as a Multi-layer Perceptron (MLP). (Pilehvar and Camacho-Collados, 2019).

Classification Head Based on the nature of the task, we use different classification or regression approaches. For the OGWiC task, we use the following classification heads:

- `Cosine + threshold (CosTH)`: Given two vector representations of different contexts, we use a threshold-based classifier that utilizes the cosine similarity between the vectors. For these cosine similarity values, the classifier optimizes thresholds per language by minimizing a custom loss function, Krippendorff's α in our case, to determine the labels as follows:

$$\text{minimize} \quad L(\mathbf{y}, \hat{\mathbf{y}}|\theta) = 1 - \alpha(\mathbf{y}, \hat{\mathbf{y}}_\theta),$$

  where $\mathbf{y}, \hat{\mathbf{y}}$ are gold labels and predicted cosine similarities respectively, α is Krippendorff's α and $\hat{\mathbf{y}}_\theta$ is a mapping of cosine similarities to thr ordinal labels based onthresholds θ. We optimize thresholds per language.

- `Linear Regression (LR)`: The Linear Regression (Pedregosa et al., 2012) predicts continuous distribution of values by optimizing the Mean Square Error between a linear combination of the features and the ground truth. In our case, given the concatenated vector as input, Linear Regression predicts continuous values. The semantic proximity labels on a scale of 1 to 4 are then mapped from these predicted continuous values based on pre-defined thresholds based on rounding to the next integer, see Equation 5.

$$\text{threshold}(y_{\text{pred}}) = \begin{cases} 1, & \text{if } y_{\text{pred}} < 1.5 \\ 2, & \text{if } 1.5 \leq y_{\text{pred}} < 2.5 \\ 3, & \text{if } 2.5 \leq y_{\text{pred}} < 3.5 \\ 4, & \text{else} \end{cases} \tag{5}$$

- `Multilayer Perceptron (MLP)`: A Multilayer Perceptron (MLP) (Rosenblatt, 1958) is a feedforward artificial neural network that learns complex patterns and perform tasks like classification and regression. It consists of input layers, hidden layers and a output layer. In the WiC task (Pilehvar and Camacho-Collados, 2019), this approach has been used as a baseline. Given the concatenated vector as input, we use the MLP classifier to predict the semantic proximity label. We try to optimize the batch size, activation function, hidden layer size and alpha parameters, see Table 8 in appendix A.

For the DisWiC task, we use the following classification heads:

- `Multilayer Perceptron (MLP)`: Given the concatenated vectors as input, we use the MLP regressor which unlike the MLP Classifier model use MSE loss function and linear activation function to predict the the continuous disagreement labels. We optimize the batch size, activation function, hidden layer size and alpha parameters as well along with early stopping to prevent the model from overfitting.
- `Linear Regression`: Given the concatenated vector as input features, we use Linear Regression to predict the continuous disagreement values.

For the NoiseWiC task, we use logistic regression as a classification head. Logistic regression is a model used for binary classification tasks (Cox, 2018), predicting the probability that a given input belongs to either of the classes. It uses a sigmoid function to map predictions to a 0-1 probability range. Logistic regression generally uses 0.5 as a threshold value to map the probabilities to the binary labels. The probabilities greater than or equal to 0.5 are mapped to the label 1 and vise versa. In our case, given the concatenated vector as input, the logistic regression model is used detect the "noise" label.

5.1 Upperbound Metric

We explore an upperbound metric, which refers to the maximum performance a model can achieve on a given task. The main aim of an Upperbound is to set the model performance into context and to understand what we can expect from the model's performance and provide context to that performance. Model performance is typically expected to fall between the baseline and the Upperbound. For the OGWiC task, we compute the Upperbound metric by iteratively calculating Krippendorff's α between a single, excluded annotation and the median label built from the remaining annotations, weighted by their share of total annotations. For the DisWiC task, we compute the Upperbound metric by iteratively calculating Spearman's rank correlation between the mean disagreement of an excluded annotator pair and the mean disagreement label derived from the remaining annotations. Instances must have at least four annotators, as the definition of the disagreement measure requires at least two annotators for its calculation.

5.2 Baseline Models

5.2.1 Baseline XLM-R embedder

`XLM-R` : XLM-R (eXtreme Language Model Roberta) is an extension of RoBERTa that uses self-supervised training techniques to achieve state-of-the-art performance in cross-lingual understanding. It has been used as the underlying language model for fine-tuning XL-Lexeme (Cassotti et al., 2023). It was trained to learn robust representations from large-scale multilingual data (Conneau et al., 2019).We use the boolean mask to identify and extract subwords corresponding to the target token, extract the corresponding embeddings for the target subwords, and aggregate them using mean pooling to obtain the target token embedding. It is paired with CosTH model and Linear Regression model as classification heads for the OGWiC and DisWiC tasks respectively.

5.2.2 Majority Baseline

For the NoiseWic task, we employ a majority class baseline that assigns the most frequently occurring class in the train dataset to every instance in the test dataset, which, in our case, was the '0' label. This baseline provides a minimum performance threshold that a model should exceed.

5.2.3 Feature Baseline

The model architecture employs embedding features from pre-trained language models, as is common in many semantic NLP tasks (Pilehvar and Camacho-Collados, 2019; Schlechtweg et al., 2020). We engineer a set of simple linguistic features that correlate with noise or disagreement, including lexical complexity, grammatical complexity, and context richness.For the DisWiC task, we engineer features such as character length and the presence of non-alphabetic characters in the context to evaluate their impact on performance, using an MLP to predict disagreement labels.

6 Experiments

Our experiments aim to predict a median semantic proximity, mean disagreement or noise label based on the input usages. We experiment with different components of our model and compare their performances for this task. Also, we explore the factors influencing the disagreements through our experiments. The code for these experiments is available online.[1]

For generating the contextualized word embeddings, we primarily use XL-Lexeme, with XLM-R serving as the baseline model. For each of the subtasks, the models are fit on the training data in two ways: (i) per language, i.e., hyperparameters or thresholds are learned per language, and (ii) on the entire training data available. We experiment with various hyperparameter values for different classification heads across different tasks, see Appendix A. For OGWiC task, we used the default parameters for the scikit-learn linear regression model, as there were very few tunable parameters `n_jobs`, `fit_intercept`, and `copy_X`. Similarly, for the Cosine+Threshold model (CosTH), we implement it without hyperparameter tuning due to the lack of tunable parameters. In case of the DisWiC task, for the Linear Regression classification head, we again use the default parameters. For the MLP model in both OGWiC and DisWic tasks, we perform grid search over the specified hyperparameter grid, see Table 8 in Appendix A, fitting the model with each combination on the training data and evaluating its performance on the development data using the Spearman correlation as scoring metric. It keeps track of the best-performing combination and outputs the best score and hyperparameters at the end. We choose the hyperparameters for our grid by relying on Pilehvar and Camacho-Collados (2019), who use a solver 'Adam', batch size of 32 and hidden layer size 100. We take these values and expand our grid. We also take default parameters of the scikit-learn MLP in the parameter grid.

Apart from that, we also included some parameters like the hidden layer size and learning rate from Chai et al. (2021, p. 6). We also give standard scaler as an option in the parameter grid to improve the overall performance of the MLP. The

[1] `https://github.com/choppa98/Supervised-semantic-proximity-detection`

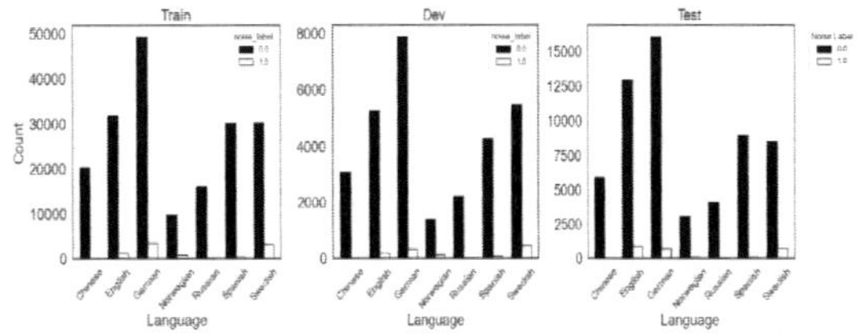

Figure 1: Label distribution for NoiseWiC task per language.

NoiseWiC dataset, refer Figure 1 is highly skewed with the majority label being 0. Especially, in languages like chinese and russian there is little to no presence of the noise label 1.0, as you can see in the Figure 4. In order to address this class imbalance and to avoid any bias associated with it, we omit instances of these languages while carrying out our experiments. Also, we employ a sampling strategy to downsample the majority class to match the size of the minority class. After downsampling, each language group is a balanced dataset with equal number of instances from both classes, see Figure 5 in Appendix A.

Apart from this, we also conduct an error analysis on the disagreed instances. We went through annotator comments for various patterns of disagreements and manually inspect the corresponding contexts to understand reasons for '0' annotations and annotator disagreements.

7 Results and Analysis

For the OGWiC task, as shown in Table 3, the Cosine+Threshold model achieves the best performance among classification heads, with an average Krippendorff's α of 0.67 on the development data and 0.58 on the test data. While XL-Lexeme + MLP shows relatively high performance in the "All data' setting (α of 0.55 on development, 0.42 on test), it performs lower in the "Per Lang" setting (α of 0.37 on development, 0.28 on test). The baseline model, XLM-R with Cosine+Threshold, underperforms (α of 0.25 on development, 0.12 on test). XL-Lexeme+Linear Regression performs poorest across all languages and settings. For ZH (Chinese), models generally performed better on development data but poorly on test data. NO (Norwegian) shows consistently low performance across models. For EN (English), both XL-Lexeme+CosTH and XL-Lexeme+MLP achieve moderately high results, while for DE (German) and SV (Swedish), XL-Lexeme+CosTH performs particularly well.

For the DisWiC task, the XL-Lexeme+MLP model shows best performance with average Spearman's ρ of 0.16 on development and 0.15 on test data in the "All Data" setting. In the "Per Lang" setting, it achieves 0.16 on test data but only 0.11 on development data. The MLP model shows high variability across languages, with ZH and NO achieving higher Spearman's ρ on test data. ES (Spanish) and EN exhibited consistently low values across settings and splits. The Linear Regression model yielded lower results (Spearman's ρ of 0.11 on development, 0.10 on test in "All data" setting). The baseline XLM-R+Linear regression model gives similar average Spearman's ρ as XL-Lexeme under "All data" setting, with ZH showing relatively higher ρ on both development and test data. The Upperbound metric for DisWiC provides inaccurate comparison results due to insufficient data for Chinese and Norwegian i.e, each instance in these languages has been annotatated by less than four annotators. For the NoiseWiC task, XLM-R+Logistic Regression achieves best results with average accuracy of 0.62 on development and 0.59 on test data (Krippendorff's α of 0.24 and 0.14 respectively). XL-Lexeme+Logistic Regression achieves 0.58 on both sets, performing particularly well for EN and SV. ES consistently shows lower scores, similar to the DisWiC task.

Model	Setting	Split	AVG	ZH	EN	DE	NO	RU	ES	SV
XLM-R + CosTH	Lang	Dev	.25	.51	.17	.3	.03	.27	.44	.05
		Test	.12	.06	.10	.27	.12	.11	.17	.02
XL-Lexeme + CosTH	Lang	Dev	**.67**	**.77**	**.66**	**.75**	**.52**	.62	.62	**.75**
		Test	.58	.38	.65	.72	.51	.55	**.65**	.60
XL-Lexeme + LR	All	Dev	.20	.37	.09	.33	.20	.05	.24	.15
		Test	.16	.04	.26	.15	.06	.15	.26	.18
	Lang	Dev	.10	.11	.19	.31	-.08	.13	-.13	.19
		Test	.09	.06	.04	.15	.03	.22	.22	-.07
XL-Lexeme + MLP	All	Dev	.55	.63	.49	.65	.48	.47	.48	.68
		Test	.42	.35	.49	.39	.37	.44	.51	.40
	Lang	Dev	.37	.17	.17	.60	.24	.32	.50	.59
		Test	.28	.20	.36	.36	.23	.32	.34	.13
Upperbound	All	Dev	.96	1.	.97	.92	.97	.95	.96	.96
		Test	.95	1.	.97	.88	.94	.96	.96	.95

Table 3: Krippendorff's α for OGWiC task. All = 'All Data', Lang = 'Per Lang'.

8 Analysis

As we observe in Section 7, for the OGWiC task, the models show promising results with highest α being 0.67 on development data and 0.58 on test data. But the models performed rather poorly on the DisWiC and the NoiseWic tasks. In case of the DisWiC task, the number of annotators significantly impacted performance, with Chinese and Norwegian having few annotators (most instances annotated by less than four). For analyzing annotator disagreement levels (0.66, 1.33, 3.0), instances from the English dataset reveal that fewer annotators can lead to more consistent labeling as their variation becomes more predictable.

For the instances with the disagreement label 3.0, among the annotators, it was observed that most of the disagreements, see example in Appendix A, occurred in the presence of a "0" label which corresponds to the "cannot decide" label. Another common pattern observed was that the highly disagreed instances had mostly two annotators whose judgments were [1, 4], which means either annotator agrees that the meaning of the target lemma is identical in both the contexts or completely unrelated. This pattern originates from the task definition: Only in the case of two annotators the maximum disagreement score of 3.0 can be reached. Generally, more annotators lead to a decrease in the score. This is because, with more annotators, the pairwise distances between some individual labels must be either small or zero, resulting in lesser maximal possible disagreement.

For example, refer to Appendix A, that had a mean disagreement of 1.33, the annotator judgments varied with all the annotators mostly having unique judgment per instance. In the cases, see Example 10 in Appendix A, where a mean disagreement of 0.66 was observed, the judgments mostly corresponding to a pattern of only one annotator disagreeing with the rest of the group. Key factors affecting these disagreement levels include grammatical errors, misspelled words, lack of context, and complex language misinterpretation. Likewise, annotator uncertainty in many cases raises questions about annotator reliability in meaning annotation tasks. Additionally, on analyzing various noise patterns, the background knowledge about various domains also determined the annotator's assignment of the '0' label. All these factors indicate the influence of the underlying data properties, such as ambiguity, which in turn point to data uncertainty.

Model	Setting	Split	AVG	ZH	EN	DE	NO	RU	ES	SV
XLM-R + LR	All	Dev	.11	.31	.07	.16	.12	.05	.02	.07
		Test	.11	.38	.06	.09	.07	.04	.07	.08
	Lang	Dev	.02	.01	-.05	.09	.07	-.01	-.01	.04
		Test	.05	.10	.01	.13	.04	.11	.05	-.11
Feature Baseline	All	Dev	-.00	.03	-.04	.01	-.05	.02	.00	.02
		Test	-.00	-.00	-.00	.00	-.03	-.01	-.01	.02
XL-Lexeme + LR	All	Dev	.11	.16	.01	.06	.26	.002	.03	.21
		Test	.10	.30	.02	.03	.06	.07	.05	.18
	Lang	Dev	.10	.11	.19	**.31**	-.08	.13	-.13	.19
		Test	.09	.06	.04	.15	.03	**.22**	**.22**	-.07
XL-Lexeme + MLP	All	Dev	.16	.36	.03	.11	.33	.06	.05	.15
		Test	.15	.45	**.07**	.07	.10	.13	.08	.16
	Lang	Dev	.11	.06	.04	.11	**.35**	.04	-.02	**.23**
		Test	**.16**	**.48**	.04	.11	.25	.04	.06	.16
Upperbound	All	Dev	.16		-.09	.16		.32	.21	.20
		Test	.18		.07	.04		.22	.08	.48

Table 4: Spearman's ρ for DisWiC task.All = 'All Data', Lang = 'Per Lang'.

Model	Split	AVG	EN	DE	NO	ES	SV
Majority Baseline	Dev	.5	.5	.5	.5	.5	.5
	Test	.5	.5	.5	.5	.5	.5
XLM-R +Logistic Reg	Dev	**.62**	.57	**.67**	**.70**	.55	.65
	Test	.59	.59	.65	.47	**.60**	.63
XL-Lexeme +Logistic Reg	Dev	.58	**.61**	.59	.55	.48	**.68**
	Test	.58	.59	.63	.58	.48	.63

Table 5: Accuracy for NoiseWiC task.

9 Conclusion

In this study, we have formulated the OGWiC task, the DisWiC and the NoiseWiC task. We focus on predicting semantic proximity, disagreement, and noise labels using contextualized word embeddings across multiple languages. For OGWiC, the combination of XL-Lexeme with a Cosine + Threshold approach achieved the highest Krippendorff's α scores of 0.67 on the development data and 0.58 on the test data. In DisWiC, the MLP classification head significantly outperformed Linear Regression, particularly when trained per language, with hyperparameter tuning enhancing performance in languages like Chinese and Norwegian. NoiseWiC had challenges due to class imbalance, especially in languages with sparse noise labels, which we addressed through downsampling; however, model performance remained low, as indicated by the Krippendorff's α scores. Across tasks, XL-Lexeme consistently outperformed the baseline XLM-R, especially in language-specific setups. Training strategies: whether using all data or per language, played a crucial role, with per-

Model	Split	AVG	EN	DE	NO	ES	SV
XLM-R +Logistic Reg	Dev	**.24**	.09	**.33**	**.39**	.10	.29
	Test	.14	.17	.30	-.21	**.20**	.25
XL-Lexeme +Logistic Reg	Dev	.13	**.21**	.16	.06	-.11	**.36**
	Test	.15	.19	.27	.15	-.08	.26

Table 6: Krippendorff's α for NoiseWiC task.

language tuning improving performance. Further, our analysis of results lays a stepstone for future work especially for the DisWiC task.

Limitations

When instances are annotated by different numbers of people, it becomes tricky to make direct comparisons of disagreement levels between those instances. Take two cases: when an instance has two annotators versus three annotators, the maximum possible disagreement between them will be inherently different. This variation in annotator numbers may help explain why we see different performance patterns across languages. For instance, the Chinese dataset stands out because every instance in this language has been annotated by two annotators. Going forward, we should do two things: first, explore alternative ways to measure disagreement, and second, ensure that all instances receive the same number of annotations to make comparisons more meaningful. Also, for the noise detection, the high imbalance in labels especially for Russian and Chinese pose a challenge.

Acknowledgments

This work is strongly based on a master thesis written at the Institute for Natural Language Processing at the University of Stuttgart (Choppa, 2024). Work by Michael Roth was funded by the DFG Emmy Noether program (RO 4848/2-1). Dominik Schlechtweg has been funded by the research program 'Change is Key!' supported by Riksbankens Jubileumsfond (under reference number M21-0021).

References

Anna Aksenova, Ekaterina Gavrishina, Elisei Rykov, and Andrey Kutuzov. 2022. RuDSI: Graph-based word sense induction dataset for Russian. In *Proceedings of TextGraphs-16: Graph-based Methods for Natural Language Processing*, pages 77–88, Gyeongju, Republic of Korea. Association for Computational Linguistics.

Carlos Santos Armendariz, Matthew Purver, Matej Ulčar, Senja Pollak, Nikola Ljubešić, and Mark Granroth-Wilding. 2020. CoSimLex: A resource for evaluating graded word similarity in context. In *Proceedings of the Twelfth Language Resources and Evaluation Conference*, pages 5878–5886, Marseille, France. European Language Resources Association.

Susan Windisch Brown. 2008. Choosing sense distinctions for WSD: Psycholinguistic evidence. In *Proceedings of the 46th Annual Meeting of the Association for Computational Linguistics on Human Language Technologies: Short Papers*, pages 249–252, Stroudsburg, PA, USA.

Pierluigi Cassotti, Lucia Siciliani, Marco de Gemmis, Giovanni Semeraro, and Pierpaolo Basile. 2023. Xl-lexeme: Wic pretrained model for cross-lingual lexical semantic change. In *Proceedings of the 61th Annual Meeting of the Association for Computational Linguistics*, Online. Association for Computational Linguistics.

Soo See Chai, Whye Lian Cheah, Kok Luong Goh, Yee Hui Robin Chang, Kwan Yong Sim, and Kim On Chin. 2021. A multilayer perceptron neural network model to classify hypertension in adolescents using anthropometric measurements: A cross-sectional study in sarawak, malaysia. *Computational and Mathematical Methods in Medicine*, 2021(1):2794888.

Jing Chen, Emmanuele Chersoni, Dominik Schlechtweg, Jelena Prokic, and Chu-Ren Huang. 2023. ChiWUG: A graph-based evaluation dataset for Chinese lexical semantic change detection. In *Proceedings of the 4th International Workshop on Computational Approaches to Historical Language Change*, Singapore. Association for Computational Linguistics.

Tejaswi Choppa. 2024. Supervised semantic proximity noise and disagreement detection. Master thesis, University of Stuttgart.

Alexis Conneau, Kartikay Khandelwal, Naman Goyal, Vishrav Chaudhary, Guillaume Wenzek, Francisco Guzmán, Edouard Grave, Myle Ott, Luke Zettlemoyer, and Veselin Stoyanov. 2019. Unsupervised cross-lingual representation learning at scale. *arXiv preprint arXiv:1911.02116*.

D. R. Cox. 2018. The regression analysis of binary sequences. *Journal of the Royal Statistical Society: Series B (Methodological)*, 20(2):215–232.

A. P. Dawid and A. M. Skene. 1979. Maximum likelihood estimation of observer error-rates using the em algorithm. *Journal of the Royal Statistical Society. Series C (Applied Statistics)*, 28(1):20–28.

Jacob Devlin, Ming-Wei Chang, Kenton Lee, and Kristina Toutanova. 2019. BERT: Pre-training of deep bidirectional transformers for language understanding. In *Proceedings of the 2019 Conference of the North American Chapter of the Association for Computational Linguistics: Human Language Technologies, Volume 1 (Long and Short Papers)*, pages 4171–4186, Minneapolis, Minnesota. Association for Computational Linguistics.

Katrin Erk, Diana McCarthy, and Nicholas Gaylord. 2013. Measuring word meaning in context. *Computational Linguistics*, 39(3):511–554.

Patrick Hanks. 2000. Do word meanings exist? *Computers and the Humanities*, 34(1/2):205–215.

Anna Hätty, Dominik Schlechtweg, and Sabine Schulte im Walde. 2019. SURel: A gold standard for incorporating meaning shifts into term extraction. In *Proceedings of the 8th Joint Conference on Lexical and Computational Semantics*, pages 1–8, Minneapolis, MN, USA.

Adam Kilgarriff. 1977. What is word sense disambiguation good for? In *Proc. Natural Language Processing in the Pacific Rim (NLPRS '97)*, Phuket, Thailand.

Klaus Krippendorff. 2018. *Content Analysis: An Introduction to Its Methodology*. SAGE Publications.

Sinan Kurtyigit, Maike Park, Dominik Schlechtweg, Jonas Kuhn, and Sabine Schulte im Walde. 2021. Lexical Semantic Change Discovery. In *Proceedings of the 59th Annual Meeting of the Association for Computational Linguistics and the 11th International Joint Conference on Natural Language Processing (Volume 1: Long Papers)*, Online. Association for Computational Linguistics.

Andrey Kutuzov and Lidia Pivovarova. 2021. Rushifteval: a shared task on semantic shift detection for russian. *Komp'yuternaya Lingvistika i Intellektual'nye Tekhnologii: Dialog conference*.

Andrey Kutuzov, Samia Touileb, Petter Mæhlum, Tita Enstad, and Alexandra Wittemann. 2022. NorDiaChange: Diachronic semantic change dataset for Norwegian. In *Proceedings of the Thirteenth Language Resources and Evaluation Conference*, pages 2563–2572, Marseille, France. European Language Resources Association.

Qianchu Liu, Edoardo M Ponti, Diana McCarthy, Ivan Vulić, and Anna Korhonen. 2021. Am2ico: Evaluating word meaning in context across low-resource languages with adversarial examples. *arXiv preprint arXiv:2104.08639*.

Federico Martelli, Najla Kalach, Gabriele Tola, and Roberto Navigli. 2021. SemEval-2021 task 2: Multilingual and cross-lingual word-in-context disambiguation (MCL-WiC). In *Proceedings of the 15th International Workshop on Semantic Evaluation (SemEval-2021)*, pages 24–36, Online. Association for Computational Linguistics.

Roberto Navigli. 2009. Word sense disambiguation: a survey. *ACM Computing Surveys*, 41(2):1–69.

Fabian Pedregosa, Gaël Varoquaux, Alexandre Gramfort, Vincent Michel, Bertrand Thirion, Olivier Grisel, Mathieu Blondel, Peter Prettenhofer, Ron Weiss, Vincent Dubourg, Jake VanderPlas, Alexandre Passos, David Cournapeau, Matthieu Brucher, Matthieu Perrot, and Edouard Duchesnay. 2012. Scikit-learn: Machine learning in python. *CoRR*, abs/1201.0490.

Matthew Peters, Mark Neumann, Mohit Iyyer, Matt Gardner, Christopher Clark, Kenton Lee, and Luke Zettlemoyer. 2018. Deep contextualized word representations. In *Proceedings of the 2018 Conference of the North American Chapter of the Association for Computational Linguistics: Human Language Technologies*, pages 2227–2237, New Orleans, LA, USA.

Mohammad Taher Pilehvar and Jose Camacho-Collados. 2019. WiC: the word-in-context dataset for evaluating context-sensitive meaning representations. In *Proceedings of the 2019 Conference of the North American Chapter of the Association for Computational Linguistics: Human Language Technologies, Volume 1 (Long and Short Papers)*, pages 1267–1273, Minneapolis, Minnesota. Association for Computational Linguistics.

Barbara Plank, Dirk Hovy, and Anders Søgaard. 2014. Linguistically debatable or just plain wrong? In *Proceedings of the 52nd Annual Meeting of the Association for Computational Linguistics (Volume 2: Short Papers)*, volume volume 2, pages 507–511. Association for Computational Linguistics.

Alessandro Raganato, Tommaso Pasini, Jose Camacho-Collados, and Mohammad Taher Pilehvar. 2020. Xl-wic: A multilingual benchmark for evaluating semantic contextualization. *arXiv preprint arXiv:2010.06478*.

Julia Rodina and Andrey Kutuzov. 2020. RuSemShift: a dataset of historical lexical semantic change in Russian. In *Proceedings of the 28th International Conference on Computational Linguistics*, pages 1037–1047, Barcelona, Spain (Online). International Committee on Computational Linguistics.

Frank Rosenblatt. 1958. The perceptron: a probabilistic model for information storage and organization in the brain. *Psychological review*, 65 6:386–408.

Fardin Ahsan Sakib, A H M Rezaul Karim, Saadat Hasan Khan, and Md Mushfiqur Rahman. 2023. Intent detection and slot filling for home assistants: Dataset and analysis for Bangla and Sylheti. In *Proceedings of the First Workshop on Bangla Language Processing (BLP-2023)*, pages 48–55, Singapore. Association for Computational Linguistics.

Dominik Schlechtweg. 2023. *Human and Computational Measurement of Lexical Semantic Change*. Ph.D. thesis, University of Stuttgart, Stuttgart, Germany.

Dominik Schlechtweg, Pierluigi Cassotti, Bill Noble, David Alfter, Sabine Schulte im Walde, and Nina Tahmasebi. 2024. More DWUGs: Extending and evaluating word usage graph datasets in multiple languages. In *Proceedings of the 2024 Conference on Empirical Methods in Natural Language Processing*, Miami, Florida. Association for Computational Linguistics.

Dominik Schlechtweg, Tejaswi Choppa, Wei Zhao, and Michael Roth. 2025. The CoMeDi shared task: Median judgment classification & mean disagreement ranking with ordinal word-in-context judgments. In *Proceedings of the 1st Workshop on Context and Meaning–Navigating Disagreements in NLP Annotations*, Abu Dhabi, UAE.

Dominik Schlechtweg, Barbara McGillivray, Simon Hengchen, Haim Dubossarsky, and Nina Tahmasebi. 2020. SemEval-2020 Task 1: Unsupervised Lexical Semantic Change Detection. In *Proceedings of the 14th International Workshop on Semantic Evaluation*, Barcelona, Spain. Association for Computational Linguistics.

Dominik Schlechtweg, Sabine Schulte im Walde, and Stefanie Eckmann. 2018. Diachronic Usage Relatedness (DURel): A framework for the annotation of lexical semantic change. In *Proceedings of the 2018 Conference of the North American Chapter of the Association for Computational Linguistics: Human Language Technologies*, pages 169–174, New Orleans, Louisiana.

Dominik Schlechtweg, Nina Tahmasebi, Simon Hengchen, Haim Dubossarsky, and Barbara McGillivray. 2021. DWUG: A large Resource of Diachronic Word Usage Graphs in Four Languages. In *Proceedings of the 2021 Conference on Empirical Methods in Natural Language Processing*, pages 7079–7091, Online and Punta Cana, Dominican Republic. Association for Computational Linguistics.

Dominik Schlechtweg, Shafqat Mumtaz Virk, Pauline Sander, Emma Sköldberg, Lukas Theuer Linke, Tuo Zhang, Nina Tahmasebi, Jonas Kuhn, and Sabine Schulte im Walde. 2023. The durel annotation tool: Human and computational measurement of semantic proximity, sense clusters and semantic change. *Preprint*, arXiv:2311.12664.

Victor S. Sheng, Foster Provost, and Panagiotis G. Ipeirotis. 2008. Get another label? improving data quality and data mining using multiple, noisy labelers. In *Proceedings of the 14th ACM SIGKDD International Conference on Knowledge Discovery and Data Mining*, KDD '08, page 614–622, New York, NY, USA. Association for Computing Machinery.

Charles Spearman. 1904. The proof and measurement of association between two things. *American Journal of Psychology*, 15:88–103.

Chen Sun, Abhinav Shrivastava, Saurabh Singh, and Abhinav Gupta. 2017. Revisiting unreasonable effectiveness of data in deep learning era. *Preprint*, arXiv:1707.02968.

Alexandra Uma, Tommaso Fornaciari, Anca Dumitrache, Tristan Miller, Jon Chamberlain, Barbara Plank, Edwin Simpson, and Massimo Poesio. 2021a. SemEval-2021 task 12: Learning with disagreements. In *Proceedings of the 15th International Workshop on Semantic Evaluation (SemEval-2021)*, pages 338–347, Online. Association for Computational Linguistics.

Alexandra Uma, Tommaso Fornaciari, Dirk Hovy, Silviu Paun, Barbara Plank, and Massimo Poesio. 2021b. Learning from disagreement: A survey. *Journal of Artificial Intelligence Research*, 72:1385–1470.

Ji Xin, Raphael Tang, Yaoliang Yu, and Jimmy Lin. 2021. The art of abstention: Selective prediction and error regularization for natural language processing. In *Proceedings of the 59th Annual Meeting of the Association for Computational Linguistics and the 11th International Joint Conference on Natural Language Processing (Volume 1: Long Papers)*, pages 1040–1051, Online. Association for Computational Linguistics.

Frank D. Zamora-Reina, Felipe Bravo-Marquez, and Dominik Schlechtweg. 2022. LSCDiscovery: A shared task on semantic change discovery and detection in Spanish. In *Proceedings of the 3rd International Workshop on Computational Approaches to Historical Language Change*, Dublin, Ireland. Association for Computational Linguistics.

Tuo Zhang. 2023. An ordinal formulation of the graded word-in-context task. Master thesis, University of Stuttgart.

A Appendix

(6) `Context 1`: The public, gene- /z/ **rally**, remained indifferent, notwithstanding the marvellous things which were related of the terri tory which had been ceded to the company.

(7) `Context 2`: Once or twice I have known him touch nerves that go close to the heart; but gene **rally**, he is no master of the feelings.

`Observation`: misspelled, grammatically incorrect

`Judgments` : [1, 0, 0, 4]

`Mean Disagreement Label` : 3.0

`Comments available` : '', 'same word, but incomplete', 'generally?', 'UNK; I think the intended meaning of the target word might be generally in both sentences']

(8) `Context 1`: Willoughby's as the family possess and will submit for examination, carefully searched, in the hope that some **record** may be found in his hand-writing, sufficiently clear to establish the fact that my mother was the wife of the elder Captain Allen.

(9) `Context 2`: For the **record**, your information is inaccurate on Governor Rockefeller's visit on Sept. 21.

`Judgments` : [3, 4, 2]

`Mean Disagreement Label` : 1.333

`Comments available` : ['', 'If "for the record" is used metaphorically and not literally in sentence 2, then a rating of 3 would be more appropriate.', ''] On other front,

`Observation`: Context 1 talks about a physical record like a book or document whereas Context 2 refers to stating a fact or information.

(10) `Context 1`: Ari arrived at Kibbutz Revivim Tuesday **afternoon**, at the peak of the sun's arc across

`Context 2`: Old shopping lists and ticket stubs and wads of listed newsprint come falling around Pafko in the faded **afternoon**.

`Judgments` : [3, 4, 4]

`Mean Disagreement Label` : 0.66

`Observation` : Both refer to the mid day time frame, also referring to how the afternoon looks like

`Comments available` : ['daylight versus actual day', '', '']

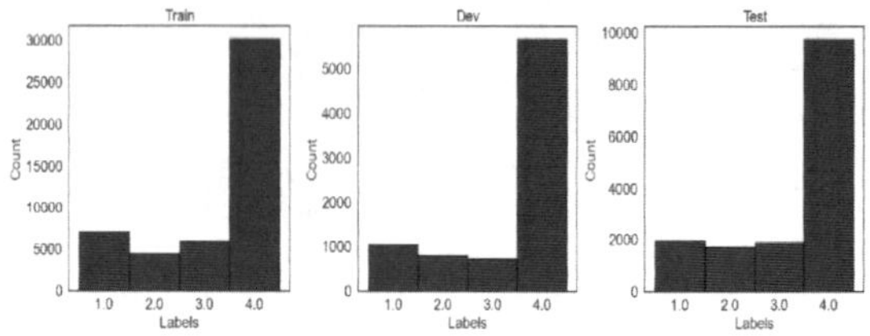

Figure 2: Label Distribution for OGWiC task.

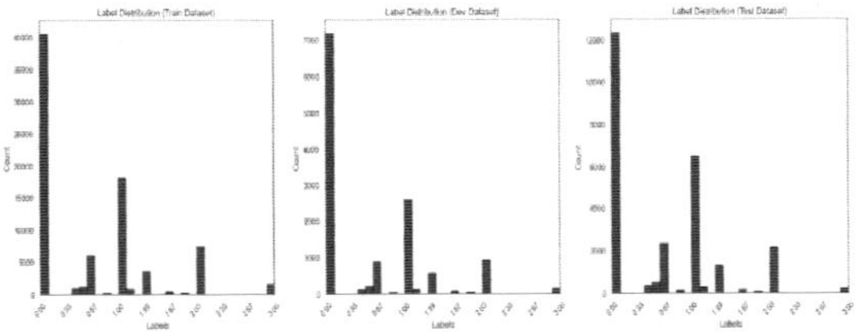

Figure 3: Label distribution for DisWiC task.

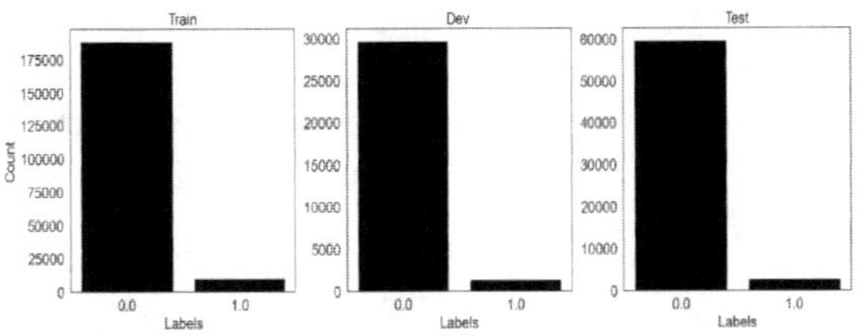

Figure 4: Label distribution for NoiseWiC task.

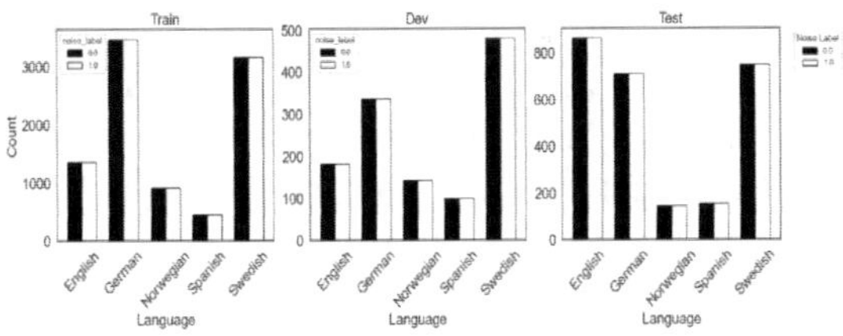

Figure 5: Label distribution for NoiseWiC task per language after downsampling.

Dataset	LG	Reference	JUD	VER	KRI	SPR
DWUG	DE	Schlechtweg et al. (2021)	63K	3.0.0	.67	.61
DWUG Res.	DE	Schlechtweg et al. (2024)	10K	1.0.0	.59	.7
DiscoWUG	DE	Kurtyigit et al. (2021)	28K	2.0.0	.59	.57
RefWUG	DE	Schlechtweg (2023)	4k	1.1.0	.67	.7
DURel	DE	Schlechtweg et al. (2018)	6k	3.0.0	.54	.59
SURel	DE	Hätty et al. (2019)	5k	3.0.0	.83	.84
DWUG	EN	Schlechtweg et al. (2021)	69K	3.0.0	.63	.55
DWUG Res.	EN	Schlechtweg et al. (2024)	7K	1.0.0	.56	.59
DWUG	ES	Zamora-Reina et al. (2022)	62k	4.0.1	.53	.57
DWUG	SV	Schlechtweg et al. (2021)	55K	3.0.0	.67	.62
DWUG Res.	SV	Schlechtweg et al. (2024)	16K	1.0.0	.56	.65
ChiWUG	CH	Chen et al. (2023)	61k	1.0.0	.60	.69
RuSemShift	RU	Rodina and Kutuzov (2020)	8k	1.0.0	.52	.53
RuShiftEval	RU	Kutuzov and Pivovarova (2021)	30k	1.0.0	.56	.55
RuDSI	RU	Aksenova et al. (2022)	6k	1.0.0	.41	.56
NorDiaChange	NO	Kutuzov et al. (2022)	19k	1.0.0	.71	.74

Table 7: Datasets used for our task. All are annotated under DURel scale. Spearman and Krippendorff values for RuShiftEval are calculated as average across all time bins. LG: Language; JUD: Number of judgments; VER: Dataset version; KRI: Krippendorff's α; SPR: Weighted mean of pairwise Spearman correlations; Res.: Resampled.

Parameter	Values
activation	relu, tanh
solver	Adam
hidden layer sizes	10, 50, 100
alpha	0.0001, 0.001, 0.01, 0.1
batch size	32, auto, 50, 100
scaler	StandardScaler(), None

Table 8: Parameter grid used for tuning MLP.

Hyperparameter	Model	Task	ZH	EN	DE	NO	RU	ES	SV
Activation	MLP	OGWiC	relu	relu	relu	relu	relu	relu	relu
Alpha			.0001	.0001	.0001	.0001	.0001	.0001	.0001
Batch Size			10	10	10	10	10	10	10
Hidden Layers			(10,)	(10,)	(10,)	(10,)	(10,)	(10,)	(10,)
Scaler			yes	yes	yes	None	yes	yes	yes
Solver			adam	adam	adam	adam	adam	adam	adam
Activation	MLP	OGWiC	tanh	tanh	relu	relu	tanh	tanh	tanh
Alpha			.001	.1	.0001	.001	.1	.1	.0001
Batch Size			auto	auto	auto	100	100	auto	100
Hidden Layers			(50,)	(50,)	(50,)	(50,)	(100,)	(100,)	(100,)
Scaler			None	yes	yes	yes	yes	yes	yes
Solver			adam	adam	adam	adam	adam	adam	adam

Table 9: Final set of hyperparameters for MLP per task in 'Per Lang' setting.

Hyperparameter	Model	Task	Value
Activation	MLP	OGWiC	relu
Alpha			.0001
Batch Size			auto
Hidden Layers			(100,)
Scaler			None
Solver			adam
Activation	MLP	DisWiC	relu
Alpha			.001
Batch Size			auto
Hidden Layers			(50,)
Scaler			yes
Solver			adam

Table 10: Final set of hyperparameters for MLP in 'All Data' setting

GRASP at CoMeDi Shared Task: Multi-Strategy Modeling of Annotator Behavior in Multi-Lingual Semantic Judgments

David Alfter
GRIDH
University of Gothenburg
Sweden
david.alfter@gu.se

Mattias Appelgren
CLASP
University of Gothenburg
Sweden
mattias.appelgren@gu.se

Abstract

This paper presents the GRASP team's systems for the CoMeDi 2025 shared task on disagreement prediction in semantic annotation. The task comprises two subtasks: predicting median similarity scores and mean disagreement scores for word usage across multiple languages including Chinese, English, German, Norwegian, Russian, Spanish, and Swedish. For subtask 1, we implement three approaches: Prochain, a probabilistic chain model predicting sequential judgments; FARM, an ensemble of five fine-tuned XLM-RoBERTa models; and THAT, a task-specific model using XL-Lexeme with adaptive thresholds. For subtask 2, we develop three systems: LAMP, combining language-agnostic and monolingual models; BUMBLE, using optimal language combinations; and DRAMA, leveraging disagreement patterns from FARM's outputs. Our results show strong performance across both subtasks, ranking second overall among participating teams. The probabilistic Prochain model demonstrates surprisingly robust performance when given accurate initial judgments, while our task-specific approaches show varying effectiveness across languages.

1 Introduction

The growing importance of modeling annotator disagreement in NLP has emerged as a crucial challenge for developing more robust and nuanced language understanding systems. While traditional approaches often treat divergent annotations as noise to be filtered out, recent work suggests that systematic patterns in annotator disagreement can provide valuable insights into linguistic ambiguity, contextual interpretation, and the inherent complexity of language understanding tasks (Uma et al., 2021; Leonardelli et al., 2023).

The 2025 Workshop on Context and Meaning - Navigating Disagreements in NLP Annotations (CoMeDi)[1] addresses this challenge through a shared task focused on predicting patterns of annotator disagreement across multiple languages. The task encompasses seven languages (Chinese, English, German, Norwegian, Russian, Spanish, and Swedish), drawing from various semantic change datasets as shown in Table 1. This multilingual scope provides a unique opportunity to explore how annotator disagreement patterns manifest across different linguistic and cultural contexts.

In this paper, we present a range of approaches for modeling annotator behavior and predicting disagreement patterns. Our methods span from probabilistic modeling of sequential judgments to neural architectures specifically designed to capture the nuanced nature of semantic annotation tasks. Through these diverse approaches, we aim to contribute to the broader understanding of how to effectively model and utilize annotator disagreement in NLP systems.

2 Related Work

Prior work on modeling annotator disagreement falls into several key areas. Early approaches treated disagreement primarily as noise to be filtered out through measures like inter-annotator agreement (Artstein and Poesio, 2008) or adjudication (Passonneau, 2004). However, recent work has shown that systematic patterns in annotator disagreement can provide valuable linguistic insights (Plank et al., 2014; Pavlick and Kwiatkowski, 2019).

In the context of semantic annotation, several studies have specifically examined disagreement patterns in word sense annotation. Erk et al. (2013) introduced a graded approach to word sense, showing that annotators often perceive multiple valid interpretations rather than discrete senses. This finding was further supported by Jurgens (2014),

[1] https://comedinlp.github.io/

Proceedings of Context and Meaning: Navigating Disagreements in NLP Annotation, pages 78–89
January 19, 2025.

Language	Datasets (version) [citation]
Chinese	ChiWUG (1.0.0) [Chen et al. (2023)]
English	DWUG_EN (3.0.0), DWUG_EN_resampled (1.0.0) [Schlechtweg et al. (2024)]
German	DWUG_DE (3.0.0), DWUG_DE_resampled (1.0.0), DiscoWUG (2.0.0), RefWUG (1.1.0) [Schlechtweg et al. (2024), Kurtyigit et al. (2021)]
	DURel (3.0.0) [Schlechtweg et al. (2018)]
	SURel (3.0.0) [Hätty et al. (2019)]
Norwegian	NorDiaChange1, NorDiaChange2 [Kutuzov et al. (2022)]
Russian	RuSemShift_1, RuSemShift_2 [Rodina and Kutuzov (2020)]
	RuShiftEval1, RuShiftEval2, RuShiftEval3 [Kutuzov and Pivovarova (2021)]
	RuDSI [Aksenova et al. (2022)]
Spanish	DWUG_ES (4.0.1) [Schlechtweg et al. (2024)]
Swedish	DWUG_SV (3.0.0), DWUG_SV_resampled (1.0.0) [Schlechtweg et al. (2024)]

Table 1: Overview of Semantic Change Datasets by Language

who demonstrated that disagreements often reflect genuine semantic ambiguity rather than annotator error.

Cross-lingual aspects of semantic annotation have been explored in various contexts. Bender and Friedman (2018) highlighted how linguistic and cultural differences can lead to systematic variations in annotation patterns across languages. This work was extended by Chang et al. (2014), who showed that annotation disagreements often reflect genuine cross-linguistic differences in semantic categorization.

Recent work has increasingly focused on computational approaches to modeling annotator behavior. Uma et al. (2021) demonstrated the effectiveness of learning annotator-specific patterns for improving overall annotation quality. Similarly, Davani et al. (2022) showed how multi-task learning can help capture individual annotator preferences while maintaining consistent predictions.

3 Approaches

The shared task consists of two sub-tasks. For sub-task 1, participants are asked to predict the *median* similarity score of a word in two sentences based on multiple human annotations (between 2 and 7). For sub-task 2, participants are asked to predict the mean disagreement of human annotators given a target word and two example contexts.

3.1 Sub-task 1

We approach sub-task 1 in two different ways: first, we use a simple method that relies on probabilities *between* human judgments. We predict the probability of each judgment given the previous judgment(s). Second, we model annotators using two different architectures: XLM-RoBERTa (Conneau et al., 2020) and XL-Lexeme (Cassotti et al., 2023). XL-Lexeme is a WordEncoder model that has been fine-tuned on Word-in-Context tasks and thus should be an apt choice to model the semantic closeness of target words given two sentences.

3.1.1 Prochain

Our first system, Prochain (probabilistic chain), is a non-parametric probabilistic model. While the human judgments are made independently, our model exploits potential underlying patterns in these independent assessments to create a probabilistic framework for prediction. This approach assumes that even though judges make decisions independently, there exist statistical relationships between different judgment aspects that can be leveraged for prediction.

For training, given a tuple of three judgments (j_1, j_2, j_3), we calculate the frequency distribution of j_2 given j_1, and of j_3 given (j_1, j_2). We then normalize these frequency distributions to obtain probability distributions, as shown in Equations 1 and 2.

$$P(j_2|j_1) = \frac{\text{count}(j_1, j_2)}{\text{count}(j_1)} \quad (1)$$

$$P(j_3|j_1, j_2) = \frac{\text{count}(j_1, j_2, j_3)}{\text{count}(j_1, j_2)} \quad (2)$$

For prediction, given a first judgment j_1, we predict j_2 as a probability distribution based on the normalized frequencies observed during training. Similarly, given (j_1, j_2), we predict j_3 as a probability distribution based on the observed frequencies of j_3 for each combination of (j_1, j_2) in the training data.

Since this method requires the first judgment to be calculated by other means, we use the training data and XL-Lexeme to calculate the cosine similarity between the target word in the two sentences for each item in the training data, then map this continuous value to a discrete value j_0 as shown in Equation 3, then learn mappings between the predicted value j_0 and j_1 in the training data, as we did for j_2 and j_3.

$$j_0 = \begin{cases} 1 & \text{if sim} < 0.4 \\ 2 & \text{if } 0.4 \leq \text{sim} < 0.6 \\ 3 & \text{if } 0.6 \leq \text{sim} < 0.8 \\ 4 & \text{if sim} \geq 0.8 \end{cases} \quad (3)$$

At prediction time, for the prediction of the first judgment, we calculate the cosine similarity between the target word in the two sentences, map this value to a discrete value, then use the Prochain method to predict 11 values, of which we take the most frequently predicted value as j_1.

3.1.2 FARM

Our second system, FARM (Five Adapted Roberta Models), is an XLM-Roberta-base model which is fine-tuned for sentence classification, in the standard way, i.e. a classification head is placed on the special first token, $\langle s \rangle$. To model the disagreement between judgments we create 5 separate "datasets" and train a model on each of these sets. The datasets vary simply in which label we select as the target. If J is the set of judgments for a particular pair of sentences then dataset d_i labels the pair with $j_{imod|J|}$.

For prediction we simply have each of the five models predict their output and then take the median of the 5 predictions.

Each of the Roberta models is trained for 3 epochs using learning rate $2e^{-5}$ and 200 warmup steps. A batch size of 8, a linear learning rate scheduler, the ADAM optimizer, optimized against cross-entropy loss. We use the hugging face trainer interface with any unmentioned arguments left as the default.

3.1.3 THAT

Our third system, THAT (Task-specific Human-like Adaptive Thresholds), is a fine-tuned XL-Lexeme model (Cassotti et al., 2023). The model is trained to embed two sentences such that the cosine similarity between the sentences is inverse proportional to to the label between them, i.e., sentences which are scored as 4 are closer together while sentences which are labeled 1 are further apart. The model is trained to minimize the contrastive loss (Hadsell et al., 2006) as described in in Cassotti et al. (2023).

At prediction time we calculate the cosine similarity between the sentences and we then set three thresholds, t_1, t_2, t_3. We label a sentence pair as 1 if $cosine(s_1, s_2) < t_1$, 2 if its less than t_2, 3 if its less than t_3 and 4 otherwise. We tune the thresholds on the dev-set using the following algorithm.

We begin the thresholds regularly spaced: $t_1 = 0.4, t_2 = 0.6, t_3 = 0.8$ we then vary the thresholds between -0.05, 0, or $+0.05$ from the base threshold. This creates 3^3 different possible threshold combinations. We evaluate each against the dev-set, selecting the threshold which gives the highest score. We then repeat the process until we converge on stable threshold values.

We found that the method converged such that $t_1 = t_2 = t_3$ which means in practice that the best results were gained when we simply predicted 1 or 4.

However, for the purpose of this task we wanted to actually model disagreement between annotators. One way in which annotators may be different is that they have different thresholds for what they think is for example a 3 vs 4. We model this by creating 5 different threshold functions. The thresholds are random perturbations around the optimal threshold. These are not validated directly on the dev set. We then select the median value as the actual label. Given that they all rely on the same underlying similarity function the main benefit of this method is to find examples which are close to the decision boundary and perhaps changing their label from for example 1 to 2.

3.2 Subtask 2

We approach sub-task 2 in two different ways: first, we use feature-engineering to extract features from the sentences and target words. The features were specifically developed for the shared task. We then train regression models on the features, with the target mean disagreement as label. Second, we use the output from our FARM model to calculate disagreement.

Systems 1 and 2 are feature-based systems using a common set of features described in the next section and XGBoost as regressor (Chen and Guestrin,

2016). We performed a hyper-parameter search to fix the best parameters using the dev set. For tagging, we use spacy (Honnibal et al., 2020), and for WordNet features, we use nltk (Bird et al., 2009). For preprocessing, we use pymorphy2 (Korobov, 2015) to lemmatize Russian and jieba[2] to tokenize Chinese. All other languages are transformed to lowercase.

3.2.1 Feature extraction

NLP features We use various NLP features to represent the example contexts. The features are: cosine similarities between context 1 and 2 based on XLM-RoBERTa embeddings of the target token, and between each context (CLS token) and the target word (target token embedding), as well as cosine similarities based on XL-Lexeme, the length of each context, and the length difference in characters between the two contexts, and between each context and the target word, as well as the ratio of lengths between the two contexts, word overlap between the two contexts, fuzzy ratios between the two contexts, and each context and the target word, NER overlap between the two contexts, n-gram overlap ($n = 2$ and $n = 3$) between the two contexts, the position of the target word in each context, whether the target word has the same (1) part-of-speech, (2) NER tag, (3) dependency relation in the two contexts, and WordNet features for supported languages (all except Russian and German): the number of lemmas in the first synset, the depth of the first synset, and the number of hypernyms and hyponyms.

Psycholinguistic features We use concreteness, imageability, familiarity and age-of-acquisition from the MRC database (Wilson, 1988). Since this database only contains data for English, we fine-tuned XLM-RoBERTa models on each of the features for 3 epochs, then use these models to predict the features for all languages.

Prototype features We calculate sense prototypes for each target word using a custom algorithm.[3] The algorithm is an iterative, non-parametric approach to inducing word sense prototypes from contextual representations using the XL-Lexeme transformer model. The core induction process performs multiple iterations (default: 51) where each iteration processes contexts in random order, maintaining a set of induced sense prototypes while comparing new contextualized embeddings with existing prototypes using cosine similarity, either merging similar senses or creating new prototypes based on a similarity threshold. The prototype merging strategy computes pairwise similarities between sense representations, identifies the most similar pairs across different iteration results, and creates aggregate prototypes by averaging the vector representations, using a similarity threshold to control the granularity of sense distinctions. The algorithm builds consensus across iterations by identifying the most frequent number of induced senses (mode), filtering iteration results to retain only those matching the modal number of senses, aligning similar senses across different iterations through similarity-based matching, and creating final sense prototypes by merging aligned sense representations. In the final stage, the algorithm assigns sense labels to the induced prototypes, maps each context back to its most similar prototype, and creates a mapping between context IDs and sense labels. This approach allows for dynamic sense discovery without pre-specifying the number of senses, while maintaining consistency through multiple iterations and consensus building.

After running the algorithm, we assign each word its closest prototype vector. For a target word t and two contexts, we then use the cosine similarity between the prototypes p_1 and p_2, and between each prototype and each target word embedding (t_1 to p_1, t_1 to p_2, t_2 to p_1 and t_2 to p_2).

On length differences Two of the less straightforward features might be differences in context length and between contexts and target words. Let us imagine two contexts for the target word *bark*:

- The bark was rough
- The bark was rough and dark brown, typical of old oak trees in this forest that had weathered many storms

A longer context provides more specific information and constraints about what the target word means (tree bark), while the shorter context leaves more room for ambiguity (it could be dog bark or tree bark). This difference in specificity could lead annotators to have more disagreement with shorter contexts due to lack of disambiguating information, and show more agreement with longer contexts that provide clear contextual clues.

For the difference in length between the words and the contexts, it can be said that a short target word in a long context usually has clear situational grounding, while a longer target phrase in a short

[2]https://github.com/fxsjy/jieba
[3]https://github.com/daalft/senseprototypeinduction

context might lack sufficient contextual support for judgment. This could lead to systematic patterns in annotator disagreement based on these length relationships.

Feature importance Given the large number of features, we use CorrelationAttributeEval from WEKA (Frank et al., 2016) with ten-fold cross-validation to calculate feature importance, and find that all features are important to the task, with the most predictive features being character overlap of trigrams, word overlap between sentences, and familiarity. See Appendix A for the full list of features. Table 9 in the Appendix lists the average merit and rank of each feature.

3.2.2 LAMP

Our first submission, LAMP (Language Agnostic, Monolingual, Prochain), uses a combination of models to produce a result. We train one language-agnostic model on all languages, as well as one model per language. We also include Prochain with an iteration count of 3, based on which we calculate disagreement. We then average all predictions to arrive at the final prediction.

3.2.3 BUMBLE

Our second submission, BUMBLE (Best Universal Model By Language Ensemble), uses a single model to predict the disagreement. We train different models on all possible combinations of languages (single-language models, two languages, ... up to all languages), then select the best model for each language based on its score on the dev set. Results show that the best models are two- or three-language models, but that these models do not always include the language they are predicting.

3.2.4 DRAMA

Our third submission, Disagreement Rating Across Multiple Answers (DRAMA), uses the five judgments generated from FARM and calculates the difference scores from those judgments. I.e. FARM, being 5 different fine-tuned Roberta models output five different judgments J and while FARM calculates the median value over these five judgments, DRAMA calculates the mean difference score as described in the task:

$$D(J) = \frac{1}{|J|} \sum_{(j_1,j_2)\in J} (|j_1 - j_2|) \tag{4}$$

Due to the fact that we use 5 judgments while the actual data uses a varying number of judgments which is usually lower than 5 (e.g. 2 for Chinese) the scores are likely to be higher on average than the true data. However, if the models have successfully modeled the variation in the data, i.e., that more ambiguous utterances have more variance, then the correlation score would still reflect this.

4 Results and Analysis

Tables 2 and 3 summarize our results on the test set for Tasks 1 and 2 respectively. All of our submitted systems demonstrate strengths in specific languages and scenarios, suggesting that different approaches capture different aspects of annotator behavior.

Language	Prochain	FARM	THAT
Chinese	**0.332**	0.177	0.317
German	0.619	0.515	**0.656**
English	0.565	**0.608**	0.555
Norwegian	0.469	0.285	**0.589**
Russian	0.464	0.344	**0.487**
Spanish	0.593	0.582	**0.636**
Swedish	0.556	0.481	**0.648**
Overall	0.514	0.428	**0.555**

Table 2: Results for task 1 according to Krippendorff's α. The best results per language are indicated in bold.

Language	LAMP	DRAMA	BUMBLE
Chinese	0.265	0.498	**0.539**
German	**0.135**	0.123	0.108
English	0.062	**0.097**	0.041
Norwegian	0.269	**0.317**	0.272
Russian	0.110	0.159	**0.167**
Spanish	0.102	0.101	**0.115**
Swedish	0.204	0.233	**0.296**
Overall	0.164	0.218	**0.220**

Table 3: Results for task 2 calculated according to equation 4. The best results per language are indicated in bold.

4.1 Task 1

For predicting median similarity scores, our task-specific model THAT achieved the best overall performance (α = 0.555), followed by Prochain (α = 0.514) and FARM (α = 0.428). Several interesting patterns emerge from these results:

1. The systems consistently performed better on Germanic languages, with particularly strong results for German (THAT: 0.656), Swedish (THAT: 0.648), and English (FARM: 0.608). This pattern holds across all three systems, suggesting that either these languages share helpful structural similarities, or their annotators demonstrate more consistent judgment patterns.
2. Despite its simplicity, Prochain performed surprisingly well, even outperforming FARM overall. This suggests that sequential dependencies between judgments might be more important than previously thought. When provided with correct initial judgments on development data, Prochain achieves remarkably high performance (see Section 5.2), indicating strong predictability in how annotators influence each other's subsequent judgments.
3. All systems struggled most with Chinese data, with the best performance being Prochain's α = 0.332. This might be attributed to several factors:
    - The extremely skewed label distribution (83% label 4)
    - The fundamental differences in how word meanings are constructed in Chinese
    - The smaller number of annotators per item in the Chinese dataset

4.2 Task 2

The disagreement prediction task proved more challenging overall, with markedly different patterns from Task 1: BUMBLE (0.220) and DRAMA (0.218) performed similarly overall but showed distinct strengths across languages. Notably, the best performance was achieved on Chinese (0.539 with BUMBLE) - a striking contrast to Task 1 where Chinese was the most challenging language.

BUMBLE's language combination strategy revealed that optimal performance often came from models trained on two or three languages, but surprisingly, these optimal combinations didn't always include the target language. This suggests the existence of cross-linguistic patterns in annotator disagreement that transcend individual language boundaries.

4.3 Overall

In the context of other participating teams, our systems achieved competitive results: Second place overall in both tasks, *first* place for Chinese, English, and Norwegian in Task 2, and *second* place for Russian, Spanish, and Swedish in both tasks.

These results suggest that our multi-strategy approach, combining probabilistic modeling, neural architectures, and feature engineering, successfully captures different aspects of annotator behavior across languages.

5 Discussion

5.1 Label distribution

Overall, we notice that the data labels are strongly skewed towards label 4, as illustrated in Table 4. For all languages, most of the labels are 4, and on average, label 1 comes second. This might explain why THAT was gravitating towards a binary threshold, i.e., dividing the data into labels 1 and 4.

	1	2	3	4
Overall	0.150	0.094	0.130	0.630
Chinese	0.009	0.043	0.120	0.830
German	0.130	0.210	0.170	0.500
Russian	0.230	0.032	0.170	0.650
Norwegian	0.140	0.032	0.088	0.770
Spanish	0.210	0.088	0.210	0.500
English	0.230	0.170	0.140	0.460
Swedish	0.200	0.089	0.090	0.620

Table 4: Label distribution for median judgments task 1. Percentage of samples given a particular label in the train-set.

5.2 Prochain

The Prochain method is surprisingly strong in subtask 1, despite its simplicity, *if* the first judgment is given and correct. This is confirmed by the results on the development data for subtask 1: when taking the first judgment from the development data label file, and predicting a second and third judgment using PROCHAIN, then calculating the median value, we reach results of 0.938 on average,as illustrated in Table 5.

5.3 THAT – DRAMA

Table 6 shows the results of DRAMA and THAT2 (calculating disagreement on the output of THAT; we did not submit THAT2 run) on the dev data of the second task. The NaN numbers for Chinese come from the fact that in the dev-set there is no disagreement which means that the Spearman rank

Language	Krippendorff's α
Average	0.938
Chinese	1.000
English	0.950
German	0.902
Norwegian	0.948
Russian	0.862
Spanish	0.962
Swedish	0.939

Table 5: Results of Prochain if the first judgment is taken from the gold labels

cannot calculate a difference. A surprising fact is how poorly XL-Lexeme with 5 different thresholds performs. It was our best model in the first subtask, however, it seems that the thresholding technique does not align with the difference observed in the human judges. This would suggest that the judges do not have an equivalent difference space to XL-Lexeme in their heads but different thresholds for judging something a 2 or a 3. Our choice of thresholds may also have been suboptimal.

	DRAMA	THAT2
German	0.158	0.049
Russian	0.028	0.043
Swedish	0.125	0.083
Spanish	0.014	-0.051
English	0.084	0.051
Chinese	NAN	NAN
Norwegian	0.275	0.0551
All	0.114	0.0383

Table 6: Results for DRAMA and THAT2 on the dev set

5.4 The lack of disagreement in Chinese data

We noticed that in the Chinese data for task 1, no disagreement was found between annotators. In addition, only two annotations were present. While puzzling at first, this may well be due to differences in annotation procedure. It is conceivable that annotations were consolidated to resolve disagreements before the data was released. However, the data paper states that they follow the same guidelines as other data sets (Chen et al., 2023).

5.5 The case of English

An unexpected finding in our results is the particularly challenging nature of English data for disagreement prediction, despite the language's extensive resources and representation in training data. While English achieves moderate performance in median prediction (Task 1) with $\alpha = 0.565$, it shows strikingly low correlation scores in disagreement prediction (Task 2), with even our best system DRAMA achieving only 0.097. Several factors may contribute to this counterintuitive result. First, the English dataset demonstrates more balanced label distribution (46% label 4 compared to the overall average of 63%), suggesting annotators may be making more nuanced distinctions rather than defaulting to high similarity judgments. Second, English's rich polysemy and extensive metaphorical usage may lead to more genuine cases of ambiguity, making annotator disagreement patterns less systematic and therefore harder to predict. This hypothesis is supported by the fact that even our more sophisticated neural approaches failed to capture these patterns effectively.

6 Conclusion

The GRASP team's participation in the CoMeDi shared task has led to several important insights into modeling annotator disagreement across multiple languages. Our diverse approach, implementing both probabilistic and neural methods, proved effective across both subtasks, securing second place overall.

The strong performance of our simple Prochain model highlights the value of probabilistic approaches in capturing annotator behavior, while the varying success of our more complex models across languages suggests that language-specific factors play a crucial role in disagreement prediction.

The skewed label distribution toward label 4 significantly influenced model behavior, particularly affecting our threshold-based approaches. Future work could focus on better handling this class imbalance and developing more robust cross-lingual disagreement modeling techniques.

Acknowledgements

The authors would like to thank Pierluigi Cassotti for sharing the code to fine-tune XL-Lexeme. This work has in part been funded by the research program Change is Key! supported by Riksbankens Jubileumsfond (under reference number M21-0021).

References

Anna Aksenova, Ekaterina Gavrishina, Elisei Rykov, and Andrey Kutuzov. 2022. RuDSI: Graph-based word sense induction dataset for Russian. In *Proceedings of TextGraphs-16: Graph-based Methods for Natural Language Processing*, pages 77–88, Gyeongju, Republic of Korea. Association for Computational Linguistics.

Ron Artstein and Massimo Poesio. 2008. Inter-coder agreement for computational linguistics. *Computational linguistics*, 34(4):555–596.

Emily M Bender and Batya Friedman. 2018. Data statements for natural language processing: Toward mitigating system bias and enabling better science. *Transactions of the Association for Computational Linguistics*, 6:587–604.

Steven Bird, Ewan Klein, and Edward Loper. 2009. *Natural language processing with Python: analyzing text with the natural language toolkit.* " O'Reilly Media, Inc.".

Pierluigi Cassotti, Lucia Siciliani, Marco DeGemmis, Giovanni Semeraro, and Pierpaolo Basile. 2023. XL-LEXEME: WiC pretrained model for cross-lingual LEXical sEMantic changE. In *Proceedings of the 61st Annual Meeting of the Association for Computational Linguistics (Volume 2: Short Papers)*, pages 1577–1585, Toronto, Canada. Association for Computational Linguistics.

Angel Chang, Manolis Savva, and Christopher D Manning. 2014. Learning spatial knowledge for text to 3D scene generation. In *Proceedings of the 2014 conference on empirical methods in natural language processing (EMNLP)*, pages 2028–2038.

Jing Chen, Emmanuele Chersoni, Dominik Schlechtweg, Jelena Prokic, and Chu-Ren Huang. 2023. ChiWUG: A graph-based evaluation dataset for Chinese lexical semantic change detection. In *Proceedings of the 4th International Workshop on Computational Approaches to Historical Language Change*, Singapore. Association for Computational Linguistics.

Tianqi Chen and Carlos Guestrin. 2016. XGBoost: A Scalable Tree Boosting System. In *Proceedings of the 22nd ACM SIGKDD International Conference on Knowledge Discovery and Data Mining*, KDD '16, pages 785–794, New York, NY, USA. ACM.

Alexis Conneau, Kartikay Khandelwal, Naman Goyal, Vishrav Chaudhary, Guillaume Wenzek, Francisco Guzmán, Edouard Grave, Myle Ott, Luke Zettlemoyer, and Veselin Stoyanov. 2020. Unsupervised Cross-lingual Representation Learning at Scale. *Preprint*, arXiv:1911.02116.

Aida Mostafazadeh Davani, Mark Díaz, and Vinodkumar Prabhakaran. 2022. Dealing with disagreements: Looking beyond the majority vote in subjective annotations. *Transactions of the Association for Computational Linguistics*, 10:92–110.

Katrin Erk, Diana McCarthy, and Nicholas Gaylord. 2013. Measuring word meaning in context. *Computational Linguistics*, 39(3):511–554.

Eibe Frank, Mark A Hall, and Ian H Witten. 2016. *The WEKA workbench.* Morgan Kaufmann.

Raia Hadsell, Sumit Chopra, and Yann LeCun. 2006. Dimensionality reduction by learning an invariant mapping. *2006 IEEE Computer Society Conference on Computer Vision and Pattern Recognition (CVPR'06)*, 2:1735–1742.

Anna Hätty, Dominik Schlechtweg, and Sabine Schulte im Walde. 2019. SURel: A gold standard for incorporating meaning shifts into term extraction. In *Proceedings of the 8th Joint Conference on Lexical and Computational Semantics*, pages 1–8, Minneapolis, MN, USA.

Matthew Honnibal, Ines Montani, Sofie Van Landeghem, Adriane Boyd, et al. 2020. spaCy: Industrial-strength Natural Language Processing in Python.

David Jurgens. 2014. An analysis of ambiguity in word sense annotations. In *Proceedings of the Ninth International Conference on Language Resources and Evaluation (LREC'14)*, pages 3006–3012.

Mikhail Korobov. 2015. Morphological analyzer and generator for russian and ukrainian languages. In Mikhail Yu. Khachay, Natalia Konstantinova, Alexander Panchenko, Dmitry I. Ignatov, and Valeri G. Labunets, editors, *Analysis of Images, Social Networks and Texts*, volume 542 of *Communications in Computer and Information Science*, pages 320–332. Springer International Publishing.

Sinan Kurtyigit, Maike Park, Dominik Schlechtweg, Jonas Kuhn, and Sabine Schulte im Walde. 2021. Lexical Semantic Change Discovery. In *Proceedings of the 59th Annual Meeting of the Association for Computational Linguistics and the 11th International Joint Conference on Natural Language Processing (Volume 1: Long Papers)*, Online. Association for Computational Linguistics.

Andrey Kutuzov and Lidia Pivovarova. 2021. Rushifteval: a shared task on semantic shift detection for russian. *Komp'yuternaya Lingvistika i Intellektual'nye Tekhnologii: Dialog conference.*

Andrey Kutuzov, Samia Touileb, Petter Mæhlum, Tita Enstad, and Alexandra Wittemann. 2022. NorDiaChange: Diachronic semantic change dataset for Norwegian. In *Proceedings of the Thirteenth Language Resources and Evaluation Conference*, pages 2563–2572, Marseille, France. European Language Resources Association.

Elisa Leonardelli, Gavin Abercrombie, Dina Almanea, Valerio Basile, Tommaso Fornaciari, Barbara Plank, Verena Rieser, Alexandra Uma, and Massimo Poesio. 2023. SemEval-2023 task 11: Learning with disagreements (LeWiDi). In *Proceedings of the 17th International Workshop on Semantic Evaluation (SemEval-2023)*, pages 2304–2318, Toronto, Canada. Association for Computational Linguistics.

Rebecca J Passonneau. 2004. Computing reliability for coreference annotation. In *4th International Conference on Language Resources and Evaluation, LREC 2004*, pages 1503–1506. European Language Resources Association (ELRA).

Ellie Pavlick and Tom Kwiatkowski. 2019. Inherent disagreements in human textual inferences. *Transactions of the Association for Computational Linguistics*, 7:677–694.

Barbara Plank, Dirk Hovy, and Anders Søgaard. 2014. Learning part-of-speech taggers with inter-annotator agreement loss. In *Proceedings of the 14th Conference of the European Chapter of the Association for Computational Linguistics*. Association for Computational Linguistics.

Julia Rodina and Andrey Kutuzov. 2020. RuSemShift: a dataset of historical lexical semantic change in Russian. In *Proceedings of the 28th International Conference on Computational Linguistics*, pages 1037–1047, Barcelona, Spain (Online). International Committee on Computational Linguistics.

Dominik Schlechtweg, Pierluigi Cassotti, Bill Noble, David Alfter, Sabine Schulte im Walde, and Nina Tahmasebi. 2024. More DWUGs: Extending and evaluating word usage graph datasets in multiple languages. In *Proceedings of the 2024 Conference on Empirical Methods in Natural Language Processing*, Miami, Florida. Association for Computational Linguistics.

Dominik Schlechtweg, Sabine Schulte im Walde, and Stefanie Eckmann. 2018. Diachronic Usage Relatedness (DURel): A framework for the annotation of lexical semantic change. In *Proceedings of the 2018 Conference of the North American Chapter of the Association for Computational Linguistics: Human Language Technologies*, pages 169–174, New Orleans, Louisiana.

Alexandra N Uma, Tommaso Fornaciari, Dirk Hovy, Silviu Paun, Barbara Plank, and Massimo Poesio. 2021. Learning from disagreement: A survey. *Journal of Artificial Intelligence Research*, 72:1385–1470.

Michael Wilson. 1988. MRC psycholinguistic database: Machine-usable dictionary, version 2.00. *Behavior research methods, instruments, & computers*, 20(1):6–10.

A Feature list

Feature Name	Description
cosine_sim_sent1_sent2	BERT embedding cosine similarity between the two sentences
cosine_sim_sent1_target	BERT embedding cosine similarity between first sentence and target word
cosine_sim_sent2_target	BERT embedding cosine similarity between second sentence and target word
len_diff_sent1_sent2	Absolute character length difference between sentences
len_ratio_sent1_sent2	Ratio of first sentence length to second sentence length
len_diff_sent1_target	Character length difference between first sentence and target
len_diff_sent2_target	Character length difference between second sentence and target
word_overlap_sent1_sent2	Jaccard similarity of word sets between sentences
word_overlap_sent1_target	Jaccard similarity between first sentence words and target word
word_overlap_sent2_target	Jaccard similarity between second sentence words and target word
fuzz_ratio_sent1_sent2	Levenshtein ratio between the two sentences
fuzz_ratio_sent1_target	Levenshtein ratio between first sentence and target
fuzz_ratio_sent2_target	Levenshtein ratio between second sentence and target
ner_count_sent1	Number of named entities in first sentence
ner_count_sent2	Number of named entities in second sentence
ner_overlap	Number of shared named entities between sentences
char_ngram_overlap_2	Overlap of character bigrams between sentences
char_ngram_overlap_3	Overlap of character trigrams between sentences
target_position_sent1	Relative position of target word in first sentence
target_position_sent2	Relative position of target word in second sentence
sent1_length	Word count of first sentence
sent2_length	Word count of second sentence
length_diff	Absolute difference in sentence word counts
word_overlap	Jaccard similarity of lowercased words
same_pos	Binary indicator if target words have same POS tag
same_ner	Binary indicator if target words have same NER tag
same_dep	Binary indicator if target words have same dependency relation
corpus_frequency	Brown corpus frequency (English only)
avg_word_vec_similarity	Cosine similarity of averaged spaCy word vectors
num_synsets	Number of WordNet synsets for target word
num_lemmas	Number of lemmas in target word's synsets
first_synset_depth	Depth of first synset in WordNet hierarchy
num_hypernyms	Number of hypernyms for first synset
num_hyponyms	Number of hyponyms for first synset
xl_similarity	XL-Lexeme embedding cosine similarity between the two sentences

Table 7: Features Extracted for Disagreement Prediction (NLP features)

Feature Name	Description
conc	Concreteness
imag	Imageability
fam	Familiarity
aoa	Age-of-acquisition
proto_sim	Cosine similarity between the prototypes (p1, p2) of the target word in both sentences
proto_sim_sent1	Cosine similarity between the target word embedding in sentence 1 (t1) and its prototype (p1)
proto_sim_sent2	Cosine similarity between the target word embedding in sentence 2 (t2) and its prototype (p2)
cross_proto_sim1	Cross-prototype similarity: target word embedding from sentence 1 (t1) to prototype from sentence 2 (p2)
cross_proto_sim2	Cross-prototype similarity: target word embedding from sentence 2 (t2) to prototype from sentence 1 (p1)

Table 8: Features Extracted for Disagreement Prediction (Psycholinguistic and prototype features)

Average Merit	Average Rank	Attribute
0.119 ± 0.003	1.0 ± 0.00	char_ngram_overlap_3
0.107 ± 0.003	2.0 ± 0.00	word_overlap_sent1_sent2
0.093 ± 0.003	3.3 ± 0.46	char_ngram_overlap_2
0.089 ± 0.003	3.8 ± 0.60	len_diff_sent1_target
0.085 ± 0.002	4.9 ± 0.30	len_diff_sent2_target
0.079 ± 0.002	6.0 ± 0.00	same_pos
0.067 ± 0.002	8.1 ± 0.94	num_lemmas
0.067 ± 0.002	8.1 ± 0.94	num_synsets
0.066 ± 0.002	8.5 ± 1.12	word_overlap
0.064 ± 0.002	9.3 ± 1.00	sent2_length
0.054 ± 0.003	11.0 ± 0.00	sent1_length
0.044 ± 0.002	12.0 ± 0.00	len_diff_sent1_sent2
0.035 ± 0.002	13.1 ± 0.30	same_ner
0.032 ± 0.004	14.1 ± 0.70	word_overlap_sent2_target
0.026 ± 0.002	15.7 ± 0.64	cosine_sim_sent1_sent2
0.027 ± 0.002	16.0 ± 1.48	conc
0.024 ± 0.003	16.8 ± 1.17	avg_word_vec_similarity
0.022 ± 0.003	17.7 ± 0.90	x1_p1
0.018 ± 0.004	19.7 ± 1.42	aoa
0.018 ± 0.001	19.9 ± 0.83	corpus_frequency
0.016 ± 0.003	21.1 ± 1.45	x1_p2
0.015 ± 0.002	21.9 ± 1.04	length_diff
0.014 ± 0.002	22.2 ± 1.40	word_overlap_sent1_target
0.010 ± 0.002	24.4 ± 1.20	same_dep
0.010 ± 0.002	25.0 ± 0.63	cosine_sim_sent2_target
0.007 ± 0.003	26.1 ± 0.94	imag
0.004 ± 0.004	27.6 ± 1.96	fuzz_ratio_sent1_sent2
0.003 ± 0.002	27.8 ± 1.08	len_ratio_sent1_sent2
0.001 ± 0.003	29.2 ± 1.25	x2_p2
-0.002 ± 0.002	30.9 ± 1.37	cosine_sim_sent1_target
-0.004 ± 0.003	31.6 ± 1.28	p1_p2
-0.008 ± 0.003	33.8 ± 0.98	x2_p1
-0.008 ± 0.002	34.1 ± 0.94	xl_sim
-0.010 ± 0.004	34.6 ± 1.56	fuzz_ratio_sent2_target
-0.012 ± 0.002	35.5 ± 1.02	fuzz_ratio_sent1_target
-0.017 ± 0.003	37.5 ± 1.12	target_position_sent1
-0.018 ± 0.003	38.0 ± 0.77	target_position_sent2
-0.019 ± 0.003	38.2 ± 0.98	first_synset_depth
-0.051 ± 0.005	40.4 ± 0.49	num_hyponyms
-0.051 ± 0.002	40.6 ± 0.49	num_hypernyms
-0.101 ± 0.003	42.0 ± 0.00	fam

Table 9: Feature ranking by average merit (correlation with target variable). Positive values indicate features positively correlated with annotator agreement, while negative values indicate features correlated with disagreement.

Funzac at CoMeDi Shared Task: Modeling Annotator Disagreement from Word-In-Context Perspectives

Olufunke O. Sarumi[1], Charles Welch[2], Lucie Flek[3], Jörg Schlötterer[1,4]
[1]University of Marburg, [2]McMaster University, [3]University of Bonn, [4]University of Mannheim
{sarumio,joerg.schloetterer}@uni-marburg.de[1], cwelch@mcmaster.ca[2], flek@bit.uni-bonn.de[3]

Abstract

In this work, we evaluate annotator disagreement in Word-in-Context (WiC) tasks exploring the relationship between contextual meaning and disagreement as part of the CoMeDi shared task competition. While prior studies have modeled disagreement by analyzing annotator attributes with single-sentence inputs, this shared task incorporates WiC to bridge the gap between sentence-level semantic representation and annotator judgment variability. We describe three different methods that we developed for the shared task, including a feature enrichment approach that combines concatenation, element-wise differences, products, and cosine similarity, Euclidean and Manhattan distances to extend contextual embedding representations, a transformation by Adapter blocks to obtain task-specific representations of contextual embeddings, and classifiers of varying complexities, including ensembles. The comparison of our methods demonstrates improved performance for methods that include enriched and task-specfic features. While the performance of our method falls short in comparison to the best system in subtask 1 (OGWiC), it is competitive to the official evaluation results in subtask 2 (DisWiC).

1 Introduction

Disagreement in annotation tasks has been widely studied, with various methods proposed to address it (Leonardelli et al., 2023). One of the most common approaches is majority voting (Nguyen et al., 2017), where the most frequently chosen annotation is treated as the correct label. Recent research explores alternatives to this traditional majority voting paradigm, modeling individual annotators and their labels to predict perspectives, aiming to account for individual differences in judgment (Plepi et al., 2022; Mostafazadeh Davani et al., 2022; Oluyemi et al., 2024) and exploring the use of demographic information to cluster annotators, using these clusters to model disagreement (Deng et al., 2023). However, fewer authors considered the role of contextual information in pairwise sentences, which can shed light on the root causes of disagreement (Pilehvar and Camacho-Collados, 2019; Armendariz et al., 2020). Understanding these causes may reveal ambiguities in data and help to gain insights into why annotators diverge in their judgments.

While not explicitly posed as such, we view the CoMeDi shared task (Schlechtweg et al., 2025) in light of these recent trends, offering potential avenues for a better understanding of contextual ambiguities and their consequences on annotator disagreement. This shared task involves modeling disagreement in word sense annotation for the Word-in-Context (WiC) task, where annotators provide judgments on the relatedness of two word uses in a sentence pair, rated on an ordinal scale from 1 (homonymy) to 4 (identity). It includes two subtasks: Median Judgment Classification, which predicts the median of annotator ratings as an ordinal classification task evaluated with Krippendorff's α, and Mean Disagreement Ranking, which quantifies the magnitude of disagreement between annotators by ranking instances based on pairwise absolute differences evaluated with Spearman's ρ. From the methods we developed, the inclusion of task-specific representations obtained by transformations of contextual embeddings via Adapter blocks outperformed our other methods in predicting the median in the OGWiC task, In the DisWiC task, the best performance among our approaches alternated between this method and an ensemble of XGBoost and CatBoost on enriched feature combinations of contextual embeddings.

We made submissions to the shared task at the post evaluation phase and make our implementation publicly available.[1]

[1]https://github.com/funzac/comedi

Proceedings of Context and Meaning: Navigating Disagreements in NLP Annotation, pages 90–96
January 19, 2025.

2 Shared Task

The shared task is subdivided into two subtasks, Median Judgment Classification with Ordinal Word-in-Context Judgments (OGWiC) and Mean Disagreement Ranking with Ordinal Word-in-Context Judgments (DisWiC). In both tasks, a training instance consists of (i) a pair of two contexts (each context is a sentence or paragraph), (ii) a target word (lemma) that appears in both contexts, (iii) ordinal ratings by multiple annotators of how related the meanings of the lemma are in the two contexts on a scale from 1 (completely unrelated) to 4 (identical). Each instance contains additional information on the language of contexts, lemmas, and indices of the target word. The two tasks differ in their prediction targets:

OGWiC Predict the median rating. Predictions are evaluated by the ordinal version of Krippendorf's α against the ground truth median ratings.

DisWiC Predict the mean disagreement, i.e., the mean of average pairwise differences in relatedness ratings and rank by magnitude of disagreement. Predictions are evaluated by Spearman's ρ against ground truth disagreement ranking.

3 System Description

Following the setup of the baseline method provided by the task organizers, our system builds upon contextual embeddings of the lemma in both contexts, obtained from the XLM-RoBERTa (XLM-R[2]) transformer model (Conneau et al., 2020). We investigated three methods (XLM-R, XLMR + Ensemble, XLM-R + Adapter), featuring different classifiers in the ordinal classification task OGWiC and different regressors in the DisWiC task. We additionally enriched the input to XLMR + Ensemble and XLM-R + Adapter by pairwise comparisons of the contextual embeddings, such as element-wise difference. The XLM-R + Adapter method further includes the transformation of the contextual embeddings in the input to a task-specific representation.

3.1 CoMeDi Baselines

The baseline methods provided by the task organizers start from contextual embeddings e_1 and e_2 of the lemma in context 1 and context 2 respectively. These contextual embeddings are obtained from a pre-trained XLM-RoBERTa model. Specifically, e_1 and e_2 are the mean of the last hidden states of the hidden states corresponding to the subword tokens of the lemma in each respective context.

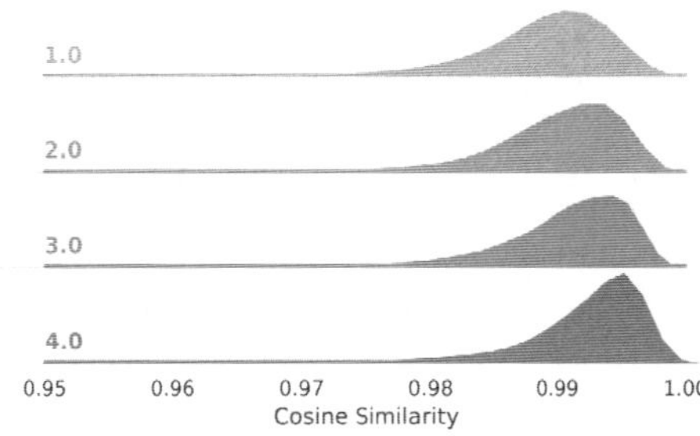

Figure 1: Densities of cosine similarity (x-axis) of context embeddings e_1 and e_2 vs median similarity rating (y-axis). Note that the x-axis does not start at 0.

In the DisWiC task, the contextual embeddings are concatenated to obtain an input representation $f = [e_1|e_2]$ (where | denotes concatenation) for a Linear Regression model. The dependent variable in the linear regression is the average disagreement of annotators.

In the OGWiC task, the organizers first calculate the cosine similarity between e_1 and e_2 and place them into four bins, corresponding to the median judgement values. The bin boundaries are directly optimized with respect to the target measure of the task, Krippendorf's α.

3.2 XLM-R

Our XLM-R method uses the concatenation of contextual embeddings $f = [e_1|e_2]$ as input in both, the OGWiC classification and the DisWiC regression task.

Analyzing the cosine similarities between pairs of contextual embeddings (e_1 and e_2) in the OGWiC task, we discovered that these are hardly separable into distinct bins (see Figure 1). Therefore, we decided to cast the task as multi-class classification, aiming to predict the median similarity judgement per instance. On the concatenation of contextual embeddings $f = [e_1|e_2]$, we train a simple linear classification head with dropout.

This method for the DisWiC task is almost identical to the baseline, only adding dropout to the linear regression head.

[2]https://huggingface.co/FacebookAI/xlm-roberta-base

3.3 Feature Enrichment

Inspired by Reimers and Gurevych (2019), we enrich the original input $f = [e_1|e_2]$, i.e., the concatenation of contextual embeddings, by pairwise comparisons and similarity measures of the two embeddings. Specifically, we extend f to $f_e = [e_1|e_2|e_1 - e_2|e_1 * e_2|C|E|M]$ where "$-$" and "$*$" indicate element-wise difference and multiplication, and C, E, and M indicate cosine similarity, Euclidean and Manhattan distance. We use this extended feature representation f_e as input in both, XLM-R + Adapter and XLM-R + ensemble for both tasks (OGWiC and DisWiC).

3.4 XLM-R + Adapter

In this method, we first transform the original contextual embeddings $e1$ and e_2 in the input $f_e = [e_1|e_2|e_1 - e_2|e_1 * e_2|C|E|M]$ (cf. section 3.3) to task-specific representations e'_1 and e'_2, followed by a classification/regression network on the adapted representations $f_a = [e'_1|e'_2|e_1|e_2|e_1 - e_2|e_1 * e_2|C|E|M]$. For the transformation, we use the architecture of adapter blocks (Houlsby et al., 2019), which is a bottleneck architecture with down-projection, GELU activation, dropout for regularization, up-projection, and a residual connection. We use a separate adapter block for each transformation $e_1 \rightarrow e'_1$ and $e_2 \rightarrow e'_2$.

The classification/regression network consists of two hidden layers of size 512 and 256 with GELU activation, each preceded by layer normalization and followed by dropout, and a final linear classification (OGWiC) or regression (DisWic) head.

The adapter blocks are jointly trained with the classification/regression network, turning the contextual embeddings into a task-specific representation: While the contextual embeddings are obtained from a frozen XLM-RoBERTa model optimized for language modeling, their transformation is optimized for the classification/regression task.

3.5 XLM-R + Ensemble

We train the two ensemble methods, CatBoost (Prokhorenkova et al., 2018) and XGBoost (Chen and Guestrin, 2016), independently on the enriched input $f_e = [e_1|e_2|e_1 - e_2|e_1 * e_2|C|E|M]$ (cf. section 3.3). We then combine their predictions, effectively forming an ensemble of ensembles. In the OGWiC task, we weigh the predictions of the CatBoost and XGBoost classifiers with 0.4 and 0.3 in the combined prediction (linear combination). In the DisWiC task we weigh the CatBoost and XGBoost regressors with 0.4 and 0.6 (weighted average).

3.6 Hyper-parameters

We train all our networks (including adapter blocks) for 10 epochs with a learing rate of 1e-4, AdamW optimizer, batch size of 32 and dropout rate of 0.2.

We train both ensemble models (XGBoost and CatBoost) with a learning rate of 0.05, a maximum depth of 6, and 500 iterations/estimators. Additionally, we set the column sub-sampling rate in XGBoost to 0.8.

We keep all other hyper-parameters at the default values provided by their respective libraries.

4 Dataset

Separate datasets were provided for OGWiC and DisWiC task. However, the uses of a word, i.e., a lemma in one particular context are identical for both tasks. That is, both tasks have the same set of available contexts and lemmas. Yet, the instances per task differ in the extent that they make use of the combinatorial options to combine different contexts for the same lemma and do not necessarily make use of all combinatorial options (probably due to the unavailability of ratings). From what we observed, instances in the OGWiC task are a subset of the instances in DisWiC, discarding instances where no meaningful median of the ratings can be obtained. For both tasks (OGWiC and DisWiC), the datasets were divided into pre-defined train, dev and test splits. The OGWiC task data includes 47.8K training, 8.3K dev and 15.3K test instances in different languages from prior work, specifically Chinese (Chen et al., 2023), German (Schlechtweg et al., 2024), Russian (Kutuzov and Pivovarova, 2021; Aksenova et al., 2022), English (Schlechtweg et al., 2018), Swedish (Schlechtweg et al., 2024), Spanish (Zamora-Reina et al., 2022), and Norwegian (Kutuzov et al., 2022). The DisWiC task data includes 82.2K training, 13.1K dev and 26.7K test instances from the same languages. Table 1 details the training set statistics per language.

5 Results

In Table 2, we compare our three models (XLM-R, XML-R + Adapter, XML-R + Ensemble) to each other, to the baselines provided by the task organizers, and to the best performing submission in the

	AVG	ZH	DE	EN	NO	RU	ES	SV
Available Set of Contexts and Lemmas								
Unique Contexts	7,844	1,119	12,141	6,565	1,222	24,848	2,757	6,256
Unique lemmas	74	28	117	31	56	189	70	30
Context length	218	58	3,369	1,167	352	4,278	1,410	1,397
OGWiC								
Instances	6,833	10,833	8,279	5,910	4,504	8,029	4,821	5,457
DisWiC								
Instances	11,740	20,461	13,690	10,831	6,041	12,698	9,339	9,117

Table 1: Training set statistics of both tasks (OGWiC and DisWiC) per language (ISO codes in column headings) and on average (AVG, rounded to the nearest integer). The set of *available* contexts and lemmas is identical in both tasks (top part), but the use of possible combinations differs in the two tasks, yielding varying amounts of training instances across tasks (bottom part). Unique contexts is the amount of unique contexts, unique lemmas the amount of unique words in consideration and context length is the average number of words per context (rounded to the nearest integer).

	AVG	ZH	DE	EN	NO	RU	ES	SV
OGWiC (Krippendorff's α)								
Baseline	0.123	0.059	0.274	0.102	0.124	0.112	0.175	0.018
XLM-R	0.174	0.068	0.185	0.280	0.025	0.192	0.375	0.091
XLM-R + Adapter	**0.340**	**0.187**	**0.396**	**0.394**	**0.283**	**0.341**	**0.435**	**0.347**
XLM-R + Ensemble	0.242	-0.052	0.199	0.347	0.217	0.316	0.330	0.337
Top Submission	0.656	0.424	0.723	0.723	0.668	0.623	0.748	0.675
DisWiC (Spearman's ρ)								
Baseline	0.118	0.387	0.093	0.064	0.076	0.049	0.077	0.081
XLM-R	0.083	0.398	0.067	0.016	-0.118	0.045	0.052	0.119
XLM-R + Adapter	0.146	0.402	0.127	**0.092**	0.113	**0.091**	**0.103**	0.097
XLM-R + Ensemble	**0.170**	**0.433**	**0.167**	0.056	**0.178**	0.076	0.088	**0.194**
Top Submission	0.226	0.301	0.204	0.078	0.286	0.175	0.187	0.350

Table 2: Results on the test sets of both subtasks (OGWiC and DisWiC, evaluation metric in parentheses) per language (ISO codes in column headings) and on average (AVG). We compare our methods against the baselines provided by the task organizers (cf. section 3.1 and the best performing system (Deep Change) at the time of evaluation of the competition (indicated by "Top Submission" in the table). Best scores of our methods in **bold** and best overall underlined.

shared task. Since the shared task is still open for participation, post-evaluation results are subject to change. Therefore, we compare against the official evaluation results from within the competition and report corresponding scores for the best submission. By average scores, our XLM-R + Adapter method would have ranked 5th in the OGWiC task and the XLM-R + Ensemble method 3rd in DisWiC.

In the OGWiC task, XLM-R + Adapter consistently performs best across all languages among our methods, but falls short in comparison to the best submission. On average, also the simple XLM-R method performs better than the baseline.

In the DisWiC task, best performance among our models varies between XLM-R + Adapter and XLM-R + Ensemble. While XLM-R + Ensemble outperforms the best submission on Chinese language and XLM-R + Adapter performs better than the best submission on English, scores of the best submission are highest on the remaining five languages and on average. In comparison to the Linear Regression baseline as provided by the organizers, the addition of dropout in XLM-R seems to be harmful rather than helpful.

6 Discussion

Expectably, our methods with enriched features and more complex classifiers/regressor (XLM-R + Adapter and XLM-R) outperform our baseline of a simple classification/regression head directly on top of the concatenation of contextual embeddings (XLM-R). This behavior is consistent across languages, except for Chinese, where the XLM-R + Ensemble performs worst among all methods (including the CoMeDi baseline) in the OGWiC task. Generally, the subset of Chinese instances reveals interesting patterns. Despite that Chinese has the highest number of training instances in both tasks, performance is almost opposite between the two tasks: Chinese has the lowest score among almost all methods in OGWiC (and in particular the lowest score in the best submission), whereas it has the highest score among almost all methods in DisWiC (second-highest in best submission). We hypothesize that this gap may be rooted in the set of available contexts, which is smallest for Chinese, despite Chinese having the highest amount of training instances in both tasks. That means, several contexts must appear in multiple instance whereas for example the Russian instances could be constructed almost exclusively from unique contexts (each instance is a pair of two contexts, i.e., 12698*2 = 25396 unique contexts would be required for every context to appear only once, whereas 24848 unique contexts are available). Since our methods build on contextual embeddings, for contexts that appear a lot of times, they might learn to rely on patterns in the corresponding contextual embeddings that are determined by context only and try to use these as shortcuts. This behavior might work in DisWiC, if the disagreement of annotators is governed by context rather than the lemma, but fail in the prediction of the relatedness of the actual lemma. However, that is only one potential explanation, while other components in the pipeline of our methods or differences in the task/data configuration may offer equally valid explanations. We also do not know details about the best performing submission and hence cannot judge whether that explanation would hold for it.

In the initial submission, we related the performance of individual methods to properties of the data for different languages, such as duplicated contexts. However, we noticed a mistake in the definition/calculation of duplicated contexts and that these conclusions were drawn erroneously. Therefore, we dropped this part of the discussion in the final submission.

7 Conclusion

In this shared task paper, we introduced multiple methods that incorporate extensions of contextual embeddings by pairwise comparison, such as element-wise difference and similarity measures, and additonal transformations of these embeddings by Adapter blocks to task-specific representations. We use the contextual embeddings (and their extensions) with classifiers and regressors of varying complexity.

While the performance of our methods falls short in comparison to the best submission in the OGWiC task, it is competitive in terms of official evaluation results in the DisWiC task.

We are curiously looking forward to the descriptions of the other systems and plan to investigate potential options to combine approaches and ideas to advance future research on disagreement modeling in multilingual and multi-contextual settings.

Limitations

This study focuses exclusively on WiC tasks involving seven specific languages, leaving the generalization of the models to other languages outside the scope of this shared task uncertain. Additionally, our approach is limited to the methods described in this work. Future research could explore the performance of these models across a wider range of languages and investigate the impact of alternative fine-tuning strategies on their overall effectiveness.

Acknowledgments

Part of the research that led to this submission has been supported with funding by Hessian.AI. Any opinions, findings, conclusions, or recommendations in this material are those of the authors and do not necessarily reflect the views of Hessian.AI.

References

Anna Aksenova, Ekaterina Gavrishina, Elisei Rykov, and Andrey Kutuzov. 2022. RuDSI: Graph-based word sense induction dataset for Russian. In *Proceedings of TextGraphs-16: Graph-based Methods for Natural Language Processing*, pages 77–88, Gyeongju, Republic of Korea. Association for Computational Linguistics.

Carlos Santos Armendariz, Matthew Purver, Senja Pollak, Nikola Ljubešić, Matej Ulčar, Ivan Vulić, and Mohammad Taher Pilehvar. 2020. SemEval-2020 task 3: Graded word similarity in context. In *Proceedings of the Fourteenth Workshop on Semantic Evaluation*, pages 36–49, Barcelona (online). International Committee for Computational Linguistics.

Jing Chen, Emmanuele Chersoni, Dominik Schlechtweg, Jelena Prokic, and Chu-Ren Huang. 2023. ChiWUG: A graph-based evaluation dataset for Chinese lexical semantic change detection. In *Proceedings of the 4th Workshop on Computational*

Approaches to Historical Language Change, pages 93–99, Singapore. Association for Computational Linguistics.

Tianqi Chen and Carlos Guestrin. 2016. Xgboost: A scalable tree boosting system. In *Proceedings of the 22nd ACM SIGKDD International Conference on Knowledge Discovery and Data Mining, San Francisco, CA, USA, August 13-17, 2016*, pages 785–794. ACM.

Alexis Conneau, Kartikay Khandelwal, Naman Goyal, Vishrav Chaudhary, Guillaume Wenzek, Francisco Guzmán, Edouard Grave, Myle Ott, Luke Zettlemoyer, and Veselin Stoyanov. 2020. Unsupervised cross-lingual representation learning at scale. In *Proceedings of the 58th Annual Meeting of the Association for Computational Linguistics*, pages 8440–8451, Online. Association for Computational Linguistics.

Naihao Deng, Xinliang Zhang, Siyang Liu, Winston Wu, Lu Wang, and Rada Mihalcea. 2023. You are what you annotate: Towards better models through annotator representations. In *Findings of the Association for Computational Linguistics: EMNLP 2023*, pages 12475–12498, Singapore. Association for Computational Linguistics.

Neil Houlsby, Andrei Giurgiu, Stanislaw Jastrzebski, Bruna Morrone, Quentin de Laroussilhe, Andrea Gesmundo, Mona Attariyan, and Sylvain Gelly. 2019. Parameter-efficient transfer learning for NLP. In *Proceedings of the 36th International Conference on Machine Learning, ICML 2019, 9-15 June 2019, Long Beach, California, USA*, volume 97 of *Proceedings of Machine Learning Research*, pages 2790–2799. PMLR.

Andrey Kutuzov and Lidia Pivovarova. 2021. Rushifteval: a shared task on semantic shift detection for russian. *Komp'yuternaya Lingvistika i Intellektual'nye Tekhnologii: Dialog conference*.

Andrey Kutuzov, Samia Touileb, Petter Mæhlum, Tita Enstad, and Alexandra Wittemann. 2022. NorDiaChange: Diachronic semantic change dataset for Norwegian. In *Proceedings of the Thirteenth Language Resources and Evaluation Conference*, pages 2563–2572, Marseille, France. European Language Resources Association.

Elisa Leonardelli, Gavin Abercrombie, Dina Almanea, Valerio Basile, Tommaso Fornaciari, Barbara Plank, Verena Rieser, Alexandra Uma, and Massimo Poesio. 2023. SemEval-2023 task 11: Learning with disagreements (LeWiDi). In *Proceedings of the 17th International Workshop on Semantic Evaluation (SemEval-2023)*, pages 2304–2318, Toronto, Canada. Association for Computational Linguistics.

Aida Mostafazadeh Davani, Mark Díaz, and Vinodkumar Prabhakaran. 2022. Dealing with disagreements: Looking beyond the majority vote in subjective annotations. *Transactions of the Association for Computational Linguistics*, 10:92–110.

An Thanh Nguyen, Byron Wallace, Junyi Jessy Li, Ani Nenkova, and Matthew Lease. 2017. Aggregating and predicting sequence labels from crowd annotations. In *Proceedings of the 55th Annual Meeting of the Association for Computational Linguistics (Volume 1: Long Papers)*, pages 299–309, Vancouver, Canada. Association for Computational Linguistics.

Sarumi Oluyemi, Béla Neuendorf, Joan Plepi, Lucie Flek, Jörg Schlötterer, and Charles Welch. 2024. Corpus considerations for annotator modeling and scaling. In *Proceedings of the 2024 Conference of the North American Chapter of the Association for Computational Linguistics: Human Language Technologies (Volume 1: Long Papers)*, pages 1029–1040, Mexico City, Mexico. Association for Computational Linguistics.

Mohammad Taher Pilehvar and Jose Camacho-Collados. 2019. WiC: the word-in-context dataset for evaluating context-sensitive meaning representations. In *Proceedings of the 2019 Conference of the North American Chapter of the Association for Computational Linguistics: Human Language Technologies, Volume 1 (Long and Short Papers)*, pages 1267–1273, Minneapolis, Minnesota. Association for Computational Linguistics.

Joan Plepi, Béla Neuendorf, Lucie Flek, and Charles Welch. 2022. Unifying data perspectivism and personalization: An application to social norms. In *Proceedings of the 2022 Conference on Empirical Methods in Natural Language Processing*, pages 7391–7402, Abu Dhabi, United Arab Emirates. Association for Computational Linguistics.

Liudmila Ostroumova Prokhorenkova, Gleb Gusev, Aleksandr Vorobev, Anna Veronika Dorogush, and Andrey Gulin. 2018. Catboost: unbiased boosting with categorical features. In *Advances in Neural Information Processing Systems 31: Annual Conference on Neural Information Processing Systems 2018, NeurIPS 2018, December 3-8, 2018, Montréal, Canada*, pages 6639–6649.

Nils Reimers and Iryna Gurevych. 2019. Sentence-BERT: Sentence embeddings using Siamese BERT-networks. In *Proceedings of the 2019 Conference on Empirical Methods in Natural Language Processing and the 9th International Joint Conference on Natural Language Processing (EMNLP-IJCNLP)*, pages 3982–3992, Hong Kong, China. Association for Computational Linguistics.

Dominik Schlechtweg, Pierluigi Cassotti, Bill Noble, David Alfter, Sabine Schulte im Walde, and Nina Tahmasebi. 2024. More DWUGs: Extending and evaluating word usage graph datasets in multiple languages. In *Proceedings of the 2024 Conference on Empirical Methods in Natural Language Processing*, Miami, Florida. Association for Computational Linguistics.

Dominik Schlechtweg, Tejaswi Choppa, Wei Zhao, and Michael Roth. 2025. The CoMeDi shared task: Median judgment classification & mean disagreement ranking with ordinal word-in-context judgments. In *Proceedings of the 1st Workshop on Context and Meaning–Navigating Disagreements in NLP Annotations*, Abu Dhabi, UAE.

Dominik Schlechtweg, Sabine Schulte im Walde, and Stefanie Eckmann. 2018. Diachronic usage relatedness (DURel): A framework for the annotation of lexical semantic change. In *Proceedings of the 2018 Conference of the North American Chapter of the Association for Computational Linguistics: Human Language Technologies, Volume 2 (Short Papers)*, pages 169–174, New Orleans, Louisiana. Association for Computational Linguistics.

Frank D. Zamora-Reina, Felipe Bravo-Marquez, and Dominik Schlechtweg. 2022. LSCDiscovery: A shared task on semantic change discovery and detection in Spanish. In *Proceedings of the 3rd Workshop on Computational Approaches to Historical Language Change*, pages 149–164, Dublin, Ireland. Association for Computational Linguistics.

FuocChuVIP123 at CoMeDi Shared Task: Disagreement Ranking with XLM-Roberta Sentence Embeddings and Deep Neural Regression

Chu Duong Huy Phuoc
University of Information Technology
Vietnam National University - Ho Chi Minh City, Vietnam
23521229@gm.uit.edu.vn

Abstract

This paper presents results of our system for CoMeDi Shared Task, focusing on Subtask 2: Disagreement Ranking. Our system leverages sentence embeddings generated by the paraphrase-xlm-r-multilingual-v1 model, combined with a deep neural regression model incorporating batch normalization and dropout for improved generalization. By predicting the mean of pairwise judgment differences between annotators, our method explicitly targets disagreement ranking, diverging from traditional "gold label" aggregation approaches. We optimized our system with a customized architecture and training procedure, achieving competitive performance in Spearman correlation against mean disagreement labels. Our results highlight the importance of robust embeddings, effective model architecture, and careful handling of judgment differences for ranking disagreement in multilingual contexts. These findings provide insights into the use of contextualized representations for ordinal judgment tasks and open avenues for further refinement of disagreement prediction models.

1 Introduction

The CoMeDi Shared Task Subtask 2: Mean Disagreement Ranking with Ordinal Word-in-Context Judgments (DisWiC) (Schlechtweg et al., 2025) focuses on predicting annotator disagreement in semantic similarity judgments. Participants were tasked to rank word-use pairs based on the mean of pairwise absolute differences in annotations, highlighting disagreement rather than consensus. This task builds on recent research emphasizing the importance of capturing variability in linguistic judgments for complex, ambiguous datasets. Evaluations were using Spearman's correlation.

In this paper, we present an embedding-based approach that uses SentenceTransformer (paraphrase-xlm-r-multilingual-v1) with base model is XLM-RoBERTa (Conneau et al., 2020) to generate contextual embeddings for word-use pairs. These embeddings were combined in a deep regression model with Batch Normalization, Dropout, and an optimized learning rate scheduler to enhance performance. The model was fine-tuned to predict disagreement scores efficiently, demonstrating the potential of leveraging advanced multilingual embeddings and robust neural architectures for capturing semantic complexities in multilingual datasets.

2 Related Work

Annotation disagreements in NLP, particularly in tasks involving meaning in context, pose challenges to data quality and model reliability. Early studies, such as (Artstein and Poesio, 2008) and (Hovy et al., 2013), explored inter-annotator agreement and aggregation methods to address inconsistencies. Recent works have shifted toward leveraging disagreements as valuable signals. For instance, (Basile et al., 2021) introduced perspectivism to embrace diverse annotator viewpoints, while (Mostafazadeh Davani et al., 2022) and (Mostafazadeh Davani et al., 2022) utilized disagreements to train models better suited for subjective tasks. In Word-in-Context (WiC) tasks, (Schlechtweg et al., 2018) proposed the DURel framework to capture semantic relatedness using ordinal scales, with subsequent studies, such as (Uma et al., 2021), focusing on preserving disagreement information through alternative label aggregation methods. This Subtask 2 builds on this foundation by explicitly modeling disagreement using mean pairwise judgment differences, evaluated via Spearman's correlation (Zar, 2005), offering a novel perspective on handling annotation variability.

3 Task Description

The CoMeDi shared task, part of the COLING 2025 workshop (Schlechtweg et al., 2025), consists

Proceedings of Context and Meaning: Navigating Disagreements in NLP Annotation, pages 97–102
January 19, 2025.

of two subtasks focusing on predicting disagreements in word sense annotation in context (WiC). The first subtask (OGWiC) involves predicting the median of annotator judgments on an ordinal scale (1-4) for word usage pairs, treating this as an ordinal classification task. The second subtask (DisWiC) aims to rank instances based on the mean disagreement between annotators, measured by pairwise absolute differences in judgments. Both subtasks rely on datasets such as the DWUG EN dataset (Schlechtweg et al., 2024) and will be evaluated using Krippendorff's α (Krippendorff, 2018) for OGWiC and Spearman's ρ for DisWiC.

3.1 Dataset

We conducted our experiments using the dataset provided by the organizers for training and evaluation. The dataset includes samples from seven languages: Chinese (Chen et al., 2023), English (Schlechtweg et al., 2024), German (Schlechtweg et al., 2024), Norwegian (Kutuzov et al., 2022), Russian (Rodina and Kutuzov, 2020); (Kurtyigit et al., 2021), Spanish (Zamora-Reina et al., 2022), and Swedish (Schlechtweg et al., 2024). Tables 1 and 2 summarize its key characteristics.

The training dataset contains more samples than the development set, ranging from 1,222 for Norwegian to 24,891 for Russian. On average, context length varies widely, with Spanish having the longest at 84.72 tokens and Chinese the shortest at 1.00 token. German has the largest maximum context length of 1,643 tokens, while Chinese remains the smallest at 1 token. This diversity in sample sizes and context lengths across languages poses challenges for model generalization but provides a strong foundation for evaluating multilingual methods.

Languages	# Samples	Avg. Len.	Max Len.
Chinese	20.46	1.00	1.00
English	10.83	31.91	176.00
German	13.69	39.39	1643.00
Norwegian	6.04	47.49	346.00
Russian	12.69	24.88	356.00
Spanish	9.33	84.72	480.00
Swedish	9.11	34.89	376.00

Table 1: Training dataset statistics.

4 System Overview

Our system tackles the shared task by combining neural sentence embeddings and a deep regression model to predict mean disagreement rankings for the DWUGs dataset (Schlechtweg et al., 2024). The primary steps include: (i) generating semantic representations using multilingual pre-trained models, (ii) concatenating embeddings for context pairs, (iii) training a regression model to predict mean disagreement values.

Languages	# Samples	Avg. Len.	Max Len.
Chinese	3.09	1.00	1.00
English	1.90	32.01	169.00
German	2.59	33.52	376.00
Norwegian	871	52.89	452.00
Russian	1,932	23.98	352.00
Spanish	1,269	82.19	493.00
Swedish	1.41	33.66	305.00

Table 2: Development dataset statistics.

4.1 Semantic Representations

We employ the SentenceTransformer *paraphrase-xlm-r-multilingual-v1* model to generate semantic embeddings for sentence pairs. This model is based on XLM-RoBERTa (Conneau et al., 2020), a transformer architecture fine-tuned for multilingual sentence representation tasks. Given a context sentence, C, the embedding function $E(C)$ produces a 768-dimensional vector:

$$E(C) \in \mathbb{R}^{768}$$

For each data sample, two contexts C_1 and C_2 are processed, and their embeddings are concatenated:

$$X = [E(C_1), E(C_2)] \in \mathbb{R}^{1536}$$

4.2 Deep Regression Model

We propose a deep feedforward neural network to map concatenated embeddings to mean disagreement scores. The model architecture consists of: Input Layer: 1536-dimensional concatenated embeddings. Hidden Layers: Four fully connected layers with dimensions [512, 256, 128, 64], each followed by BatchNorm and dropout ($p = 0.3$). Output Layer: A single neuron for regression output. Each hidden layer uses ReLU activation, and the loss function is Mean Squared Error (MSE):

$$\mathcal{L} = \frac{1}{N} \sum_{i=1}^{N} (y_i - \hat{y}_i)^2$$

where y_i and $\hat{y}_i$ are the ground truth and predicted scores.

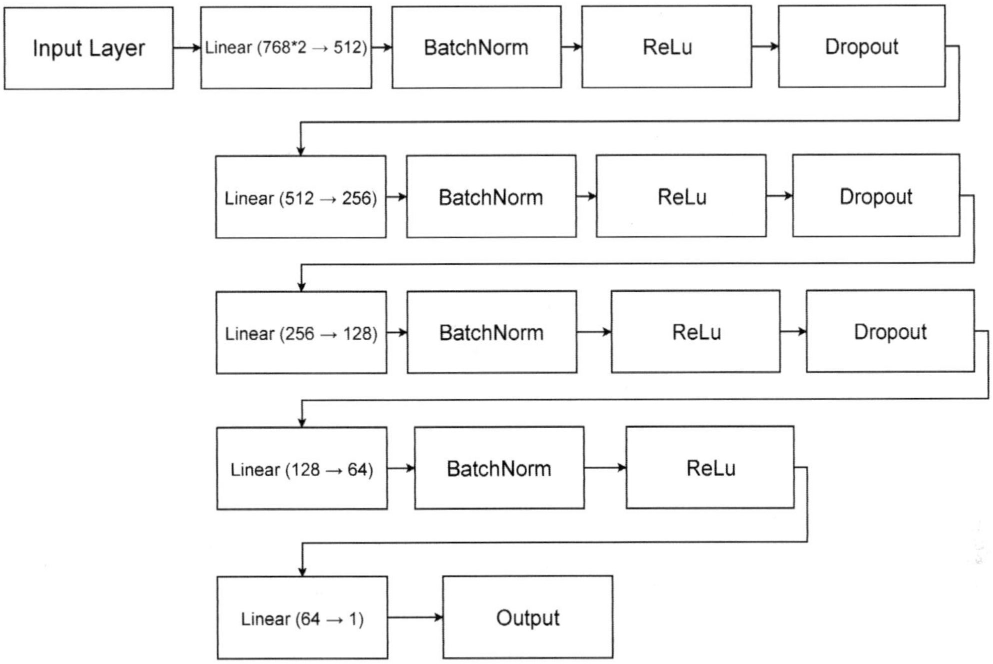

Figure 1: The structure of Deep Regression model.

4.3 XLM-RoBERTa

As illustrated in Figure 2, the structure of XLM-RoBERTa (Conneau et al., 2020) consists of three main components: Embedding Layers, Transformer Encoders, and a final layer for handling specific tasks. During the model's training process, the input is a sequence of tokens, starting with the [CLS] character. The representation of the sequence is extracted from the vector C, corresponding to the [CLS] token. This vector is passed through a Fully Connected Layer and then processed using the sigmoid activation function to convert the output into a probability value. This value is optimized through the cross-entropy loss function.

4.4 Training Strategy

The model is trained using the AdamW optimizer with weight decay and an initial learning rate of 10^{-4}. To prevent overfitting, we employ learning rate scheduling via `ReduceLROnPlateau`, reducing the learning rate by a factor of 0.5 if the validation loss does not improve for three consecutive epochs. Gradients are clipped (Chen et al., 2020) to a maximum norm for stability:

$$\text{f}(g) = \min\left(1, \frac{\text{max\_grad\_norm}}{\|g\|_2}\right) \cdot g$$

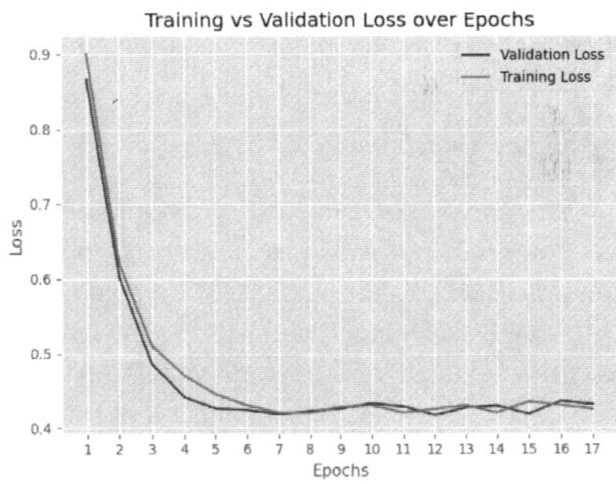

Figure 3: Training and validation loss while training.

4.5 Evaluation Metrics

The system's performance is evaluated using Spearman's Rank Correlation Coefficient (ρ) (Zar, 2005) between the predicted and true mean disagreement rankings. This metric is defined as:

$$\rho = 1 - \frac{6\sum_{i=1}^{N} d_i^2}{N(N^2 - 1)}$$

where d_i is the difference between the ranks of corresponding predicted and ground truth values, and N is the total number of samples.

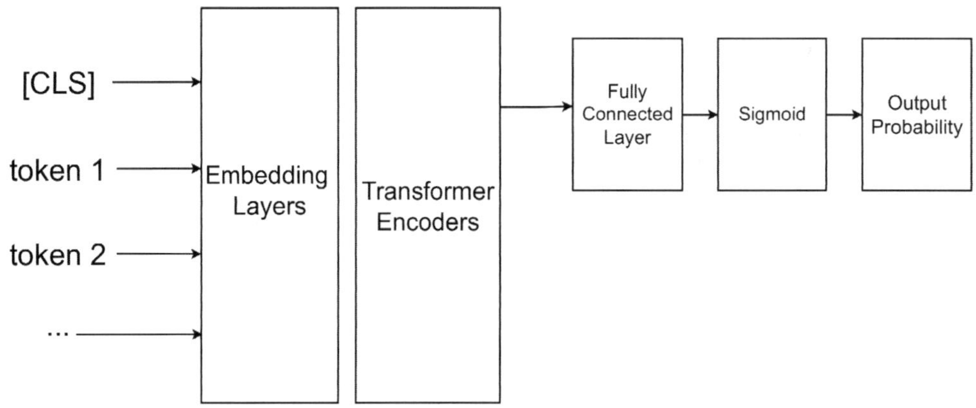

Figure 2: Structure of BERT and XLM-RoBERTa.

Phase	Team	Subtask2 (spearman)							
		AVG	ZH	EN	DE	NO	RU	ES	SV
Evaluation	deep-change	**0.226 (1)**	0.301 (7)	**0.078 (1)**	**0.204 (1)**	**0.286 (1)**	**0.175 (1)**	**0.187 (1)**	**0.350 (1)**
	GRASP	0.220 (2)	**0.539 (1)**	0.042 (5)	0.108 (2)	0.272 (2)	0.167 (2)	0.115 (2)	0.296 (2)
	FuocChuVIP123 (ours)	0.124 (4)	0.362 (4)	0.018 (7)	0.099 (3)	0.156 (4)	0.050 (6)	0.012 (7)	0.172 (3)
Post evaluation	deep-change	**0.281 (1)**	**0.574 (1)**	**0.143 (1)**	**0.241 (1)**	**0.294 (1)**	**0.194 (1)**	**0.161 (1)**	**0.360 (1)**
	GRASP	0.220 (2)	0.539 (2)	0.042 (3)	0.108 (3)	0.272 (2)	0.167 (2)	0.115 (2)	0.296 (2)
	funzac	0.170 (3)	0.433 (3)	0.056 (2)	0.167 (2)	0.178 (3)	0.076 (3)	0.088 (3)	0.194 (3)

Table 3: Top 3 results of Subtask 2.

5 Experimental setup

For the shared task, we used a custom deep regression model built with a multi-layer perceptron (MLP) architecture, which was trained to predict mean disagreement scores from sentence embeddings. The embeddings were generated using the Sentence-Transformer model paraphrase-xlm-r-multilingual-v1, which was fine-tuned for multilingual text. We trained the model for 17 epochs with a batch size of 32 with PyTorch. The AdamW optimizer was used with an initial learning rate of 0.0001, and we applied a learning rate scheduler (ReduceLROnPlateau) with a patience of 3 epochs and a factor of 0.5 to reduce the learning rate when the validation loss plateaued. The model also utilized batch normalization and dropout layers to prevent overfitting.The training data was split into training and validation sets with an 80-20% split. For evaluation, we used the mean squared error (MSE) loss for training and Spearman's rank correlation coefficient to assess the performance of the model. Regarding data preprocessing, we used the raw contexts from the dataset without extensive cleaning. We merged the necessary information from training and development sets to construct the input for our model. No lemmatization or punctuation removal was applied as the dataset was in multilingual form, and we decided to focus on the context and target token indices for each pair of words. Our model was evaluated on the development set, and we used Spearman's rank correlation as the primary evaluation metric.

6 Results

Table 3 lists the evaluation phase scores of the top three contenders for subtask 2 as well as our system. During this phase, submission scores and leaderboards were hidden. For Subtask 2, our team ranked 3rd out of 7 teams in the evaluation phase. We focused solely on Subtask 2 and did not participate in Subtask 1. The models of the top-performing teams utilized a variety of strategies. Our approach involved using embeddings generated from a pre-trained multilingual transformer model (XLM-R) to capture context information. These embeddings were then fed into a deep neural network model with batch normalization layers, which we trained to predict the "mean disagreement" score for each pair of contexts. We conducted a series of experiments with different hyperparameters and fine-tuned the model, which allowed us to achieve notable improvements in performance. In the evaluation phase, our team faced challenges, particularly with the Latin languagues, which proved to be more complex due to its size and variability. This likely contributed to our lower score of 0.124 on average during the evaluation.

7 Conclusion

In this paper, we presented our approach to Subtask 2 of the CoMeDi Shared Task, focusing on predicting disagreement rankings in multilingual word-in-context judgments. By leveraging sentence embeddings from the pre-trained paraphrase-xlm-r-multilingual-v1 model and a deep regression network with batch normalization, our method achieved competitive performance, ranking 3rd among 7 teams. Our results highlight the potential of multilingual embeddings and robust neural architectures for handling disagreement in semantic similarity tasks. Future work could explore further refinements to address language-specific complexities and improve overall model performance.

8 Limitations

Our system, while achieving competitive performance, has several limitations. First, it struggled with Latin-based languages like Spanish, highlighting challenges with XLM-RoBERTa embeddings for specific linguistic nuances. Second, the approach relied heavily on embedding quality, which may not fully capture fine-grained word-use differences. Additionally, the system focused solely on mean disagreement scores without modeling the underlying causes of annotator disagreement, such as cultural or subjective biases.

References

Ron Artstein and Massimo Poesio. 2008. Survey article: Inter-coder agreement for computational linguistics. *Computational Linguistics*, 34(4):555–596.

Valerio Basile, Federico Cabitza, Andrea Campagner, and Michael Fell. 2021. Toward a perspectivist turn in ground truthing for predictive computing. *CoRR*, abs/2109.04270.

Jing Chen, Emmanuele Chersoni, Dominik Schlechtweg, Jelena Prokic, and Chu-Ren Huang. 2023. ChiWUG: A graph-based evaluation dataset for Chinese lexical semantic change detection. In *Proceedings of the 4th International Workshop on Computational Approaches to Historical Language Change*, Singapore. Association for Computational Linguistics.

Xiangyi Chen, Steven Z. Wu, and Mingyi Hong. 2020. Understanding gradient clipping in private sgd: A geometric perspective. In *Advances in Neural Information Processing Systems*, volume 33, pages 13773–13782. Curran Associates, Inc.

Alexis Conneau, Kartikay Khandelwal, Naman Goyal, Vishrav Chaudhary, Guillaume Wenzek, Francisco Guzmán, Edouard Grave, Myle Ott, Luke Zettlemoyer, and Veselin Stoyanov. 2020. Unsupervised cross-lingual representation learning at scale. In *Proceedings of the 58th Annual Meeting of the Association for Computational Linguistics*, pages 8440–8451, Online. Association for Computational Linguistics.

Dirk Hovy, Taylor Berg-Kirkpatrick, Ashish Vaswani, and Eduard Hovy. 2013. Learning whom to trust with MACE. In *Proceedings of the 2013 Conference of the North American Chapter of the Association for Computational Linguistics: Human Language Technologies*, pages 1120–1130, Atlanta, Georgia. Association for Computational Linguistics.

Klaus Krippendorff. 2018. *Content Analysis: An Introduction to Its Methodology*, 4 edition. SAGE Publications.

Sinan Kurtyigit, Maike Park, Dominik Schlechtweg, Jonas Kuhn, and Sabine Schulte im Walde. 2021. Lexical Semantic Change Discovery. In *Proceedings of the 59th Annual Meeting of the Association for Computational Linguistics and the 11th International Joint Conference on Natural Language Processing (Volume 1: Long Papers)*, Online. Association for Computational Linguistics.

Andrey Kutuzov, Samia Touileb, Petter Mæhlum, Tita Enstad, and Alexandra Wittemann. 2022. NorDiaChange: Diachronic semantic change dataset for Norwegian. In *Proceedings of the Thirteenth Language Resources and Evaluation Conference*, pages 2563–2572, Marseille, France. European Language Resources Association.

Aida Mostafazadeh Davani, Mark Díaz, and Vinodkumar Prabhakaran. 2022. Dealing with disagreements: Looking beyond the majority vote in subjective annotations. *Transactions of the Association for Computational Linguistics*, 10:92–110.

Julia Rodina and Andrey Kutuzov. 2020. RuSemShift: a dataset of historical lexical semantic change in Russian. In *Proceedings of the 28th International Conference on Computational Linguistics*, pages 1037–1047, Barcelona, Spain (Online). International Committee on Computational Linguistics.

Dominik Schlechtweg, Pierluigi Cassotti, Bill Noble, David Alfter, Sabine Schulte im Walde, and Nina Tahmasebi. 2024. More DWUGs: Extending and evaluating word usage graph datasets in multiple languages. In *Proceedings of the 2024 Conference on Empirical Methods in Natural Language Processing*, Miami, Florida. Association for Computational Linguistics.

Dominik Schlechtweg, Tejaswi Choppa, Wei Zhao, and Michael Roth. 2025. The CoMeDi shared task: Median judgment classification & mean disagreement ranking with ordinal word-in-context judgments. In *Proceedings of the 1st Workshop on Context and Meaning–Navigating Disagreements in NLP Annotations*, Abu Dhabi, UAE.

Dominik Schlechtweg, Sabine Schulte im Walde, and Stefanie Eckmann. 2018. Diachronic Usage Relatedness (DURel): A framework for the annotation of lexical semantic change. In *Proceedings of the 2018 Conference of the North American Chapter of the Association for Computational Linguistics: Human Language Technologies*, pages 169–174, New Orleans, Louisiana.

Alexandra Uma, Tommaso Fornaciari, Dirk Hovy, Silviu Paun, Barbara Plank, and Massimo Poesio. 2021. Learning from disagreement: A survey. *J. Artif. Intell. Res.*, 72:1385–1470.

Frank D. Zamora-Reina, Felipe Bravo-Marquez, and Dominik Schlechtweg. 2022. LSCDiscovery: A shared task on semantic change discovery and detection in Spanish. In *Proceedings of the 3rd International Workshop on Computational Approaches to Historical Language Change*, Dublin, Ireland. Association for Computational Linguistics.

Jerrold H. Zar. 2005. Spearman rank correlation.

JuniperLiu at CoMeDi Shared Task: Models as Annotators in Lexical Semantics Disagreements

Zhu Liu[1*], **Zhen Hu**[2*], **Ying Liu**[1]
[1]School of Humanities, Tsinghua University, Beijing, China
[2]College of Engineering, Beijing Forestry University, Beijing, China
liuzhu22@mails.tsinghua.edu.cn, huzhen@bjfu.edu.cn

Abstract

We present the results of our system for the CoMeDi Shared Task, which predicts majority votes (Subtask 1) and annotator disagreements (Subtask 2). Our approach combines model ensemble strategies with MLP-based and threshold-based methods trained on pretrained language models. Treating individual models as virtual annotators, we simulate the annotation process by designing aggregation measures that incorporate continuous relatedness scores and discrete classification labels to capture both majority and disagreement. Additionally, we employ anisotropy removal techniques to enhance performance. Experimental results demonstrate the effectiveness of our methods, particularly for Subtask 2. Notably, we find that standard deviation on continuous relatedness scores among different model manipulations correlates with human disagreement annotations compared to metrics on aggregated discrete labels. The code will be published at https://github.com/RyanLiut/CoMeDi_Solution.

1 Introduction

Lexical semantic similarity is a classical task that encompasses various forms, including multi-choice sense selection (Navigli, 2009), binary classification (Pilehvar and Camacho-Collados, 2019), and contextual word similarity (Islam and Inkpen, 2008), among others. However, the potential disagreements among annotators, arising from the inherent vagueness and continuous nature of meaning, have received comparatively less attention. To address these complexities, the CoMedi workshop (Context and Meaning - Navigating Disagreements in NLP Annotations[1]) introduced a Shared Task with two subtasks (Schlechtweg et al., 2025). Subtask 1 involves predicting the median judgment classification across four candidate labels, which represent the degree of similarity for a target word in context. Subtask 2 focuses on predicting annotator disagreement, which can be interpreted as a form of predictive uncertainty estimation (Gal, 2016).

In this paper, we first conceptualize the two subtasks as corresponding to two fundamental statistical properties of a Gaussian distribution: the mean and variance. Subsequently, we model each system, parameterized by specific variables, as an individual human annotator. These variables encompass both homogeneous factors, such as layers within the same model, and heterogeneous factors across different models. To address the tasks, we employ MLP-based and threshold-based approaches to generate continuous relatedness [2] scores and discrete classification labels, respectively. Additionally, we incorporate techniques for anisotropy removal to mitigate geometric biases inherent in embedding spaces. Finally, we propose diverse strategies for model ensembling to enhance performance. Our results demonstrate the effectiveness of threshold-based methods combined with anisotropy removal and MLP-based approaches. For Subtask 2, the findings further highlight the advantages of aggregating relatedness scores over discrete labels in capturing annotator disagreement.

2 Related Work

Probing for Contextual Word Meaning Tasks capturing word meaning in context include word sense disambiguation (WSD) (Navigli, 2009), which selects the most appropriate sense, and WiC (Pilehvar and Camacho-Collados, 2019), which determines semantic equivalence across contexts. Extending these, relatedness scoring provides a continuous measure of semantic relatedness.

*These authors contributed equally.
[1]https://comedinlp.github.io/

[2]We distinguish *similarity* from *relatedness*, with the task focusing on annotating relatedness scores.

Proceedings of Context and Meaning: Navigating Disagreements in NLP Annotation, pages 103–112
January 19, 2025.

The CoMeDi Shared Task reframes WiC as an ordinal classification task with four labels indicating relatedness degrees. Probing methods include MLP-based approaches (Tenney et al., 2019; Pilehvar and Camacho-Collados, 2019), which train dense networks, and threshold-based methods (Pilehvar and Camacho-Collados, 2019; Vulić et al., 2020; Liu et al., 2024), which optimize relatedness thresholds for pretrained representations. Since embeddings are often anisotropic (Ethayarajh, 2019), techniques like centering (Sahlgren et al., 2016) and standardization (Timkey and van Schijndel, 2021) are applied to improve representation quality.

Uncertainty Estimation Subtask 2 models annotator disagreement, aligning with the study of uncertainty estimation (UE), widely explored in computer vision (Gal, 2016) and robust AI (Stutz, 2022). UE arises from data uncertainty (aleatoric, linked to inherent data ambiguity like annotation disagreement) and model uncertainty (epistemic, due to biased learning on out-of-distribution data) (Gal, 2016). Researchers (Liu and Liu, 2023) combine these areas to model semantic uncertainty in sense selection. While Bayesian (Vazhentsev et al., 2022) and non-Bayesian (Szegedy et al., 2016) methods often use label probabilities, our threshold-based method lacks this feature. Instead, we treat the process as model ensemble (Lakshminarayanan et al., 2017) and propose aggregation measures.

Annotator Disagreement Annotator disagreement is common in lexical semantics tasks, such as word sense disambiguation (WSD) (Navigli, 2009; Chklovski and Mihalcea, 2003), due to the subjective and ambiguous nature of meaning (Navigli, 2008). While many studies resolve disagreement through majority voting, others exploit it by reframing tasks as multi-label classification (Conia and Navigli, 2021) or training on multiple judgments (Uma et al., 2021).

In this paper, we model annotator disagreement as uncertainty estimation, as both involve (1) output variability, (2) data noise [3], and (3) similar evaluation metrics.

3 System Overview

Most systems use MLP-based (Tenney et al., 2019; Pilehvar and Camacho-Collados, 2019) and threshold-based (Pilehvar and Camacho-Collados, 2019; Vulić et al., 2020; Liu et al., 2024) methods. They extract representations from pretrained language models, then MLP-based methods train a network to predict discrete labels (Subtask 1) or continuous values (Subtask 2). Threshold-based methods learn a threshold selector to map similarity scores to labels. However, naive baselines often fall short, as shown in Section 5. In our system, we applied anisotropy removal to the baseline code (Schlechtweg et al., 2025) and used a classifier-based method for comparison. For Subtask 1, we apply techniques to make data points more isotropic. For Subtask 2, we ensemble models, treating them as annotators, and use various strategies to model disagreement.

3.1 Formulation as Parameter Estimation

For a target word w appearing in a pair of contexts c_i and c_j, annotators from a hypothetical human space $\mathcal{H}$ provide a judgment score $s \in \mathcal{R}$, where higher values indicate greater similarity in meaning between c_i and c_j. These scores form a judgment distribution p on $\mathcal{R}$, which we assume follows a Gaussian distribution, $p \sim \mathcal{N}(\mu, \sigma^2)$, as it is a natural statistical choice (Jaynes, 2003). Here, μ represents the consensus similarity, while σ reflects disagreement among annotators.

In practice, the continuous Gaussian distribution is discretized due to the finite number of annotators and graded annotations. Nonetheless, we adopt the Gaussian framework to unify the two tasks: Subtask 1 estimates μ, while Subtask 2 estimates σ.

3.2 Subtask 1: Anisotropy Removal

Contextual representations are known to be anisotropic (Ethayarajh, 2019), clustering in a narrow region of the space. This inflates similarity scores, reducing their discriminative power in meaning-related tasks. For example, even unrelated words often exhibit high similarity. We adopt three techniques to reduce anisotropy: (1) centering by subtracting the mean vector (2) normal standardization (3) All-but-the-top (Mu and Viswanath, 2018): subtracting the projection on the component of the largest variance.

3.3 Subtask 2: Model Ensembling

To model annotator disagreement, we treat each model or its manipulation as an annotator and use three measures to reflect uncertainty. We explore

[3] Annotator disagreement can be viewed as label noise, contributing to data uncertainty—a key component of irreducible uncertainty.

three ensembling strategies: (1) homogeneous aggregation with model manipulations (e.g., layer and anisotropy removal), (2) heterogeneous ensembling across different models, and (3) a mixed approach combining both. After each model forward pass, we obtain a discrete label using the threshold-based model [4] and a continuous relatedness score. We apply three measures: standard deviation (STD) for continuous scores, mean pairwise absolute judgment differences (MPD) for discrete labels (as used in Subtask 2), and variation ratio (VR), the ratio of values not equal to the mode, commonly used in uncertainty estimation (Gal, 2016).

4 Experiment Setup

4.1 Task Description

The Shared Task in the workshop of CoMeDi (Schlechtweg et al., 2025) includes two subtasks. The first aims to predict a discrete label (from 1 to 4) to show the relatedness of the target word in two contexts while the second obtains a continuous value to indicate the disagreement. The task data was sampled from multilingual datasets, involving 7 languages, i.e., Chinese (Chen et al., 2023), English (Schlechtweg et al., 2021, 2024), German (Schlechtweg et al., 2018, 2021, 2024; Hätty et al., 2019; Kurtyigit et al., 2021; Schlechtweg, 2023), Norwegian (Kutuzov et al., 2022), Russian (Rodina and Kutuzov, 2020; Kutuzov and Pivovarova, 2021; Aksenova et al., 2022), Spanish (Zamora-Reina et al., 2022), Swedish (Schlechtweg et al., 2021, 2024).

4.2 Models

Our study focuses on threshold-based methods using pre-trained models: XLM-RoBERTa-base, XLM-RoBERTa-large (Conneau, 2019), BERT-multi-base (Pires, 2019), and Llama-7B (Touvron et al., 2023). For encoder-only models, we extract target word representations directly, while for the decoder-only Llama-7B, we use a prompt-based method (Liu and Liu, 2023) to extract the final colon representation. Inspired by in-context learning (Jiang et al., 2024), we apply layer-wise manipulations (centering, standardization, and all-but-the-top) to reduce anisotropy.

We discretize the continuous similarity scores into labels using a threshold selector based on the shared task baseline. The selector employs the Nelder-Mead method (Nelder and Mead, 1965) to optimize bin edges for Krippendorff's α, starting with evenly spaced bins and iteratively refining them. For Subtask 2, we explore model ensembling strategies (homo, hetero, mixed) and different measures (STD, MPD, VR), and also evaluate an MLP-based approach (details in Appendix 10.1).

4.3 Evaluation Phase Setting

During the evaluation phase, we selected models based on the development set.

For **Subtask 1**, we employ a threshold-based method using XLM-RoBERTa-base as the pre-trained model, except for Chinese and Russian (BERT-multi-base) and Norwegian (LERT-base-chinese). Representations are extracted from the 10th layer for XLM-RoBERTa-base and the final layer for other models. We apply normal standardization except for Norwegian to address anisotropy and utilized the threshold selection method from the official baseline code (Schlechtweg et al., 2025). Specifically,

For **Subtask 2**, we fine-tune an MLP regressor to predict disagreement scores, following the baseline methodology. It comprised of two linear layers and a ReLU activation function. For Swiss, we train for 50 epochs with a batch size of 32, while for other languages, we use 200 epochs with a batch size of 16. The learning rate is 1e-2 with a 0.1 dropout rate. We utilize AdamW for optimization with a warm-up ratio of 0.1.

4.4 Post Evaluation Phase Setting

For **Subtask 1**, we use the 25th layer of Llama and the 11th layer of XLM-RoBERTa-Base for all languages, with an MLP-based method fine-tuned using training data. All model representations are standardized to remove anisotropy. For the MLP-based model, we train for 50 epochs with a batch size of 128, an initial learning rate of 1e-2, and apply a dropout rate of 0.1 to prevent overfitting.

For **Subtask 2**, we employ ensembling strategies to significantly improve performance. We report two results from our ensembling methods. The first (ensembling) applies the same strategy across all languages: standardization with layer 24, no standardization with layer 16, centering with layer 24, and all-but-the-top with layer 16, all on Llama-7B. The second (ensembling*) presents language-specific ensembling strategies, as in Table 6.

[4]For Subtask 2, we use the majority of judgment scores as the GT label, avoiding the median to handle decimals.

Participator	Method	AVG	ZH	EN	DE	NO	RU	ES	SV
kuklinmike	-	**0.656**	**0.424**	**0.732**	0.723	**0.668**	**0.623**	**0.748**	**0.675**
comedy_baseline_2	-	0.583	0.379	0.654	**0.728**	0.515	0.550	0.656	0.601
daalft	-	0.555	0.317	0.555	0.656	0.589	0.487	0.636	0.648
ours	Thr* (XLM-R-B)	0.271	0.140	0.507	0.492	0.080	0.128	0.330	0.224
ours	Thr (LLM)	**0.451**	-0.090	0.474	**0.696**	**0.445**	**0.444**	**0.623**	**0.566**
ours	Thr (XLM-R-B)	0.339	**0.148**	**0.524**	0.485	0.240	0.301	0.348	0.325
ours	MLP	0.338	0.128	0.369	0.371	0.351	0.329	0.411	0.407

Table 1: Results for Subtask 1. The upper part shows the evaluation phase, and the lower part the post-evaluation phase. "Thr" denotes threshold-based methods, and "Thr*" indicates language-specific model selections. The same applies to other tables.

Participator	Method	AVG	ZH	EN	DE	NO	RU	ES	SV
kuklinmike	-	**0.226**	0.301	0.078	0.204	**0.286**	**0.175**	**0.187**	0.350
daalft	-	0.220	**0.539**	0.042	0.108	0.272	0.167	0.115	0.296
comedy_baseline_2	-	0.163	0.485	0.060	0.085	0.235	0.116	0.078	0.079
ours	MLP	0.082	0.358	0.038	0.022	-0.042	0.067	0.040	0.090
ours	ensembling	0.205	0.274	0.117	0.236	0.279	0.101	0.073	0.353
ours	ensembling*	0.220	0.347	**0.118**	**0.242**	0.283	0.108	0.078	**0.364**

Table 2: Evaluation results (upper part) and post-evaluation results (lower part) for Subtask 2. The method *ensembling** integrates language-specific ensembling strategies, while *ensembling* uses the strategy with the best average score across all languages.

5 Results

We present the results in Table 1 and Table 2 on the **test** set. The upper sections show evaluation phase scores submitted to the leaderboard, while the lower sections display post-evaluation results using public answers. We then conduct abalation studies on the **development** set in later sections.

In the evaluation phrase, for **Subtask 1**, our threshold-based method achieved moderate results, with LERT-base-chinese performing relatively better for Norwegian, though with limitations. For **Subtask 2**, we fine-tuned an MLP to predict disagreement scores but observed limited performance, prompting alternative methods in the post-evaluation phase.

In the post-evaluation phase, for **Subtask 1**, the threshold-based model performed comparably to the MLP-based model, while large language models (LLMs) showed superior results, highlighting their potential. For **Subtask 2**, our results matched the evaluation phase's top performances, confirming the effectiveness of the ensembling approach.

5.1 Abalation Study on Subtask 1

Figure 1 shows the average performance change with different anisotropy removal methods across layers. The large gap between removal and non-removal emphasizes the importance of this technique. Performance improves with higher layers, except for a drop in the last one or two layers. Standardization consistently performs best across all layers.

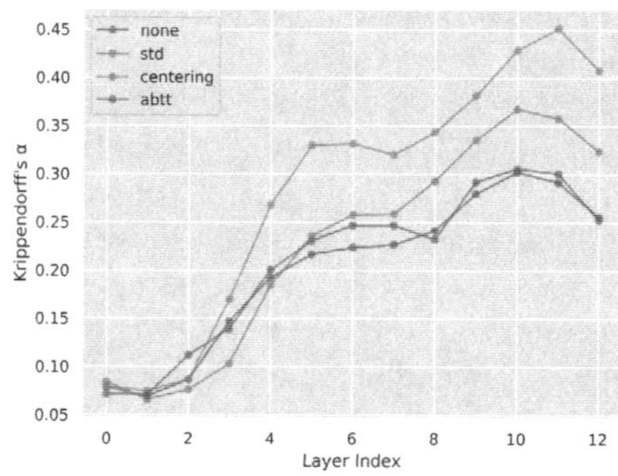

Figure 1: Performance of different types of anisotropy removal with the increase of layer index. 0 indicates the input embedding. "abtt" means all-but-the-top.

Figure 2 displays the performance of different models. Since Llama-7B is a decoder-only model with significantly more parameters and training data, its optimal result (Layer 25) serves as an upper bound [5]. The results show that XLM-RoBERTa-base outperforms all other models, including its larger counterpart.

[5] We attempt representations of different layers from Llama-7B, and the optimal layer index is 25.

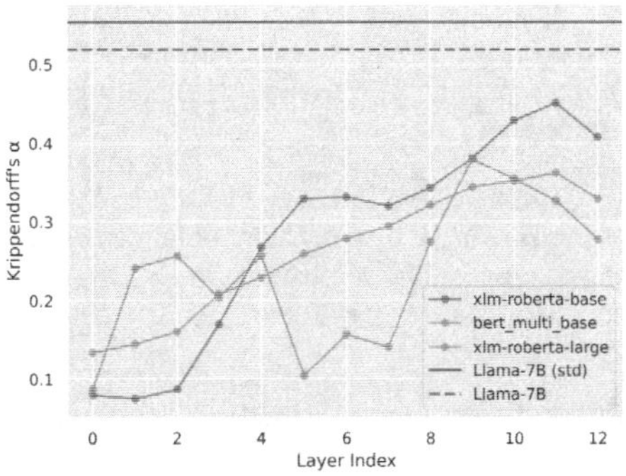

Figure 2: Performance of different models as the layer index increases. The optimal result (Layer 25) for Llama-7B and its standardized version are shown as the upper bound.

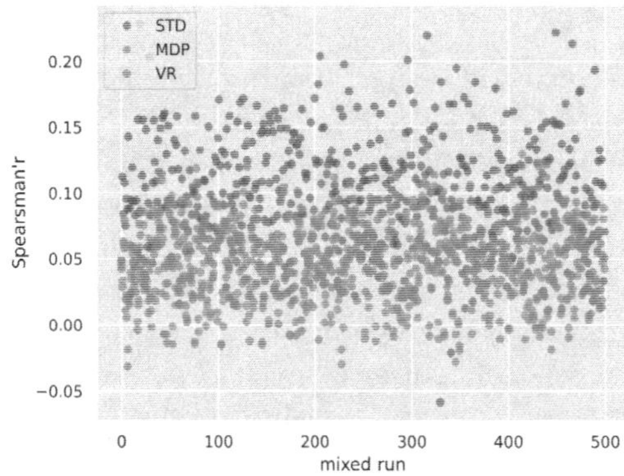

Figure 3: Performance of three types of measures across 500 random runs.

5.2 Abalation Study on Subtask 2

In this section, we analyze various factors influencing ensembling performance, including the choice of measure and model selection. We evaluate four candidate models i.e., XLM-RoBERTa-base, XLM-RoBERTa-large, BERT-multi-base, and Llama-7B, with four types of anisotropy removal and four layer levels. For layer levels, we extract layers 1, 4, 7, 10 for encoder-only models, and layers 8, 16, 24, 32 for the Llama model, yielding 64 possible model configurations. We use a threshold-based method for each model to obtain both a continuous similarity score and a discrete classification label, as we have done in Subtask 1. We randomly select a subset of 4 models from these possibilities, referred to as "mixed". Additionally, we experiment with homogeneous aggregation (using the same model) and heterogeneous aggregation (using different models). For homogeneous aggregation, we choose Llama-7B due to its superior performance. For each category, we sample 500 model subsets, obtaining both their classification labels using a threshold-based method and relatedness scores based on pre-trained embeddings. We first evaluate three measures (STD, MPD, and VR) in the mixed setting, selecting the best one to compare different category choices.

Measure Figure 3 presents the results for three measures. In most cases, STD on a continuous similarity score outperforms the others, while MDP slightly exceeds VR on the discrete classification labels . This suggests that similarity scores have an advantage over discrete labels due to the robustness of continuous values. Label prediction can be seen as a discretization of the continuous counterpart, leading to a loss of precision. Thus, we select STD as our final measure.

Type	1	2	3	4	5
homo	**0.237**	**0.235**	**0.235**	**0.234**	**0.233**
hete	0.217	0.216	0.215	0.209	0.201
mixed	0.228	0.222	0.219	0.213	0.203

Table 3: Top five groups for strategies of model selections

Model Selection Table 3 shows the top five results for three ensemble strategies. The specific model groups are listed in Tabel 7. Homogeneous model manipulations (homo) outperform mixed ensembles, while combining different models yields the worst performance. This suggests that model variance can still serve as an effective alternative, aligning with the use of dropout in uncertainty estimation (Gal, 2016).

6 Conclusion

We present our system for two subtasks released on CoMeDi Shared Task. We first formalize these tasks as parameter estimation where Subtask 1 estimates a mean and Subtask 2 the variance for a hypothetical Gaussian distribution. Then we mainly adopt threshold-based method with different techniques of anisotropy removal to classify the label for Subtask 1. Inspired by the area of uncertainty estimation, we utilize model ensembling with various strategies to select models and measures to reflect disagreement for Subtask 2. Experiments show the effectiveness of our method.

7 Limitations

We acknowledge several limitations in our system. First, the model training process utilizes data from all languages without considering their unique linguistic characteristics. For instance, Chinese exhibits rich formation rules (Zheng et al., 2021), yet lacks the morphological complexity found in Western languages, potentially leading to distinct patterns of disagreement. Second, our parameter estimation for the Gaussian distribution does not account for the estimation of the mean, which could be incorporated into Subtask 1 for a more comprehensive approach. Furthermore, in Subtask 2, we employ the median of all annotations as an independent label for the model instead of using individual annotations. This approach may introduce inconsistencies with our formulation of *models as annotators*. Lastly, while our experiments highlight the potential of large language models (LLMs) compared to pretrained language models, future work will focus on exploring more effective strategies for extracting lexical representations from LLMs.

8 Ethics Statement

We do not foresee any immediate negative ethical consequences arising from our research.

9 Acknowledgements

The authors thank the anonymous reviewers for their valuable comments and constructive feedback on the manuscript. This work is supported by the 2018 National Major Program of Philosophy and Social Science Fund "Analyses and Researches of Classic Texts of Classical Literature Based on Big Data Technology" (18ZDA238) and Research on the Long-Term Goals and Development Plan for National Language and Script Work by 2035 (ZDA145-6).

References

Anna Aksenova, Ekaterina Gavrishina, Elisei Rykov, and Andrey Kutuzov. 2022. RuDSI: Graph-based word sense induction dataset for Russian. In *Proceedings of TextGraphs-16: Graph-based Methods for Natural Language Processing*, pages 77–88, Gyeongju, Republic of Korea. Association for Computational Linguistics.

Jing Chen, Emmanuele Chersoni, Dominik Schlechtweg, Jelena Prokic, and Chu-Ren Huang. 2023. ChiWUG: A graph-based evaluation dataset for Chinese lexical semantic change detection. In *Proceedings of the 4th International Workshop on Computational Approaches to Historical Language Change*, Singapore. Association for Computational Linguistics.

Timothy Chklovski and Rada Mihalcea. 2003. Exploiting agreement and disagreement of human annotators for word sense disambiguation. In *Recent Advances in Natural Language Processing*.

Simone Conia and Roberto Navigli. 2021. Framing word sense disambiguation as a multi-label problem for model-agnostic knowledge integration. In *Proceedings of the 16th Conference of the European Chapter of the Association for Computational Linguistics: Main Volume*, pages 3269–3275.

A Conneau. 2019. Unsupervised cross-lingual representation learning at scale. *arXiv preprint arXiv:1911.02116*.

Kawin Ethayarajh. 2019. How contextual are contextualized word representations? comparing the geometry of bert, elmo, and gpt-2 embeddings. In *Proceedings of the 2019 Conference on Empirical Methods in Natural Language Processing and the 9th International Joint Conference on Natural Language Processing (EMNLP-IJCNLP)*, pages 55–65, Hong Kong, China. Association for Computational Linguistics.

Yarin Gal. 2016. *Uncertainty in Deep Learning*. Phd thesis, University of Cambridge.

Anna Hätty, Dominik Schlechtweg, and Sabine Schulte im Walde. 2019. SURel: A gold standard for incorporating meaning shifts into term extraction. In *Proceedings of the Eighth Joint Conference on Lexical and Computational Semantics (*SEM 2019)*, pages 1–8, Minneapolis, Minnesota. Association for Computational Linguistics.

Aminul Islam and Diana Inkpen. 2008. Semantic text similarity using corpus-based word similarity and string similarity. *ACM Transactions on Knowledge Discovery from Data*, 2(2):10:1–10:25.

Edwin T Jaynes. 2003. *Probability theory: The logic of science*. Cambridge university press.

Ting Jiang, Shaohan Huang, Zhongzhi Luan, Deqing Wang, and Fuzhen Zhuang. 2024. Scaling sentence embeddings with large language models. In *Findings of the Association for Computational Linguistics: EMNLP 2024*, pages 3182–3196, Miami, Florida, USA. Association for Computational Linguistics.

Sinan Kurtyigit, Maike Park, Dominik Schlechtweg, Jonas Kuhn, and Sabine Schulte im Walde. 2021. Lexical Semantic Change Discovery. In *Proceedings of the 59th Annual Meeting of the Association for Computational Linguistics and the 11th International Joint Conference on Natural Language Processing (Volume 1: Long Papers)*, Online. Association for Computational Linguistics.

Andrey Kutuzov and Lidia Pivovarova. 2021. Rushifteval: a shared task on semantic shift detection for russian. *Komp'yuternaya Lingvistika i Intellektual'nye Tekhnologii: Dialog conference*.

Andrey Kutuzov, Samia Touileb, Petter Mæhlum, Tita Enstad, and Alexandra Wittemann. 2022. NorDiaChange: Diachronic semantic change dataset for Norwegian. In *Proceedings of the Thirteenth Language Resources and Evaluation Conference*, pages 2563–2572, Marseille, France. European Language Resources Association.

Balaji Lakshminarayanan, Alexander Pritzel, and Charles Blundell. 2017. Simple and scalable predictive uncertainty estimation using deep ensembles. *Advances in neural information processing systems*, 30.

Zhu Liu, Cunliang Kong, Ying Liu, and Maosong Sun. 2024. Fantastic semantics and where to find them: Investigating which layers of generative LLMs reflect lexical semantics. In *Findings of the Association for Computational Linguistics: ACL 2024*, pages 14551–14558, Bangkok, Thailand. Association for Computational Linguistics.

Zhu Liu and Ying Liu. 2023. Ambiguity meets uncertainty: Investigating uncertainty estimation for word sense disambiguation. In *Findings of the Association for Computational Linguistics: ACL 2023*, pages 3963–3977.

Jiaqi Mu and Pramod Viswanath. 2018. All-but-the-top: Simple and effective postprocessing for word representations. In *International Conference on Learning Representations*.

Roberto Navigli. 2008. A structural approach to the automatic adjudication of word sense disagreements. *Natural Language Engineering*, 14(4):547–573.

Roberto Navigli. 2009. Word sense disambiguation: A survey. *ACM computing surveys (CSUR)*, 41(2):1–69.

John A. Nelder and Roger Mead. 1965. A simplex method for function minimization. *The Computer Journal*, 7(4):308–313.

Mohammad Taher Pilehvar and Jose Camacho-Collados. 2019. Wic: the word-in-context dataset for evaluating context-sensitive meaning representations. In *Proceedings of NAACL-HLT*, pages 1267–1273.

T Pires. 2019. How multilingual is multilingual bert. *arXiv preprint arXiv:1906.01502*.

Julia Rodina and Andrey Kutuzov. 2020. RuSemShift: a dataset of historical lexical semantic change in Russian. In *Proceedings of the 28th International Conference on Computational Linguistics*, pages 1037–1047, Barcelona, Spain (Online). International Committee on Computational Linguistics.

Magnus Sahlgren, Amaru Cuba Gyllensten, Fredrik Espinoza, Ola Hamfors, Jussi Karlgren, Fredrik Olsson, Per Persson, Akshay Viswanathan, and Anders Holst. 2016. The gavagai living lexicon. In *Proceedings of the Tenth International Conference on Language Resources and Evaluation (LREC 2016)*, Paris, France. European Language Resources Association (ELRA).

Dominik Schlechtweg. 2023. *Human and computational measurement of lexical semantic change*. Ph.D. thesis, University of Stuttgart, Germany.

Dominik Schlechtweg, Pierluigi Cassotti, Bill Noble, David Alfter, Sabine Schulte im Walde, and Nina Tahmasebi. 2024. More DWUGs: Extending and evaluating word usage graph datasets in multiple languages. In *Proceedings of the 2024 Conference on Empirical Methods in Natural Language Processing*, Miami, Florida. Association for Computational Linguistics.

Dominik Schlechtweg, Tejaswi Choppa, Wei Zhao, and Michael Roth. 2025. The CoMeDi shared task: Median judgment classification & mean disagreement ranking with ordinal word-in-context judgments. In *Proceedings of the 1st Workshop on Context and Meaning–Navigating Disagreements in NLP Annotations*, Abu Dhabi, UAE.

Dominik Schlechtweg, Sabine Schulte im Walde, and Stefanie Eckmann. 2018. Diachronic usage relatedness (DURel): A framework for the annotation of lexical semantic change. In *Proceedings of the 2018 Conference of the North American Chapter of the Association for Computational Linguistics: Human Language Technologies, Volume 2 (Short Papers)*, pages 169–174, New Orleans, Louisiana. Association for Computational Linguistics.

Dominik Schlechtweg, Nina Tahmasebi, Simon Hengchen, Haim Dubossarsky, and Barbara McGillivray. 2021. DWUG: A large resource of diachronic word usage graphs in four languages. In *Proceedings of the 2021 Conference on Empirical Methods in Natural Language Processing*, pages 7079–7091, Online and Punta Cana, Dominican Republic. Association for Computational Linguistics.

David Stutz. 2022. Understanding and improving robustness and uncertainty estimation in deep learning. *Saarländische Universitäts-und Landesbibliothek*.

Christian Szegedy, Vincent Vanhoucke, Sergey Ioffe, Jon Shlens, and Zbigniew Wojna. 2016. Rethinking the inception architecture for computer vision. In *Proceedings of the IEEE conference on computer vision and pattern recognition*, pages 2818–2826.

Ian Tenney, Patrick Xia, Berlin Chen, Alex Wang, Adam Poliak, R Thomas McCoy, Najoung Kim, Benjamin Van Durme, Samuel R Bowman, Dipanjan Das, et al. 2019. What do you learn from context? probing for sentence structure in contextualized word representations. In *7th International Conference on Learning Representations, ICLR 2019*.

William Timkey and Marten van Schijndel. 2021. All bark and no bite: Rogue dimensions in transformer language models obscure representational quality. In *Proceedings of the 2021 Conference on Empirical Methods in Natural Language Processing (EMNLP)*, pages 4527–4546, Online and Punta Cana, Dominican Republic. Association for Computational Linguistics.

Hugo Touvron, Thibaut Lavril, Gautier Izacard, Xavier Martinet, Marie-Anne Lachaux, Timothée Lacroix, Baptiste Rozière, Naman Goyal, Eric Hambro, Faisal Azhar, et al. 2023. Llama: Open and efficient foundation language models. *arXiv preprint arXiv:2302.13971*.

Alexandra N Uma, Tommaso Fornaciari, Dirk Hovy, Silviu Paun, Barbara Plank, and Massimo Poesio. 2021. Learning from disagreement: A survey. *Journal of Artificial Intelligence Research*, 72:1385–1470.

Artem Vazhentsev, Gleb Kuzmin, Artem Shelmanov, Akim Tsvigun, Evgenii Tsymbalov, Kirill Fedyanin, Maxim Panov, Alexander Panchenko, Gleb Gusev, Mikhail Burtsev, et al. 2022. Uncertainty estimation of transformer predictions for misclassification detection. In *Proceedings of the 60th Annual Meeting of the Association for Computational Linguistics (Volume 1: Long Papers)*, pages 8237–8252.

Ivan Vulić, Edoardo Maria Ponti, Robert Litschko, Goran Glavaš, and Anna Korhonen. 2020. Probing pretrained language models for lexical semantics. In *Proceedings of the 2020 Conference on Empirical Methods in Natural Language Processing (EMNLP)*, pages 7222–7240, Online. Association for Computational Linguistics.

Frank D. Zamora-Reina, Felipe Bravo-Marquez, and Dominik Schlechtweg. 2022. LSCDiscovery: A shared task on semantic change discovery and detection in Spanish. In *Proceedings of the 3rd International Workshop on Computational Approaches to Historical Language Change*, Dublin, Ireland. Association for Computational Linguistics.

Hua Zheng, Lei Li, Damai Dai, Deli Chen, Tianyu Liu, Xu Sun, and Yang Liu. 2021. Leveraging word-formation knowledge for Chinese word sense disambiguation. In *Findings of the Association for Computational Linguistics: EMNLP 2021*, pages 918–923, Punta Cana, Dominican Republic. Association for Computational Linguistics.

10 Appendix

10.1 MLP-based Methods

We attempt the MLP-based method in two subtasks, freezing XLM-RoBERTa-base model parameters to obtain the vector representation of the target word, and training a classifier or a regression model downstream. MLP1 is a linear layer, MLP2 represents two linear layers, and uses the ReLU activation function.

In Subtask 1, we use the cross-entropy loss function to train a classifier. The results on the development dataset are shown in Table 4. We find that two linear layers achieve better results. We attempt to use a weighted cross-entropy loss function to alleviate the problem of sample imbalance, but shows slight improvement. We compare the results of different layers of the model and find that the vector representation of the shallower layers(11th) achieves better results. We attempt layer fusion and average pooling of the vectors in the last 4 layers, which results in more stable improvements.

Training settings for the MLP-based method in Subtask 1: 50 epochs, batch size of 128, 1e-2 learning rate, AdamW optimizer, and a dropout rate of 0.1 to improve generalization.

In Subtask 2, we use the mean square error loss function to train a regression model that directly predicts continuous values of inconsistent labeling of target words, similar to the baseline provided by the official source. The results on the development dataset are shown in Table 5. We find that two linear layers are worse than a single linear layer.

We try multiple different hyperparameter settings on Task 2. In MLP1, we ultimately chose 200 epochs, batch size of 16, while in MLP2, we chose 50 epochs, batch size of 32. Other training settings: 1e-2 learning rate, AdamW optimizer, and a dropout rate of 0.1.

10.2 Model Groups

We use letters to denote different models: A, B, C, and D represent Llama-7B, XLM-RoBERTa-base, BERT-multi-base, and XLM-RoBERTa-large, respectively.

For encoder-only models, h, i, j, and k indicate layers 1, 4, 7, and 10, respectively; whereas in large language models (LLMs), these symbols correspond to layers 8, 16, 24, and 32.

X, Y, Z, and W correspond to four standardization methods: non-standard, std, centering, and all-but-the-top.

Model groups for specific languages. We experiment with various model groups, and different groups achieve the best results in different languages. Table 2 shows the best results for the test dataset in Subtask 2, and the specific model groups are shown in Table 6.

Top 5 model groups. We employ three ensemble strategies, and the top five results of each strategy on the development dataset of Subtask 2 are presented in Table 3, with corresponding model groups shown in Table 7.

Method	AVG	ZH	EN	DE	NO	RU	ES	SV
MLP1	0.191	0.105	-0.140	0.192	0.337	0.276	0.418	0.151
weighted loss	0.240	0.361	0.110	0.166	0.156	0.255	0.354	0.277
layer11	0.265	0.267	0.009	0.261	0.357	0.298	0.341	0.321
MLP2	0.407	0.519	0.268	**0.609**	0.360	0.265	0.565	0.262
layer11	0.418	0.530	**0.384**	0.511	**0.416**	0.311	0.576	0.198
last4layer	**0.429**	**0.509**	0.229	0.570	0.306	**0.416**	**0.584**	**0.386**

Table 4: Evaluation results for Subtask 1 in MLP-based methods. The upper part presents the outcomes of using a single linear layer as a classifier, where "weight loss" indicates the employment of a weighted cross-entropy loss function, and "layer11" denotes utilizing the vector representations from the 11th layer of the language model. The lower part illustrates the results obtained by employing two linear layers as classifiers, showing the performance of the 11th layer of the model as well as the outcome after applying average pooling to the last four layers of the model.

Method	AVG	ZH	EN	DE	NO	RU	ES	SV
MLP1	**0.128**	**0.323**	**0.088**	**0.179**	**0.132**	**0.061**	0.026	0.083
MLP2	0.098	0.232	-0.061	0.131	0.119	0.020	**0.061**	**0.187**

Table 5: Evaluation results for Subtask 2 in MLP-based methods, demonstrating the results of Multi-Layer Perceptrons (MLPs) with different numbers of layers.

Language	Model Groups
Chinese	AiX-AkX-AhX-AkW
English	AjZ-AiX-AjX-AjW
German	AhW-AjX-AjW-AjZ
Norwegian	AjZ-AiX-AjX-AjW
Russian	AiX-AiW-AkW-AkZ
Spanish	AhY-AiZ-AhX-AhW
Swedish	AiX-AkY-AjZ-AjY

Table 6: The optimal model groups for each specific language for the development set in Subtask 2.

Type	1	2	3	4	5
homo	**AjY-AjZ-AiX-AiW**	**AjY-AiW-AjZ-AjX**	**AjX-AiX-AiW-AjY**	**AjZ-AiX-AjX-AjW**	**AiX-AjZ-AjX-AhX**
hete	AjY-BkW-ChZ-DkX	AjY-BiX-ChW-DjX	AjY-BkW-CiX-DiW	AjZ-BkW-ChY-DhW	AjY-BhW-ChY-DiX
mixed	AjX-ChX-AiX-AjZ	AjY-AiX-AjW-ChY	AkW-ChX-AjY-AjW	AjZ-ChY-DhX-DkX	ChX-AkY-AiX-AiW

Table 7: Top five model groups when ensembling models for Subtask 2.

MMLabUIT at CoMeDi Shared Task: Text Embedding Techniques versus Generation-Based NLI for Median Judgment Classification

Le Duc Tai[1,2], Trong-Tai Dam Vu[1,2], Dang Van Thin[1,2],
[1]University of Information Technology-VNUHCM, Ho Chi Minh City, Vietnam
[2]Vietnam National University, Ho Chi Minh City, Vietnam
23521374@gm.uit.edu.vn, {taidvt,thindv}@uit.edu.vn

Abstract

This paper presents our approach in the COLING 2025 - CoMeDi task in 7 languages, focusing on sub-task 1: Median Judgment Classification with Ordinal Word-in-Context Judgments (OGWiC). Specifically, we need to determine the meaning relation of one word in two different contexts and classify the input into 4 labels. To address sub-task 1, we implement and investigate various solutions, including (1) Stacking, Averaged Embedding techniques with a multilingual BERT-based model; and (2) utilizing a Natural Language Inference approach instead of a regular classification process. All the experiments were conducted on the P100 GPU from the Kaggle platform. To enhance the context of input, we perform Improve Known Data Rate and Text Expansion in some languages. For model focusing purposes Custom Token was used in the data processing pipeline. Our best official results on the test set are 0.515, 0.518, and 0.524 in terms of Krippendorff's α score on task 1. Our participation system achieved a Top 3 ranking in task 1. Besides the official result, our best approach also achieved 0.596 regarding Krippendorff's α score on Task 1.

1 Introduction

The CoMeDi 2025 shared-task (Schlechtweg et al., 2025) aims to investigate and model disagreements in word sense annotation within context. Specifically, the task focuses on predicting the median annotator judgment for word usage pairs based on an ordinal scale and exploring the linguistic and semantic factors that contribute to annotation disagreement. Two sub-tasks were proposed for participants in this shared task. The first challenge called Median Judgment Classification with Ordinal Word-in-Context Judgments, aims to measure the meaning of a word in two different contexts by classifying them into four ordinal judgments: "homonymy", "polysemy", "context variance", and "identity". While the second task, Mean Disagreement Ranking with Ordinal Word-in-Context Judgments aims to predict the mean of pairwise absolute judgment differences between annotators.

In general, the data annotation process is often hindered by disagreements among annotators and misunderstandings in daily communication. These challenges stem from the inherent ambiguity of language, where a single word can have multiple meanings and word meanings can shift based on context. Such ambiguity can significantly impact communication quality, leading to misinterpretations and reduced clarity. Addressing these issues is essential to improve the accuracy and reliability of both human and automated communication. As a result, in this paper, we present our solutions for Task 1 - Median Judgment Classification with Ordinal Word-in-Context Judgments in the CoMeDi 2025 shared-task (Schlechtweg et al., 2025). Specifically, we employ two different approaches to address this task: (1) stacking and average text embedding methods, and (2) BERT-based and generative-based models with natural language inference, combined with custom tokens.

2 Related Works

In recent years, researchers have made significant advancements in linguistic features such as Named Entity Recognition and part-of-speech tagging. However, there has been limited exploration of utilizing BERT-based models with Natural Language Processing approaches or custom tokens. An early SemEval shared task, Task 3, was introduced by (Armendariz et al., 2020), which had a substantial impact on advancing research in grading word similarity within context. This challenge is closely related to our CoMeDi task (Schlechtweg et al., 2025). A study by Hettiarachchi and Ranasinghe (2020) proposed an innovative method to enhance model performance using Stacked Embeddings. In this approach, different word embeddings are con-

Proceedings of Context and Meaning: Navigating Disagreements in NLP Annotation, pages 113–121
January 19, 2025.

catenated to create a final vector. By combining embeddings from various learning techniques, this method integrates their distinct characteristics. Additionally, average embeddings, which consider the mean of weights across different layers, are used to merge the information learned at each layer. Cosine similarity is then computed to generate predictions.

The work by Costella Pessutto et al. (2020) introduced a technique called BabelEncoding, which significantly improved word similarity grading in the context of Croatian. BabelEncoding involves three key steps: translation, multi-embedding extraction using BERT and Mono Word Embeddings, and the calculation of weighted averages. Chen et al. (2020) enhanced prediction results by incorporating sentence structure and TF-IDF (term frequency-inverse document frequency) features along with BERT word embeddings. In their approach, TF-IDF features were integrated into a masking layer of the BERT model, rather than just feeding the input text into BERT alone. Meanwhile, Gamallo (2020) proposed an innovative solution for word similarity tasks by combining BERT word embeddings with Dependency-Based Contextualization. This technique improves inference by considering the contextual meaning of a word in a sequence, taking into account the static embeddings of syntactically related words to the target word.

3 Task Description

The **CoMeDi (Contextual Meaning Disagreement)** shared-task[1] focuses on exploring and modeling disagreements in annotator judgments regarding word meanings in specific contexts. The primary goal is to understand and predict these disagreements in "Word-in-Context" (WiC) scenarios, where the meaning of a word can change based on its usage. There are two sub-tasks proposed to address as described below.

3.1 Task 1: Median Judgment Classification with Ordinal Word-in-Context Judgments (OGWiC)

In Task 1, the goal is to predict the median of annotator judgments for each word use pair in the WiC data. Each use pair consists of two instances of the same target word in different contexts. Annotators rate the relatedness of these instances on an ordinal scale from 1 to 4. This task can also be framed as a classification problem, where the objective is to categorize the relationship between the two instances into one of four classes: "homonymy", "polysemy", "context variance", and "identity".

3.2 Task 2: Mean Disagreement Ranking with Ordinal Word-in-Context Judgments (DisWiC)

In Task 2, the purpose task is to predict the mean of pairwise judgment differences between annotators for each use pair. This task involves ranking instances based on the level of disagreement observed in annotators' ratings. Unlike Task 1, which focuses on classification, Task 2 explicitly aims to capture and rank instances with higher annotator disagreement, providing insight into areas where word meanings are more subjective or ambiguous.

3.3 Dataset descriptions

The dataset provided by the competition includes seven languages (Chinese, English, German, Norwegian, Russian, Spanish, and Swedish), based on various data sets on semantic change as shown in Table 1. This multilingual scope provides a unique opportunity to explore how annotator disagreement patterns manifest across different linguistic and cultural contexts.

4 Methodology

In this section, we present three approaches for Task 1 in CoMeDi shared tasks in detail.

4.1 Data Processing

Our initial experiments focused on three dataset variations: raw, cleaned, and lemmatized. Specifically, we applied lemmatization and punctuation removal as part of the data cleaning process. However, these pre-processing steps did not lead to improved accuracy. Consequently, we simplified the cleaning process by removing only special characters, hashtags, and URLs.

Given the imbalanced nature of the dataset, we employed the stratified K-fold cross-validation technique (Bates et al., 2023) with $K = 10$ to mitigate the effects of data imbalance on the models. Stratified cross-validation ensures that the class distribution remains consistent across folds, thereby reducing bias in performance estimation caused by unequal class distributions in random splits. This approach enables a more reliable evaluation of model performance across diverse subsets of the data.

[1] https://comedinlp.github.io/

Table 1: Dataset Information for the Median Judgment Task.

Language	Dataset[version]
Chinese	ChiWUG[1.0.0] (Chen et al., 2023)
English	DWUG_EN [3.0.0], DWUG_EN_resampled [1.0.0] (Schlechtweg et al., 2024)
German	DWUG_DE [3.0.0], DWUG_DE_resampled [1.0.0], DiscoWUG [2.0.0], RefWUG [1.1.0] ((Schlechtweg et al., 2024) (Kurtyigit et al., 2021))
	DURel [3.0.0] (Schlechtweg et al., 2018)
	SURel [3.0.0] (Hätty et al., 2019)
Norwegian	NorDiaChange1, NorDiaChange2 (Kutuzov et al., 2022)
Russian	RuSemShift_1, RuSemShift_2 (Rodina and Kutuzov, 2020)
	RuShiftEval1, RuShiftEval2, RuShiftEval3 (Kutuzov and Pivovarova, 2021)
	RuDSI (Aksenova et al., 2022)
Spanish	DWUG_ES [4.0.1] (Schlechtweg et al., 2024)
Swedish	DWUG_SV [3.0.0], DWUG_SV_resampled [1.0.0] (Schlechtweg et al., 2024)

For data augmentation, we employed back-translation, applying it to entire sentences while preserving the target word. However, this method did not yield significant improvements, probably due to contextual alterations introduced during the translation process. Consequently, we opted not to use the back-translation technique to address the imbalance problem.

4.2 Stack Embedding

To create a final representation of each word-use pair, we combine BERT-based embeddings from different pre-trained language models, including $\text{mBERT}_{\text{large}}$ (Pires et al., 2019) and $\text{XLM-RoBERTa}_{\text{large}}$ (Conneau et al., 2019). These models are used to extract the embedding features of BERT words. Stacked embeddings are created by concatenating vectors from multiple embedding models to form a final, richer representation. This approach leverages the complementary characteristics of different embeddings, enabling the models to generalize across domains and adapt more effectively during fine-tuning. Let v_i^{stk} represent the final or stacked word vector corresponding to the word i, and v_{model_i} represent the vector obtained by using the embedding model m. The stacked vector is formed as shown below:

$$v_i^{\text{stk}} = \begin{bmatrix} v_{\text{model}_1,i} \\ v_{\text{model}_2,i} \\ \vdots \\ v_{\text{model}_m,i} \end{bmatrix} \quad (1)$$

After extracting the Stack Embedding features, we calculated Cosine Similarity and followed the baseline approach provided by the organizers. As shown in Table 2, the results on the test set demonstrated the performance of this approach.

Table 2: The result of Stacking Embedding method.

Model	Data	Krippendorff's α
BERT	Raw	0.267
BERT	Clean	**0.312**
XLM-Roberta	Raw	0.217
XLM-Roberta	Clean	0.201

4.3 Averaged Embedding

Instead of stacking the different representations, we also compute the average of the weights across different layers to combine the information learned by each layer. This approach is called an average embedding approach. For word i, the average embedding v_i^{avg} is calculated by considering the last l layers, as shown in Equation 2. The weights in the last layer are represented by the vector v_i^{-1}, and k denotes the number of layers selected for this calculation. The formula of the average embedding technique is presented below.

$$v_i^{\text{avg}} = \frac{v_i^{-l} + \cdots + v_i^{-1}}{k} = \frac{1}{k}\sum_{l=1}^{k} v_i^{(l)} \quad (2)$$

Because each layer returns a distinct embedding and different layers of transformer-based models often capture different types of information, the lower layers tend to capture more syntactic features, such as sentence structure and grammar, while higher layers capture more semantic information, such as word meaning and sentence context. Average Embedding provides a more robust representation of

Table 3: The result of Average Embedding method.

Model	Data	Krippendorff's α
BERT	Raw	0.193
BERT	Clean	**0.341**
XLM-Roberta	Raw	0.229
XLM-Roberta	Clean	0.231

a word by reducing the impact of noisy or outlier activations in individual layers. It also helps reduce the dimensionality of the feature space, creating a more compact representation of the word or sentence. By combining both syntactic and semantic features, Average Embedding can improve the quality of the input embeddings for model fine-tuning. After extracting the Average Embedding features, we computed the Cosine Similarity and followed the baseline approach provided by the organizers. The results of the test set are shown in Table 3.

4.4 Natural Language Inference

Natural Language Inference (NLI) is the task of determining whether a "hypothesis" is true (entailment), false (contradiction), or undetermined (neutral) given a "premise". NLI can also be treated as a classification task, but there are some key differences between the two. NLI requires two text inputs, labeled as "hypothesis" and "premise", and the model needs to classify the relationship between them into one of three possible labels. Our team observed that NLI bears a strong resemblance to Task 1: Median Judgment Classification with Ordinal Word-in-Context Judgments, as both tasks involve classifying or grading the relationship between two textual elements. In task 1, the goal is to classify the similarity of two words, which is conceptually similar to determining the relationship between two sentences in NLI. Therefore, conducting experiments in Task 1 using NLI could prove promising.

Our team experimented with two strategies, including:

- **Fine-tuning the original language models on NLI task**: The list of language models includes mBERT [2] (Devlin et al., 2018), XLM-R[3] (Conneau et al., 2019) and XLM-R [4] (Liu et al., 2019).
- **Fine-tuning the language models trained NLI task**: The purpose of this task is to continue fine-tuning the model that is trained on the NLI task for the OGWiC task. We choose the XLM-R-XNLI model[5] as the main language model for this strategy.

Initially, our team conducted experiments on small models due to GPU resource limitations with the aim of testing whether our approach was effective. These initial experiments confirmed that BERT-based models performed better than the stacking and average embedding methods. Subsequently, we analyzed larger BERT-based models, such as *FacebookAI/xlm-roberta-large* and *FacebookAI/roberta-large*.

Even though large BERT-based classification approaches yielded better results than stacking and average embedding methods, as shown in table 4, the results demonstrated that the large BERT-based classification approach achieved Krippendorff's α scores of 0.381 and 0.419, surpassing the best scores of the stacking and average embedding methods, which were 0.312 and 0.341, respectively.

Additionally, our team examined the performance of a BERT-based model previously trained on the Natural Language Inference (NLI) task. As expected, the *joeddav/xlm-roberta-large-xnli* model significantly outperformed the other two large-sized models.

4.5 Generative-based Model Approach

In this approach, using a generative-based model, our team opted to experiment with the BART model (Lewis et al., 2020) by adapting it for a classification task through fine-tuning. BART functions as a denoising auto-encoder designed for pretraining sequence-to-sequence models. It is trained by intentionally introducing noise into text and then learning to reconstruct the original content.

The model employs a standard Transformer-based neural machine translation framework, which, while straightforward, effectively generalizes over other models such as BERT (with its bidirectional encoder) and GPT (with its left-to-right decoder), along with recent pretraining approaches. For fine-tuning BART for sequence classification tasks, the model processes the input through both the encoder and decoder. The last hidden state of the final token in the decoder is then fed into a new linear classifier for multi-class prediction. This

[2] google-bert/bert-base-multilingual-cased

[3] FacebookAI/xlm-roberta-large

[4] FacebookAI/roberta-large

[5] joeddav/xlm-roberta-large-xnli

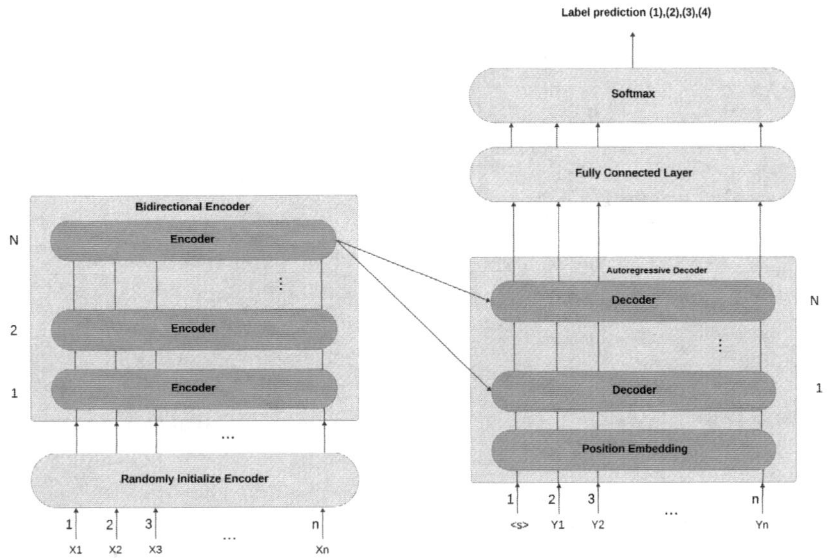

Figure 1: BART Architecture fine-tune for NLI task.

Table 4: The experimental results of BERT-based classification and NLI approach on the test set.

Model	**Method**	**Krippendorff's** α
facebook/bart-large-mnli	Natural Language Inference	**0.518**
joeddav/xlm-roberta-large-xnli	Natural Language Inference	0.482
FacebookAI/roberta-large	Classification	0.419
FacebookAI/xlm-roberta-large	Classification	0.381
google-bert/bert-base-multilingual-cased	Classification	0.356

approach resembles the use of the CLS token in BERT; however, an additional token is appended to the input's end, enabling the final token's representation in the decoder to attend to all decoder states generated from the full input sequence.

Similar to the BERT-based approach, we used a tokenizer to tokenize the two inputs, which were then fed into BART. Moreover, we utilized the pre-trained *facebook/bart-large-mnli* (Lewis et al., 2019) model, which was trained on the MNLI (Williams et al., 2018) dataset. The generative-based model achieved remarkable results compared to the BERT-based model, as shown in Table 4.

4.6 Custom Token

Given the promising results achieved by pre-trained BERT-based models on Natural Language Inference tasks, we sought to further explore this approach. While pre-trained Natural Language Inference models offer significant advantages, a key challenge arises in directing the model's focus to specific target words rather than entire sentences. To address this, our team introduced a Custom Token technique designed to enhance the model's attention to target words. Our analysis suggests that by incorporating Custom Tokens around target words, the model can allocate greater attention to these specific words, leading to subtle improvements in prediction accuracy. The following example illustrates the application of Custom Tokens:

Original input:

Context1: *"Esposito has gone for an afternoon walk and fallen asleep, his walking stick in his hand, one knee bent, his head pillowed on a stone."*

Context2: *"Old shopping lists and ticket stubs and wads of listed newsprint come falling around Pafko in the faded afternoon."*

Custom Token

Context1: *"Esposito has gone for an <target> afternoon </target> walk and fallen asleep, his walking stick in his hand, one knee bent, his head pillowed on a stone."*

Context2: *"Old shopping lists and ticket stubs and wads of listed newsprint come falling around Pafko in the faded <target> afternoon </target>."*

Custom tokens help clarify for the model which parts of the input are significant for the task. Thus, with the help of Custom Token, we combined this technique with the Natural Language Inference approach, and our team has recognized a slight improvement in accuracy, which is 0.524 in terms of Krippendorff's α.

4.7 Improve Known Data Rate

In this research, we used pre-trained embedding models, which meant that the dataset included tokens like names of people, organizations, locations, and other entities that weren't part of the model's original vocabulary. To create consistency and make the data more recognizable for the model during embedding generation, we replaced these unfamiliar names of people, organizations, locations, and other entities that weren't part of the model's original vocabulary with more common ones. This transformation was done automatically using the Named Entity Recognition (NER) task, based on the approach described by (Pakhale, 2023). Identified named entities, detected with spaCy (Honnibal and Montani, 2017) tools, were substituted in place of the unknown tokens. The example transformation is shown below:

Original: "**Esposito** *has gone for an afternoon walk and fallen asleep, his walking stick in his hand, one knee bent, his head pillowed on a stone."*

Improve Known Data Rate: "**Person** *has gone for an afternoon walk and fallen asleep, his walking stick in his hand, one knee bent, his head pillowed on a stone."*

As you can see in the example transformation, *"Esposito"* is replaced with *"Person"*. However, due to the limitation of time and resources our team could only perform Improve Known Data Rate transformation in English and Swedish.

5 Experimental Setup

5.1 Data and Evaluation Metrics

We conducted experiments exclusively on the dataset provided by the organizer for training models and testing approaches in this shared task. Table 5 summarizes key information about the training and testing datasets, while Table 6 provides general statistics and the distribution of four classes in the training dataset. By observing the class polarity in Table 6, we note that the ratio between the classes is unbalanced. Specifically, the total samples in classes (1), (2), and (3) are fewer than the total samples in class (4). This imbalance could introduce bias during fine-tuning.

Table 5: The information of the experimental dataset.

Information	Training set	Validation set	Test set
Number of samples	47833	8287	15332
Number of tokens	2990377	436735	985402
The average length	40.41	37.94	40.74
The maximum length	1643	493	605

Imbalanced data was one of the main challenges that competitors needed to address while implementing distinct techniques to achieve optimal results. To handle the imbalance in class labels, our team utilized data augmentation techniques, one of the most effective methods for addressing this issue. Data augmentation helps mitigate bias in performance estimation. Specifically, we applied the back-translation method to classes (1), (2), and (3) to reduce data polarity and make the class distribution less imbalanced.

However, the back-translation method proved suboptimal for addressing the imbalance issue. When translating input while preserving the target word, changes in the sentence's context may negatively impact the prediction of the target word. As shown in Table 5, the number of samples in the training dataset is significantly higher than in the testing dataset, enabling our models to train effectively and generalize well. Additionally, we perform some data cleaning processes before fine-tuning models:

- **Noise Removal:** We observed that there are a lot of noises, such as punctuation and special characters, in the dataset. We found that these noises are not necessary for the sentence-level dataset. Therefore, we remove it from the samples.

- **Text Expansion:** we also perform text expansion in English for example: "*I'll*" into "*I will*" or "*he'd*" into "*he would*". Text expansion was utilized for consistency of data purposes, and this can help the model to generalize better.

Table 6: The statistic of class distribution beyond dataset.

Class samples	Homonymy	Polysemy	Context variance	Identity
Training set	7099	4 510	5967	30257
Validation set	1055	817	739	5676
Full dataset	8154	5327	6706	35933

5.2 System Settings

We conducted our training process using HuggingFace (Wolf et al., 2020), and all BERT-based models were trained for 10 epochs. The AdamW optimizer was utilized to optimize the models. We selected a learning rate of 5e-5,3e-5 for BERT-based models. The batch sizes were set to 16 and 32, the random seed was set to 221, and the maximum token length was 512.

Due to computational resource limitations, we had to adjust system settings for fine-tuning the BART-MNLI model (Lewis et al., 2019). Specifically, we reduced the batch size to 8 and employed gradient accumulation to effectively train on larger effective batch sizes. This technique allows us to accumulate gradients over multiple smaller batches before updating the optimizer, mitigating memory constraints. Furthermore, we utilized mixed precision training (FP16) and gradient checkpointing to accelerate training and reduce memory usage. Mixed precision training combines 16-bit and 32-bit floating-point operations, enabling efficient training of large-scale models like transformers. Dynamic loss scaling was employed to maintain numerical stability. Given GPU limitations, we trained BART for only 6 epochs and opted for the AdaFactor optimizer, known for its efficiency in training large models, instead of AdamW. All models were evaluated using the metric provided by the task organizers. Our team leveraged a P100 GPU, available for up to 30 free hours per week on Kaggle, for computational resources.

6 Main Result

The official evaluation phase and post-evaluation phase submission results are presented in Table 7. The *facebook/bart-large-mnli* model with NLI, custom token, and average embedding on Chinese achieved the highest Krippendorff's α score of 0.596. In the official evaluation phase, we submitted predictions created with *joeddav/xlm-roberta-large-xnli* with Improve Known Data Rate and Custom Token for NLI, and *facebook/bart-large-mnli* fine-tuned for NLI, which attained a Krippendorff's alpha score of 0.524 and 0.518, respectively. Furthermore, in the last submission we submitted *joeddav/xlm-roberta-large-xnli* combined with Improve Known Data Rate which only achieved 0.515 in Krippendorff's alpha.

Through experimentation, our team observed that all classification or natural language inference approaches performed worse in Chinese compared to the stacking and average embedding methods. As a result, we utilized stacking and average embeddings exclusively for Chinese and found that average embedding outperformed stacking embedding in this context.

By combining different techniques, we leveraged the advantages of each method, leading to better results overall. Additionally, our team's official ranking in the top 3rd position demonstrates promising results in Task 1: Median Judgment Classification with Ordinal Word-in-Context Judgments (OGWiC).

7 Conclusion and Future Work

In this paper, we present our approaches for the shared task CoMeDi 2025 (Schlechtweg et al., 2025), Task 1: Median Judgment Classification with Ordinal Word-in-Context Judgments (OGWiC). Our methods achieved a top 3rd ranking in the official hard-label evaluation of Task 1 shown in Table 8 and achieved the final result by using *joeddav/xlm-roberta-large-xnli* combined with Custom token and Improve Know Data Rate technique which results in 0.524 final scores. Moreover, pretrained BART models on NLI task also achieve 0.518 and *joeddav/xlm-roberta-large-xnli* combined with Improve Know Data Rate only achieve 0.515 in Krippendorff's α.

We introduced various methods and combinations, including stacking, averaged embedding techniques, natural language inference, a generative-based model approach combined with custom tokens, and improved known data rates. Through experimentation and analysis, our approaches yielded promising results for Task 1. Moreover, our approaches can bring novelty in examining how word

Table 7: All evaluation and post-evaluation results.

Model	Method	Score
facebook/bart-large-mnli	NLI + Custom Token + Average Embedding(Chinese)	**0.596**
joeddav/xlm-roberta-large-xnli	NLI + Custom Token + Improve Known Data Rate	**0.524**
facebook/bart-large-mnli	Natural Language Inference	**0.518**
joeddav/xlm-roberta-large-xnli	NLI + Improve Known Data Rate	0.515
joeddav/xlm-roberta-large-xnli	Natural Language Inference	0.482
Baseline		0.123

meaning changes based on different contexts because the former research only uses the text embedding method for this task while our team's main approach is leveraging the power of not only BERT-based models but also generative-based models. We believe these methods apply to real-world tasks due to their low computational cost compared to large language model-based approaches.

Additionally, by analyzing the results, we observed that preprocess stages like data cleaning and data augmentation can improve the clarity and consistency of data representation which can further enhance performance.

Ranking	Team	score
Top 1	Deep-Change	0.656
Top 2	GRASP	0.583
Top 4	JuniperLiu	0.271
Baseline	-	0.123
Ours (Top 3)	**MMLabUIT**	**0.524**

Table 8: Official Results for Task 1: Median Judgment Classification with Ordinal Word-in-Context Judgments

Acknowledgements

This research was supported by The VNUHCM-University of Information Technology's Scientific Research Support Fund.

References

Anna Aksenova, Ekaterina Gavrishina, Elisei Rykov, and Andrey Kutuzov. 2022. RuDSI: Graph-based word sense induction dataset for Russian. In *Proceedings of TextGraphs-16: Graph-based Methods for Natural Language Processing*, pages 77–88, Gyeongju, Republic of Korea. Association for Computational Linguistics.

Carlos Santos Armendariz, Matthew Purver, Senja Pollak, Nikola Ljubešić, Matej Ulčar, Ivan Vulić, and Mohammad Taher Pilehvar. 2020. SemEval-2020 task 3: Graded word similarity in context. In *Proceedings of the Fourteenth Workshop on Semantic Evaluation*, pages 36–49, Barcelona (online). International Committee for Computational Linguistics.

Stephen Bates, Trevor Hastie, and Robert Tibshirani. 2023. Cross-validation: what does it estimate and how well does it do it? *Journal of the American Statistical Association*, pages 1–12.

Jing Chen, Emmanuele Chersoni, Dominik Schlechtweg, Jelena Prokic, and Chu-Ren Huang. 2023. ChiWUG: A graph-based evaluation dataset for Chinese lexical semantic change detection. In *Proceedings of the 4th International Workshop on Computational Approaches to Historical Language Change*, Singapore. Association for Computational Linguistics.

Weilong Chen, Xin Yuan, Sai Zhang, Jiehui Wu, Yanru Zhang, and Yan Wang. 2020. Ferryman at SemEval-2020 task 3: Bert with TFIDF-weighting for predicting the effect of context in word similarity. In *Proceedings of the Fourteenth Workshop on Semantic Evaluation*, pages 281–285, Barcelona (online). International Committee for Computational Linguistics.

Alexis Conneau, Kartikay Khandelwal, Naman Goyal, Vishrav Chaudhary, Guillaume Wenzek, Francisco Guzmán, Edouard Grave, Myle Ott, Luke Zettlemoyer, and Veselin Stoyanov. 2019. Unsupervised cross-lingual representation learning at scale. *CoRR*, abs/1911.02116.

Lucas Rafael Costella Pessutto, Tiago de Melo, Viviane P. Moreira, and Altigran da Silva. 2020. BabelEnconding at SemEval-2020 task 3: Contextual similarity as a combination of multilingualism and language models. In *Proceedings of the Fourteenth Workshop on Semantic Evaluation*, pages 59–66, Barcelona (online). International Committee for Computational Linguistics.

Jacob Devlin, Ming-Wei Chang, Kenton Lee, and Kristina Toutanova. 2018. BERT: pre-training of deep bidirectional transformers for language understanding. *CoRR*, abs/1810.04805.

Pablo Gamallo. 2020. CitiusNLP at SemEval-2020 task 3: Comparing two approaches for word vector contextualization. In *Proceedings of the Four-*

teenth Workshop on Semantic Evaluation*, pages 275–280, Barcelona (online). International Committee for Computational Linguistics.

Anna Hätty, Dominik Schlechtweg, and Sabine Schulte im Walde. 2019. SURel: A gold standard for incorporating meaning shifts into term extraction. In *Proceedings of the 8th Joint Conference on Lexical and Computational Semantics*, pages 1–8, Minneapolis, MN, USA.

Hansi Hettiarachchi and Tharindu Ranasinghe. 2020. BRUMS at SemEval-2020 task 3: Contextualised embeddings for predicting the (graded) effect of context in word similarity. In *Proceedings of the Fourteenth Workshop on Semantic Evaluation*, pages 142–149, Barcelona (online). International Committee for Computational Linguistics.

Matthew Honnibal and Ines Montani. 2017. spacy: Industrial-strength natural language processing in python. Explosion AI. Available at https://spacy.io.

Sinan Kurtyigit, Maike Park, Dominik Schlechtweg, Jonas Kuhn, and Sabine Schulte im Walde. 2021. Lexical Semantic Change Discovery. In *Proceedings of the 59th Annual Meeting of the Association for Computational Linguistics and the 11th International Joint Conference on Natural Language Processing (Volume 1: Long Papers)*, Online. Association for Computational Linguistics.

Andrey Kutuzov and Lidia Pivovarova. 2021. Rushifteval: a shared task on semantic shift detection for russian. *Komp'yuternaya Lingvistika i Intellektual'nye Tekhnologii: Dialog conference*.

Andrey Kutuzov, Samia Touileb, Petter Mæhlum, Tita Enstad, and Alexandra Wittemann. 2022. NorDiaChange: Diachronic semantic change dataset for Norwegian. In *Proceedings of the Thirteenth Language Resources and Evaluation Conference*, pages 2563–2572, Marseille, France. European Language Resources Association.

Mike Lewis, Yinhan Liu, Naman Goyal, Marjan Ghazvininejad, Abdelrahman Mohamed, Omer Levy, Veselin Stoyanov, and Luke Zettlemoyer. 2019. BART: denoising sequence-to-sequence pre-training for natural language generation, translation, and comprehension. *CoRR*, abs/1910.13461.

Mike Lewis, Yinhan Liu, Naman Goyal, Marjan Ghazvininejad, Abdelrahman Mohamed, Omer Levy, Veselin Stoyanov, and Luke Zettlemoyer. 2020. BART: Denoising sequence-to-sequence pre-training for natural language generation, translation, and comprehension. In *Proceedings of the 58th Annual Meeting of the Association for Computational Linguistics*, pages 7871–7880, Online. Association for Computational Linguistics.

Yinhan Liu, Myle Ott, Naman Goyal, Jingfei Du, Mandar Joshi, Danqi Chen, Omer Levy, Mike Lewis, Luke Zettlemoyer, and Veselin Stoyanov. 2019. Roberta: A robustly optimized BERT pretraining approach. *CoRR*, abs/1907.11692.

Kalyani Pakhale. 2023. Comprehensive overview of named entity recognition: Models, domain-specific applications and challenges. *arXiv preprint arXiv:2309.14084*.

Telmo Pires, Eva Schlinger, and Dan Garrette. 2019. How multilingual is multilingual BERT? In *Proceedings of the 57th Annual Meeting of the Association for Computational Linguistics*, pages 4996–5001, Florence, Italy. Association for Computational Linguistics.

Julia Rodina and Andrey Kutuzov. 2020. RuSemShift: a dataset of historical lexical semantic change in Russian. In *Proceedings of the 28th International Conference on Computational Linguistics*, pages 1037–1047, Barcelona, Spain (Online). International Committee on Computational Linguistics.

Dominik Schlechtweg, Pierluigi Cassotti, Bill Noble, David Alfter, Sabine Schulte im Walde, and Nina Tahmasebi. 2024. More DWUGs: Extending and evaluating word usage graph datasets in multiple languages. In *Proceedings of the 2024 Conference on Empirical Methods in Natural Language Processing*, Miami, Florida. Association for Computational Linguistics.

Dominik Schlechtweg, Tejaswi Choppa, Wei Zhao, and Michael Roth. 2025. The CoMeDi shared task: Median judgment classification & mean disagreement ranking with ordinal word-in-context judgments. In *Proceedings of the 1st Workshop on Context and Meaning–Navigating Disagreements in NLP Annotations*, Abu Dhabi, UAE.

Dominik Schlechtweg, Sabine Schulte im Walde, and Stefanie Eckmann. 2018. Diachronic Usage Relatedness (DURel): A framework for the annotation of lexical semantic change. In *Proceedings of the 2018 Conference of the North American Chapter of the Association for Computational Linguistics: Human Language Technologies*, pages 169–174, New Orleans, Louisiana.

Adina Williams, Nikita Nangia, and Samuel Bowman. 2018. A broad-coverage challenge corpus for sentence understanding through inference. In *Proceedings of the 2018 Conference of the North American Chapter of the Association for Computational Linguistics: Human Language Technologies, Volume 1 (Long Papers)*, pages 1112–1122. Association for Computational Linguistics.

Thomas Wolf, Lysandre Debut, Victor Sanh, Julien Chaumond, Clement Delangue, Anthony Moi, Pierric Cistac, Tim Rault, Remi Louf, Morgan Funtowicz, Joe Davison, Sam Shleifer, Patrick von Platen, Clara Ma, Yacine Jernite, Julien Plu, Canwen Xu, Teven Le Scao, Sylvain Gugger, Mariama Drame, Quentin Lhoest, and Alexander Rush. 2020. Transformers: State-of-the-art natural language processing. In *Proceedings of the 2020 Conference on Empirical Methods in Natural Language Processing: System Demonstrations*, pages 38–45, Online. Association for Computational Linguistics.

ABDN-NLP at CoMeDi Shared Task: Predicting the Aggregated Human Judgment via Weighted Few-Shot Prompting

Ying Xuan Loke[1] **Dominik Schlechtweg**[2] **Wei Zhao**[1]
[1]University of Aberdeen [2]University of Stuttgart
y.loke.22@abdn.ac.uk
schlecdk@ims.uni-stuttgart.de
wei.zhao@abdn.ac.uk

Abstract

Human annotation is notorious for being subjective and expensive. Recently, Schlechtweg et al. (2025) introduced the CoMeDi shared task aiming to address this issue by predicting human annotations on the semantic proximity between word uses, and estimating the variation of the human annotations. However, distinguishing the proximity between word uses can be challenging, when their semantic difference is subtle. In this work, we focus on predicting the aggregated annotator judgment of semantic proximity by using a large language model fine-tuned on 20 examples with various proximity classes. To distinguish nuanced proximity, we propose a weighted few-shot approach that pays greater attention to the proximity classes identified as important during fine-tuning. We evaluate our approach in the CoMeDi shared task across 7 languages. Our results demonstrate the superiority of our approach over zero-shot and standard few-shot counterparts. While useful, the weighted few-shot should be applied with caution, given that it relies on development sets to compute the importance of proximity classes, and thus may not generalize well to real-world scenarios where the distribution of class importance is different[1].

1 Introduction

Human annotation, which leverages human annotators to create gold-standard labels, has been an essential step when curating training data for machine learning tasks. However, this process is particularly challenging due to the subjective nature of human judgment. Such subjectivity may result in significant disagreements among human annotators, giving rise to poor quality of gold-standard labels—which may further trouble the reliability of models trained on these labels. While many efforts have focused on using aggregation to mitigate disagreements among annotators (Uma et al., 2021; Leonardelli et al., 2023), very few works studied the fundamental aspects of disagreements, such as the complexity and underlying causes that may lead to disagreements in human annotation.

Recently, Schlechtweg et al. (2025) introduced the CoMeDi 2025 shared task, which investigates annotation disagreements in semantic proximity between word uses through two subtasks: (i) predicting the aggregated judgment among human annotators, and (ii) predicting the variation of annotations by estimating the level of disagreement in annotating semantic proximity.

In this work, we focus on the first subtask and build our approaches upon the work by Yadav et al. (2024), which leverages large language models (LLMs) to produce human judgments of semantic proximity. We refer to their approach as automating human judgment. Approaches of this kind have been shown to incur a much lower cost in annotation compared to using human annotators to do so (Gilardi et al., 2023). Our main contribution is to introduce a weighted few-shot learning approach that prompts LLMs to predict human judgments of the proximity class between word uses, on an ordinal scale ranging from 1 to 4, and fine-tunes LLMs on 20 examples to help them learn how such judgments are made. Our few-shot approach differs from the standard one in that important proximity classes receive greater attention during fine-tuning.

2 Task Description

The CoMeDi 2025 shared task explores annotation disagreements through two subtasks, both of which are based on human Word-in-Context (WiC) judgments across seven languages. Each data instance contains a target word w with a pair of uses u_1 and u_2, where each usage conveys a context-specific meaning. Each use pair associates with a human

[1]Our implementation is made publicly available at https://github.com/yingxuaaaaaan/automating-semantic-proximity-annotation

Proceedings of Context and Meaning: Navigating Disagreements in NLP Annotation, pages 122–128
January 19, 2025.

Target word: chairman
Usage 1: ..out of respect to the chairman's cough...
Usage 2: Ronald J. Gidwitz, chairman, Illinois State Board of Education..

Human judgments: [3, 4, 4]
Median of judgments: 4
Mean pairwise difference of judgments: 0.667

Figure 1: A running example for the target word 'chairman'. The semantic proximity of the two uses are judged by three annotators as context variance (3), identity (4) and identity (4), respectively.

judgment on an ordinal relatedness scale ranging from 1 to 4. The judgment reflects the semantic proximity between a pair of uses, interpreted as homonymy (1), polysemy (2), context variance (3), and identity (4), respectively. An running example is illustrated in Figure 1. The subtask descriptions are outlined as follows:

- Subtask 1: For each use pair (u_1, u_2), participants are asked to predict the median of annotator judgments regarding semantic proximity of the two uses. Predictions are evaluated against the median labels using the ordinal version of Krippendorff's α (Krippendorff, 2018).
- Subtask 2: For each use pair (u_1, u_2), participants are asked to predict the level of annotation disagreement in semantic proximity between the two uses. The level of disagreement is calculated as the mean of pairwise absolute judgment differences among annotators. Predictions are evaluated against the mean disagreement labels using Spearman's ρ (Spearman, 1961).

3 Our System

In this work, our focus is on subtask 1. Our system leverages GPT-4o-mini to predict the aggregated annotator judgment per use pair through prompting. We experiment with three prompting setups: zero-shot, standard few-shot and weighted few-shot.

Zero-shot. Our prompt and model configuration are based on the template by Yadav et al. (2024). The prompt is designed to automate the annotation of semantic proximity by prompting LLMs to follow human annotation guidelines to produce a judgment for each use pair. Additionally, they found that model performance is affected greatly by model hyperparameters such as temperature and top-p, which control the diversity and randomness of the model output. We adopt the model configuration from their work and set both top-p and temperature to 0.9.

Standard few-shot. Our prompt in the standard few-shot setup extends upon the zero-shot prompt by providing a small number of examples for GPT-4o-mini to learn annotator judgments on proximity classes. For instance, in the n-shot setup, we randomly sample n equally sized data instances per judgment (proximity) class from **development data** and incorporate these instances into the prompt. In this case, we assume the four judgment classes are equally important.

Weighted few-shot. Our preliminary results showed that performance gaps between judgment (proximity) classes are substantial (e.g., the judgment class 1 is often the most difficult class for GPT-4o-mini to predict, cf., Figure 5). Additionally, we found that the number of data instances per judgment class is imbalanced (see Figure 4). This indicates that the four judgment classes are not equally important. Based on these observations, we propose a weighted few-shot scheme: we first compute the importance per judgment class, and for each class we randomly sample data instances from **development data** based on the class importance—**the more important a judgment class is, the greater attention it will receive**, i.e. that we will sample many more data instances of that class compared to other classes for fine-tuning GPT-4o-mini. As a result, this approach will prioritize model improvement on important classes. We consider two implementations of class importance, based on: (a) **class frequency** and (b) **class difficulty**. For (a), the importance of each class is estimated based on the percentage of data instances belonging to that class. We use these percentages as probabilities for sampling data instances in each class. Note that we compute importance separately for each language. For (b), we refer the importance of each class to the model performance of that class. To do so, we compute the inverted F_1 score (the harmonic mean of precision and recall) for each class, and normalize it across the four classes, denoted by:

$$p_i = \frac{{F_1}^{-1}(i)}{\sum_{j\in(1,2,3,4)} {F_1}^{-1}(j)}$$

where p_i is the importance of the i-th class that we use as the probability for sampling data instances belonging to that class from development data. Alternative measures for estimating class difficulty are mostly based on entropy (Capecchi and Moller, 1968; Li et al., 2019; Juszczuk et al., 2021), which we will explore in future work.

Note that we use the raw texts without applying lemmatization or removing punctuation, nor do we explore advanced LLMs such as GPT-4o and Llama 3. Instead, our system focuses on showcasing the use of our weighted few-shot prompting for predicting the aggregated annotator judgment in semantic proximity, and therefore our system performance might be suboptimal.

In the case that prompting GPT-4o-mini does not generate a ordinal judgment class for a use pair, we assign Judgment 0 to that use pair and treat it as an outlier. We note that such cases are very rare in our experiments, and therefore their impact on model performance is expected to be small.

Prompt engineering. Our prompt builds upon the template by Yadav et al. (2024), with the following modifications. Firstly, we provide examples by appending them to the prompt; doing so will not update model weights while Yadav et al. (2024) submit a fine-tuning job to the OpenAI server that will update model weights. Secondly, we restrict the formatting of model response to include the identifiers of each use pair, to which we observe performance gains on development sets. We attribute performance gains to the fact that including identifiers help avoid mismatches between a judgment class prediction and the corresponding use pair. Mismatch may happen in our setup as we prompt GPT-4o-mini in batch, i.e., judgment classes for a batch of use pairs are predicted at once. Note that such identifiers are added to the prompt only in the few-shot setup, as we observe that, without providing examples to fine-tune the model, identifiers are sometimes not generated in model responses.

We additionally experimented with including a language identifier in the prompt to state which language each use pair belongs to, but this is not helpful. Our prompt in the zero-shot setup is displayed in Figure 2. The prompt in the standard and weighted few-shot setups is provided in Figure 3.

[SYSTEM]
You are a highly trained text data annotation tool capable of providing subjective responses. Rate the semantic similarity of the target word in these sentences 1 and 2. Consider only the objects/concepts the word forms refer to: ignore any common etymology and metaphorical similarity! Ignore case! Ignore number (cat/Cats = identical meaning). If target is emoji then rate by its contextual function. Homonyms (like bat the animal vs bat in baseball) count as unrelated. Output numeric rating: 1 is unrelated; 2 is distantly related; 3 is closely related; 4 is identical in meaning. Your response should align with a human's succinct judgment. Please respond in the format:
[USER]
Keyword (target word): <value>
Sentence 1: <value>
Sentence 2: <value>

Please provide a judgment as a single integer. For example, if your judgment is Identical, then provide 4. If your judgment is Unrelated, provide 1.

Figure 2: Our prompt in the zero-shot setup.

4 Experimental Setup

Datasets. The CoMeDi shared task provides datasets for seven languages: Chinese, English, German, Norwegian, Russian, Spanish, and Swedish. These were sampled from publicly available datasets (Schlechtweg et al., 2018; Schlechtweg, 2023; Schlechtweg et al., 2021; Hätty et al., 2019; Rodina and Kutuzov, 2020; Kutuzov and Pivovarova, 2021; Kurtyigit et al., 2021; Aksenova et al., 2022; Kutuzov et al., 2022; Zamora-Reina et al., 2022; Chen et al., 2023) and supplemented with unpublished data (Schlechtweg et al., 2024). Each dataset is divided into three splits: train, development, and test sets. Table 1 presents the data statistics for these datasets. We observed class imbalance in terms of the percentage of instances per judgment class (see Figure 4).

	Train set		Dev set		Test set	
Languages	#data	#tgts	#data	#tgts	#data	#tgts
Russian	8029	189	1126	28	2285	55
Swedish	5457	30	871	5	1345	9
Spanish	4821	70	621	10	1497	20
Norwegian	4494	56	611	8	1380	16
English	5910	31	863	5	2444	10
Chinese	10833	28	2532	4	3240	8
German	8279	116	1663	17	3141	34

Table 1: Statistics of the CoMeDi datasets. '#tgts' denotes the number of target words; '#data' means the number of use pairs.

Class imbalance. In the zero-shot setup, the imbalance of judgment classes will not harm GPT-4o-mini, as we do not fine-tune the model on the CoMedi datasets. For the standard few-shot setup, we provide equally sized examples to fine-tune the

```
[SYSTEM]
You are a highly trained text data annotation tool
capable of providing subjective responses. Rate the
semantic similarity of the target word in these
sentences 1 and 2. Consider only the objects/
concepts the word forms refer to: ignore any common
etymology and metaphorical similarity! Ignore case!
Ignore number (cat/Cats = identical meaning). If
target is emoji then rate by its contextual function.
Homonyms (like bat the animal vs bat in baseball)
count as unrelated. Output numeric rating: 1 is
unrelated; 2 is distantly related; 3 is closely related;
4 is identical in meaning. Your response should align
with a human's succinct judgment. Please respond in
the format:

Identifier1: <value>
Identifier2: <value>
Rating: <value>

### Examples ###
[USER]
Identifier1: <value>
Identifier2: <value>
Keyword (target word): <value>
Sentence 1: <value>
Sentence 2: <value>

[ASSISTANT]
Identifier1: <value>
Identifier2: <value>
Rating: <value>
```

Figure 3: Our prompt in the few-shot setup.

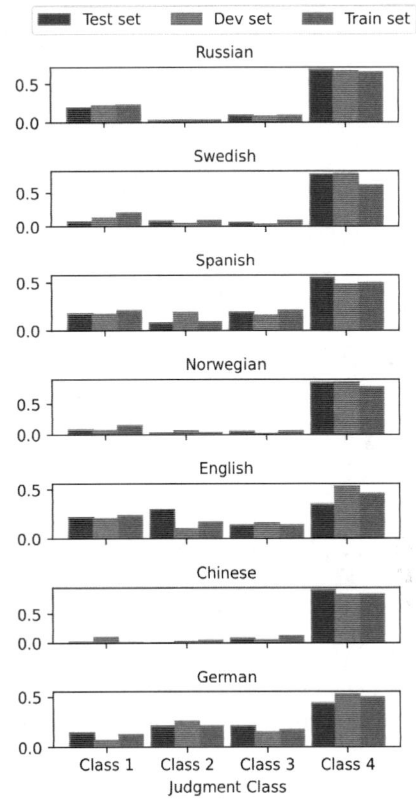

Figure 4: Class frequency distributions across train, dev and test sets, where y-axis shows the percentage of instances per judgment class.

model via in-context learning, aiming to avoid sampling bias stemming from data imbalance.

However, we hypothesize that equally sized sampling is suboptimal because it does not make use of prior knowledge from developments sets, such as class frequency and difficulty distributions. Integrating such knowledge into the few-shot learning process might be useful. For instance, if judgment class 4 is the most popular or most difficult class, providing more examples of that class to fine-tune the model would prioritize model improvement on important classes. Nevertheless, there is no guarantee that the class frequency and difficulty distributions are the same (or comparable) across data splits, but we assume that the difficulty distribution is more consistent than the frequency distribution across splits, as the test set could contain any number of instances per judgment class while the class difficulty reflects its inherent complexity, less affected by data splits.

Results. Table 2 compares our approach in various setups on the CoMeDi test set for the post-evaluation subtask 1. Overall, our approach based on GPT-4o-mini in the zero-shot setup yields moderate Krippendorff scores in most cases, indicating moderate agreement between model and human judgments in semantic proximity. We see our approach performs poorly in Norwegian and Chinese, meaning that GPT-4o-mini may struggle to understand these two languages.

Secondly, we see "standard few-shot", which fine-tunes GPT-4o-mini on totaling 20 examples across 4 classes through in-context learning, is useful. It outperforms the counterpart in the zero-shot setup on average (0.403 vs. 0.388). This is not surprising, as few-shot learning help GPT-4o-mini learn how human judgments are made. Additionally, we observe that our weighted few-shot approach relying on 'frequency' achieves the best performance on average among the four setups. This is because class frequency distributions are generally consistent in both dev and test sets (see Figure 4). In contrast, we see the weighted few-shot relying on 'difficulty' performs only slightly better than 'standard few-shot', which we attribute to the fact that class difficulty distributions differ

Setup	Russian	Swedish	Spanish	Norwegian	English	German	Chinese	Avg
zero-shot (n=0)	0.504	0.351	0.491	0.207	0.610	0.529	0.026	0.388
standard few-shot (n=20)	0.423	0.441	**0.587**	0.197	**0.626**	0.675	-0.127	0.403
weighted few-shot (frequency, n=20)	0.478	**0.509**	0.569	**0.431**	0.625	0.673	**0.209**	**0.499**
weighted few-shot (difficulty, n=20)	**0.512**	0.389	0.543	0.183	0.600	**0.690**	-0.056	0.408
deep-change (Kuklin and Arefyev, 2025)	**0.623**	**0.675**	**0.748**	**0.668**	**0.732**	**0.723**	**0.424**	**0.656**
comedi-baseline (Schlechtweg et al., 2025)	0.112	0.018	0.175	0.124	0.102	0.274	0.059	0.123

Table 2: Krippendorff's results from GPT-4o-mini on the test set in the post-evaluation CoMeDi subtask 1. "deep-change" is the best-performing system in the CoMeDi leaderboard.

across data splits to a large degree (see Figure 5).

Our approach, even in the zero-shot, performs much better than comedi-baseline—which relies on XLM-R coupled with a threshold-based classifier tuned on training data. This means prompting LLMs could yield very competitive results. However, our approach lags behind deep-change—which fine-tunes the Word-in-Context model on the training data of the shared task; this is because deep-change benefits greatly from fine-tuning on the full training data that is 300-500 times larger than the number of training examples we provided in the few-shot setups.

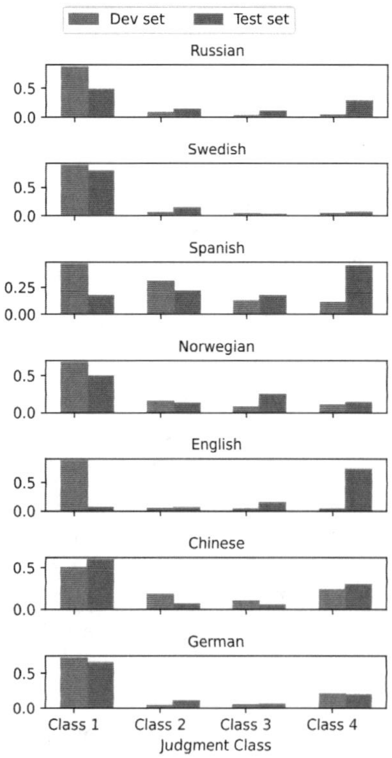

Figure 5: Class difficulty distributions across train, dev and test sets, where y-axis shows the inverted F_1 score per class after normalization.

5 Conclusions

In this work, we leverage a large language model to predict the aggregated human judgment of the semantic proximity between word uses. In particular, we explore several few-shot learning approaches for the model to learn annotator judgments through fine-tuning. Our results demonstrate that our weighted few-shot approach outperforms standard few-shot and zero-shot approaches.

Limitations. In the shared task setup, the class frequency distributions generally are consistent across data splits for all languages. However, such alignment is not guaranteed in real-world scenarios. If distributions differ across splits, performance gains from weighted few-shot learning may become small or even disappear. While class difficulty distributions might be consistent and are not affected much by data splits, but giving greater attention to difficult classes may not be useful in the case that such classes are rare in test sets. As such, how best to leverage prior knowledge (class difficulty and frequency distributions) does not have a straightforward answer, and the standard few-shot learning is still useful when the reliability of prior knowledge is uncertain. Additionally, our findings are based on a single LLM and might differ when we use other LLMs. Moreover, our approach is sub-optimal: further improvements could benefit from cleaning up datasets, using stronger LLMs, fine-tuning on a large number of examples in few-shot setups, developing a new approach combining both class frequency and difficulty factors, and others.

Acknowledgements

We thank the anonymous reviewers for their thoughtful feedback that greatly improved the texts. Dominik Schlechtweg has been funded by the research program 'Change is Key!' supported by Riksbankens Jubileumsfond (under reference number M21-0021).

References

Anna Aksenova, Ekaterina Gavrishina, Elisei Rykov, and Andrey Kutuzov. 2022. RuDSI: Graph-based word sense induction dataset for Russian. In *Proceedings of TextGraphs-16: Graph-based Methods for Natural Language Processing*, pages 77–88, Gyeongju, Republic of Korea. Association for Computational Linguistics.

Vittorio Capecchi and Frank Moller. 1968. Some applications of the entropy to the problems of classification. *Quality & Quantity*, 2.

Jing Chen, Emmanuele Chersoni, Dominik Schlechtweg, Jelena Prokic, and Chu-Ren Huang. 2023. ChiWUG: A graph-based evaluation dataset for Chinese lexical semantic change detection. In *Proceedings of the 4th International Workshop on Computational Approaches to Historical Language Change*, Singapore. Association for Computational Linguistics.

Fabrizio Gilardi, Meysam Alizadeh, and Maël Kubli. 2023. Chatgpt outperforms crowd workers for text-annotation tasks. *Proceedings of the National Academy of Sciences*, 120(30):e2305016120.

Anna Hätty, Dominik Schlechtweg, and Sabine Schulte im Walde. 2019. SURel: A gold standard for incorporating meaning shifts into term extraction. In *Proceedings of the 8th Joint Conference on Lexical and Computational Semantics*, pages 1–8, Minneapolis, MN, USA.

Przemysław Juszczuk, Jan Kozak, Grzegorz Dziczkowski, Szymon Głowania, Tomasz Jach, and Barbara Probierz. 2021. Real-world data difficulty estimation with the use of entropy. *Entropy*, 23(12):1621.

Klaus Krippendorff. 2018. *Content analysis: An introduction to its methodology*. Sage publications.

Mikhail Kuklin and Nikolay Arefyev. 2025. Deepchange at CoMeDi: the cross-entropy loss is not all you need. In *Proceedings of the 1st Workshop on Context and Meaning–Navigating Disagreements in NLP Annotations*, Abu Dhabi, UAE.

Sinan Kurtyigit, Maike Park, Dominik Schlechtweg, Jonas Kuhn, and Sabine Schulte im Walde. 2021. Lexical Semantic Change Discovery. In *Proceedings of the 59th Annual Meeting of the Association for Computational Linguistics and the 11th International Joint Conference on Natural Language Processing (Volume 1: Long Papers)*, Online. Association for Computational Linguistics.

Andrey Kutuzov and Lidia Pivovarova. 2021. Rushifteval: a shared task on semantic shift detection for russian. *Komp'yuternaya Lingvistika i Intellektual'nye Tekhnologii: Dialog conference*.

Andrey Kutuzov, Samia Touileb, Petter Mæhlum, Tita Enstad, and Alexandra Wittemann. 2022. NorDiaChange: Diachronic semantic change dataset for Norwegian. In *Proceedings of the Thirteenth Language Resources and Evaluation Conference*, pages 2563–2572, Marseille, France. European Language Resources Association.

Elisa Leonardelli, Gavin Abercrombie, Dina Almanea, Valerio Basile, Tommaso Fornaciari, Barbara Plank, Verena Rieser, Alexandra Uma, and Massimo Poesio. 2023. SemEval-2023 task 11: Learning with disagreements (LeWiDi). In *Proceedings of the 17th International Workshop on Semantic Evaluation (SemEval-2023)*, pages 2304–2318, Toronto, Canada. Association for Computational Linguistics.

Lusi Li, Haibo He, and Jie Li. 2019. Entropy-based sampling approaches for multi-class imbalanced problems. *IEEE Transactions on Knowledge and Data Engineering*, 32(11):2159–2170.

Julia Rodina and Andrey Kutuzov. 2020. RuSemShift: a dataset of historical lexical semantic change in Russian. In *Proceedings of the 28th International Conference on Computational Linguistics*, pages 1037–1047, Barcelona, Spain (Online). International Committee on Computational Linguistics.

Dominik Schlechtweg. 2023. *Human and Computational Measurement of Lexical Semantic Change*. Ph.D. thesis, University of Stuttgart, Stuttgart, Germany.

Dominik Schlechtweg, Pierluigi Cassotti, Bill Noble, David Alfter, Sabine Schulte im Walde, and Nina Tahmasebi. 2024. More DWUGs: Extending and evaluating word usage graph datasets in multiple languages. In *Proceedings of the 2024 Conference on Empirical Methods in Natural Language Processing*, Miami, Florida. Association for Computational Linguistics.

Dominik Schlechtweg, Tejaswi Choppa, Wei Zhao, and Michael Roth. 2025. The CoMeDi shared task: Median judgment classification & mean disagreement ranking with ordinal word-in-context judgments. In *Proceedings of the 1st Workshop on Context and Meaning–Navigating Disagreements in NLP Annotations*, Abu Dhabi, UAE.

Dominik Schlechtweg, Sabine Schulte im Walde, and Stefanie Eckmann. 2018. Diachronic Usage Relatedness (DURel): A framework for the annotation of lexical semantic change. In *Proceedings of the 2018 Conference of the North American Chapter of the Association for Computational Linguistics: Human Language Technologies*, pages 169–174, New Orleans, Louisiana.

Dominik Schlechtweg, Nina Tahmasebi, Simon Hengchen, Haim Dubossarsky, and Barbara McGillivray. 2021. DWUG: A large Resource of Diachronic Word Usage Graphs in Four Languages. In *Proceedings of the 2021 Conference on Empirical Methods in Natural Language Processing*, pages 7079–7091, Online and Punta Cana, Dominican Republic. Association for Computational Linguistics.

Charles Spearman. 1961. The proof and measurement of association between two things.

Alexandra N Uma, Tommaso Fornaciari, Dirk Hovy, Silviu Paun, Barbara Plank, and Massimo Poesio. 2021. Learning from disagreement: A survey. *Journal of Artificial Intelligence Research*, 72:1385–1470.

Sachin Yadav, Tejaswi Choppa, and Dominik Schlechtweg. 2024. Towards automating text annotation: A case study on semantic proximity annotation using gpt-4. *arXiv preprint arXiv:2407.04130*.

Frank D. Zamora-Reina, Felipe Bravo-Marquez, and Dominik Schlechtweg. 2022. LSCDiscovery: A shared task on semantic change discovery and detection in Spanish. In *Proceedings of the 3rd International Workshop on Computational Approaches to Historical Language Change*, Dublin, Ireland. Association for Computational Linguistics.

Automating Annotation Guideline Improvements using LLMs: A Case Study

Adrien Bibal[1], Nathaniel Gerlek[1], Goran Muric[1], Elizabeth Boschee[2,*], Steven Fincke[2,*], Mike Ross[3,*], Steven N. Minton[1]
[1]InferLink Corporation
[2]Information Sciences Institute (ISI), University of Southern California
[3]Meta AI
[*]These authors equally contributed to this work and are listed by alphabetical order.
{abibal,ngerlek,gmuric,sminton}@inferlink.com,
{boschee,sfincke}@isi.edu, mikeross@meta.com

Abstract

Annotating texts can be a tedious task, especially when texts are noisy. At the root of the issue, guidelines are not always optimized enough to be able to perform the required annotation task. In difficult cases, complex workflows are designed to be able to reach the best possible guidelines. However, crowdsource workers are commonly recruited to go through these complex workflows, limiting the number of iterations over the workflows, and therefore, the possible results because of the slow speed and the high cost of workers. In this paper, our case study, based on the entity recognition problem, suggests that LLMs can help produce guidelines of high quality (inter-annotator agreement going from 0.593 to 0.84 when improving WNUT-17's guidelines), while being faster and cheaper than crowdsource workers.

1 Introduction

Designing guidelines making every annotator agree on their annotations is a difficult and tedious process. Such a task can be even more difficult in the context of noisy texts, common in fast-paced online communication especially on platforms such as X (formerly known as Twitter). Such texts can be filled with typos, with specific tokens (e.g., Twitter handles and hashtags in the context of Tweets) and with interjections (such as, for instance, "mmmmhhhh"). Furthermore, texts to annotate can lack context, because of the nature of the text (e.g., an isolated Tweet) or because of its collection (e.g., when the logical connection between the elements of a discussion has been lost).

These challenges can lead to many iterations over the guidelines to clarify to the annotators how to annotate. The classic iterative workflow is, (1) to have an expert designing the guidelines, (2) to have annotators annotating with these guidelines, (3) to compute an inter-annotator agreement (IAA) to check if the guidelines are clear enough. If there are not clear enough, Steps 1 to 3 are performed again until an acceptable IAA is reached (Pustejovsky and Stubbs, 2012).

Expense and time issues related to the multiple iterations over the workflow are commonly reduced by working with crowd workers (when compared to, e.g., in-premise recruitment). However, this is sometimes not enough when working with complex workflows (Pradhan et al., 2022). Indeed, the number of iterations to reach good guidelines can be very large, and processes sometimes never converge.

In this paper, we suggest via a case study that complex annotation workflows can be automated with large language models (LLMs), producing quality guidelines, while significantly reducing the cost and time needed to go through such workflows (more than 700 times cheaper and more than 300 times faster). Furthermore, using LLMs to automate such workflows also has the benefit of avoiding human biases, such as post-rationalizing to stick to their choices when suggested to reconsider them.

2 Related Work on the Optimization of Guidelines

This section introduces the related work on optimizing guidelines using complex annotation workflows. Please note that we use, as done in the literature, the term "workers" to refer to the people involved in the workflow used to optimize the guidelines. Indeed, "annotators" only corresponds to the subset of workers who perform the annotation work in the workflow. Also, note that we do not restrict our presentation of the literature to annotations in natural language processing, as relevant workflows have been proposed to annotate other items than sentences or words, such as

Proceedings of Context and Meaning: Navigating Disagreements in NLP Annotation, pages 129–144
January 19, 2025.

images and websites.

When dealing with the task of improving annotation guidelines, the classic approach is MAMA, or Model-Annotate-Model-Annotate (Pustejovsky and Stubbs, 2012). The idea is simple: the annotation task needs to be modeled, through guidelines, then evaluated via a proper annotation task, from which will follow a revision of the guidelines, and so on. In order to evaluate the guidelines, the agreement between the annotators (or IAA for inter-annotator agreement) is generally used (Pustejovsky and Stubbs, 2012).

Other, more complex, workflows have been developed over time, but with an ever increasing investment in time and money. Bernstein et al. (2010) proposed a Find-Fix-Verify workflow. This workflow can be adapted to very different scenarios, but in our context, Find (the first step) corresponds to asking workers to find ambiguous elements in the guidelines given some examples to annotate. Based on the identified issues in the guidelines, workers, in the Fix step, propose alternatives to each problematic element in the guidelines. The last step, Verify, then consists in asking new workers to vote for the best alternative.

Drapeau et al. (2016) later introduced a Justify-Reconsider workflow that leverages rationales from the workers. In the Justify phase, workers provide rationales for their annotations. Then, after reading the rationales from other workers, each worker is given the possibility to reconsider their annotations. While this workflow can provide more accurate annotations, it stops short of improving the guidelines.

In a similar fashion, Chang et al. (2017) proposed a Vote-Explain-Categorize workflow that also leverages rationales. The first stage, Vote, is the annotation stage, with the addition of an option for the annotators to express their uncertainty. The examples showing disagreement or uncertainty are then selected for the Explain step, where workers are asked to provide a rationale for these selected labels. Finally, the Categorize stage consists, for each worker, in choosing a label based on the explanations.

In both their work, Drapeau et al. (2016) and Chang et al. (2017) noted the difficulty of obtaining quality rationales in the workflow. Wang et al. (2018) developed a solution that they called "Rewarding the Brave" to pay workers based on the effectiveness of their rationales in convincing other workers.

Instead of only asking for a rationale, a discussion between the workers using a chat platform can also be envisioned (Schaekermann et al., 2018; Chen et al., 2019). This solution has been found to be effective, but comes with a significant increase in time.

Bragg et al. (2018) proposed a Work-Filter-Diagnose-Clarify/GenTest-Organize-Refine workflow. The first stage, Work, corresponds to the annotation step in our case. Based on this annotation work, examples causing disagreement are selected in the Filter stage. Then, in the Diagnose stage, another set of workers analyze the disagreement on each example to identify if it is best to clarify the guidelines (Clarify stage) or to add the problematic examples to the guidelines (GenTest stage). In the Organize stage, a clustering approach then automatically organizes the various propositions made by the new set of workers to clarify the task. Finally, in the Refine stage, the guideline makers then take inspiration from the worker's propositions to improve the task and the guidelines.

WingIt is a solution to spot ambiguous cases and to propose improvements to the guidelines (VK Chaithanya and Quinn, 2018). The workers have the possibility to ask questions and to propose answers to these questions. The guideline makers can then choose to pick from the suggested answers, or make their own.

In a subsequent work, VK Chaithanya et al. (2019) proposed TaskMate, which is a 5-stage workflow: Identify-Resolve-Merge-Verify-Select. The Identify stage corresponds to the questions and answers of WingIt. However, instead of the guideline makers having to evaluate and select an answer, the workers themselves vote, in the Resolve stage, for the best answer to each question. Based on all the votes, the workers are then asked to propose new guidelines in the Merge stage. In the Verify stage, the workers have to check if the new proposed instructions indeed clarify the original ambiguities. Finally, among all the newly proposed instructions that pass the check, the workers have to vote again, in the Select stage, for the improved instructions that will be included in the new version of the guidelines.

Finally, directly inspired by the Find-Fix-Verify workflow of Bernstein et al. (2010), Pradhan et al. (2022) proposed a Find-Resolve-Label workflow. The Find stage is similar to the one of Bernstein et al. (2010). In the Resolve stage, the guideline makers select some of the ambiguous examples and integrate them as examples in the guidelines. The Verify stage is then an annotation task with the guidelines and the ambiguous examples.

Note that focusing on improving the guidelines may not be the only solution to the problem. Chen and Zhang (2023) showed that two dimensions can be considered when dealing with the problem: (1) how much the texts to annotate are ambiguous and (2) how much the guidelines are ambiguous. If the texts to annotate are ambiguous, the solution can be to modify the texts themselves. However, if text ambiguity is not the main issue, then the guidelines probably are. It may then be worth improving the guidelines. Note that the solution proposed here can only be applied if modifying the texts to annotate is an option.

Many, if not all of these workflows, require multiple iterations, which is not doable in practice. While cost and time are regular concerns for these workflows, the new advances with large language models (LLMs) may allow for a solution: swapping crowdsource workers with LLMs. However, the question is: can LLMs go through a complex workflow and produce good guidelines? We propose in this paper a case study exploring this question. However, before that, we present in the next section the workflow developed for our case study.

3 Workflow Used in our Case Study

While some parts of the literature showed that developing and using complex workflows with workers are costly and time-consuming, other parts highlighted the advance of LLMs in the domain. Gilardi et al. (2023) showed, for instance, that GPT models outperform crowdsource workers in terms of accuracy on annotation tasks. At the same time, it has been shown that LLMs can follow annotation guidelines closely, and their agreement is on par with the agreement of human annotators among themselves (Fonseca and Cohen, 2023). Furthermore, in the case where pre-trained LLMs are not good enough at following guidelines, Sainz et al. (2024) have shown that LLMs can be fine-tuned to be specifically better at that.

This section introduces the workflow developed for our case study. We present in Section 3.1 the different phases of the workflow. Section 3.2 will then discuss its automation.

3.1 Annotate-Justify-Reconsider-Fix

Inspired by the literature and various internal tests, we developed Annotate-Justify-Reconsider-Fix as a pattern for the workflow in our case study (see the left part of Figure 1). The first phase of the workflow, "Annotate", is self-explanatory: annotators are first asked to annotate, given certain guidelines.

In the "Justify" phase, each annotator is asked to justify their annotations (or lack thereof) in two situations: (1) if there is a disagreement on an annotation, and (2) if the annotator did not annotate an element, while other annotators did. This phase is separated from the first one for two reasons: (1) because asking for a rationale is not necessary if everyone agrees on the annotation, and (2) because what is not annotated, but could be, is only known after some annotations are provided. During this phase, the workers can change their mind about their annotation.

In the third phase, "Reconsider", the annotators are asked to reconsider their annotations considering the other annotators' rationales. In addition to choosing their final annotations, the annotators are asked to suggest changes to the guidelines. Seeing different arguments for the same annotation often makes ambiguities in the guidelines more visible.

Finally, in the "Fix" phase, the annotators are asked to compile their suggested changes to the guidelines to re-write the guidelines. The objective of this phase is twofold. First, the guideline makers do not have to interpret the annotator's suggestions to perform the changes. Second, suggestions are given, during Phase 3, per annotation. This means that annotators did not necessarily have the big picture in mind when they provided their suggestions. Because of that, some suggestions may be contradictory. The annotator is therefore the best person to provide the global changes that best reflect the sum of their local changes.

After the merge of all the guidelines proposed in the Fix Phase by the workers, a new iteration over the workflow can begin. This process continues until a desirable inter-annotator agreement (IAA) is reached.

Now that the different components of the workflow have been presented, next section will describe how they are automated with LLMs.

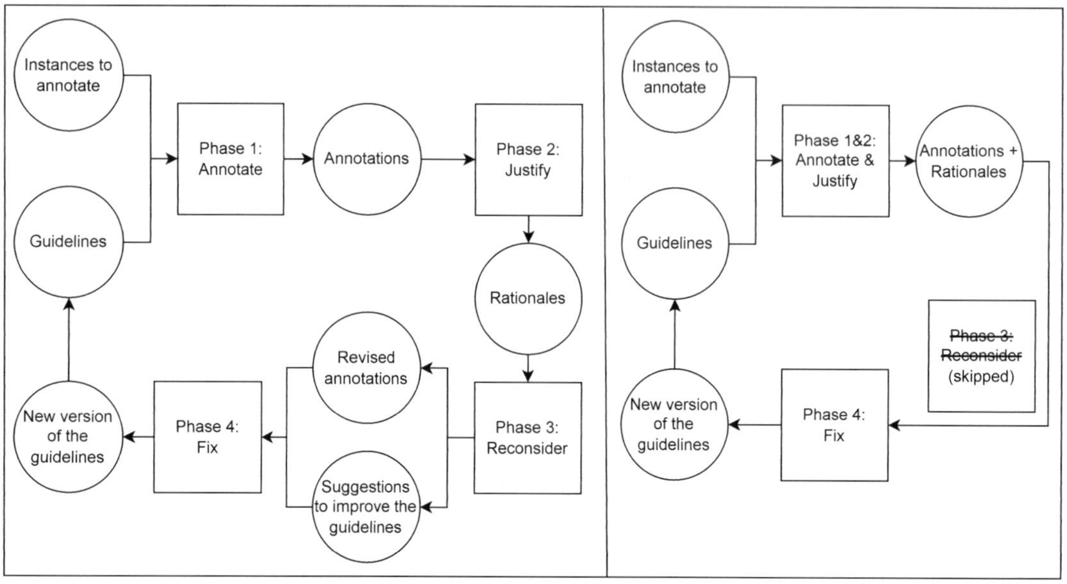

Figure 1: On the left, the workflow developed for our case study with workers. On the right, version of the workflow adapted for automation.

3.2 From Workers to LLMs

In order to automate the workflow, LLMs are used replace workers in all phases of the workflow, as well as the staff member optimizing the guidelines. To do so, two types of LLMs are used: annotator LLMs and an optimizer LLM. We define the annotator LLMs as models that are developed to provide annotations based on particular guidelines and an input text to annotate. On the other hand, we define the optimizer LLM as the model doing the task of the guideline makers: collecting guideline suggestions in order to define new guidelines for the next iteration of the workflow.

One key element to mention in the automation is that LLMs do not have the same attention issues and biases as people. For instance, we noted in our internal tests a clear bias from people to stick to their previous choices. Indeed, some annotators seem to prefer to post-rationalize their choices, even when difficult to defend, rather than to admit that they may have made a mistake. While LLMs have their own attention issues and biases (e.g., forgetting long-distance context because of their architecture and/or training), these are definitely not the same as the ones of people (e.g., being inattentive due to their fatigue). This has implications, mainly, on the "Justify" and "Reconsider" phases. During preliminary internal tests, we could see that an important advantage of Justify is that it forces workers to double-check their annotations. However, LLMs generally do not need this double-check.

Another difference between the workflow for people and for LLMs is that Phases 1 and 2 are mixed for LLMs. This is because the time required to write a rationale for each annotation is far less of an issue than it is with people. Also, asking LLMs for a rationale actually improves their annotations, as it is similar to a chain-of-thought strategy (Wei et al., 2022).

Concerning Phase 3, "Reconsider", we observed that people can have very different levels of expertise and knowledge when annotating. "Reconsider" is therefore quite important when an "expert" among the annotators can provide a rationale that will convince the other annotators. While the variance in expertise on different subjects can be high between human annotators, current pretrained LLMs have a high degree of knowledge across the board. We noticed during our internal tests that the Reconsider phase was not that important for LLMs, while it was quite critical for human annotators. Because of that, we removed the LLM calls to reconsider in the automated workflow. The LLM-based workflow is shown in the right part of Figure 1.

Based on this workflow and its automation, we present an experiment in the next section. The goal of our case study is to discuss the quality of guidelines that can be produced by such a methodology, while also giving some numbers on the increase in speed and decrease in cost when using LLMs.

4 Experiment

This section presents an experiment, for our case study, comparing workers and LLMs going through the workflow. In order to make this comparison, we first explain our experimental setup in Section 4.1. We then go through the details of the annotation work done with workers on a Prolific, crowdsourcing platform, in Section 4.2. Finally, we present our insights in Section 4.3.

4.1 Experimental Setup

In order to give a fair shot to the LLM considered in this case study, we use one of the best models to this date[1]: GPT-4o-08-06 [2]. The temperatures of the annotator LLMs and the optimizer were set to 0.9 and 0 respectively. The prompts are provided in Appendix A.

To compare the automation of our workflow with workers going through it, we consider the entity recognition (ER) problem. In ER, the goal is to detect entities in sentences in order to then assign one or more categories to them.

As the sources of the problem can both be in ambiguities of the texts to annotate and in ambiguities of the guidelines (Chen and Zhang, 2023), we consider a dataset that expresses these two issues: WNUT-17 (Derczynski et al., 2017). The dataset features ambiguous sentences such as Tweets, along with guidelines that are not entirely optimized to annotate these ambiguous sentences. 20 sentences selected at random, and containing multiple entities, were considered for the experiment.

Next section presents how workers have been recruited to go through our workflow with the ER problem applied to the WNUT-17 dataset.

4.2 Crowdsourcing

The workflow developed for this case study has requirements to consider when choosing a crowdsourcing platform. First, the same workers are sometimes required to work on connected phases. For instance, the "Justify" phase requires that the workers justify their annotations provided during the "Annotation" phase. Second, as the workflow is quite complex, a platform that allows the staff member managing the annotation (or annotation manager) to redirect workers to some forms, spreadsheets, etc. outside the platform is necessary. Based on these constraints, Prolific [3] was chosen. The only filter used to recruit workers was their fluency in English. A bonus payment was provided to incentivize workers to do a meaningful job (as suggested by "Rewarding the Brave" of Wang et al. (2018)).

4.3 Insights

This section presents the insights gained from the comparison between the worker-based and LLM-based workflow. We perform our case study in two parts: correctness insights, and time and cost-related insights.

In order to get the data needed to perform this comparison, workers went through the workflow once, and then redid the Annotation phase. 16, 10, 8 and 12 workers went through, respectively, Phases 1, 2, 3 and then Phase 1 again.

Note that the Fix Phase (Phase 4) had to be simulated by us, because only 2 workers provided one suggestion each to change the guidelines. We hypothesize that this issue is due to the low motivation of workers on crowdsourcing platforms (despite the possibility of receiving a bonus). We elaborate on this in Section 5.2. Our simulation of what the workers could propose as changes to the guidelines revolved around the question "what changes the workers would have wanted to see in the guidelines when they wrote their arguments?"

4.3.1 Correctness Analysis

In order to get some insights about the correctness of the LLM-produced guidelines, we propose a qualitative and a quantitative assessment. First, we compare the two solutions after one iteration. Second, we produced a new round of annotations with both the original and the LLM-produced guidelines.

Let us start with the comparison after one iteration. The rationale behind this test is that, first, each iteration over the workflow is independent to the others, and can therefore be analyzed separately. Second, the improvement of the guidelines is front-loaded – most of the changes are performed at the beginning. Comparing the worker-based and LLM-based solutions on the first im-

[1]As per LMArena (https://lmarena.ai/?leaderboard) at the time of the experiment.

[2]https://platform.openai.com/docs/models/gpt-4o

[3]https://www.prolific.com/

proved guidelines can give us an idea of their respective amount and quality of changes. The comparison between the worker-based and LLM-based solutions is shown in Table 2 and Table 3 of Appendix B.

When comparing the guidelines, it can be seen that the LLM-based solution not only added elements to the guidelines, but also provided a lot of reformulations and additional examples. For instances, fully circular definitions like "*location: Names that are locations*" have been replaced by more meaningful descriptions, such as "*location: Names that are specific geographic locations or landmarks*". In the case of the worker-based solution, the changes are very localized. This is due to (1) workers not really providing suggestions to change the guidelines, and due to (2) the difficulty to make changes by having all examples of the dataset in mind. These points have repeatedly been shortcomings in the internal tests we made.

To obtain a quantitative understanding of the quality of the LLM solution, we conducted an additional experiment. The objective of this experiment is to compare the IAA produced by the original guidelines with the guidelines produced after the last iteration over the workflow by the LLMs. Because making sure that the guidelines are followed is paramount in this experiment, we decided to not rely on crowdsource workers. Instead, we mobilized 8 staff members, and each was instructed to annotate given two sets of guidelines (the original WNUT-17 guidelines before starting the workflow and the LLM-improved ones), while paying close attention to the guidelines. The LLM-improved guidelines can be seen in Table 4 of Appendix C.

The results of this experiment are shown in Table 1. One initial observation is that the IAA is only barely better with the LLM-based guidelines when compared to the original ones, before iterating over the workflow (first row of Table 1). This is due to three issues creating disagreements independently to the quality of the guidelines: intrinsically unclear entities, annotators' lack of knowledge about entities and inattention mistakes.

The issue related to intrinsically unclear entities is well-known in the literature (Chen and Zhang, 2023). In some situations, the context does not help annotators decide for their annotation, e.g. in "*Stairs : po jaket MU sampai tgl 8 jan IDR 175rb @Bagusr18971897 PIN 32783FC8 SMS 081912233358*". This sentence will often lead to disagreements, even when very good guidelines are considered. By analyzing all the sentences to annotate and the entities identified by the annotators, we tagged all intrinsically unclear entities. After removing such entities (25 left over 39), the IAA of the original and LLM guidelines become 0.558 and 0.613 respectively. As can be seen, the original gap in IAA of 0.011 enlarges to 0.055 when dropping this source of disagreements.

Annotators' lack of knowledge about certain entities is another important source of disagreements. Indeed, disagreements between annotators can occur when annotators lack the relevant knowledge. In order to identify the disagreements that were caused by a lack of knowledge, we interviewed the annotators based on annotations that seemed odd. We spotted these odd annotations by identifying all the entities for which an internet search could easily clarify what the entity is. For instance, "*Real*" in "*RT @KaiWayne : I think Big Sam was misquoted when he said he could manage Real. What he actually said was he could manage a real ale.*" corresponds to Real Madrid (the football club), but one annotator annotated it as a Person. The reason for this particular annotation is that, without knowing that Real is Real Madrid, one can see Real as a singer who is managed by Big Sam. Dropping the entities where at least one annotator showed a lack of knowledge (26 left over 39) leads to IAAs of 0.441 and 0.474 (gap of 0.033). Note that the IAAs are lower than when all entities were considered. This is because entities with a high agreement can be dropped because only one annotator showed a lack of knowledge.

Finally, inattention mistakes is another issue that causing disagreements. Even if the guidelines are perfect, annotators can miss entities to annotate, and can also miss or forget particular instructions in the guidelines. During the interview mentioned above, we became aware of and noted some inattention mistakes made by the annotators. When dropping the entities with attention issues (34 left over 39), the IAAs become 0.463 and 0.478 (gap of 0.015). Again, like in the case of the lack of knowledge, some entities were dropped despite having high agreement, explaining the lower IAAs.

A final overview of the true impact of optimizing the guidelines can then be provided by dropping entities belonging to any of these three issues (11 left over 39). By doing so, the disagreements

Selected Entities	Original Guidelines	LLM-based Guidelines
All entities	0.488 [0.484, 0.491]	0.499 [0.496, 0.502]
All entities, excluding intrinsically unclear entities	0.558 [0.555, 0.562]	0.613 [0.608, 0.617]
All entities, excluding lack of knowledge	0.441 [0.436, 0.446]	0.474 [0.469, 0.479]
All entities, excluding inattention mistakes	0.463 [0.46, 0.466]	0.478 [0.475, 0.482]
All entities, excluding all 3 issues	0.593 [0.588, 0.599]	**0.84 [0.836, 0.845]**

Table 1: Comparisons, in different situations, of the inter-annotator agreement (Fleiss' Kappa) between the original WNUT-17 guidelines (before iterating over the workflow) and the ones improved by the LLM-based solution after 4 iterations. 95% confidence intervals calculated by a bootstrap sampling with 1,000 samples are provided.

that are compared are mainly about the changes in the guidelines, and less about issues independent to the quality of these guidelines. In that situation, the IAAs for the original guidelines and the LLM-based guidelines are 0.593 and 0.84 respectively (gap of 0.247).

It therefore seems like LLMs can produce guideline changes that greatly reduce the disagreement between annotators. However, it also seems like the benefit of these changes can be hidden by disagreements caused by other issues. Each of these issues must therefore be handled alongside the guidelines.

4.3.2 Cost and Time-related Analysis

While it seems evident that the LLM-based solution saves money and time, when compared to the worker-based solution, we conducted experiments to quantitatively assess this gap. Indeed, while it is intuitive that LLMs are faster and cheaper, we argue that it is important to be able to put numbers on these intuitions.

During these experiments, we could observe that going through the annotation workflow with LLMs was more than 300 times faster and more than 700 times cheaper than with crowdsource workers. Many details about these experiments, including the time and cost per phase, can be found in Appendix D.

5 Discussion

While the insights provided above had the objective to shed more light on the difference between crowdsource workers and LLMs going through complex annotation workflows, this section focuses on additional points to discuss.

5.1 Annotation Manager's Time

In addition to the time and cost of the task itself, a non-negligible time is also spent by the annotation manager on tangential sub-tasks, such as coordinating the workers, ensuring that everything goes smoothly, checking their work (and acting when cheating is found), answering messages, etc. None of these sub-tasks are required when working with LLMs.

However, one can argue that the time needed to code and debug the LLM-based solution is, on the other hand, not required for the worker-based solution. A counter-argument to that would be that implementing the LLM-based solution is needed once, while coordinating/managing workers is to be done every time workers work with the workflow.

In both solutions, though, it is difficult to measure the required time. For instance, assessing the time needed to implement the LLM solution would require several coders coding the solution from scratch and taking their average time as an estimate. We leave this analysis as a future work.

5.2 Quality of Workers' Work

The poor quality of work in crowdsourcing platforms, as well as cheating, is well known and documented in the literature (Gadiraju et al., 2015; Xia, 2024). This kind of behavior, seen in multiple occasions during our study, has three main consequences in our context.

First, poor quality guidelines are obtained, which increases the number of iterations over the workflow that are needed to reach good quality guidelines and labels. Second, low effort can sometimes be hard to detect. Indeed, our study is based on the fact that texts can be noisy and annotating can be difficult. Because of that, it is difficult to differentiate between semi-random annotations and honest annotations misled by the noisy nature of texts. Third, a significant amount of the annotation manager's time must be spent detecting and acting on these cases (see the previous section). This has the effect of indirectly increasing the cost of the worker-based version of the workflow. We argue that these consequences can be avoided when using LLMs.

5.3 Speed and Cost Improvement of LLMs vs. Crowd Workers

While our study is a snapshot in the history of LLMs, current trends indicate that the performance of LLMs will continue to evolve and improve. Along with their quality, their speed and cost is also expected to improve. If we consider the GPT-family of models as an example, the cost of GPT-4 was initially of $0.03 and $0.06 per 1k input and output tokens respectively. However, GPT-4o-mini currently shows, being only slightly below GPT-4o in benchmarks, for a price more than 100 times cheaper than GPT-4.

Speed-wise, many efforts are put by academia and industry in designing new hardware (such as new GPUs), as well as in strategies for LLMs to run quicker on these pieces of hardware (e.g., FlashAttention (Dao et al., 2022), AWQ (Lin et al., 2024), etc.). It is therefore expected that LLMs will increase in speed over time, making the gap between workers and LLMs larger and larger.

5.4 Nature of Disagreements between LLMs and between People

We observed during our experiments that the nature of disagreements happens to be different for LLMs and people. A typical example of that is Twitter handles (such as @JohnDoe). During all our experiments, people kept struggling with Twitter handles. Understandably, it is not clear, in the original WNUT-17 guidelines, if using @JohnDoe at the beginning of a Tweet to indicate that the message is about John Doe makes @JohnDoe a "person" entity.

However, LLMs seem to generally agree on the fact that Twitter handles are not entities with the original WNUT-17 guidelines. Examples of LLM rationales for not annotating Twitter handles are provided in Appendix E.

This difference between people and LLMs makes that Twitter handles are always one the first things to clarify, for people, in the guidelines. For LLMs, however, it is something to clarify in a later stage. For instance, while the first iteration did not contain references to Twitter handles (see Table 3 in Appendix B), it is only at the second iteration that LLMs consider it worth it to mention them.

5.5 On Subjective Annotation Tasks

In our case study, we assumed that multiple interpretations of an annotation indicated an issue with either the annotation guidelines or the text being annotated. However, some annotation tasks are intrinsically subjective. For instance, annotating a piece of text as "well written" or not often depends on the perspective of the annotator. Two changes in our setup are needed to accommodate such a task.

First, the notion of agreement needs to be changed. Instead of checking if the annotators agree with each other, one may check if the distribution of annotations is expected. For instance, the percentage of administrative texts that are "understandable" (given a definition of what "understandable" means in the guidelines) should be close to an expected percentage given in the literature for a certain population.

Second, annotator LLMs should integrate personas such that the distribution of personas corresponds to the population simulated by the LLMs for the subjective annotation task.

6 Conclusion

In this paper, we presented a case study on automating complex annotation workflow. We provided some insights about using LLMs for the automation of such workflows. In particular, our case study suggests that LLMs can produce guidelines of good quality: from an inter-annotator agreement of 0.596 (original WNUT-17 guidelines) to 0.84 (LLM-improved guidelines). We also noted that the gap in cost and time required by workers and LLMs to go through the workflow was significantly large, with LLMs going more than 300 times quicker through the workflow, for a cost per annotator that is more than 700 times cheaper.

Based on our case study, we urge the community to develop LLM-specific workflows, as our case study seems to indicate that LLMs are well-suited for the task. However, further work is needed to identify the datasets and tasks for which humans are superior than LLMs when going through annotation workflows. Thanks to that, a subsequent future work can be to categorize datasets and tasks for the community to better understand when to leverage crowdsource workers and when to develop LLM-based systems.

7 Limitations of our Case Study

One limitation of our study is that it is assessed on one dataset (WNUT-17) and one task (Entity Recognition) only. While it is true that multiplying the datasets and tasks would strengthen our conclusions, we believe that our case study is enough to convey some insights about the use of LLMs to automate complex annotation workflows. Furthermore, we also believe that cost and time-wise, the gap is so large that it is very unlikely to be disproved by analyzing many datasets and tasks.

However, an interesting future work would be to find particular datasets and tasks for which our conclusions would not hold. In particular, this means finding a dataset and a task for which people are a lot superior when going through annotation workflows than LLMs.

Acknowledgments

No data collection or experimentation was conducted by Meta. The workflow automation described in this paper was based on work supported by the Air Force Research Laboratory under Contract No. FA8750-22-C-0511 and by the Army ASA(ALT) SBIR CCoE under Contract No. W51701-24-C-0127. The experiments with crowd workers described here were carried out as part of InferLink's commercial activities. Any opinions, findings and conclusions or recommendations expressed in this material are those of the authors and do not necessarily reflect the views of the funders.

References

Michael S Bernstein, Greg Little, Robert C Miller, Björn Hartmann, Mark S Ackerman, David R Karger, David Crowell, and Katrina Panovich. 2010. Soylent: A word processor with a crowd inside. In *Proceedings of the Annual ACM Symposium on User Interface Software and Technology*, pages 313–322.

Jonathan Bragg, Mausam, and Daniel S Weld. 2018. Sprout: Crowd-powered task design for crowdsourcing. In *Proceedings of the Annual ACM Symposium on User Interface Software and Technology*, pages 165–176.

Joseph Chee Chang, Saleema Amershi, and Ece Kamar. 2017. Revolt: Collaborative crowdsourcing for labeling machine learning datasets. In *Proceedings of the CHI Conference on Human Factors in Computing Systems*, pages 2334–2346.

Quan Ze Chen and Amy X Zhang. 2023. Judgment Sieve: Reducing uncertainty in group judgments through interventions targeting ambiguity versus disagreement. *Proceedings of the ACM on Human-Computer Interaction (HCI)*, 7(CSCW2):1–26.

Quanze Chen, Jonathan Bragg, Lydia B Chilton, and Dan S Weld. 2019. Cicero: Multi-turn, contextual argumentation for accurate crowdsourcing. In *Proceedings of the CHI Conference on Human Factors in Computing Systems*, pages 1–14.

Tri Dao, Dan Fu, Stefano Ermon, Atri Rudra, and Christopher Ré. 2022. FlashAttention: Fast and memory-efficient exact attention with IO-awareness. *Advances in Neural Information Processing Systems (NeurIPS)*, 35:16344–16359.

Leon Derczynski, Eric Nichols, Marieke Van Erp, and Nut Limsopatham. 2017. Results of the WNUT2017 shared task on novel and emerging entity recognition. In *Proceedings of the Workshop on Noisy User-generated Text*, pages 140–147.

Ryan Drapeau, Lydia Chilton, Jonathan Bragg, and Daniel Weld. 2016. Microtalk: Using argumentation to improve crowdsourcing accuracy. In *Proceedings of the AAAI Conference on Human Computation and Crowdsourcing*, volume 4, pages 32–41.

Marcio Fonseca and Shay B Cohen. 2023. Can large language models follow concept annotation guidelines? A case study on scientific and financial domains. *arXiv:2311.08704*.

Ujwal Gadiraju, Ricardo Kawase, Stefan Dietze, and Gianluca Demartini. 2015. Understanding malicious behavior in crowdsourcing platforms: The case of online surveys. In *Proceedings of the Annual ACM Conference on Human Factors in Computing Systems*, pages 1631–1640.

Fabrizio Gilardi, Meysam Alizadeh, and Maël Kubli. 2023. ChatGPT outperforms crowd workers for text-annotation tasks. *Proceedings of the National Academy of Sciences*, 120(30):e2305016120.

Ji Lin, Jiaming Tang, Haotian Tang, Shang Yang, Wei-Ming Chen, Wei-Chen Wang, Guangxuan Xiao, Xingyu Dang, Chuang Gan, and Song Han. 2024. AWQ: Activation-aware weight quantization for on-device LLM compression and acceleration. *Proceedings of Machine Learning and Systems*, 6:87–100.

Vivek Krishna Pradhan, Mike Schaekermann, and Matthew Lease. 2022. In search of ambiguity: A three-stage workflow design to clarify annotation guidelines for crowd workers. *Frontiers in Artificial Intelligence*, 5:828187.

James Pustejovsky and Amber Stubbs. 2012. *Natural Language Annotation for Machine Learning: A guide to corpus-building for applications*. O'Reilly Media, Inc.

Oscar Sainz, Iker García-Ferrero, Rodrigo Agerri, Oier Lopez de Lacalle, German Rigau, and Eneko Agirre. 2024. GoLLIE: Annotation guidelines improve zero-shot information-extraction. In *International Conference on Learning Representations (ICLR)*.

Mike Schaekermann, Joslin Goh, Kate Larson, and Edith Law. 2018. Resolvable vs. irresolvable disagreement: A study on worker deliberation in crowd work. *Proceedings of the ACM on Human-Computer Interaction (HCI)*, 2(CSCW):1–19.

Manam VK Chaithanya, Dwarakanath Jampani, Mariam Zaim, Meng-Han Wu, and Alexander J. Quinn. 2019. Taskmate: A mechanism to improve the quality of instructions in crowdsourcing. In *Companion Proceedings of The World Wide Web Conference*, pages 1121–1130.

Manam VK Chaithanya and Alexander J. Quinn. 2018. Wingit: Efficient refinement of unclear task instructions. In *Proceedings of the AAAI Conference on Human Computation and Crowdsourcing*, volume 6, pages 108–116.

Meihong Wang, Yuling Sun, Jing Yang, and Liang He. 2018. Enabling the disagreement among crowds: A collaborative crowdsourcing framework. In *IEEE International Conference on Computer Supported Cooperative Work in Design (CSCWD)*, pages 790–795.

Jason Wei, Xuezhi Wang, Dale Schuurmans, Maarten Bosma, Fei Xia, Ed Chi, Quoc V Le, Denny Zhou, et al. 2022. Chain-of-thought prompting elicits reasoning in large language models. *Advances in Neural Information Processing Systems (NeurIPS)*, 35:24824–24837.

Huichuan Xia. 2024. Tragedy of the commons in crowd work-based research. *ACM Journal on Responsible Computing*, 1(1):4:1–4:25.

A Prompts Used in the LLM-based Solution

The LLM-based solution is built upon three components: annotator LLMs, an ensemble of these annotator LLMs and a guideline optimizer LLM. The prompt used for the annotator LLMs is the following:

> You are an expert in annotating entities in texts. You will be provided with annotation guidelines and, based on them, you will have to annotate the entities in a sentence. Here are the guidelines about the entities to annotate: [GUIDELINES]
>
> Each entity has two versions (B- and I-) depending on if a token starts the entity (B-) or not (I-). For instance, in the sentence "I'm Chuck Norris", "Chuck" should be annotated as B-person because "Chuck" starts the entity "Chuck Norris" and "Norris" should be annotated as I-person because "Norris" doesn't start the entity "Chuck Norris".
>
> The list of all entities available for annotation is therefore the following: [LIST OF POSSIBLE ANNOTATION CATEGORIES]
>
> Given the guidelines, what is the entity type of each of the following tokens [TOKENS IN THE SENTENCE TO ANNOTATE] in "[SENTENCE TO ANNOTATE]"? Think step-by-step and answer with a JSON containing two keys: (1) "reasoning", which will contain a list with your reasoning for each annotation, and (2) "annotation", which will contain your annotation only. Your annotation in the "annotation" key of the JSON must contain a list of entities in the format [O,O,B-person,I-person,I-person,O,B-location].

where all elements in brackets are elements to be provided in the prompt.

For the guideline optimizer LLM, the prompt is the following:

> You are an expert in making annotation guidelines better. You will be provided with annotation guidelines and some elements on which there is some disagreements. Your goal is to improve the provided guidelines to reduce the disagreement between the annotators. Here are the annotation guidelines to improve: "[CURRENT GUIDELINES]"
>
> These guidelines currently have an inter-annotator agreement of [INTER-ANNOTATOR AGREEMENT]. The disagreement is mainly because of disagreements between these elements: [EXAMPLES OF DISAGREEMENT]

> Provide a new version of these guidelines in order to solve these disagreements. When updating the guidelines, make them so that there will not be new disagreements on the following sentences that will be annotated: [SENTENCES USED IN THE ANNOTATION PROCESS]
>
> The only thing you can do is to clarify the description of categories in order to reduce future disagreements. In other words, only change the description of person, location, corporation, product, creative work and group. If you want to provide examples in the descriptions about what to do or not do, invent examples, i.e. do not take examples from the dataset. Finally, do not mention the B and I of the categories in the description (e.g., B-group and I-group). Instead, mention the category itself (e.g., group).
>
> Answer with nothing else but a string corresponding to the new guidelines you propose.

where all elements in brackets are elements to be provided in the prompt.

B Examples of Guideline Improvements

Tables 2 and 3 show comparisons of the original WNUT-17 guidelines with the worker-based improvements after one iteration (Table 2) and with the LLM-based improvements after one iteration (Table 3).

C Experimental Guidelines

Table 4 shows the resulting guidelines after four iterations over the LLM-based workflow. The amount of agreements resulting from these guidelines has been assessed in Section 4.3.1, with the results reported in Table 1.

D Cost and Time Insights

Table 5 reports the time taken by workers to go through each phase of the workflow. 16, 10, 8 and 12 workers went through Phases 1, 2, 3 and then Phase 1 again in the workflow. Going through the workflow once, and then annotating again, spanned roughly one week and a half. This is due to several factors. First of all, all workers did not start at the same time – a worker can hold onto a sheet for 30 minutes, then can decide that they do not want to work on it, releasing the sheet for another worker 30 minutes after the first ones started. However, this accounts for only short delays. Most important delays are due to the fact that some phases are connected (e.g., Phase 2 and Phase 1, as Phase 2 is about asking for rationales related to annotations in Phase 1). Because of that, the annotation manager had to wait until the workers from Phase 1 were available again to do the second phase. Lastly, many workers had issues with the platform, and a significant number of them cheated (tried to get the completion code, in order to be paid, without doing the task), did not do the task in its entirety or did it in a seemingly random way. Because of that, a significant amount of time of the annotation manager was required to handle these issues. Section 5.1 elaborates on that.

In comparison, going through the workflow once, and then annotating again, is performed in 18.43 seconds by the LLMs (see Table 6). Indeed, the average runtime to perform the annotation with the initial guidelines is 5.83 seconds per LLM per instance/sentence. As all the calls to the LLMs are parallelized, having 10 annotator LLMs and 20 sentences to annotate still is 5.83 seconds in total on average. Runtime of going through the workflow once and then annotating is therefore the sum of the runtime for the annotation (which is parallelized), the optimization of the guidelines (only one call to an LLM) and the re-annotation (which is also parallelized).

Cost-wise, the cost of an LLM is generally computed in two different ways, depending on the situation: either the LLM is self hosted, or it is accessed via an API. In the first case, the cost of the LLM is the cost of the infrastructure used to work with the LLM. For example, if Amazon AWS is used with a specific instance (e.g., an ml.t3.medium), then the cost per hour of this instance multiplied by the time needed to complete the workflow will define the cost. If the model is not self hosted, but rather accessed via an API, then the cost is generally dependent on the number of tokens in the input and output (with input and output tokens varying in price).

In our case, as GPT-4o was used in this study, the cost is per token. The number of input and output tokens needed for each phase, as well as the corresponding costs, are presented in Table 6. The average number of input and output tokens for 10

Initial guidelines (before any iteration)	Worker-based solution after 1 iteration
• person: Names of people (e.g. Virginia Wade). Don't mark people that don't have their own name. Include punctuation in the middle of names. Fictional people can be included, as long as they're referred to by name (e.g. Harry Potter).	• person: Names of people (e.g. Virginia Wade). Don't mark people that don't have their own name. Include punctuation in the middle of names. Fictional people can be included, as long as they're referred to by name (e.g. Harry Potter). Usernames are considered a name to identify a person (e.g. @JohnDoe).
• location: Names that are locations (e.g. France). Don't mark locations that don't have their own name. Include punctuation in the middle of names. Fictional locations can be included, as long as they're referred to by name (e.g. Hogwarts).	• location: Names that are locations (e.g. France). Don't mark locations that don't have their own name. Include punctuation in the middle of names. Fictional locations can be included, as long as they're referred to by name (e.g. Hogwarts). Twitter handles about locations should be considered as locations.
• corporation: Names of corporations (e.g. Google). Don't mark locations that don't have their own name. Include punctuation in the middle of names.	• corporation: Names of corporations (e.g. Google). Don't mark locations that don't have their own name. Include punctuation in the middle of names. Twitter handles for corporations should be considered as corporations.
• product: Name of products (e.g. iPhone). Don't mark products that don't have their own name. Include punctuation in the middle of names. Fictional products can be included, as long as they're referred to by name (e.g. Everlasting Gobstopper). It's got to be something you can touch, and it's got to be the official name.	• product: Name of products (e.g. iPhone). Don't mark products that don't have their own name. Include punctuation in the middle of names. Fictional products can be included, as long as they're referred to by name (e.g. Everlasting Gobstopper). It's got to be something you can touch, and it's got to be the official name.
• creative_work: Names of creative works (e.g. Bohemian Rhapsody). Include punctuation in the middle of names. The work should be created by a human, and referred to by its specific name.	• creative_work: Names of creative works (e.g. Bohemian Rhapsody). Include punctuation in the middle of names. The work should be created by a human, and referred to by its specific name.
• group: Names of groups (e.g. Nirvana, San Diego Padres). Don't mark groups that don't have a specific, unique name, or companies (which should be marked corporation).	• group: Names of groups (e.g. Nirvana, San Diego Padres). Don't mark groups that don't have a specific, unique name (e.g. "a group of runners" is not a specific name, as opposed to "Los Angeles Runners"), or companies (which should be marked as corporations). Twitter handles can be considered as specific, unique names for groups.

Table 2: Guidelines improved after 1 iteration over the workflow for the worker-based solution. The first column of the table shows the initial guidelines. Highlighted in green are the changes made by the solution.

annotators and 20 sentences in the table are computed by taking the average for 1 annotator LLM annotating 1 sentence, multiplied by 200 (for the 200 calls corresponding to 10 annotator LLMs annotating 20 sentences). The result is an approximate cost of $4 to go through the complex workflow with 10 annotator LLMs and 20 sentences.

Concerning crowd workers, the cost related to workers depends on two variables: the time a specific phase takes for them and the rate per hour paid to the workers. The time needed for workers to go through each phase of the workflow is reported in Table 5. It can be seen that, in addition to being significantly slower, as each phase takes roughly 30 minutes per worker, the cost of each phase per worker is around $4, $5 and $10 for an hourly rate of $8, $10 and $20 respectively ($8 per hour being the minimum on Prolific). Therefore, at the cost of having one worker going through one phase of the workflow with 20 sentences, while

Initial guidelines (before any iteration)	LLM-based solution after 1 iteration
• person: Names of people (e.g. Virginia Wade). Don't mark people that don't have their own name. Include punctuation in the middle of names. Fictional people can be included, as long as they're referred to by name (e.g. Harry Potter).	• person: Names of people, including titles or roles when they are part of a name (e.g., President Lincoln). Do not mark generic titles or roles without a specific name. Include punctuation in the middle of names. Fictional people can be included, as long as they're referred to by name (e.g., Harry Potter).
• location: Names that are locations (e.g. France). Don't mark locations that don't have their own name. Include punctuation in the middle of names. Fictional locations can be included, as long as they're referred to by name (e.g. Hogwarts).	• location: Names that are specific geographic locations or landmarks (e.g., Eiffel Tower, France). Do not mark generic terms like "park" or "river" without a specific name. Include punctuation in the middle of names. Fictional locations can be included, as long as they're referred to by name (e.g., Hogwarts).
• corporation: Names of corporations (e.g. Google). Don't mark locations that don't have their own name. Include punctuation in the middle of names.	• corporation: Names of corporations or companies (e.g., Google, Microsoft). Do not mark generic terms like "store" or "company" without a specific name. Include punctuation in the middle of names.
• product: Name of products (e.g. iPhone). Don't mark products that don't have their own name. Include punctuation in the middle of names. Fictional products can be included, as long as they're referred to by name (e.g. Everlasting Gobstopper). It's got to be something you can touch, and it's got to be the official name.	• product: Names of tangible products or items (e.g., iPhone, Coca-Cola). Do not mark services or intangible products. Include punctuation in the middle of names. Fictional products can be included, as long as they're referred to by name (e.g., Everlasting Gobstopper). It must be something you can touch, and it must be the official name.
• creative_work: Names of creative works (e.g. Bohemian Rhapsody). Include punctuation in the middle of names. The work should be created by a human,and referred to by its specific name.	• creative_work: Names of creative works such as books, songs, movies, or artworks (e.g., Bohemian Rhapsody, The Great Gatsby). Include punctuation in the middle of names. The work should be created by a human, and referred to by its specific name.
• group: Names of groups (e.g. Nirvana, San Diego Padres). Don't mark groups that don't have a specific, unique name, or companies (which should be marked corporation).	• group: Names of groups, teams, or bands (e.g., Nirvana, San Diego Padres). Do not mark generic terms like "team" or "band" without a specific name. Do not mark companies, which should be marked as corporation.

Table 3: Guidelines improved after 1 iteration over the workflow for the LLM-based solution. The first column of the table shows the initial guidelines. Green highlights correspond to elements added by the LLM optimizer, red ones correspond to what has been deleted, and orange ones to reformulations.

being paid the minimal hourly rate on Prolific, one can have 10 annotator LLMs doing an entire iteration over the workflow.

E LLM Rationales for not Annotating Twitter Handles

During our experiments, we could see that knowing if a Twitter handles was an entity or not was an important issues for workers. However, this was generally not a primary concern for LLMs, for which clarifying Twitter handles came at a later stage of the process. Table 7 shows some examples of LLM rationales for not annotating Twitter handles.

Initial guidelines (before any iteration)	LLM-based solution after 4 iterations
• person: Names of people (e.g. Virginia Wade). Don't mark people that don't have their own name. Include punctuation in the middle of names. Fictional people can be included, as long as they're referred to by name (e.g. Harry Potter).	• person: Names of people, including titles or roles when they are part of a name (e.g., President Lincoln). Do not mark generic titles or roles without a specific name. Include punctuation in the middle of names. Fictional people can be included, as long as they're referred to by name (e.g., Harry Potter). Social media handles or usernames that clearly refer to a person should also be marked as person. Do not mark possessive forms or contractions as person unless they are part of a name. Do not mark standalone words or punctuation that are not part of a person's name.
• location: Names that are locations (e.g. France). Don't mark locations that don't have their own name. Include punctuation in the middle of names. Fictional locations can be included, as long as they're referred to by name (e.g. Hogwarts).	• location: Names that are specific geographic locations or landmarks (e.g., Eiffel Tower, France). Do not mark generic terms like "park" or "river" without a specific name. Include punctuation in the middle of names. Fictional locations can be included, as long as they're referred to by name (e.g., Hogwarts). Do not mark dates, days of the week, or months as locations. Do not mark standalone words or punctuation that are not part of a location's name.
• corporation: Names of corporations (e.g. Google). Don't mark locations that don't have their own name. Include punctuation in the middle of names.	• corporation: Names of corporations or companies (e.g., Google, Microsoft). Do not mark generic terms like "store" or "company" without a specific name. Include punctuation in the middle of names. Do not mark groups, teams, or bands as corporations. Do not mark standalone words or punctuation that are not part of a corporation's name.
• product: Name of products (e.g. iPhone). Don't mark products that don't have their own name. Include punctuation in the middle of names. Fictional products can be included, as long as they're referred to by name (e.g. Everlasting Gobstopper). It's got to be something you can touch, and it's got to be the official name.	• product: Names of tangible products or items (e.g., iPhone, Coca-Cola). Do not mark services or intangible products. Include punctuation in the middle of names. Fictional products can be included, as long as they're referred to by name (e.g., Everlasting Gobstopper). It must be something you can touch, and it must be the official name. Do not mark generic terms like "truck" or "car" unless they are part of a specific product name. Do not mark verbs, actions, standalone words, or punctuation related to products.
• creative_work: Names of creative works (e.g. Bohemian Rhapsody). Include punctuation in the middle of names. The work should be created by a human,and referred to by its specific name.	• creative_work: Names of creative works such as books, songs, movies, or artworks (e.g., Bohemian Rhapsody, The Great Gatsby). Include punctuation in the middle of names. The work should be created by a human, and referred to by its specific name. Do not mark parts of a date or time as creative works. Do not mark conjunctions, prepositions, standalone words, or punctuation as part of creative works unless they are part of the official title.
• group: Names of groups (e.g. Nirvana, San Diego Padres). Don't mark groups that don't have a specific, unique name, or companies (which should be marked corporation).	• group: Names of groups, teams, or bands (e.g., Nirvana, San Diego Padres). Do not mark generic terms like "team" or "band" without a specific name. Do not mark companies, which should be marked as corporation. Social media handles or usernames that clearly refer to a group should also be marked as group. Do not mark standalone words or punctuation that are not part of the group's name.

Table 4: Guidelines improved after 4 iterations over the workflow for the LLM-based solution. The first column of the table shows the initial guidelines. Green highlights correspond to elements added by the LLM optimizer, red ones correspond to what has been deleted, and orange ones to reformulations.

Phase	Median time needed for the phase (with min and max)
Phase 1 (Annotation)	28:54 minutes (15:47 minutes - 53:23 minutes)
Phase 2 (Justify)	25:10 minutes (8:29 minutes - 55:30 minutes)
Phase 3 (Reconsider)	23:12 minutes (12:46 minutes - 1:02:52 hour)
Phase 1 (Annotation w/ new guidelines)	34:54 minutes (14:32 minutes - 49:50 minutes)
Total	1:52:10 hour (51:12 minutes - 3:41:35 hours)

Table 5: Time required by the workers to go through each phase of the workflow. The number of workers who went through each of these phases is 16, 10, 8 and 12 for, respectively, Phases 1, 2, 3 and then Phase 1 again.

Phase	Avg # input tokens per LLM	Avg # output tokens per LLM	Cost	Avg runtime
Annotation + Justify	771	499	\$0.0069175	5.83 sec
Modifying the guidelines	1871	472	\$0.0093975	5.9 sec
Annotation w/ new guidelines	784	503	\$0.00699	6.7 sec
Total for 1 annotator and 1 sentence	3429	1174	\$0.0203125	18.43 sec
Total for 10 annotators and 20 sentences	685,800	234,800	\$4.0625	18.43 sec

Table 6: Number of input and output tokens needed for each phase per annotator LLM, and the corresponding cost and runtime for GPT-4o. The information is reported for each instance/sentence on average ("# input tokens" and "# out tokens"). At the time of this analysis, the cost of GPT-4o was \$0.0025/1K input tokens and \$0.01/1K output tokens. The input prompt for the annotation includes the instructions for the task, the guidelines of WNUT17 and the sentence to annotate. The average runtime from multiple annotators and sentences do not scale because all the annotations are done in parallel. Please note that for speed and accuracy reasons, Phase 1 and 2 are mixed for LLMs, and because the results are mostly similar before and after Phase 3 (see Section 3.2), Phase 3 is skipped in the automation of the workflow.

Entity	Sentence	LLM's Rationale
@TeenThings	RT @TeenThings : I love waking up in the middle of the night knowing i have more time to sleep. #teenthings #comedownwithlove	This seems to be a Twitter handle, which doesn't correspond to named entities like person, location, etc. in the context of physical entities, so it's labeled as 'O'.
		This is a Twitter handle. While it typically represents a user or group, it doesn't fit neatly into the provided categories like person, group, or corporation. As handles aren't named entities per se, it will also be annotated as 'O'.
		Appears to be a social media username. It doesn't fit any provided entity categories (person, location, corporation, etc.). Annotated as O.
@KaulitzClub	@KaulitzClub Hahaha! We dance, eat, drink, and talk EVERYTIME we get together. And it's been this way for like years now!	This appears to be a social media handle or username rather than a name of a person, location, corporation, product, creative work, or group. Thus, it should be marked as 'O'.
		It appears to be a username or a handle, but it doesn't fit into any of the specified annotation categories, such as person or group. Thus, it is marked as O.
		This could be a group or corporation, but based on the given format, it's a social media handle. Without specific context identifying it as a named entity, it's marked as O.

Table 7: Examples of LLM rationales for *not* annotating Twitter handles with the original WNUT-17 guidelines. Please note that 'O' is used by the models to say that it is not an entity.

Ambiguity and Disagreement in Abstract Meaning Representation

Shira Wein
Amherst College
swein@amherst.edu

Abstract

Abstract Meaning Representation (AMR) is a graph-based semantic formalism which has been incorporated into a number of downstream tasks related to natural language understanding. Recent work has highlighted the key, yet often ignored, role of ambiguity and implicit information in natural language understanding. As such, in order to effectively leverage AMR in downstream applications, it is imperative to understand to what extent and in what ways ambiguity affects AMR graphs and causes disagreement in AMR annotation. In this work, we examine the role of ambiguity in AMR graph structure by employing a taxonomy of ambiguity types and producing AMRs affected by each type. Additionally, we investigate how various AMR parsers handle the presence of ambiguity in sentences. Finally, we quantify the impact of ambiguity on AMR using disambiguating paraphrases at a larger scale, and compare this to the measurable impact of ambiguity in vector semantics.

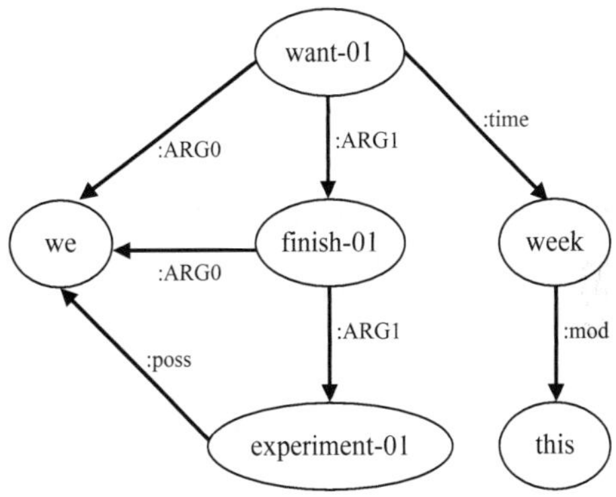


```
(w1 / want-01
    :ARG0 (w2 / we)
    :ARG1 (f / finish-01
        :ARG1 (e / experiment-01
            :poss w2)
        :ARG0 w2)
    :time (w3 / week
        :mod (t / this)))
```

Figure 1: The AMR annotation for the sentence "we want to finish our experiments this week," as a graph (top) and as a string in PENMAN notation (bottom).

1 Introduction

Abstract Meaning Representation (AMR; Banarescu et al., 2013) is a semantic representation which formally encodes the meaning of a sentence or phrase in the form of a rooted, directed graph. Figure 1 shows an example AMR graph of a sentence, in both PENMAN (string-based) and graph-based form. AMR has recently been leveraged for a range of downstream tasks (Wein and Opitz, 2024). While progress has been made on incorporating AMR for engineering purposes, there has not yet been consideration for how ambiguity affects AMR graph structure.

Ambiguity is a key factor in understanding the meaning of a sentence (Zipf, 1949; Piantadosi et al., 2012) and is also a pain point for current NLP systems (Yuan et al., 2023; Liu et al., 2023), making this an important consideration for formal semantic representations such as AMR. Further, ambiguity in the form of "differences in interpretation" is cited as one of the primary causes of disagreement in AMR annotation (§2.1). Therefore, if we want to effectively leverage AMR as a meaning representation for downstream tasks, it is important to investigate how ambiguity affects AMR given the critical role ambiguity plays in meaning.

In this work, we investigate the role of ambiguity on English AMR graph structure by (1) examining which *types* of ambiguity affect graph structure, (2) determining how three top-performing text-to-AMR parsers handle ambiguity in text, and (3) measuring the effect of ambiguity on AMR in comparison to vector semantics.

First (in §3), in order to assess which types of ambiguity affect AMR graph structure, we apply the ambiguity taxonomy from Li et al. (2024). Using the ambiguous sentences and their possible

Proceedings of Context and Meaning: Navigating Disagreements in NLP Annotation, pages 145–154
January 19, 2025.

interpretations provided from Li et al. (2024); Liu et al. (2023), we parse the sentences into AMR graphs for each interpretation, with the notion that if the ambiguous sentence breaks down into multiple AMRs (with the AMR graph being dependent upon interpretation), then the type of ambiguity present in the sentence affects AMR.

Second (in §4), we examine how ambiguity in text is handled by text-to-AMR parsers. Text-to-AMR parsing is the task of automatically converting a sentence or phrase into its corresponding AMR annotation. We elicit parses of the ambiguous sentences from three high-performing AMR parsers and assess whether they parse AMRs corresponding to the same or different interpretations.

Third (in §5), for a large set of disambiguating paraphrases of ambiguous sentences, we measure AMR graph overlap (via Smatch (Cai and Knight, 2013)) and BERTscores (Zhang et al., 2019) of the sentences in order to see a broader picture of the measurable effect of ambiguity on both forms of semantic representations.

2 Background

2.1 AMR Disagreement

Abstract Meaning Representation (AMR) is a semantic representation which reflects "who does what to whom," capturing the core concepts and relationships of elements of meaning (Banarescu et al., 2013). AMRs are rooted, directed graphs in which the nodes correspond with concepts in the sentence and edges indicate the relationships between those concepts; the root typically reflects the main action verb. AMR was originally designed for English but has since been extended to a number of other languages (Wein and Schneider, 2024). Annotation is fairly lightweight but still requires annotator training. Inter-annotator agreement (IAA) is often calculated using Smatch (Cai and Knight, 2013), a hill-climbing algorithm which measures graph overlap on a scale from 0 to 1; 1 indicates graph isomorphism and 0 indicates no shared graph attributes.

In existing AMR corpora, reported IAA has ranged from 0.71 to 0.89. Numerous causes have been cited as the reason for annotator disagreement. Persian AMR (Takhshid et al., 2022), Portuguese AMR (Sobrevilla Cabezudo and Pardo, 2019), Korean AMR (Choe et al., 2020), Spanish AMR (Wein et al., 2022), and Chinese AMR (Li et al., 2016) all cited different *interpretations of sentences* as being causes of different AMR graphs. Specific sources of difference included modality, conjunctive markers with multiple meanings, and verb sense labels. Thus, it is important to investigate how ambiguity, as it relates to different possible interpretations of sentences, quantitatively affects AMR annotation.

Multilingual issues, such as a lack of in-language frame sets or individual collocations not represented in the guidelines (Takhshid et al., 2022; Sobrevilla Cabezudo and Pardo, 2019; Choe et al., 2020), errors (Li et al., 2016; Sobrevilla Cabezudo and Pardo, 2019; Oral et al., 2024; Wein et al., 2022), and confusion with guidelines (Sobrevilla Cabezudo and Pardo, 2019; Choe et al., 2020; Wein et al., 2022) were also cited as causes of annotator disagreement. English AMR (Banarescu et al., 2013) did not describe causes of annotator disagreement.

2.2 Related Work on Ambiguity in Symbolic Representations

As we do for AMR in this work, prior work has considered the role of ambiguity in other symbolic representations. In particular, prior work investigated the impact of ambiguous input on semantic parsing with regard to synchronous context free grammars (Arthur et al., 2015), logical forms (Stengel-Eskin et al., 2023), and synactic parse trees (Church and Patil, 1982).

Dumitrache et al. (2019) produced a crowd-annotated FrameNet corpus which contains multiple annotations per frame and disagreement-based confidence scores, as opposed to the single most-chosen frame, in order to account for ambiguity in the text which would alter the frame annotation. Similarly, Vossen et al. (2018) created a data-to-text corpus with incorporated referential ambiguity.

On the other hand, it is also possible to *address* the presence of ambiguity using formal representations. Koller et al. (2008) addressed scope ambiguity by computing the most likely reading using a regular tree grammar and Duan et al. (2016) used CCG to produce disambiguating paraphrases.

3 Effect of Each Type of Ambiguity on AMR Graphs

In this section, we investigate which types of ambiguity have an effect on AMR via analysis on a small dataset.

3.1 Data and Approach to AMR Parsing

We extract the ambiguous sentences and their individual interpretations from Li et al. (2024), which contains sentences collected from various sources plus newly generated sentences, and an appendix with taxonomically annotated sentences from the AmbiEnt dataset (Liu et al., 2023). We use all of the sentences included in the work, which results in 25 sentences occupying 11 categories of ambiguity, with two or three sentences per category.

We produce AMRs for each interpretation by automatically parsing (1) the original ambiguous sentence, (2) the first interpretation, and (3) the second interpretation, using SPRING (Bevilacqua et al., 2021). We manually write the sentences corresponding to the two interpretations based on the descriptions of the source of ambiguity provided in Li et al. (2024). Then, we manually fix any errors in the automatically parsed AMRs and ensure that they do in fact represent the two distinct possible interpretations of the ambiguous sentence.

In producing and analyzing the AMRs, we determine whether, for each of the explored types of ambiguity, different AMR graph structures are necessary to reflect the individual interpretations. If different AMR graph structures result from each interpretation, this indicates that *the type of ambiguity has an effect on AMR graph structure*.

3.2 Results

The results for this experiment, with different AMRs being parsed for the individual interpretations indicating the ambiguity has an effect on AMR, can be found in Table 1.

Of the 11 types of ambiguity, four (syntactic, elliptical, idiomatic, and coreferential) have an effect on the AMR graph for all sentences in that category, five (collective, implicative, presuppositional, generic, and type/token) have no effect on AMR for any sentences in that category, and two (lexical and scopal) have mixed effects. All AMR graphs along with their interpretations and IDs (which ambiguity they contain) can be found in Appendix A.

Type of Ambiguity	Sent. 1	Sent. 2	Sent. 3
Lexical	X	✓	
Syntactic	✓	✓	✓
Scopal	X	✓	
Elliptical	✓	✓	✓
Collective	X	X	
Implicative	X	X	
Presuppositional	X	X	
Idiomatic	✓	✓	
Coreferential	✓	✓	
Generic	X	X	X
Type/Token	X	X	

Table 1: For each type of ambiguity, shows which sentences have the same (X) versus different (check) AMRs for both interpretations, where having different AMRs indicates that the ambiguity does have an effect on AMR graph structure for that sentence.

Consistent effect. Syntactic ambiguity consistently has an effect on AMR graph structure because it changes argument placement. For example, in the case of "superfluous hair remover," for the interpretation *remover of superfluous hair remover*, superfluous modifies hair, whereas for the *hair remover which is superfluous* interpretation, superfluous modifies remover.

Elliptical and coreferential ambiguity consistently affect AMR graph structure because they dictate the content of the coreferent concept. For example, for elliptical ambiguity, "Peter walked his dog, and Dan did, too" could indicate that Dan walked either his own or Peter's dog, which is represented differently in AMR because the dog walked by Dan will either be possessed by Peter or Dan. For coreferential ambiguity, such as "Abby told Brittney that she upset Courtney" the `:ARG0` of *upset*, i.e. the actor doing the upsetting, will be either Abby or Brittney depending on the interpretation.

Idioms are incorporated in AMR as special frames. Therefore, whether the idiom is the intended meaning or the literal interpretation is the intended meaning will change whether the special frame is used (e.g. `(z1 / kick_bucket-05)` versus `(z1 / kick-01 :ARG1 (z2 / bucket))` for "kick the bucket").

Mixed effects. Lexical ambiguity sometimes has an effect on AMR graph structure depending on whether one interpretation receives special treatment in AMR. For example "bank" is not represented differently if it is a financial or river bank, but "speaker" could be represented as `(z1 / person :ARG0-of (z2 / speak-01))` or `(z1 / speaker)` if it is a person speaking or a loudspeaker, respectively. This is indicative of the fact that people are rooted by `person` in AMR, and other entities such as organizations would receive similar treatment, and thus would similarly induce an AMR divergence based on lexical ambiguity.

Scope is not represented in AMR and as a result, scopal ambiguity generally should not affect AMR graph structure. However, for the sentence "he wants to attend a school in New York," the emphasis could change based on the interpretation to have the school be an argument of `be-located-at-91` or have location be a modifier of the school.

No effect. The types of ambiguity which do not have an effect on AMR graph structure generally rely on commonsense knowledge or assumptions, which are not incorporated into AMR. For example, "the students wrote a paper" (which is affected by collective/distributive ambiguity) is represented the same in AMR whether the students wrote a paper together or individually.

Similarly, implicative, presuppositional, and generic/non-generic ambiguity all rely on assumptions about content not contained in the sentence, which therefore does not affect AMR structure, since implied content does not appear in an AMR annotation.

Type/token ambiguity can be closer to underspecification than outright ambiguity, as in the case of "you should visit Norway in the summer." This is represented the same in AMR whether it is interpreted as "you should visit Norway *this* summer" or "you should visit Norway during *a* summer," but they would differ if the text explicitly said "this/a summer."

4 AMR Parsers and Ambiguity

In this section we investigate how text-to-AMR parsers handle the presence of ambiguity in text, using the same data as in §3.

Methodology. For this experiment, we test how ambiguity affects the output of the SPRING (Bevilacqua et al., 2021), XFM-BART-large, and T5-based text-to-AMR parsers.[1]

Results. For all cases except for two where the ambiguity resulted in two different AMR structures (one for each interpretation), the three parsers produced graphs corresponding with the same interpretation.

The first case where the parsers produced different interpretations was due to an error made by the T5-based parser, which for the sentence "Calvin will honor his father and Otto will too" produced an AMR reflecting that Otto will honor himself. The SPRING parser also had difficulty with this sentence, as even when explicitly stating that Otto will honor Otto's father, the output still indicated that Otto too will honor Calvin's father.

The next case of different interpretation production amongst the parsers was for the sentence "My roommate and I met the lawyer for coffee, but she became ill and had to leave." The SPRING and XFM-BART-large parsers both produced AMRs indicating that the roommate became ill, while the T5-based parser produced an AMR indicating that the lawyer became ill.

In general, the parsers accommodated the ambiguity by outputting one acceptable interpretation, though ambiguity is a possible cause of parser disagreement and/or error, as demonstrated here by the two cases where parser disagreement/error did occur. Still, the quite consistent parsing of ambiguous sentences into the same meaning suggests that there is perhaps a "default" or more likely meaning for the ambiguous sentence from the perspective of text-to-AMR parsers, which is the interpretation reflected in the automatic AMR parse.

5 Overall Effect of Ambiguity on AMR Similarity

Now, we measure the quantitative impact of ambiguity on AMR by parsing a large set of disambiguating paraphrases and comparing the Smatch scores of the AMRs against their corresponding sentences' BERTscore values.

5.1 Approach to Calculating Overall Effect

For this analysis, we use the linguistically annotated sentences from the AmbiEnt dataset (Liu et al., 2023), a natural language inference test set of ambiguous sentences; the premises form disambiguating paraphrases of the original sentence (if the original sentence is ambiguous, which not all are). We use only the sentences which have disambiguations and pair their premises, resulting in 919 disambiguated sentence pairs. Then, we use the SPRING parser to produce the 1,838 AMRs of these sentences. This allows us to then calculate Smatch similarity between each of the different interpretations of the original sentence.

5.2 Results

Overall, we find that the Smatch similarity between the different AMRs of the interpretations is 0.83. The pairwise scores range from 0.17 to 1.0, with 387 of the items having a Smatch score of 1.0.[2] A number of the especially low scores (including

[1] On the AMR 3.0 dataset (Knight et al., 2020), XFM-BART-large and SPRING both achieve Smatch scores of 0.84, while the T5-based parser achieves a Smatch score of 0.82. We run all three parsers through the `amrlib` package.

[2] The variance was 0.03 and the median was 0.88.

the 0.17 case) were caused by multi-sentence differences (i.e. whether one or both AMRs were rooted by `multi-sentence`), which is not a divergence in AMR structure that conveys a difference in meaning.

One example of an AMR pair with a low Smatch score (0.67) is for the following sentence pair: "the vote was close because many people were unsure of their vote" and "the vote was close because many people abstained due to indecision." The AMRs diverge because the argument of their shared `cause-01` root either reflects the abstention or the indecision, making the AMRs quite different. However, these sentences have a BERTscore of 0.78.

The average `bert-base-uncased` BERTscore of the sentences is 0.91, noticably higher than the 0.83 average Smatch score. Thus, in line with prior work (Leung et al., 2022; Wein et al., 2023; Opitz et al., 2023), we find that AMR metrics are *even more sensitive* to finer-grained differences in meaning than embedding-based semantics. While AMR reflects finer-grained differences in meaning, in particular with respect to predicate-argument structure, BERTscore and similar vector-based representations of meaning are less sensitive to these nuances of meaning. Therefore, taking ambiguity into account is even more important when working with AMR than with vector-based models.

6 Conclusion & Future Work

In this work, we investigated the effect of ambiguity on AMR by determining whether different interpretations of ambiguous sentences result in different AMR graphs. Ultimately, we find that syntactic, elliptical, idiomatic, and coreferential ambiguity consistently affect AMR graph structure, and lexical and scopal ambiguity can also affect AMRs depending on the specific sentence. We manually examine a small amount of sentences, which makes it possible that the other types of ambiguity have edge cases which may impact an AMR; still, in our sample and as a general rule, they do not have an impact and we reason through why in §3.

The results of our experiments indicate that ambiguity not only has an effect on AMR, but likely has an even greater effect on AMR than on embedding-based semantics. Therefore, when calculating IAA, it is important for AMR dataset curators to verify to what extent ambiguity is present in the data. Further, our results suggest that when ambiguity can be resolved by presenting additional context to annotators, the extra-sentential context should be provided.

Finally, these findings motivate future work providing AMR datasets with multiple acceptable AMRs per sentence, following Dumitrache et al. (2019). Similarly to how Huang et al. (2023) created a dataset where each AMR led to the production of multiple paraphrased sentences, our work suggests the utility of datasets containing multiple AMRs per sentence (of which ours is the first).[3]

Limitations

Our qualitative analysis, though supplemented with a larger-scale quantitative analysis, is limited to the sentences contained in Li et al. (2024) and is small-scale. However, we contextualize the observed effects within the AMR schema to further unpack which types of ambiguity affect AMR generally.

While we leverage a thorough taxonomy of ambiguity for NLP, it is possible that there are other kinds of ambiguity which may be relevant. Also, this investigation is for English data, so it is yet to be seen how this would extend to other languages.

Regarding additional future work, if in the future the AmbiEnt dataset (Liu et al., 2023) is annotated with the types of ambiguity presented in Li et al. (2024), we could also quantify the effect of each category (rather than overall effect).

References

Philip Arthur, Graham Neubig, Sakriani Sakti, Tomoki Toda, and Satoshi Nakamura. 2015. Semantic parsing of ambiguous input through paraphrasing and verification. *Transactions of the Association for Computational Linguistics*, 3:571–584.

Laura Banarescu, Claire Bonial, Shu Cai, Madalina Georgescu, Kira Griffitt, Ulf Hermjakob, Kevin Knight, Philipp Koehn, Martha Palmer, and Nathan Schneider. 2013. Abstract Meaning Representation for sembanking. In *Proceedings of the 7th Linguistic Annotation Workshop and Interoperability with Discourse*, pages 178–186, Sofia, Bulgaria. Association for Computational Linguistics.

Michele Bevilacqua, Rexhina Blloshmi, and Roberto Navigli. 2021. One SPRING to rule them both: Symmetric AMR semantic parsing and generation without a complex pipeline. In *Proceedings of AAAI*.

Shu Cai and Kevin Knight. 2013. Smatch: an evaluation metric for semantic feature structures. In *Proceedings of the 51st Annual Meeting of the Association*

[3]The full set of 1838 automatically parsed AMRs from §5 are available at https://github.com/shirawein/amr-ambiguity/.

for Computational Linguistics (Volume 2: Short Papers), pages 748–752, Sofia, Bulgaria. Association for Computational Linguistics.

Hyonsu Choe, Jiyoon Han, Hyejin Park, Tae Hwan Oh, and Hansaem Kim. 2020. Building Korean Abstract Meaning Representation corpus. In *Proceedings of the Second International Workshop on Designing Meaning Representations*, pages 21–29, Barcelona Spain (online). Association for Computational Linguistics.

Kenneth Church and Ramesh Patil. 1982. Coping with syntactic ambiguity or how to put the block in the box on the table. *American Journal of Computational Linguistics*, 8(3-4):139–149.

Manjuan Duan, Ethan Hill, and Michael White. 2016. Generating disambiguating paraphrases for structurally ambiguous sentences. In *Proceedings of the 10th Linguistic Annotation Workshop held in conjunction with ACL 2016 (LAW-X 2016)*, pages 160–170, Berlin, Germany. Association for Computational Linguistics.

Anca Dumitrache, Lora Aroyo, and Chris Welty. 2019. A crowdsourced frame disambiguation corpus with ambiguity. In *Proceedings of the 2019 Conference of the North American Chapter of the Association for Computational Linguistics: Human Language Technologies, Volume 1 (Long and Short Papers)*, pages 2164–2170, Minneapolis, Minnesota. Association for Computational Linguistics.

Kuan-Hao Huang, Varun Iyer, I-Hung Hsu, Anoop Kumar, Kai-Wei Chang, and Aram Galstyan. 2023. ParaAMR: A large-scale syntactically diverse paraphrase dataset by AMR back-translation. In *Proceedings of the 61st Annual Meeting of the Association for Computational Linguistics (Volume 1: Long Papers)*, pages 8047–8061, Toronto, Canada. Association for Computational Linguistics.

Kevin Knight, Bianca Badarau, Laura Baranescu, Claire Bonial, Madalina Bardocz, Kira Griffitt, Ulf Hermjakob, Daniel Marcu, Martha Palmer, Tim O'Gorman, et al. 2020. Abstract Meaning Representation (AMR) Annotation Release 3.0. Technical Report LDC2020T02, Linguistic Data Consortium, Philadelphia, PA.

Alexander Koller, Michaela Regneri, and Stefan Thater. 2008. Regular tree grammars as a formalism for scope underspecification. In *Proceedings of ACL-08: HLT*, pages 218–226, Columbus, Ohio. Association for Computational Linguistics.

Wai Ching Leung, Shira Wein, and Nathan Schneider. 2022. Semantic similarity as a window into vector- and graph-based metrics. In *Proceedings of the 2nd Workshop on Natural Language Generation, Evaluation, and Metrics (GEM)*, pages 106–115, Abu Dhabi, United Arab Emirates (Hybrid). Association for Computational Linguistics.

Bin Li, Yuan Wen, Weiguang Qu, Lijun Bu, and Nianwen Xue. 2016. Annotating the little prince with Chinese AMRs. In *Proceedings of the 10th Linguistic Annotation Workshop held in conjunction with ACL 2016 (LAW-X 2016)*, pages 7–15, Berlin, Germany. Association for Computational Linguistics.

Margaret Y Li, Alisa Liu, Zhaofeng Wu, and Noah A Smith. 2024. A taxonomy of ambiguity types for nlp. *arXiv preprint arXiv:2403.14072*.

Alisa Liu, Zhaofeng Wu, Julian Michael, Alane Suhr, Peter West, Alexander Koller, Swabha Swayamdipta, Noah Smith, and Yejin Choi. 2023. We're afraid language models aren't modeling ambiguity. In *Proceedings of the 2023 Conference on Empirical Methods in Natural Language Processing*, pages 790–807, Singapore. Association for Computational Linguistics.

Juri Opitz, Shira Wein, Julius Steen, Anette Frank, and Nathan Schneider. 2023. AMR4NLI: Interpretable and robust NLI measures from semantic graphs. In *Proceedings of the 15th International Conference on Computational Semantics*, pages 275–283, Nancy, France. Association for Computational Linguistics.

Elif Oral, Ali Acar, and Gülşen Eryiğit. 2024. Abstract meaning representation of turkish. *Natural Language Engineering*, 30(1):171–200.

Steven T Piantadosi, Harry Tily, and Edward Gibson. 2012. The communicative function of ambiguity in language. *Cognition*, 122(3):280–291.

Marco Antonio Sobrevilla Cabezudo and Thiago Pardo. 2019. Towards a general Abstract Meaning Representation corpus for Brazilian Portuguese. In *Proceedings of the 13th Linguistic Annotation Workshop*, pages 236–244, Florence, Italy. Association for Computational Linguistics.

Elias Stengel-Eskin, Kyle Rawlins, and Benjamin Van Durme. 2023. Zero and few-shot semantic parsing with ambiguous inputs. In *The Twelfth International Conference on Learning Representations*.

Reza Takhshid, Razieh Shojaei, Zahra Azin, and Mohammad Bahrani. 2022. Persian abstract meaning representation. *arXiv preprint arXiv:2205.07712*.

Piek Vossen, Filip Ilievski, Marten Postma, and Roxane Segers. 2018. Don't annotate, but validate: a data-to-text method for capturing event data. In *Proceedings of the Eleventh International Conference on Language Resources and Evaluation (LREC 2018)*, Miyazaki, Japan. European Language Resources Association (ELRA).

Shira Wein, Lucia Donatelli, Ethan Ricker, Calvin Engstrom, Alex Nelson, Leonie Harter, and Nathan Schneider. 2022. Spanish Abstract Meaning Representation: Annotation of a general corpus. In *Northern European Journal of Language Technology, Volume 8*, Copenhagen, Denmark. Northern European Association of Language Technology.

Shira Wein and Juri Opitz. 2024. A survey of AMR applications. In *Proceedings of the 2024 Conference on Empirical Methods in Natural Language Processing*, pages 6856–6875, Miami, Florida, USA. Association for Computational Linguistics.

Shira Wein and Nathan Schneider. 2024. Assessing the cross-linguistic utility of abstract meaning representation. *Computational Linguistics*, pages 1–55.

Shira Wein, Zhuxin Wang, and Nathan Schneider. 2023. Measuring fine-grained semantic equivalence with Abstract Meaning Representation. In *Proceedings of the 15th International Conference on Computational Semantics*, pages 144–154, Nancy, France. Association for Computational Linguistics.

Yuewei Yuan, Chaitanya Malaviya, and Mark Yatskar. 2023. AmbiCoref: Evaluating human and model sensitivity to ambiguous coreference. In *Findings of the Association for Computational Linguistics: EACL 2023*, pages 1023–1030, Dubrovnik, Croatia. Association for Computational Linguistics.

Tianyi Zhang, Varsha Kishore, Felix Wu, Kilian Q Weinberger, and Yoav Artzi. 2019. Bertscore: Evaluating text generation with bert. *arXiv preprint arXiv:1904.09675*.

George Kingsley Zipf. 1949. *Human behavior and the principle of least effort: An introduction to human ecology*.

A All Categorized AMR Graphs

```
# ::snt We finally reached the bank. ::id
    lex_amb_1_interpret_1
# ::interpretations: We finally reached the
    river bank.; We finally reached the
    financial bank.
(z1 / reach-01
      :ARG0 (z2 / we)
      :ARG1 (z3 / bank)
      :time (z4 / final))

# ::snt The speaker is at the front of the
    room. ::id lex_amb_2_interpret_1
# ::interpretations: The person who is
    speaking is at the front of the room.
(z1 / person
      :ARG0-of (z2 / speak-01)
      :location (z3 / front
            :part-of (z4 / room)))

# ::snt The speaker is at the front of the
    room. ::id lex_amb_2_interpret_2
# ::interpretations: The loudspeaker is at
    the front of the room.
(z1 / speaker
      :location (z2 / front
            :part-of (z3 / room)))

# ::snt superfluous hair remover ::id
    synt_amb_1_interpret_1
# ::interpretations: remover of superfluous
    hair
(z1 / remove-01
      :ARG1 (z2 / hair
            :mod (z3 / superfluous)))

# ::snt superfluous hair remover ::id
    synt_amb_1_interpret_2
# ::interpretations: hair remover which is
    superfluous
(z1 / remove-01
      :ARG1 (z2 / hair)
      :mod (z3 / superfluous))

# ::snt The girl hit the boy with the book.
    ::id synt_amb_2_interpret_1
# ::interpretations: With the book, the girl
     hit the boy.
(z1 / hit-01
      :ARG0 (z2 / girl)
      :ARG1 (z3 / boy)
      :ARG2 (z4 / book))

# ::snt The girl hit the boy with the book.
    ::id synt_amb_2_interpret_2
# ::interpretations: The girl hit the boy
    who had the book.
(z1 / hit-01
      :ARG0 (z2 / girl)
      :ARG1 (z3 / boy
            :ARG0-of (z4 / have-03
                  :ARG1 (z5 / book))))

# ::snt He's drawing all over the bus with
    graffiti. ::id synt_amb_3_interpret_1
# ::interpretations: He is drawing graffiti
    on the surface of the bus.
(z1 / draw-01
      :ARG0 (z2 / he)
      :ARG1 (z3 / graffiti)
      :location (z4 / bus)
      :extent (z5 / all-over))

# ::snt He's drawing all over the bus with
    graffiti. ::id synt_amb_3_interpret_2
# ::interpretations He is on the bus,
    drawing graffiti.
(z1 / bus
      :location-of (z2 / he
            :ARG0-of (z3 / draw-01
                  :ARG1 (z4 / graffiti))))

# ::snt Every student read two poems. ::id
    scop_amb_1_interpret_1
# ::interpretations Every student read two (
    possibly different) poems.; Two poems
    were read by every student (same poems).
(z1 / read-01
      :ARG0 (z2 / person
            :ARG0-of (z3 / study-01)
            :mod (z4 / every))
      :ARG1 (z5 / poem
            :quant 2))

# ::snt He wants to attend a school in New
    York. ::id scop_amb_1_interpret_1
# ::interpretations There is a school in New
     York that he wants to attend.
(z1 / want-01
      :ARG0 (z2 / he)
      :ARG1 (z3 / attend-01
            :ARG0 z2
            :ARG1 (z4 / school
```

```
                    :location (z5 / city
                          :name (z6 / name
                                :op1 "New"
                                :op2 "York")))))

# ::snt He wants to attend a school in New
    York. ::id scop_amb_1_interpret_1
# ::interpretations He wants to attend
    school in New York.
(z1 / want-01
      :ARG0 (z2 / he)
      :ARG1 (z3 / attend-01
            :ARG0 z2
            :ARG1 (z4 / be-located-at-91
                  :ARG1 (z5 / school)
                  :ARG2 (z6 / city
                        :name (z6 / name
                              :op1 "New"
                              :op2 "York")))))

# ::snt Peter walked his dog, and Dan did,
    too. ::id ellip_amb_1_interpret_1
# ::interpretations Peter and Dan walked
    Peter's dog.
(z1 / walk-01
      :ARG0 (z2 / and
            :op1 (z3 / person
                  :name (z4 / name
                        :op1 "Peter"))
            :op2 (z5 / person
                  :name (z6 / name
                        :op1 "Dan")))
      :ARG1 (z7 / dog
            :poss z3))

# ::snt Peter walked his dog, and Dan did,
    too. ::id ellip_amb_1_interpret_2
# ::interpretations Peter walked his dog,
    and Dan walked his own dog.
(z1 / and
      :op1 (z2 / walk-01
            :ARG0 (z3 / person
                  :name (z4 / name
                        :op1 "Peter"))
            :ARG1 (z5 / dog
                  :poss z3))
      :op2 (z6 / walk-01
            :ARG0 (z7 / person
                  :name (z8 / name
                        :op1 "Dan"))
            :ARG1 (z9 / dog
                  :poss z7)))

# ::snt Sam loves Jess more than Jason. ::id
    ellip_amb_2_interpret_1
# ::interpretations Sam loves Jess more than
    Sam loves Jason.
  (z1 / love-01
    :ARG0 (z2 / person
          :name (z3 / name
                :op1 "Sam"))
    :ARG1 (z4 / person
          :name (z5 / name
                :op1 "Jess"))
    :ARG1-of (z6 / have-degree-91
          :ARG3 (z7 / more)
          :ARG4 (z8 / love-01
                :ARG0 z2
                :ARG1 (z9 / person
                      :name (z10 / name
                            :op1 "Jason")))))

# ::snt Sam loves Jess more than Jason. ::id
    ellip_amb_2_interpret_2
# ::interpretations Sam loves Jess more than
    Jason loves Jess.
  (z1 / love-01
    :ARG0 (z2 / person
          :name (z3 / name
                :op1 "Sam"))
    :ARG1 (z4 / person
          :name (z5 / name
                :op1 "Jess"))
    :ARG1-of (z6 / have-degree-91
          :ARG3 (z7 / more)
          :ARG4 (z8 / love-01
                :ARG0 (z9 / person
                      :name (z10 / name
                            :op1 "Jason"))
                :ARG1 z4)))

# ::snt Calvin will honor his father and
    Otto will too. ::id
    ellip_amb_3_interpret_1
# ::interpretations Calvin and Otto will
    honor Calvin's father.
(z1 / and
      :op1 (z2 / honor-01
            :ARG0 (z3 / person
                  :name (z4 / name
                        :op1 "Calvin"))
            :ARG1 (z5 / person
                  :ARG0-of (z6 / have-rel-role
                        -91
                        :ARG1 z3
                        :ARG2 (z7 / father))))
      :op2 (z8 / honor-01
            :ARG0 (z9 / person
                  :name (z10 / name
                        :op1 "Otto"))
            :ARG1 z5
            :mod (z11 / too)))

# ::snt Calvin will honor his father and
    Otto will too. ::id
    ellip_amb_3_interpret_2
# ::interpretations Calvin will honor Calvin
    's father, and Otto will honor Otto's
    father.
(z1 / and
      :op1 (z2 / honor-01
            :ARG0 (z3 / person
                  :name (z4 / name
                        :op1 "Calvin"))
            :ARG1 (z5 / person
                  :ARG0-of (z6 / have-rel-role
                        -91
                        :ARG1 z3
                        :ARG2 (z7 / father))))
      :op2 (z8 / honor-01
            :ARG0 (z9 / person
                  :name (z10 / name
                        :op1 "Otto"))
            :ARG1 (z11 / person
                  :ARG0-of (z12 / have-rel-
                        role-91
                        :ARG1 z9
                        :ARG2 (z13 / father)))
            :mod (z14 / too)))
```

```
# ::snt The students wrote a paper. ::id
    coll_amb_1_interpret_1
# ::interpretations The students wrote a
    paper together.; Each student wrote a
    paper separately.
(z1 / write-01
     :ARG0 (z2 / person
          :ARG0-of (z3 / study-01))
     :ARG1 (z4 / paper))

# ::snt Jenny and Zoe solved the puzzle. ::
    id coll_amb_2_interpret_1
# ::interpretations Jenny and Zoe each
    solved the puzzle individually.; Jenny
    and Zoe solved the puzzle together.
(z1 / solve-01
     :ARG0 (z2 / and
          :op1 (z3 / person
               :name (z4 / name
                    :op1 "Jenny"))
          :op2 (z5 / person
               :name (z6 / name
                    :op1 "Zoe")))
     :ARG1 (z7 / puzzle-01))

# ::snt Some gems in this box are fake. ::id
    impl_amb_1_interpret_1
# ::interpretations Some, and not all, gems
    in this box are fake.; Some, and perhaps
    all, gems in this box are fake.
(z1 / fake-02
     :ARG1 (z2 / gem
          :quant (z3 / some)
          :location (z4 / box
               :mod (z5 / this))))

# ::snt Carolyn had talked to two senators.
    ::id impl_amb_2_interpret_1
# ::interpretations Carolyn had talked to (
    exactly) two senators.; Carolyn had
    talked to (at least) two senators.
(z1 / talk-01
     :ARG0 (z2 / person
          :name (z3 / name
               :op1 "Carolyn"))
     :ARG2 (z4 / person
          :quant 2
          :ARG0-of (z5 / have-org-role-91
               :ARG1 (z6 / government-
                   organization
                    :name (z7 / name
                         :op1 "Senate"))))
                              )

# ::snt Jane left early too. ::id
    pres_amb_1_interpret_1
# ::interpretations (e.g. Robert left early
    .) Jane left early too.; (e.g. Jane
    arrived early.) Jane left early too.
(z1 / leave-11
     :ARG0 (z2 / person
          :name (z3 / name
               :op1 "Jane"))
     :time (z4 / early)
     :mod (z5 / too))

# ::snt The new software is also available
    in a Spanish-language version. ::id
    pres_amb_2_interpret_1
# ::interpretations The new software is also
    available in a Spanish-language version
    (in addition to older software).; The
    new software is also available in a
    Spanish-language version (in addition to
    other languages).
(z1 / available-02
     :ARG2 (z2 / software
          :ARG1-of (z3 / new-01))
     :mod (z4 / also)
     :manner (z5 / version
          :mod (z6 / language
               :name (z7 / name
                    :op1 "Spanish"))))

# ::snt kick the bucket ::id
    idiom_amb_1_interpret_1
# ::interpretations die
(z1 / kick_bucket-05)

# ::snt kick the bucket ::id
    idiom_amb_1_interpret_2
# ::interpretations hit a bucket with one's
    foot
(z1 / kick-01
     :ARG1 (z2 / bucket))

# ::snt He didn't see the big picture. ::id
    idiom_amb_2_interpret_1
# ::interpretations He didn't see the
    physical big picture.
(z1 / see-01
     :polarity -
     :ARG0 (z2 / he)
     :ARG1 (z3 / picture
          :mod (z4 / big-01)))

# ::snt He didn't see the big picture. ::id
    idiom_amb_2_interpret_2
# ::interpretations He didn't see the
    metaphorical big picture.
(z1 / see-01
     :polarity -
     :ARG0 (z2 / he)
     :ARG1 (z3 / big-picture-01))

# ::snt Abby told Brittney that she upset
    Courtney. ::id coref_amb_1_interpret_1
# ::interpretations Abby told Brittney that
    Abby upset Courtney.
(z1 / tell-01
     :ARG0 (z2 / person
          :name (z3 / name
               :op1 "Abby"))
     :ARG1 (z4 / upset-01
          :ARG0 z2
          :ARG1 (z5 / person
               :name (z6 / name
                    :op1 "Courtney")))
     :ARG2 (z7 / person
          :name (z8 / name
               :op1 "Brittney")))

# ::snt Abby told Brittney that she upset
    Courtney. ::id coref_amb_1_interpret_2
# ::interpretations Abby told Brittney that
    Brittney upset Courtney.
```

```
(z1 / tell-01
      :ARG0 (z2 / person
            :name (z3 / name
                  :op1 "Abby"))
      :ARG1 (z4 / upset-01
            :ARG0 (z5 / person
                  :name (z6 / name
                        :op1 "Brittney"))
            :ARG1 (z7 / Courtney))
      :ARG2 z5)


# ::snt My roommate and I met the lawyer for
      coffee, but she became ill and had to
     leave. ::id coref_amb_2_interpret_1
My roommate and I met the lawyer for coffee,
      but the lawyer became ill and had to
     leave.
(z1 / meet-02
      :ARG0 (z2 / and
            :op1 (z3 / person
                  :ARG0-of (z4 / have-rel-role
                        -91
                        :ARG1 (z5 / i)
                        :ARG2 (z6 / roommate)))
            :op2 z5)
      :ARG1 (z7 / lawyer)
      :purpose (z8 / coffee)
      :concession-of (z9 / and
            :op1 (z10 / become-01
                  :ARG1 z7
                  :ARG2 (z11 / ill-01
                        :ARG1 z7))
            :op2 (z12 / obligate-01
                  :ARG1 z7
                  :ARG2 (z13 / leave-11
                        :ARG0 z7))))

# ::snt My roommate and I met the lawyer for
      coffee, but she became ill and had to
     leave. ::id coref_amb_2_interpret_2
# ::interpretations My roommate and I met
     the lawyer for coffee, but my roommate
     became ill and had to leave.
(z1 / meet-02
      :ARG0 (z2 / and
            :op1 (z3 / person
                  :ARG0-of (z4 / have-rel-role
                        -91
                        :ARG1 (z5 / i)
                        :ARG2 (z6 / roommate)))
            :op2 z5)
      :ARG1 (z7 / lawyer)
      :purpose (z8 / coffee)
      :concession-of (z9 / and
            :op1 (z10 / become-01
                  :ARG1 z3
                  :ARG2 (z11 / ill-01
                        :ARG1 z3))
            :op2 (z12 / obligate-01
                  :ARG1 z3
                  :ARG2 (z13 / leave-11
                        :ARG0 z3))))

# ::snt dinosaurs ate kelp ::id
     gen_amb_1_interpret_1
# ::interpretations In general, dinosaurs
     ate kelp.; On one occasion, some
     dinosaurs ate kelp.
(z1 / eat-01
      :ARG0 (z2 / dinosaur)
      :ARG1 (z3 / kelp))

# ::snt John ate breakfast with a gold fork.
     ::id gen_amb_2_interpret_1
# ::interpretations John generally ate
     breakfast with a gold fork.; During one
     breakfast, John ate with a gold fork.
(z1 / eat-01
      :ARG0 (z2 / person
            :name (z3 / name
                  :op1 "John"))
      :ARG1 (z4 / breakfast)
      :instrument (z5 / fork
            :consist-of (z6 / gold)))

# ::snt If an athlete uses a banned
     substance, they will be disqualified
     from the competition. ::id
     gen_amb_3_interpret_1
# ::interpretations As a rule, if an athlete
     uses a banned substance, they will be
     disqualified from the competition.; If
     the referenced athlete uses a banned
     substance, they will be disqualified
     from the competition.
(z1 / disqualify-01
      :ARG1 (z2 / athlete)
      :ARG2 (z3 / compete-01
            :ARG0 z2)
      :condition (z4 / use-01
            :ARG0 z2
            :ARG1 (z5 / substance
                  :ARG1-of (z6 / ban-01))))

# ::snt I paid for the same car. ::id
     type_amb_1_interpret_1
# ::interpretations I paid for the same car
     as another person.; I paid for the same
     car twice.
(z1 / pay-01
      :ARG0 (z2 / i)
      :ARG3 (z3 / car
            :ARG1-of (z4 / same-01)))

# ::snt You should visit Norway in the
     summer. ::id type_amb_2_interpret_1
# ::interpretations You should visit Norway
     this summer.; You should visit Norway
     during a summer.
(z1 / visit-01
      :ARG0 (z2 / you)
      :ARG1 (z3 / country
            :name (z4 / name
                  :op1 "Norway"))
      :time (z5 / date-entity
            :season (z6 / summer))
      :ARG1-of (z7 / recommend-01))
```

Disagreement in Metaphor Annotation of Mexican Spanish Science Tweets

Alec Sánchez-Montero **Gemma Bel-Enguix** **Sergio-Luis Ojeda-Trueba**
Gerardo Sierra
alecm@comunidad.unam.mx gbele@iingen.unam.mx sojedat@iingen.unam.mx
gsierram@iingen.unam.mx
Universidad Nacional Autónoma de México

Abstract

Traditional linguistic annotation methods often strive for a gold standard with hard labels as input for Natural Language Processing models, assuming an underlying objective truth for all tasks. However, disagreement among annotators is a common scenario, even for seemingly objective linguistic tasks, and is particularly prominent in figurative language annotation, since multiple valid interpretations can sometimes coexist. This study presents the annotation process for identifying metaphorical tweets within a corpus of 3733 Public Communication of Science texts written in Mexican Spanish, emphasizing inter-annotator disagreement. Using Fleiss' and Cohen's Kappa alongside agreement percentages, we evaluated metaphorical language detection through binary classification in three situations: two subsets of the corpus labeled by three different non-expert annotators each, and a subset of disagreement tweets, identified in the non-expert annotation phase, re-labeled by three expert annotators. Our results suggest that expert annotation may improve agreement levels, but does not exclude disagreement, likely due to factors such as the relatively novelty of the genre, the presence of multiple scientific topics, and the blending of specialized and non-specialized discourse. Going further, we propose adopting a learning-from-disagreement approach for capturing diverse annotation perspectives to enhance computational metaphor detection in Mexican Spanish.

1 Introduction

Studies on Figurative Language Processing (FLP) have increased substantially in recent years, with metaphor as one of the main topics addressed from different computational approaches. Since most of the research related to computing and technology is carried out in English-speaking contexts, the greatest advances in computational metaphor processing have been developed for the English language, a situation that has brought an imbalance for the rest of the languages spoken on the planet. As mentioned by Sánchez-Bayona (2021), there is a gap in Spanish annotated data that can be used for automatic detection, interpretation and generation of linguistic metaphors.

As far as Mexican Spanish is concerned, works on metaphor annotation and metaphor computational processing are virtually nonexistent. Even though Natural Language Processing (NLP) approaches to the study of metaphor date back at least to the 1980s (Shutova et al., 2013), most of the research related to computing and technology is carried out in English-speaking contexts, which means the greatest advances in metaphor automatic processing have been developed for the English language. Languages like Spanish face a gap in NLP studies regarding the automatic detection, interpretation, and generation of linguistic metaphors.

To address this gap, we have explored a multi-class annotation approach to develop an annotated corpus, aiming to study both binary and future multi-class classification of metaphorical texts within the domain of Public Communication of Science (PCS) in Twitter/X. We devised this dataset would provide sufficient training data for a computational NLP model to identify and understand linguistic metaphors in Spanish texts of this particular type of discourse, where the wide use of metaphor —in contrast to specialized scientific discourse— has been pointed out, emphasizing communicative and didactic purposes, stemming from the target audience: the general public. Metaphors play a major role in PCS, as they are useful for explaining complex concepts in a way that makes them more accessible and easier to understand for the non-specialized audience (Berber Sardinha, 2007; Alexander et al., 2015; Merakchi, 2020).

During our annotation process, we noticed that human metaphor identification is a challenging process, far less intuitive than anticipated. Despite

Proceedings of Context and Meaning: Navigating Disagreements in NLP Annotation, pages 155–164
January 19, 2025.

rigorously adhering to a meticulous annotation protocol, carefully adjusted to to the linguistic characteristics of the corpus, we observed consistent disagreements among annotators on what constitutes metaphorical language in science communication. In parallel, we have held expert meetings to address the nuanced linguistic and cognitive aspects of metaphors in PCS in relation to important features of Twitter/X language use —such as brevity, interactivity, and the use of multimodality—, aiming to develop coherent annotation guidelines and a consistently annotated corpus. Through these examinations, we have pursued making the process of metaphor identification as methodical and systematic as possible. However, our annotation data has revealed the difficulty of achieving a reliable gold standard with hard labels through conventional methods, which highlights the importance of analyzing annotator disagreements more closely. Moreover, given the scarcity of research on disagreement in figurative language annotation (Weitzel et al., 2016; Sandri et al., 2023; Xiao et al.), we consider this a critical area for further exploration.

In this work, we discuss the development of our annotated corpus, from designing annotation guidelines to a focused analysis of annotator disagreement. Beyond resolving the points of disagreement to establish a gold standard, we are concerned with understanding the causes and characteristics of this divergence in the binary classification of metaphorical texts and non-metaphorical texts. For our corpus annotation, we have relied on the MATTER cycle (Pustejovsky and Stubbs, 2013) and an adaptation of the Metaphor Identification Procedure Vrije Universiteit Amsterdam (MIPVU) (Steen et al., 2010), to identify three categories of metaphors: direct metaphor, indirect metaphor, and personification metaphor. These categories were considered to detect only the presence or absence of metaphorical language in the text.

We annotated a corpus of 3733 PCS tweets published in Mexican Spanish from January 2020 to May 2023. Both our annotated dataset and the annotation guidelines are publicly available on a GitHub repository, to support future research in metaphor analysis and automatic metaphor detection. This paper is structured as follows: Section 2 outlines the linguistic metaphor annotation, including the MATTER cycle, the MIPVU method, related work in metaphor annotation, and observations about learning from disagreement. Section 3 details the annotation guidelines, while section 4 reviews a pilot testing as a key phase in improving the guidelines. Section 5 focuses on corpus annotation, encompassing inter-annotator agreement evaluation, expert annotation for disagreement cases, and subsequent guide refinements. Finally, section 6 presents conclusions and future directions for potential applications of the corpus.

2 Framework for Linguistic Metaphor Annotation

2.1 Metaphor Identification Procedure Vrije Universiteit (MIPVU)

Natural Language Processing (NLP) systems often rely on linguistic features, such as lexical patterns, syntactic structures, or semantic associations, to identify metaphorical language. To tackle this objective, NLP researchers have turned to a complementary theoretical approach, exemplified by Steen et al. (2010) work on the Metaphor Identification Procedure Vrije Universiteit (MIPVU). Originally formulated as MIP by Pragglejaz (2007), the MIPVU provides a systematic and structured methodology for identifying metaphor related words (MRWs) in text corpora, offering clear guidelines and criteria for manual annotation. Unlike the cognitive guidance of other metaphor theories —such as conceptual metaphor theory or CMT (Lakoff and Johnson, 1980)—, MIPVU operationalizes metaphor identification based on linguistic and contextual considerations. Using this approach, researchers have constructed the VUAM corpus, which stands as the most extensive dataset with annotations aimed at characterizing linguistic metaphor (Steen et al., 2010).

The MIPVU procedure involves several steps for identifying metaphorical language in text. Just like MIP, it begins with reading the text to understand its meaning, followed by identifying lexical units and establishing their contextual meaning. If a unit's contextual meaning contrasts with its basic meaning and can be understood metaphorically, it is marked as metaphorical (Pragglejaz, 2007).

In the realm of NLP, MIPVU serves as a valuable tool for automatically identifying and analyzing metaphorical language in large text corpora. By incorporating refinements such as the consideration of word class boundaries and various metaphor types, NLP systems can more accurately detect MRWs within text. Although the MIPVU methodology has been adapted to other languages (Nacey et al., 2019), Spanish has been notably omitted, resulting in a scarcity of labeled data to train supervised models (Sanchez-Bayona and Agerri, 2022).

2.2 Related Work

Research and advances in metaphor annotation in Spanish remain sparse. Notably, the work by Sanchez-Bayona and Agerri (2022) on this topic stands out. They developed the Corpus for Metaphor Detection in Spanish (CoMeta), comprising 3633 sentences from general domain texts with annotations at the token level (words with semantic content only) with binary labels. The CoMeta corpus was annotated following an adaptation of MIPVU into Spanish by the authors, representing a vital contribution to advancing metaphor research in the Spanish language.

Before CoMeta, "the only known attempt to annotate linguistic metaphor in general domain texts in Spanish is that of [Martínez] Santiago et al. (2014), who labeled a sample from SemEval 2013 dataset of the news genre employed for WSD task in Spanish" (Sánchez-Bayona, 2021, 15). Using the VUAM corpus as a benchmark and evaluating it against 9 large language models, CoMeta demonstrated lower performance results compared to English. This outcome is understandable, given the smaller size of the training set in Spanish, although this does not diminish its remarkable contribution to NLP in Spanish. However, CoMeta's binary tagging represents a certain shortcoming since it does not allow the study of the different types of automatically detected metaphors.

Agreement levels in metaphor annotation, though rarely central in literature related to computational metaphor processing, are occasionally reported but often without in-depth discussion. Among the notable cases, the (VUAM) corpus, annotated over a two-year period, achieved a high Fleiss' kappa of 0.85 (Krennmayr and Steen, 2017). Another study by Zayed (2021), focused on classifying metaphorical verbs in Twitter datasets, reported Fleiss' kappa values exceeding 0.6. Similarly, Sanchez-Bayona and Agerri (2022) involved six Spanish-speaking linguists in an evaluation of a 10% random selection of CoMeta, achieving an average Cohen's kappa of 0.631. In contrast, our study involves additional variables which may emphasize both the complexity and subjectivity of the task: a relatively unexplored genre that mixes specialized and non-specialized discourse, limited annotation time, and reliance on non-expert annotators.

In contrast to the limited studies on metaphor detection in Spanish using NLP techniques (Richi Pons-Sorolla, 2020; Uribe and Mejía, 2023), in English there have been important developments in the use of deep learning techniques and transformers for metaphor detection, as reported by Tong et al. (2021). Furthermore, noteworthy models have emerged such as MelBERT (Choi et al., 2021) and MIss RoBERTa WiLDe (Babieno et al., 2022), specifically trained for metaphor processing from fine-tuning large language models. Alternative methods have addressed metaphor detection from a cross-lingual or multilingual setting (Aghazadeh et al., 2022; Lai et al., 2023; Hülsing and Schulte Im Walde, 2024) as well as using Large Language Models (Wachowiak and Gromann, 2023).

2.3 Learning from Disagreement

In recent years, the approach known as 'learning from disagreement' has emerged in NLP as a reaction to traditional methods based on a gold standard annotation, which assumes a single objective truth underlies the annotation task. This approach challenges that epistemological assumption and, instead, it adopts a perspectivist view in which "disagreements provide useful information for learning" (Uma et al., 2021, 1389). This methodological shift is relevant for linguistic tasks like metaphor annotation, where multiple valid interpretations often coexist. By framing disagreements as a source of information for training data, FLP research can capture the diversity of perspectives, subjectivity and interpretative variability to the linguistic phenomena.

Uma et al. (2021) review the evidence for disagreements on NLP and Computer Vision (CV) tasks, pointing out that annotators might differ even on supposedly objective linguistic tasks, such as POS tagging; in some cases, even detailed annotation guidelines fail to eliminate errors or resolve "hard cases". Disagreement is even more pronounced in subjective tasks like sentiment analysis or hate speech, and it can similarly arise in tasks involving figurative language. The sources of disagreement include annotator errors, interface issues, ambiguities in the annotation scheme, item difficulty, and the inherent subjectivity of the task. Several methods have emerged to address this challenge, from aggregating crowd annotations into a single label (a form of 'silver' truth) to hybrid methods combining hard and soft labels. While hard labels assign a single definitive label to each item, soft labels capture the distribution of annotators' responses, which reflects uncertainty or variability in the data.

Evaluation of these methods contrasts traditional 'hard' metrics —e.g. F1 or accuracy— with 'soft' evaluation metrics such as cross-entropy, Jensen-Shannon divergence, and normalized entropy. The findings of Uma et al. (2021) indicate that there is no clear 'winner' among methods that do not rely on gold labels, as the best approach depends on the specific dataset. However, methods using hard labels generally perform better when evaluated with hard metrics, while those that do not assume a recoverable gold label tend to excel with soft evaluation metrics.

3 Annotation Guidelines

Development of accurate annotation guidelines was essential for the task of identifying metaphorical language in Mexican Spanish tweets, as no material available for this language variety was found. We established a group of linguists to meet and discuss the development of the guide, starting from the idea of adapting the MIPVU to this language and to the characteristics of the project. An early suggestion was to first perform a binary corpus annotation, aimed at distinguishing between metaphorical language tweets and literal language tweets. However, it was determined that focusing on the identification of specific metaphor types during annotation implied the detection of metaphorical language in the texts. This would enable annotators to classify the presence of metaphor at a binary level while subclassifying metaphorical tweets into metaphor types. Starting with a multi-class annotation system to support binary classification not only addressed the immediate objectives of the project, but also provided data for analyzing metaphor subclasses in the future.

In our guidelines, we first defined metaphor as a a conceptual relationship between a source domain and a target domain, expressed through verbal language, according to CMT's fundamental concepts (Lakoff and Johnson, 1980). Next, we examined the MRWs described by Steen et al. (2010), and decided to focus on three types of metaphors: direct (DM), indirect (IM), and personification (PM), due to the features of our corpus. Table 1 shows labeled examples of the three types of metaphors, extracted from tweets in the corpus and presented to the annotators in the guide. A more detailed explanation of our multi-class annotation schema can be found in Sánchez-Montero et al. (2024), and our guidelines can be consulted via our GitHub repository.

Since our primary goal was to detect the presence of metaphors, we utilized the identification of metaphor types as a means to this end. Therefore, we assigned general labels of 0 (non-metaphorical) and 1 (metaphorical) to the annotated tweets. In addition, our annotation focused on identifying scientific metaphors and everyday or colloquial metaphors in the corpus, both present in PCS tweets that bridge the specialized realm of science and the colloquial domain of language.

In addition to providing examples extracted from the corpus and offering guidance on how to use the annotation platform, clarifications were provided regarding the scope of the annotations, i.e. the whole set of words that should be considered within each unit tagged with a different label. It was emphasized that labels should be applied to lexical words containing relevant semantic content in all cases, like complete proper names, and for verbs, annotators were reminded to consider the type of verb for comprehensive annotation, given the complexity of Spanish verb morphology. This included simple verbs and multi-word expressions, like compound verbs, verbal periphrases, and verbal phrases.

Furthermore, it was explained that scientific terminology of metaphorical origin, such as "planetary rings", "family trees", or "neural networks", should also be marked. No further information was added on the determination of linguistic units, as annotators were presumed to have a background in linguistics. It was also emphasized that: i) all instances identified as metaphors should be marked, ii) annotators could refer to a dictionary for assistance, and iii) any problematic cases not present in the guide should be reported immediately.

4 Pilot Testing

We gathered a group of 6 native Mexican Spanish-speaking annotators to carry out a pilot test for the validation of our guidelines[1]. These annotators are undergraduate students of linguistics in the age range of 18 to 25 years old, 2 of them female and 4 male. We chose the Argilla platform

[1]The principles of the Belmont Report were followed in the data labeling process (Belmont, 1978).

Category	Annotation Example	Translation
Direct Metaphor	¿Acostumbras ver tu celular antes de dormir? ¡Tache! Te explicamos porqué este aparato es nuestro peor aliado a la hora de conciliar el sueño. ¡#RedescubreLaCiencia en el #DíaMundialDelSueño!	Do you usually watch your cell phone before going to sleep? Strike! We explain you why this device is our worst ally when it comes to falling asleep. #DiscoverScience on #WorldSleepDay!
Indirect Metaphor	¡Las mujeres a la conquista del espacio! #SpaceConCiencia y @Ciencia_UNAM presentan a @AnaC_Olvera y @TerricolaMex en una plática con @RaulGranada más allá del firmamento ¡Descubre porqué la mujer ha sido fundamental en la carrera espacial!	Women to the conquest of space! #SpaceConCiencia and @Ciencia_UNAM present @AnaC_Olvera and @TerricolaMex in a talk with @RaulGranada beyond the firmament. Find out why women have been instrumental in the space race!
Personification Metaphor	El telescopio James Webb fotografió varias galaxias que gravitan en torno de un hoyo negro que está capturando parte de su gas.	The James Webb telescope photographed several galaxies gravitating around a black hole that is capturing some of their gas.

Table 1: Examples of metaphor annotation in the guidelines including their English translation.

for corpus annotation due to its suitability for handling Spanish idiosyncrasies, including accents and the letter “ñ”, as well as other distinctive elements found in tweets such as emojis. Additionally, the platform’s ability to tokenize texts upon dataset loading proved advantageous, enhancing efficiency during the annotation task.

We evaluated a dataset of 73 tweets commonly annotated by all six annotators, randomly sampled from the corpus, using Fleiss’ Kappa coefficient (Fleiss, 1971). Our evaluation focused on a binary classification, i.e., distinguishing between tweets with metaphors and tweets without metaphors, regardless of the specific labels that annotators placed on the texts. We extracted the binary labels of each record per annotator, assigning ‘0’ to texts with no metaphor and ‘1’ to the rest of the labels used.

Once this structured dataset was determined, the Fleiss’ Kappa coefficient was calculated, resulting in a value of **0.22**. According to the Landis and Koch (1977) scale, a Kappa score like this falls within the scope of a “fair” agreement, which means that the level of inter-annotator agreement (IAA) beyond what might be expected by chance alone, but not sufficiently strong. Initially, we anticipated a lower rate of IAA given the task’s complexity for this initial phase.

During the annotation process, several common errors were identified, including the misclassification of verbs that do not personify but, being adjacent to inanimate objects words, were labeled as personificators. Additionally, concerning DMs, annotators tended to focus on identifying metaphor signals from the provided list of expressions, rather than addressing conceptual mappings, resulting in the misclassification of this type of metaphor.

Furthermore, the annotators failed to consider multiple metaphors within a text, even though the corpus presented examples of combined metaphors, such as simultaneous PMs and DMs.

Regarding annotation scope, verbs were inconsistently labeled, despite linguistic training of annotators. Oftentimes multi-word verbs were not considered, and annotations extended only to inflected verb words. Similarly, nouns were sometimes labeled without adjacent adjectives, highlighting the importance of context for accurate annotation in relation to training data for computational metaphor processing.

5 Corpus Annotation

Based on the annotation errors, some key improvements to the guide were implemented for clarity and guidance. A revised version of the annotation guide was provided to the six annotators who would be working on the full corpus. Although only four of the original pilot participants continued, the demographic profile of the corpus annotators remained consistent with that of the pilot study. Two additional annotators joined the project and also completed the same preparatory pilot test.

Based on observations from the pilot study, the revised guide minimized the theoretical content to essential information and reduced the number of examples presented. A separate document, created to outline common annotation errors from the previous phase, was also provided to the annotators.This new version of the guide also emphasized the need to focus not only on linguistic structural features but also primarily on underlying conceptual mappings within the specific context of each item.

Dataset	Agreement (%)	Fleiss' Kappa
1st Half	49.57	0.11
2nd Half	55.06	0.24

Table 2: Agreement Percentage and Cohen's Kappa Score by section of the corpus.

We also accentuated the semantic characteristics of personification markers, such as verbs or nouns that implied attributes like [+ANIMATE] and [+HUMAN]. For IMs, identified subcategories were explicitly pointed out, including scientific terminology, idioms, abstract science concepts explained through familiar terms, and implicit conceptual mappings. Finally, we decided that non-metaphorical tweets would be validated directly with no labels on the text.

Our research corpus consisted of 3733 tweets obtained via the Twitter API v2 from 19 science communicators based in Mexico. We divided this dataset into two parts: 1866 assigned to annotators A1, A2, and A3, and 1867 to annotators A4, A5, and A6. Each half of this corpus was labeled three different times to evaluate points of agreement and disagreement. We used Argilla once again for this process.

5.1 Inter-Annotator Agreement

A binary evaluation was performed for the detection of the metaphor, using both agreement percentage and Fleiss' Kappa as IAA metrics. As shown in Table 2, in the first half of the corpus, the agreement percentage was 49.57%, with a kappa value of 0.11, while in the second half the agreement increased to 55.06% and the kappa to 0.24. These values, ranging from "slight" to "fair", indicate that annotator consistency was slightly higher that would be expected by chance, although far from perfect.

To analyze IAA at a more granular level, we also evaluated each annotator pair using agreement percentage and Cohen's Kappa coefficient (Cohen, 1960). The results from this evaluation, presented in Table 3, reflect slight to fair consistency accross annotator pairs, with agreement percentages ranging from 61.36% to 79.97%, and Kappa values bewteen 0.09 and 0.38. Overall, the levels of agreement are only slightly higher than expected by chance, which means our annotation faces a significant disagreement issue and, consequently, a challenge for using the annotated data as reliable training input for a metaphor detection model.

Pair of annotators	Agreement (%)	Cohen's Kappa
A1 – A2	74.28%	0.17
A1 – A3	61.36%	0.09
A2 – A3	63.50%	0.21
A4 – A5	63.63%	0.18
A4 – A6	66.52%	0.27
A5 – A6	**79.97%**	**0.38**

Table 3: Evaluation metrics for interannotator agreement per pair of annotators in the binary classification of metaphorical and non-metaphorical tweets.

Although the results exhibit relatively low IAA in terms of Kappa coefficients, it is important to mention that, to the best of our knowledge, these are the first numerical indicators for the task of annotating metaphors in Mexican Spanish PCS tweets, so we have no point of comparison for our study. Several factors may have contributed to the considerable influence of annotator subjectivity when interpreting metaphors, including the relatively unexplored nature of this text genre, which implies a thematic diversity from astronomy and general physics to genetics and history of science, among other areas. Additionally, the hybridization of specialized and non-specialized discourse within PCS adds complexity to the task, as it demands a very nuanced understanding of context and metaphor use. We hypothesize that a direct binary classification approach from the start could contribute to a better inter-annotator agreement, by simplifying the task. Moreover, the reliance on non-expert annotators, despite their linguistics background, adds another layer of variability in their interpretation and application of metaphor categories. It should also be noted that our low agreement levels contrast with some studies reported in 2.2 that focused on specific words, such as verbs, because we chose to annotate all Spanish lexical categories. From this disagreement scenario, we sought alternative strategies to maximize the recall of possible metaphorical tweets, which could ensure a more complete representation of metaphor use in the corpus.

Table 4 shows examples of the various levels of agreement among annotators in the binary classification of tweets. The categories include: 100% agreement classified as metaphorical, 100% agreement classified as non-metaphorical, 2/3 voting as metaphorical, and 1/3 voting as metaphorical. As can be noted, the first two rows of examples demonstrate cases of unanimous agreement. In the metaphorical example, scent-based ant communication is anthropomorphized, described in terms of "vocabulary" and "words", which posits a clear metaphorical framing, straightforward for annotators to unanimously classify it as metaphorical. On the contrary, the non-metaphorical example presents factual information about alternative therapies, using direct language and lacking figurative expressions, which is easier for annotators to identify.

The last two rows present more challenging examples, as indicated by lower agreement among annotators. For the 2/3 category, neural activity during learning is compared to the process of mastering a new instrument. While this metaphorical framing is present, it can be harder to identify, likely because the description blends scientific explanation with figurative language. As for the 1/3 category, the example provides statistical information about Parkinson's disease in a straightforward, factual manner. However, the single annotator labeling it as metaphorical might have interpreted Parkinson's disease as a personified entity due to the use of the verb "affects"," which could imply an active, agent-like role, an interpretation more open to discussion. These examples illustrate the variation in annotator decisions and demonstrate the intricacies of the annotation task.

5.2 Expert Annotation in Disagreement Items

After analyzing the annotation data, we found that 1953 tweets out of 3,733 (52.3% of the corpus) exhibited perfect agreement, with 200 tweets classified as metaphorical and 1753 as non-metaphorical. Given the very small number of class 1 (metaphorical) instances, we considered additional strategies for our research, considering that class 1 is the primary focus of the task, not class 0. The remaining 1780 tweets (47.6% of the corpus) showed mixed agreement: in terms of class 1, 1229 received a 2/3 vote and 551 received a 1/3 vote. To counteract these ambiguities, we implemented an "expert annotator" strategy, following the methodology proposed by Aldama et al. (2022), where an external evaluator makes a final decision on the status of each "hard case".

Accordingly, we randomly selected 84 tweets with disagreement from the 1780 uncertain, or "hard", cases for this annotation experiment. Three linguists, who developed the annotation guide, were assigned with classifying these tweets into a binary task (1 for metaphorical, 0 for non-metaphorical). We opted for this experiment to assess the consistency of the expert annotators' decisions and compare their classifications with those of the non-expert annotators to identify any significant differences. Table 5 provides a comparison of the annotation process across the different datasets: the first half of the corpus, the second half, and the expert annotation.

As previously discussed, in the first and second corpus halves, IAA measured by Fleiss' Kappa was relatively low, even though the percentage of perfect agreement was around 50%. In terms of the voting system, 35.32% of the items in the first half received a 2/3 vote for class 1, while 30.53% of the second half did. A smaller proportion (15.11% and 14.41%, respectively) received a 1/3 vote for class 1. When looking at the expert annotation, the Fleiss' Kappa improved to 0.30, which indicates a higher level of agreement among the expert annotators, even on disagreement items, although, according to Landis and Koch (1977) agreement is still "fair". The expert group achieved a higher overall agreement rate (61.9%) and a greater average agreement per item (0.82), compared to the non-expert annotators. In addition, the proportion of tweets with a 2/3 vote dropped to 25%, while the 1/3 vote category was also smaller (13.1%) but very close to non-expert values. Although the annotation conditions are not strictly comparable —the task involves binary classification versus multiclass, with a considerably smaller sample size, among other factors—, expert annotation could be helpful in certain cases, as indicated by the average agreement per item. Nonetheless, despite the involvement of expert annotators, some disagreement persists in the classification, which stresses the complexity of the task and the need to refine annotation strategies in this context.

5.3 Guide Refinements

According to the sub-cycle of iterating modeling and annotation in the MATTER cycle (Pustejovsky and Stubbs, 2013), if we aim to create a reliable binary classification gold standard for metaphor identification, we consider refining the guide as crucial step to reduce disagreement. In our research, after evaluating IAA, we have clarified which expressions do not qualify as DMs or PMs, and have worked to define more precise subcategories for IMs. In the case of DMs, we have decided that metalinguistic clarifications (definitions, translations, etymologies), exemplifications,

Category	Example	Translation
3/3 voting as metaphorical	Las hormigas tienen un vocabulario de 20 diferentes "palabras" que dicen ¡con el aroma! ¡CuriosaMente!	Ants have a vocabulary of 20 different "words" that they say with scent! CuriousMind!
3/3 voting as non-metaphorical	¿Podemos esperar que las terapias alternativas logran algún día avances que cambien trascendentalmente nuestro presente y futuro? Es muy probable que no. Consulta nuestro tema de portada del mes de octubre. ¡Ya disponible en puestos de periódicos!	Can we expect that alternative therapies will one day achieve breakthroughs that will transcendentally change our present and future? Most likely not. Check out our October cover story. Now available on newsstands!
2/3 voting as metaphorical	Imagina que estás intentando aprender un nuevo instrumento: al principio las neuronas involucradas comienzan a tener mucha actividad, y si esta actividad se mantiene se empiezan a liberar más neurotransmisores o puede que haya un incremento de receptores.	Imagine that you are trying to learn a new instrument: at the beginning the neurons involved start to have a lot of activity, and if this activity is maintained more neurotransmitters start to be released or there may be an increase of receptors.
1/3 voting as metaphorical	-De acuerdo a la Organización Mundial de la Salud, la enfermedad de #Parkinson afecta a 1 de cada 100 personas mayores de 60 años. -Se estima que para el año 2030 habrán unas 12 millones de pacientes con Parkinson.	-According to the World Health Organization, #Parkinson's disease affects 1 in 100 people over the age of 60. -It is estimated that by 2030 there will be 12 million Parkinson's patients.

Table 4: Examples of annotator agreement levels in the binary classification of Mexican Spanish tweets including their English translation.

	First Corpus Half	Second Corpus Half	Expert Annotation
# of Annotators	3	3	3
# of Items	1866	1867	84
Fleiss' Kappa	0.11	0.24	0.30
Agreement (%)	49.57%	55.06%	61.90%
Items with Perfect Agreement	925	1028	52
2/3 Voting (Class 1)	659 (35.32%)	570 (30.53%)	21 (25%)
1/3 Voting (Class 1)	282 (15.11%)	269 (14.41%)	11 (13.1%)
Average Agreement per Item	0.71	0.74	0.82

Table 5: Inter-annotator agreement statistics for metaphor classification across different datasets and expert annotation.

comparisons within the same conceptual domain, and size comparisons should not be considered instances of DMs, despite their linguistic structure often resembling metaphorical expressions. For IMs, our new guide is more specific in delineating subtypes, which for PCS tweets include scientific terminology (e.g., "agujero negro" [black hole], "radiación infrarroja" [infrared radiation], "efecto invernadero" [greenhouse effect]), biological species names (e.g. "tiburón anguila" [frilled shark], "flor cadáver" [corpse flower]), Spanish idioms (e.g. "sentar las bases" [lay the foundations]), conceptual mappings by contrast of meanings (e.g., "hilo" [thread] in digital communication). For personification metaphors (PMs), the distinction between metonymy and personification is crucial, as they are separate phenomena, albeit closely related. We also find it important to specify that only non-human or non-animate entities should be personified, with both verbs and nominal personifiers clearly delineated and exemplified. Expert annotation can help resolve ambiguous cases. However, a gold standard is not the only possibility, as the disagreement itself can also be leveraged to refine the metaphor classification process.

6 Conclusions and Future Work

In this work, we explored the metaphor annotation process within the domain of public communication of science (PCS), with an emphasis on examining the challenges of reaching inter-annotator agreement (IAA). The frequent and meaningful disagreements observed in our corpus annotation have underscored the complexities of metaphorical language identification, where subjectivity plays a significant role. While disagreement has traditionally been regarded as a problem for Natural Language Processing, we acknowledge its strengths as a window into the diverse human interpretations of what constitutes a metaphor. Diversity in interpretation may arise from several factors, including understanding of terminology, domain-specific knowledge (particularly in scientific or technical contexts), and individual subjectivity. For instance, what one annotator perceives as a metaphor might be interpreted by another as a literal or descriptive statement.At least for this corpus, factors such as the dialect (Mexican Spanish) or the media (Twitter) do not influence the level of agreement. Since these types of tweets are written for PCS purposes, the usual writing style of social networks is not present; therefore, these publications avoid the use of confusing dialectal language.

For future work, rather than striving for perfect IAA, we propose using a probabilistic approach, based on the learning from disagreement paradigm, where soft-labeling techniques may allow us to capture different perspectives in computational metaphor detection. This type of research could benefit from approaches such as deliberate metaphor theory, as proposed by Steen (2023), since it involves greater attention to the communicative context of enunciation and cognitive models of context, with the aim of distinguishing between deliberate and non-deliberate use to interpret metaphors in context. We believe this could go beyond rigid computational categorization and embrace the multifaceted human nature of figurative language.

Another possibility is to re-annotate our dataset based on our last refinements to produce a gold standard, which, together with soft label annotations, might improve the quality of metaphor classification. Moving forward, we aim to conduct additional experiments and alternative annotation approaches that further explore the role of disagreement. Since the annotation method we followed in this study might not be the most appropriate, we propose to develop an alternative annotation protocol focused on binary annotation with emphasis on class 0 (non-metaphorical) comparisons, leveraging the fact that this is the class with the highest rate of agreement. Such an approach could provide a more nuanced perspective on annotator behavior and improve consistency in metaphorical language detection. We hypothesize that non-traditional labeling methods, such as pairwise comparisons, for linguistic metaphor annotation could address the limitations of existing metrics such as Fleiss' Kappa while generating high-quality reliable annotations.

Our findings provide an important precedent for metaphor annotation in the PCS context, showing that disagreement can be attributed to the influence of annotator subjectivity when interpreting metaphors in texts, despite the use of detailed guidelines. This subjectivity, however, should not be seen as a weakness but as an opportunity to add depth to our annotated dataset. We hope this initial work will guide future efforts on metaphor detection, classification, and figurative language analysis in scientific communication.

References

Ehsan Aghazadeh, Mohsen Fayyaz, and Yadollah Yaghoobzadeh. 2022. Metaphors in pre-trained language models: Probing and generalization across datasets and languages. In *Proceedings of the 60th Annual Meeting of the Association for Computational Linguistics (Volume 1: Long Papers)*, pages 2037–2050, Dublin, Ireland. Association for Computational Linguistics.

Nuria Aldama, Marta Guerrero, Helena Montoro, and Doaa Samy. 2022. Anotación de corpus lingüísticos: metodología utilizada en el IIC - IIC.

Marc Alexander, Fraser Dallachy, Scott Piao, Alistair Baron, and Paul Rayson. 2015. Metaphor, popular science, and semantic tagging: Distant reading with the *Historical Thesaurus of English. Digital Scholarship in the Humanities*, page fqv045.

Mateusz Babieno, Masashi Takeshita, Dusan Radisavljevic, Rafal Rzepka, and Kenji Araki. 2022. MIss RoBERTa WiLDe: Metaphor Identification Using Masked Language Model with Wiktionary Lexical Definitions. *Applied Sciences*, 12(4):2081.

Informe Belmont. 1978. Principios éticos y directrices para la protección de sujetos humanos de investigación. *Estados Unidos de Norteamérica: Reporte de la Comisión Nacional para la Protección de Sujetos Humanos de Investigación Biomédica y de Comportamiento.*

Tony Berber Sardinha. 2007. *Metáfora.* Parábola Editorial.

Minjin Choi, Sunkyung Lee, Eunseong Choi, Heesoo Park, Junhyuk Lee, Dongwon Lee, and Jongwuk Lee. 2021. MelBERT: Metaphor Detection via Contextualized Late Interaction using Metaphorical Identification Theories.

Jacob Cohen. 1960. A coefficient of agreement for nominal scales. *Educational and Psychological Measurement*, 20(1):37–46.

Joseph L. Fleiss. 1971. Measuring nominal scale agreement among many raters. *Psychological Bulletin*, 76(5):378–382.

Anna Hülsing and Sabine Schulte Im Walde. 2024. Cross-lingual metaphor detection for low-resource languages. In *Proceedings of the 4th Workshop on Figurative Language Processing (FigLang 2024)*, pages 22–34, Mexico City, Mexico (Hybrid). Association for Computational Linguistics.

Tina Krennmayr and Gerard Steen. 2017. VU amsterdam metaphor corpus. In Nancy Ide and James Pustejovsky, editors, *Handbook of Linguistic Annotation*, pages 1053–1071. Springer Netherlands.

Huiyuan Lai, Antonio Toral, and Malvina Nissim. 2023. Multilingual multi-figurative language detection. In *Findings of the Association for Computational Linguistics: ACL 2023*, pages 9254–9267, Toronto, Canada. Association for Computational Linguistics.

George Lakoff and Mark Leonard Johnson. 1980. *Metaphors we live by*. University of Chicago press.

J. Richard Landis and Gary G. Koch. 1977. The measurement of observer agreement for categorical data. *Biometrics*, 33(1):159.

Khadidja Merakchi. 2020. *The translation of metaphors in popular science from English into Arabic in the domain of astronomy and astrophysics*. Ph.D. thesis, University of Surrey. Medium: application/pdf Publisher: [object Object].

Susan Nacey, W. Gudrun Reijnierse, Tina Krennmayr, and Aletta G. Dorst. 2019. *Metaphor Identification in Multiple Languages*. Converging Evidence in Language and Communication Research. John Benjamins Publishing Company.

Pragglejaz. 2007. MIP: A method for identifying metaphorically used words in discourse. *Metaphor and Symbol*, 22(1):1–39.

J. Pustejovsky and Amber Stubbs. 2013. *Natural language annotation for machine learning*. O'Reilly Media. OCLC: ocn794362649.

Mateo Richi Pons-Sorolla. 2020. Analizador de lectura fácil 4.0: identificación de metáforas.

Elisa Sanchez-Bayona and Rodrigo Agerri. 2022. Leveraging a new spanish corpus for multilingual and cross-lingual metaphor detection. In *Proceedings of the 26th Conference on Computational Natural Language Learning (CoNLL)*, pages 228–240. Association for Computational Linguistics.

Marta Sandri, Elisa Leonardelli, Sara Tonelli, and Elisabetta Jezek. 2023. Why don't you do it right? analysing annotators' disagreement in subjective tasks. In *Proceedings of the 17th Conference of the European Chapter of the Association for Computational Linguistics*, pages 2428–2441, Dubrovnik, Croatia. Association for Computational Linguistics.

Ekaterina Shutova, Beata Beigman Klebanov, Joel Tetreault, and Zornitsa Kozareva. 2013. Proceedings of the first workshop on metaphor in NLP. Association for Computational Linguistics.

Gerard J. Steen. 2023. Thinking by metaphor, fast and slow: Deliberate metaphor theory offers a new model for metaphor and its comprehension. *Frontiers in Psychology*, 14:1242888.

Gerard J. Steen, Aletta G. Dorst, J. Berenike Herrmann, Anna Kaal, Tina Krennmayr, and Trijntje Pasma. 2010. *A Method for Linguistic Metaphor Identification: From MIP to MIPVU*, volume 14 of *Converging Evidence in Language and Communication Research*. John Benjamins Publishing Company.

Elisa Sánchez-Bayona. 2021. Detection of everyday metaphor in spanish: annotation and evaluation. Master thesis, University of the Basque Country (UPV/EHU).

Alec Sánchez-Montero, Gemma Bel-Enguix, Sergio-Luis Ojeda-Trueba, and Marisela Colín Rodea. 2024. Evaluating the development of linguistic metaphor annotation in mexican spanish popular science tweets. In *Proceedings of the 4th Workshop on Figurative Language Processing (FigLang 2024)*, pages 59–64. Association for Computational Linguistics.

Xiaoyu Tong, Ekaterina Shutova, and Martha Lewis. 2021. Recent advances in neural metaphor processing: A linguistic, cognitive and social perspective. In *Proceedings of the 2021 Conference of the North American Chapter of the Association for Computational Linguistics: Human Language Technologies*, pages 4673–4686. Association for Computational Linguistics.

Alexandra N. Uma, Tommaso Fornaciari, Dirk Hovy, Silviu Paun, Barbara Plank, and Massimo Poesio. 2021. Learning from disagreement: A survey. *Journal of Artificial Intelligence Research*, 72:1385–1470.

Stephany Nieves Uribe and Jorge Mauricio Molina Mejía. 2023. Hacia una extracción semiautomática de metáforas conceptuales en un corpus de economía a partir del procesamiento de lenguaje natural. *Estudios de Lingüística Aplicada*, (76):81–109.

Lennart Wachowiak and Dagmar Gromann. 2023. Does GPT-3 grasp metaphors? identifying metaphor mappings with generative language models. In *Proceedings of the 61st Annual Meeting of the Association for Computational Linguistics (Volume 1: Long Papers)*, pages 1018–1032, Toronto, Canada. Association for Computational Linguistics.

Leila Weitzel, Ronaldo Cristiano Prati, and Raul Freire Aguiar. 2016. *The Comprehension of Figurative Language: What Is the Influence of Irony and Sarcasm on NLP Techniques?*, pages 49–74. Springer International Publishing, Cham.

Kelaiti Xiao, Liang Yang, Xiaokun Zhang, Paerhati Tulajiang, and Hongfei Lin. Combining llm efficiency with human expertise: Addressing systematic biases in figurative language detection.

Omnia Zayed. 2021. Metaphor processing in tweets. Master's thesis, NUI Galway.

Author Index